Crown and Nobility

Blackwell Classic Histories of England

This series comprises new editions of seminal histories of England. Written by the leading scholars of their generation, the books represent both major works of historical analysis and interpretation and clear, authoritative overviews of the major periods of English history. All the volumes have been revised for inclusion in the series and include updated material to aid further study. *Blackwell Classic Histories of England* provides a forum in which these key works can continue to be enjoyed by scholars, students and general readers alike.

Published

Roman Britain
Third Edition
Malcolm Todd

England and Its Rulers: 1066–1272
Second Edition
M. T. Clanchy

Crown and Nobility: England 1272–1461
Second Edition
Anthony Tuck

Church and People: England 1450–1660
Second Edition
Claire Cross

Politics and The Nation: England 1450–1660
Fifth Edition
David Loades

Politics without Democracy 1815–1914
Second Edition
Perception and Preoccupation in British Government
Michael Bentley

Crown and Nobility
England 1272–1461

Second Edition

Anthony Tuck

BLACKWELL
Publishers

The right of Anthony Tuck to be identified as author of this work has been asserted in accordance with the Copyright, Designs and Patents Act 1988.

First edition published by Fontana 1985
Second edition published by Blackwell Publishers Ltd 1999

2 4 6 8 10 9 7 5 3 1

Blackwell Publishers Ltd
108 Cowley Road
Oxford OX4 1JF
UK

Blackwell Publishers Inc.
350 Main Street
Malden, Massachusetts 02148
USA

British Library Cataloguing in Publication Data

A CIP catalogue record for this book is available from the British Library.

Library of Congress Cataloging-in-Publication Data

Library of Congress data has been applied for.

ISBN   0 631 21461 5
                        0 631 21466 6 (pbk)

Typeset in 10.5 pt on 12 pt Sabon
by Kolam Information Services Pvt. Ltd, Pondicherry, India

Printed in Great Britain by T.J. International, Padstow, Cornwall

This book is printed on acid-free paper

Contents

Maps

Preface to the Second Edition

This book was originally commissioned by Professor Sir Geoffrey Elton and published in 1985 as a volume in the Fontana History of England series under his editorship. It was intended to accompany Peter Heath's *Church and Realm 1272–1461*, while Henry Hallam's *Rural England 1066–1348*, provided coverage of the economic and social history of England in the period from 1272 to 1348. Professor Elton asked me to write a political history of late medieval England, since other aspects of the period were covered, in large part at least, by the companion volumes.

In revising the book for its second edition, I have adhered to Professor Elton's original brief, for the incorporation of substantial discussion of ecclesiastical history and economic and social history would in effect have entailed writing a new book rather than revising the book that Elton commissioned. I have, however, used the opportunity presented by the publication of a second edition to revise parts of the original text in the light of work published since 1985, and I have added an Epilogue discussing in general terms how approaches to the political history of late medieval England have changed and developed since the first edition was published. I have also corrected a number of misprints and factual errors, and I have revised and substantially enlarged the bibliography. The Biographical Appendix of English Dukes and Earls has not been reprinted in this edition: the information contained in it is readily available elsewhere, for example in the *Handbook of British Chronology* and *The Complete Peerage*.

I am grateful to Professor Nigel Saul, of Royal Holloway University of London, for kindly agreeing to read and comment on a draft of the Epilogue.

ANTHONY TUCK
Stapleford, Cambridge
March 1999

Preface to the First Edition

In writing a book of this kind, one inevitably relies heavily on the work of many scholars who have contributed so notably to our understanding of the history of late medieval England: I hope I have adequately acknowledged my indebtedness to them in the notes. I have also incurred a number of more specific debts of gratitude: to Professor G. R. Elton for suggesting that I should write the book and for discussing the text with me; to the University of Durham for giving me a period of sabbatical leave in which the writing of the book could be completed; and to my wife for help with reading the proofs and constructing the index. Above all, however, I am grateful to Mrs Margaret Heslop for transcribing my typescript on to a word processor with great skill and accuracy, thereby making the task of revision so much easier; and to Anthony Goodman of the University of Edinburgh who very kindly read the whole book in draft, made many useful suggestions and saved me from many errors.

ANTHONY TUCK
Durham, April 1985

A Note on Translations

Quotations from primary sources in Latin or Anglo-Norman have been translated, using published translations where they exist. Quotations from primary sources in Middle English have been left in their original form.

A Note on Money

The units of account most widely used in medieval England were pounds, shillings and pence (£sd). The pound sterling was divided into twenty shillings, and the shilling into twelve pence. The mark was also used as a unit of account. It was equivalent to 13s 4d, i.e. two-thirds of a pound. Thus 1,000 marks was equivalent to £666 13s 4d.

In France, the main unit of account was the *livre tournois* (pound of Tours). It was divided into twenty *sous*, and a *sou* was divided into twelve *deniers*. The value of the *livre tournois* against the English pound varied, but in the early fourteenth century four *livres tournois* were worth one pound sterling. The *écu* was a gold coin minted by the French kings from 1337. Its relationship to the *livre tournois* varied, and its value against the English pound fluctuated. At the time of the Treaty of Brétigny, 1360, it was worth about 3s 4d, i.e. one-sixth of a pound sterling. The *franc* was a gold coin first minted in 1360, and it too was roughly equivalent to one-sixth of a pound sterling. The gold *salut* was minted by the government of Henry VI in France after 1422, and was equivalent in value to 3s 4d sterling.

Introduction

Over the two centuries which separate the Norman Conquest from the accession of Edward I, the English realm developed two characteristics which chiefly distinguished it from other polities in western Europe: a monarchy which enjoyed a high degree of authority throughout the realm and exercised that authority through institutions which were in general amenable and subordinate to the royal will; and a higher nobility which, unlike their French counterparts, did not so much aspire to a regional particularism but rather sought to exercise political influence directly over the king and his chief officers and ministers. The centre of political power in England was the king's court; the chief agents of royal power were the officers and ministers chosen by the king; and royal authority permeated from the court into virtually every part of the realm. The strength and pervasive nature of royal power in England may have their remoter origins in the achievements of the pre-Conquest kings, but they were enhanced by the work of the first three Norman kings, and taken to heights unknown elsewhere in western Europe by the energetic organizing and centralizing policies of the Angevin kings.

The attitude of the king's subjects to the strength and power of his administration was shot through with ambiguities. The legal reforms of Henry II's reign gave his subjects swifter and more efficient justice than they had previously been accustomed to, and the maintenance of order in the realm provided a welcome contrast to the civil strife of Stephen's reign. Furthermore, the crown was the fount of honour and patronage: it had much to give, and royal favour was eagerly sought for the rewards that went with it. On the other hand fiscal pressure was hard to bear, and indebtedness to the crown was used, by John at least, as a means of controlling his subjects by displays of favour or disfavour, while the cause for which much of the money was raised lacked popular appeal. For Henry II, Richard I and John the defence of their continental inheritance was their most urgent priority; but after the loss of Normandy in 1204 the fiscal and military effort required came eventually to seem unacceptable, and in the thirteenth century the English nobility showed little enthusiasm for military service overseas. One of the themes of this book will be the transformation of the English nobility's attitude to foreign war; but in John's reign the strains induced by his financial and military demands did much to provoke the political crisis of 1215.

The political conflicts of John's reign, the barons' wars of the reign of Henry III, and the conflicts between crown and nobility in the fourteenth and fifteenth century with which this book is chiefly concerned thus took place within a realm which enjoyed, in comparison with its continental neighbours, a high degree of centralization and a well-developed administrative system through which royal authority was exercised. Although, of course, the nobility were vitally concerned with the way in which the crown discharged its responsibilities for government, and although the financial, legal and military demands of the crown inevitably bore directly, and sometimes heavily, on the nobility, they did not themselves seek to discharge the functions of government or to take over the running of the administration. The nobility were not in this sense a governing class, and as long as their interests were respected, their advice sought on matters which touched their interests, and their opinions on the work of the king's advisers and ministers taken into account they expected the king and his ministers to discharge the routine functions of government.

To write in this way of the nobility, or the king's leading subjects, is however to beg the question of who these men were. A precise definition of the English nobility is impossible: it was not a caste, with entry to it defined and controlled by rigid laws and customs. At its widest, it might include all those men – perhaps over 5,000 in the mid-thirteenth century – of knightly rank and above. Men of knightly rank had military obligations to their immediate lord and to the crown which were of an honourable nature and in the thirteenth century increasingly required a degree of wealth to discharge efficiently. Such men also held office in their localities as sheriffs, coroners, and members of the multifarious commissions which the crown established as part of the work of local administration. It is not easy to draw a clear dividing line between the knightly class and those above them in the social scale. There was a tradition of fellowship amongst all those who bore arms, and those who led the opposition to Henry III looked to the knightly class, many of whom were their own tenants, for support. Even the small number of nobles who bore titles were not sharply distinguished from their fellows: titles were granted sparingly by the Angevin kings, and it is by no means clear that those who were titled enjoyed greater wealth or prestige than the most substantial of those who were not. Yet such a wide definition of nobility does not greatly advance an understanding of political conflict in late medieval England. The king's opponents were for the most part drawn from the wealthiest and most influential section of the king's subjects; during the fourteenth century there was an increasing tendency for such men to bear titles and for the *cursus honorum* to become more elaborate, while at the same time they became increasingly conscious of their separateness from the broader body of landowners; though the lesser landowners were often linked to the higher nobility by bonds of retainer. It is these men – the higher nobility – with whom this book is chiefly concerned.

Conflict between crown and nobility, however, forms only one theme in the political history of late medieval England, and although it is perhaps the dominant theme, it would be unwise to assume that such conflict was either permanent or inherent in the political structure. The caricature of late medieval English history in which the barons were forever trying to hasten the king's death, deposition or insanity while at the same time seeking to promote the ambitions of whatever false claimant to the throne they could find has no basis whatsoever in reality. The periods of conflict in the two centuries which this book covers were brief, if intense. There is some continuity of ideology and basic principle, and some self-conscious recognition of a tradition of opposition, especially in the case of Thomas of Lancaster; but there is little continuity of personnel or policy. Indeed, together with a propensity to oppose the king in particular circumstances there went a natural disposition to co-operate with him whenever possible: the nobility's sense of loyalty to the king went very deep, though it was not, as Sir Ralph Bassett pointed out in 1387, absolute or unshakeable. The nobility accepted the king's leadership in war, and looked to him as the source of honours, lands and offices. They expected much of their king in terms of good government and justice, military success, financial prudence, wise choice of counsellors, and adoption of an acceptable mode of life. It was when the nobility sensed that these expectations were not being realized that conflict developed.

By the mid-fifteenth century there seems little doubt that the English monarchy was weaker in a number of important respects than it had been at the accession of Edward I. The financial resources which the crown could call upon without the assent of parliament were minimal: late medieval kings lived off taxes, and the principle that taxation, direct and indirect, required the consent of parliament was firmly established by the end of Edward III's reign. The war in France, on which much of these financial resources were spent, gave English kings great prestige and authority when they achieved such notable victories as Crécy, Poitiers and Agincourt; but it generated political conflict when stalemate or defeat was the outcome. Indeed, it is arguable that the nobility were the real beneficiaries, in both financial and political terms, of the war, and their interest in its successful prosecution might also give rise to political conflict. Furthermore, the unfortunate personalities of Edward II, Richard II and Henry VI, and the two depositions of the fourteenth century, damaged the standing of the monarchy. The nobility brought Richard II to heel in 1386 by reminding him of the fate of his great-grandfather, and the rebellions against Henry IV in the early part of his reign derived some of their force from the rebels' professed belief that he was a usurper who deserved to suffer the same fate as his predecessor. The nobility's reluctance to remove an anointed king to whom they had sworn allegiance was not absolute; once deposition had been employed for the first time in 1327 it became the ultimate means by which an aristocratic faction could make its will prevail against a recalcitrant king.

This book, then, is above all a political narrative, taking as its main theme the relationship between the crown and the nobility in peace and war from the accession of Edward I to the deposition of Henry VI, with a brief concluding discussion of the Yorkist monarchy. It does not set out to be a general history of England, and the reader will find little on either the economy or the religious life of late medieval England. It is also a history of England rather than all those lands over which late medieval English kings claimed or exercised lordship. The Anglo-French conflict forms a central part of the book, but the internal affairs of the French kingdom are discussed only in so far as they impinge directly on the war, and the same is true of the history of Scotland and of the English lordship in Ireland. The period is treated chronologically, for only in this way can the changing nature of the relationship between crown and nobility be effectively illuminated, and the recollection of the past was itself a factor in shaping the attitudes and policies of the nobility.

I

The Reign of Edward I,

1272–1307

The chronicler Walter of Guisborough wrote of Edward I at the time of his accession that he was 'handsome, tall and elegant, standing head and shoulders above ordinary people, and young of age, not yet having completed his thirtieth year'. The author of a poem entitled 'The Praise of the Young Edward' looked back over Edward's career before his accession and described how 'while yet in his tender youth [he] went through many conflicts with a manly heart, warlike as a pard, fragrant with sweetness like a spikenard . . . he shines like a new Richard'. Such eulogies, however, stood in marked contrast to the opinion of the author of *The Song of Lewes*, writing during the barons' wars, who said of Edward: 'When he is in difficulty, he promises just what you will, but as soon as he has escaped the danger, he forgets his promise . . . The treachery or falseness by which he gains his ends he calls prudence; the way by which he arrives at his object, be it ever so crooked, is reputed to be straight; whatever may serve his purpose, it is called right; he calls lawful whatever he wills, and thinks himself absolved from the law, as though he were greater than a king; for every king is ruled by the laws which he enacts.'[1] Edward's reign was to show that both points of view had some substance, but although, as the author of 'The Praise of the Young Edward' pointed out, he had enhanced his reputation while on crusade his subjects knew him best from his conduct during the barons' wars, and the political lessons he learnt then underlay his approach to government throughout his reign. He was determined to ensure that the reins of government remained firmly in his own hands. During the barons' wars he had vigorously repudiated the view that the king should rule with the advice of a formally constituted committee of baronial advisers, and he never allowed himself to be dominated even informally by his companions, his ministers or his family. Indeed, he could prove a hard taskmaster, inadequately rewarding those who served him, and seeking to diminish the power of those who opposed him. He took an exalted view of the powers and responsibilities of the crown, and at the beginning of his reign the resolution of two outstanding problems, administrative reform and the settlement of Wales, show him acting in such a way as to place the authority and the supremacy of the crown beyond doubt.

The Period of the Statutes

One of the objects of Henry III's opponents between 1258 and 1265 had been to institute reforms in both central and local government. The decisive victory of the king's party ensured, of course, that such reforms could not be imposed by a group of magnates against the king's will, but in the years after 1265 some at least of the baronial reform programme had been implemented by Henry and his ministers. Edward I's legislative and administrative measures should be seen, therefore, in the context of the need for reform and the need at the same time to assert the jurisdictional supremacy of the crown. The large-scale inquiry into local government, for instance, which the king set up in October 1274, shortly after his return from crusading in the Holy land, where he had been at his father's death, served both purposes. It revealed substantial evidence of corruption and misgovernment by both royal and seigneurial officials while at the same time it provided information about encroachment on royal rights. Neither problem was novel: Henry III had embarked on an inquiry into the extent to which royal rights had been usurped by others, and had gone so far as to suggest that even rights granted by royal charter could be revoked. On the other hand, the investigation of abuses perpetrated by both royal and seigneurial officials had been part of the policy of the baronial reformers. While insisting on the ultimate authority of the crown, Edward was evidently prepared to take over some part of the programme put forward by the baronial reformers between 1258 and 1268. The inquiry was followed by legislation, the first Statute of Westminster, which sought to remedy the abuses perpetrated by royal officials, though with questionable success, as later inquiries into the abuses of officials were to reveal.

The problem of the usurpation of royal rights also underlay the inquiry into baronial liberties and franchises launched in 1278 and known as the *Quo Warranto* inquiry, from the opening words of the writ ordering the inquiry: 'by what warrant' is a liberty or a franchise held. If a franchise holder could not show that his privilege rested on a royal charter, it would be revoked. The principle underlying the inquiry, that the crown enjoyed supreme jurisdiction and thus all baronial jurisdiction must derive from explicit grant by the crown, was not new, and had indeed been laid down by Henry III.[2] It was, however, one thing to assert the jurisdictional supremacy of the crown, but another to cope with the political consequences of an assertion that all franchises which had no explicit written warrant should be surrendered. According to one version of Walter of Guisborough's Chronicle, Earl Warenne was summoned before the king's judges and asked by what right he held his franchises; he produced before them 'an ancient and rusty sword and said, "My lords, this is my warrant; my ancestors came with William the Conqueror and conquered their lands with the sword, and I shall defend them with the sword"'.[3] In detail the story must be false; as Dr Clanchy pointed out, it is hard to imagine even an earl brandishing a sword in the faces of the king's judges,[4] yet Warenne undoubtedly had a point. Many franchises originated in the period before written records were systematically kept, and Warenne was not the only noble who sought to rely on claims derived from the Norman Conquest. It was scarcely feasible to deprive all such nobles of their privileges, and by 1290 Edward I had reached a compromise whereby those who could show that their franchises had been held before the coronation of Richard I, which was now fixed as the time limit of legal memory, were allowed to retain them: the jurisdictional supremacy of the crown had to be tempered by some consideration for the wishes and interests of the nobility.

It would be wrong, therefore, to see Edward I's legislative programme as merely the working out of the royalist principles he had inherited from his father and which he had seen triumph after the barons' wars. For Edward's government, like that of all other medieval English kings, had to react to pressures and demands emanating from the nobility and from other sections of the community, and petitions from individuals might sometimes form the basis for general legislation. The Statute of Acton Burnell (1283), for instance, which was concerned with the problem of the recovery of debts, seems to have originated in petitions from a Flemish merchant who had failed to gain his share of the profits of his partnership with an English trader.[5] The concern of great landowners to protect the services due from their lands, and in particular to prevent the erosion of services which resulted from grants made by undertenants, underlay three of Edward's legislative enactments. The statute *Quia Emptores* of 1290 forbade subinfeudation and thus protected great lords from the loss of services when land was granted away by an undertenant. The clause *De Donis Conditionalibus* in the second Statute of Westminster, 1285, was intended to ensure that conditions attached to grants of land made by great lords on occasions such as the marriage of a daughter were observed; and the Statute of Mortmain, 1279, which forbade the gift of land to the Church without royal licence, dealt with a problem which was a source of some grievance to the great lords, since they lost the services due from land granted in this way. The immediate origin of the mortmain legislation seems to have been a quarrel between the king and Archbishop Pecham, and although Walter of Guisborough understandably described the statute as prejudicial to men of religion and to Holy Church,[6] it did not in fact put a stop to such grants but merely ensured that the king derived some useful income from selling licences to alienate land to the Church. Finally, there is little doubt that the expulsion of the Jews from England in 1290 was ordered with the encouragement of the nobility after complaints in the Easter parliament of 1290 that the Jews were impoverishing them by their usurious demands. The crown stood to lose from the expulsion, for it could no longer subject the Jews to oppressive and arbitrary taxation; but Edward was adequately compensated, in the short term at least, by the tax granted by parliament 'for this expulsion of the Jews', as Walter of Guisborough put it.[7]

The association of legislation with taxation in the parliament of 1290 should not, however, be taken to mean that the king invariably promulgated statutes in parliament, or that assemblies described as parliaments were necessarily attended by representatives of the commons as well as by the prelates and magnates and the king's councillors. Some statutes, such as Westminster I in 1275, were enacted in parliament with the consent of the 'archbishops, bishops, abbots, priors, earls, barons and the community of the land', but others were agreed only by the king's councillors. Parliament became of increasing importance during Edward's reign, but neither its powers nor its functions were precisely defined. The king's ministers, counsellors and judges were invariably present, and so were prelates and lay magnates, though the number of the latter might vary considerably. Representatives of the shires and urban communities were not always summoned, however, and their presence was thought essential only when a grant of tax was to be sought, for the king's councillors and the prelates and magnates could not give their consent on behalf of the whole tax-paying community. Indeed, the system of representation of shire and urban communities was evolved largely in response to the need to ensure that the consent of the whole population could be expressed.

Such considerations did not apply to the promulgation of legislation, where a wide measure of knowledge and consent was advisable but not essential. Nor did they apply to the doing of justice, which was one of the most important activities of Edward's parliament, though it was not a crucial or defining function. In its judicial capacity parliament dealt not only with matters which lower courts could not determine but also with petitions presented by individuals or groups of men seeking redress for all kinds of wrongs, though as early as 1280 Edward had to take steps to ensure that such petitions did not crowd out other, more important, parliamentary business. For parliament also dealt with general business placed before it by the king, 'the weighty business of his realm and of his foreign lands' as he put it in 1280,[8] and these matters were the concern of the prelates, magnates and councillors. It was to be many years before the representative element in parliament thought fit to concern themselves with such business. The importance of parliament in Edward's early years should not, however, be exaggerated: it was very much the creature of the king, and it was not until the last years of the reign, under the impact of military and financial problems, that parliament began to develop rapidly in cohesion and sophistication.

Thus Edward's policy in the years from 1274 to 1290 was characterized by a concern to root out corruption and injustice in government, by a willingness to embody in legislation some of the grievances and demands of the nobility, and by an assertion, however hedged around with compromise on the most sensitive issues, of the ultimate authority of the crown in jurisdiction. Although some of the legislation might be held to have borne hard on particular sections of the community, Edward seems to have experienced little difficulty in carrying the nobility with him in his programme of reform. Perhaps the clearest indication of his success is that the issues raised in the barons' wars now seemed dead. There was little reason to complain about the king's choice of advisers, and little reason, in the face of the inquiries and statutes of these years, to complain that the king was blind to corruption and injustice in government. Most of the personal animosities which had arisen during the barons' wars now seemed to have abated: Edward was able to call on the loyal service not just of his brother Edmund of Lancaster and his cousin Edmund of Cornwall, but also on men such as John de Vescy and Otto de Grandson. Vescy had supported de Montfort and compounded for his estates under the Dictum of Kenilworth, but he served Edward faithfully on numerous diplomatic missions until his death in 1289. Otto de Grandson, a Savoyard, was one of the most trusted and long-serving of Edward's companions, yet he appears to have aroused none of the hostility felt towards the Savoyard and Poitevin favourites of Henry III. Although Edward's manner of government should not be represented as a compromise between the two opposing principles of the barons' wars, he was well served by men who had fought for both points of view, and he united the community to such good effect that the issues which underlay the barons' wars did not revive in his lifetime.

The Conquest of Wales

The Great Seal of Edward I shows him on the obverse seated as a judge, and on the reverse mounted as a warrior. The seal symbolizes the two essential, fundamental functions of medieval kingship, and in the years before 1290 Edward must have appeared to his subjects as the embodiment of both ideals, for his creative work in legislation was accompanied by military success in Wales. Like the problems he faced at home, the question of his relationship with Wales went back directly to the period of the barons' wars, and as in his domestic legislation so in his settlement of Wales he was conscious of the need both to assert the ultimate supremacy of the crown and to pay due regard to the interests of the nobility in a land where the relationship between crown and nobles, both English and Welsh, was more complex than in England.

In the years after the Norman conquest of England, Norman adventurers had penetrated south and mid-Wales, extinguishing the numerous petty lordships they found there, and assuming for themselves the powers of the Welsh rulers they supplanted. Yet the degree of independence enjoyed by the Norman lords of the Welsh March, as the area under Norman domination may conveniently be called, has perhaps been exaggerated. They enjoyed the right to wage private war, which was denied to lords within the realm of England, and they might claim that they and they alone had jurisdictional rights over the inhabitants of the March, on the ground that the king's writ did not run there. All Marcher lordships, however, were held of the King of England, and the king's feudal superiority gave him the power, when the occasion arose, to exercise judicial supremacy over his tenants-in-chief in the March. In the first Statute of Westminster, for instance, Edward I declared that his sovereign lordship empowered him to do justice to all in the March who complained to him.[9] The jurisdictional supremacy of the crown did not stop at the Welsh March: even the native Welsh princes acknowledged their dependence on the English king. In 1273 Llywelyn ap Gruffydd, Prince of Wales, recognized that he held his principality of King Edward and hoped to take advantage of this relationship to persuade Edward to support him in his dealings with other Welsh princes and lords. At the same time, however, he believed that he should be free to deal with his own subjects without interference from the English king.

The period of the barons' wars in England, in which many important Marcher lords such as the Earl of Gloucester and the Lord Edward himself were involved, gave Llywelyn ap Gruffydd, then Lord of Snowdonia, an opportunity to expand his influence. By 1264 he had gained the support of the Welsh lords of the south, he had captured the Lord Edward's castles in North Wales, and even in Powys he had confined the Marcher lords to the lands east of the Severn. His price for supporting Simon de Montfort in 1264–5 was recognition by the English government of his title of Prince of Wales and thus his lordship over all the magnates of Wales, and even after de

Montfort's defeat and death Llywelyn pursued these objectives with the re-established government of King Henry. The outcome was the Treaty of Montgomery in 1267, in which Henry acknowledged Llywelyn as Prince of Wales and recognized his gains in Powys. For Llywelyn, the price was homage to Henry and a payment of 20,000 marks to the king for recognition of his title as prince. But the treaty provided ample material for dispute. The Earl of Hereford's inheritance in Brecon, for example, now fell under Llywelyn's lordship, and on both the Hereford and the Mortimer lands difficulties arose over the precise interpretation of the treaty. Above all, Llywelyn's part in the barons' wars and his negotiation of the Treaty of Montgomery had aroused the hostility of the Lord Edward, who had lost castles and lands in north Wales and seen his lordships in the south devastated. Both Edward himself and the other Marcher lords thus had personal reasons for seeking a reversal of the Treaty of Montgomery, and Edward could count on Marcher support in any campaign against Llywelyn.

Of more importance in provoking conflict, however, were Llywelyn's ambition and opportunism while Edward was away on crusade, and his failure to appreciate the seriousness of the divisions within his own family. After King Henry's death, Llywelyn refused to do homage to the absent Edward I and began to build a new castle at Dolforwyn, near Montgomery, on land claimed by a Marcher lord, Ralph de Tony. At the same time, Llywelyn's brother David plotted with the powerful southern lord Gruffydd ap Gwenwynwyn to overthrow Llywelyn and become Prince of Wales in his place. Llywelyn's reaction to the plot was swift: he seized Gruffydd's lordship, and both David and Gruffydd fled to England and appealed to Edward. LIywelyn continued to refuse homage to Edward except on his own terms, and, faced with the appeal from David and Gruffydd, Edward took his stand on a principle that he was later to use in the Scottish succession dispute. He argued that he could not do justice between Llywelyn and David unless Llywelyn became his vassal. Llywelyn still would not agree, and by November 1276 Edward's patience was exhausted. After consulting his magnates he decided to make war upon Llywelyn 'as a rebel and a disturber of his peace'. The feudal host assembled at Chester in August 1277. The king established his headquarters at Flint and then moved westwards to the Conway river at Deganwy. From Deganwy he sent a force by sea to take Anglesey and seize the grain harvest there. At the same time, the Marcher lords moved against Llywelyn in the south and west, and recovered much of the land they had lost under the Treaty of Montgomery. The loss of Anglesey, with its vital food supply, forced Llywelyn to come to terms with Edward. By the Treaty of Conway in November 1277, Llywelyn had to surrender the territory in north-east Wales known as the four cantrefs, which Edward had held between 1254 and the barons' wars, and he had to withdraw from all the lands in Powys and west Wales which he had gained under the Treaty of Montgomery. For the moment Edward was content to go no further: he did not intend to extinguish native Welsh rule entirely. Llywelyn was confined to Snowdonia, required to do homage to Edward, and subjected to a huge war indemnity of £50,000, though this was soon remitted. But he retained his title Prince of Wales, and the laws and customs of Wales remained in force within his much more restricted frontiers.

The Treaty of Conway was followed, however, by a firm demonstration of Edward's lordship in both military and judicial terms. The castles he established at Flint, Rhuddlan, Builth and Aberystwyth displayed the latest techniques of fortification, and must have done more than anything else to emphasize not only the territorial limits of Llywelyn's rule but also the great disparity in resources between Edward and Llywelyn. In his interpretation of his judicial supremacy over the principality, however, Edward went beyond the terms of the Treaty of Conway, and as in Scotland fifteen years later he aroused resentment by exercising in detailed and specific terms the authority which the Welsh had expected to be limited to a general overlordship. The resentment against Edward's exercise of his judicial powers in Wales ensured much popular support for a revolt by Llywelyn's brother David which broke out in 1282. David had supported Edward in the war of 1277, but felt that the lands he had received in two of the four cantrefs, Dyffryn Clwyd and Rhufoniog, were inadequate recompense for his loyalty. David made himself the champion of all those who were discontented by the activities of the English judicial commissioners in Wales, and Llywelyn rapidly concluded that his own position could only be maintained by supporting David: he could not afford to stand idly by and allow his brother to outbid him in opposition to English lordship. Accordingly, in March 1282 the two brothers planned a series of attacks on English-held castles throughout Wales.

Edward and his nobles treated the rebellion with great seriousness, and the king prepared an elaborate campaign, even calling upon contingents from Gascony to serve in his army. His strategy was essentially the same as he had pursued in 1277; indeed, it is doubtful whether the topography of north Wales would have allowed any other strategy to be considered. It was not feasible to invade Snowdonia from the south: as Roger Lestrange pointed out in a letter to the king in November 1282, 'the mountains are so difficult and repellent that no army could safely pass without putting the troops in great peril'.[10] The Marcher lords of the south and west could best be employed guarding the lands south of the mountains to prevent Llywelyn breaking out and supplies passing in. Edward mustered his forces, consisting

of about 750 cavalry and 8,000 foot soldiers, at Rhuddlan in August
1282. The king and the Earl of Lincoln then moved forward to secure
the Clwyd and Conway valleys, and crush the revolt in the four
cantrefs. At the same time Anglesey was seized in a naval operation,
and Luke de Tany, the commander, was ordered to build a bridge of
boats across the Menai Strait to Bangor. Tany was given strict instructions not to cross the bridge until Edward and Lincoln had completed
their operations in the Clwyd and Conway valleys, but he disobeyed
and on 6 November led his forces into an ambush set by the Welsh.
He himself and many of his knights were drowned. Edward replaced
him with his trusted Savoyard councillor Otto de Grandson, and had
just decided upon a winter campaign when news came to him that
Llywelyn had been killed on 11 December in a skirmish with a group
of Marcher lords near Builth. Llywelyn's death gravely weakened the
Welsh will to resist, and with Snowdonia surrounded they had little
choice but to surrender. In June 1283 David was captured and handed
over to Edward I, who later had him convicted of treason and executed. David's punishment contrasts sharply with the leniency shown
to the rebels after the barons' wars, and the similar punishment meted
out later to Scottish rebels suggests that Edward intended to demonstrate with great clarity how those of his subjects who made war
against him could expect to be treated.[11]

The settlement which Edward now imposed upon Wales was quite
different from the one which had followed the war of 1277. The war
of 1282–3 was a war of conquest, and the native Welsh principality
was extinguished. The new arrangements for the administration of
Wales were set out in the Statute of Rhuddlan, 1284, which declared
with resounding self-confidence that

> We have caused to be rehearsed before us and the leading men of our
> realm the laws and customs of those parts used hitherto: which being
> diligently heard and fully understood, we have, on the advice of the
> aforesaid leading men, abolished some of them, allowed some, and
> corrected some; and some others we have decreed are to be ordained
> and added thereunto.[12]

In practice, Edward's reforms were not as far-reaching as the pream-
ble to the statute suggested. The criminal law was brought into line
with English practices, but the Welsh civil law remained, Welsh local
officials continued to function, and the Welsh tenurial system survived. Indeed, the reorganization of government in Wales was neither
as far-reaching nor as beneficial to the crown as might have been
expected. In the four cantrefs only the extreme eastern portion was
made into a shire, the County of Flint, which was placed under the
control of the justice of Chester. The rest of that region was turned

into Marcher lordships for the men who had helped Edward to conquer it. The Earl of Lincoln received the Honour of Denbigh, Earl Warenne the lordship of Bromfield and Yale in the south-east of the region, and Reginald Grey the barony of Ruthin in the south-west. Snowdonia itself was divided into three counties, Anglesey, Caernarvonshire and Merionethshire, and placed under the control of a justice of North Wales. Finally, in 1301, the newly conquered lands were granted as an appanage to the king's eldest son, who was now created Prince of Wales. Prince Edward had been born at Caernarvon in 1284, and although the story of his presentation to the conquered Welsh as a prince who could speak no English has no basis in fact, it is not without interest for the light it casts on the popular view of the king's character.

Edward's supremacy over the Welsh was also expressed in architectural terms. He had castles built at Conway, Caernarvon, Harlech and Criccieth, while at Conway and Caernarvon walled towns were established as well, which were to form centres of English settlement and English custom in a land where urbanization was unknown. The legend still persisted in north Wales that Magnus Maximus, father of the emperor Constantine, had died at 'the fort in Arfon', and in 1282 Edward arranged for the discovery of Maximus's body and its ceremonial reburial in the church at Caernarvon. The castle which Edward built at Caernarvon was designed to symbolize this connection with imperial Rome which had been preserved in Welsh romance, and to express Edward's imperial ambition in Britain. The polygonal towers of the castle and the bands of dark masonry on the walls resemble the Theodosian wall at Constantinople, and the design of one of the towers incorporated an imperial eagle on each of its three turrets.[13]

The Marcher lordships in the rest of Wales were left alone, even though by conquering the native Welsh principality Edward had removed both the main threat to these lordships and the principal military justification for their existence. Yet incorporating them within a system of administration modelled upon that of England would almost certainly have provoked a conflict with the nobility: not until most of the lordships were in royal hands, in the time of the Tudors, was such a reorganization possible. Nonetheless, the Marcher lords had to recognize the ultimate judicial authority of the crown, and Edward's military conquest of the native principality gave him the prestige and pre-eminence with which to assert such authority.

In the 1290s royal intervention in the Marcher lordships increased substantially, the best known instance being the dispute between the Earls of Gloucester and Hereford. The dispute originated when Gloucester began building a castle at Morlais in the upper Taff valley, on land claimed by the Earl of Hereford as part of his lordship of Brecon.

War broke out between the two lords; Hereford complained to the king in the parliament of January 1290, and Edward issued a proclamation calling on both lords to cease hostilities. Gloucester ignored the proclamation, and his men raided the lordship of Brecon three times in the ensuing year. In the parliament of January 1291 Hereford complained again, and this time the king appointed a commission of inquiry under the Bishop of Ely. Gloucester ignored a summons to attend the commission at Llanthew and received support from many other Marcher lords, who refused to be sworn as a jury at the inquiry on the ground that it was 'not according to the customs of the March'.[14] The Bishop of Ely replied that for the common good the king was by his prerogative in some instances above the laws and customs of the realm, and even lords Marcher held their Marches under the crown. A jury of lesser men was empanelled, damages against Gloucester were assessed at £100, and the judges formally forbade a renewal of private war.

Hereford, however, chose to retaliate against Gloucester, despite the prohibition, and in doing so gave Edward the chance to proceed against him as well as Gloucester. Both earls were summoned to appear before the king at Abergavenny in October 1291; both were sentenced to imprisonment and loss of their lands for their presumption in believing that by virtue of their liberties in the March they could avoid the penalties they would have deserved if they had committed such acts elsewhere in the realm. The king eventually remitted the sentence of imprisonment and forfeiture, and imposed a fine of 1,000 marks on Hereford, and 10,000 marks on Gloucester, which he never paid. Edward had asserted in an unequivocal manner the principle of the ultimate judicial authority of the crown in the Marches, but the price he had to pay was high, for he created a sense of resentment, particularly in the March, which was to have an important bearing on the attitude of the Marcher lords to the king in the crisis of 1297. Edward's conflict with Hereford and Gloucester damaged his relationship with the two earls, but it also had wider significance. The arguments of the royal commissioners at Llanthew set out, in uncompromising manner, the principles on which Edward believed his authority should rest: although the Marcher lords retained many of their privileges, royal jurisdictional pressure on their lordships was intensified, and it was clear that ultimate authority here as elsewhere in Edward's dominions rested with the king.[15]

The enemies Edward made by his assertion of such principles were to create political difficulties for him after 1296, but in the early 1290s his personal prestige stood at its height. The principles of authority which he sought to establish had been effectively asserted both in administration within England and in his settlement of Wales, and they had been accomplished with little or no generalized opposition from the nobility. Indeed, the campaign in Wales had been carried out with the military and political support of the nobility, especially perhaps the Earls of Lincoln, Warwick and Warenne, and William de Valence Lord of Pembroke. Their service was rewarded, if only modestly, and even Edward's intervention in the quarrel between Gloucester and Hereford did not provoke any general aristocratic opposition. The nearest Edward came to encountering a coalition against him was the refusal of those summoned to the inquiry at Llanthew to be empanelled as jurors. His dispute with Gloucester and Hereford might have been transformed into a more general revolt against his authority in the March, for other lords such as Richard Fitzalan of Oswestry and Clun and Edmund Mortimer of Wigmore had reason to be aggrieved by Edward's policy, but his military prestige in the aftermath of the conquest of Wales and the financial pressure he could bring against recalcitrant nobles inhibited any more general expressions of discontent.

The Welsh wars and their aftermath, therefore, placed no great strain on relations between Edward I and the nobility; nor did they lead to prolonged financial burdens on the realm, though their immediate cost was great. The nobility called to service in Edward's armies by virtue of their feudal tenure refused the king's suggestion that they should be paid wages, but the household troops, men-at-arms and archers, and others who brought retinues to the war were paid. The fleet had to be paid and supplied, and over £60,000 was spent on castle building. The money was found by loans, mainly from the Italian bankers of Lucca, the Riccardi, and from the proceeds of a tour around England to raise loans undertaken by John Kirkby, the king's Treasurer. In 1283 the king seized the proceeds of a crusading tax which had been deposited in churches throughout the realm (though protests forced him to return most of it), and parliament voted a tax of one-thirtieth on movable goods. The clergy also granted a tax. It has been estimated that the war cost £150,000, and the money was raised by these various expedients; but the difficulties the king experienced, and the desperate measures he was forced to adopt showed that even a brief and successful war could not be accomplished without some financial strain.

From 1294 onwards, however, the whole scale of Edward's military operations changed dramatically as he became involved in almost continuous conflict, first with France and then with Scotland. Edward faced unprecedented problems over recruiting, supplying and financing his armies, and the strains of war gave rise to a major political crisis in 1297, the repercussions of which did much to determine the course of Edward's last years.

The Scottish Succession

Although Edward's handling of the affairs of Scotland shows some similarities to his Welsh policy, the two countries and the two wars were in reality very different in character, perhaps more different than Edward himself ever fully appreciated. Throughout the thirteenth century there had been antagonism and warfare between the English and the Welsh, and the wars had something of the character of colonial enterprises. On the other hand, the native princes of Wales had never sought to deny their feudal dependence on England, though Llywelyn was reluctant actually to do homage to Edward, and Edward frequently exercised his judicial rights over both the Marcher lordships and the native Welsh principality. The position of Scotland, however, was different. The Scottish kings were neither crowned nor anointed but they and the Scottish nobles were unwilling to accept the English claim to overlordship, which Edward had asserted as recently as 1278, when Alexander III had nevertheless maintained that he owed homage to the English king only for the lands he held in England. Nevertheless the Scottish nobility, many of whom were members of Anglo-Norman families which had migrated peacefully to Scotland in the reign of David I (1124–53), Malcolm IV (1153–65) and William the Lion (1165–1214), had close ties with their English counterparts. Such men as Robert Bruce of Annandale, John Balliol of Barnard Castle and Gilbert de Umfraville Earl of Angus held substantial estates on both sides of the border. Despite the English claim to overlordship, relations between the two realms had for the most part been peaceful during the thirteenth century, and it is perhaps significant that whereas Llywelyn of Wales had sought to marry Eleanor, daughter of Simon de Montfort, Alexander III had married Margaret, daughter of Henry III, and had made no attempt to take advantage of the barons' wars to pursue his family's traditional, though by then formally renounced, claim to Northumberland and Cumberland. Furthermore, although there were important social and linguistic differences within Scotland, and the topography of the country made effective centralized government difficult, it possessed an organized and developed political structure, with institutions modelled to a great extent on those of England, and, as events were to show, its political community had some sense of cohesion.

Edward I's interest in Scotland before 1292 was of a different kind from his concerns in Wales. He had never, of course, been a landowner in Scotland, and there was no group of powerful noblemen in the north comparable to the Marcher lords in Wales to influence his policy towards Scotland: the emergence of a northern Marcher nobility in England and a specifically Scottish aristocracy north of the border is one of the more important consequences, rather than a cause, of the war with Scotland. Many lords and knights in northern England and in Scotland had links with both countries, and might look both to the English and to the Scottish court for advancement. To such men, a prolonged war between the two kingdoms might produce a difficult conflict of allegiance, as well as presenting a threat to their lands and offices in one country or the other.[16] For his part, Edward's main concern was to ensure that Scotland remained stable and well governed, neither courted by England's enemies nor plunged into civil war. Although in 1278 he had reserved the right to assert the English claim to overlordship at some time in the future, there is no reason to believe that he had formed a plan for the conquest of Scotland and was merely waiting for an opportunity to put it into effect.

The stability of Scotland depended on the continuity and fitness of the ruling house of Canmore, the descendants of Malcolm III, and it was the dynasty's failure in the direct line which provoked a political crisis leading eventually to Edward's intervention. In March 1286, Alexander III was killed when he fell over a cliff while riding to see his wife at Kinghorn in Fife. All his children had died in his lifetime, and his sole remaining heir was his three-year-old granddaughter Margaret, daughter of King Erik II of Norway. The Scottish nobility seem to have accepted the prospect of a minority with some equanimity. A boat was sent to bring Queen Margaret home from Norway, and at the same time the Scottish nobles opened negotiations with Edward I for the marriage of Margaret to the young Prince Edward of Caernarvon. In an atmosphere of cordiality, indicative of the good relations between the realms which had developed in the course of the century, Edward and the Scottish nobles reached agreement, embodied in the Treaty of Birgham of July 1290. The union between the two kingdoms which was to follow the marriage of Margaret and Edward was to be personal only. Scotland was to retain its separate parliament and other institutions, and, of great significance in view of what was shortly to occur, appeals from Scotland were not to be heard in the English king's court, nor were the Scottish nobility to be liable to military service in England.[17] Had the treaty been implemented, Anglo-Scottish relations might have embarked on a quite different course; but Margaret was taken ill on her journey home and died at Kirkwall in September 1290.

A full-scale crisis over the Scottish succession now ensued, and the rivalries of the noble families, which had largely been kept under control as long as Margaret lived, came into the open and threatened civil war. The Bishop of St Andrews, understandably concerned at the prospect of bloodshed, asked Edward to come to the border and arbitrate in the succession dispute. Edward acceded to the bishop's request and met the Scottish nobles at a parliament at Norham in

November 1291. In a tactic reminiscent of his treatment of David and Llywelyn in Wales he insisted that he could not give judgement unless the Scottish nobility accepted his feudal overlordship and thus placed themselves within his jurisdiction, a real point cleverly exploited to gain a political advantage. The Scottish nobility were taken aback by Edward's request and stated that 'they have no knowledge of your right, nor did they ever see it claimed and used by you or your ancestors; therefore they answer you, as far as in them lies, that they have no power to reply to your statement in default of a lord to whom the demand ought to be addressed and who will have power to make answer about it'. Eventually, however, they gave way and agreed to recognize him as overlord; indeed, the only alternative was civil war. Edward then received the claims of the various contenders.[18] Some were of little worth, such as those from the various illegitimate descendants of recent Scottish kings; one, that of John Hastings, rested on the principle that the realm of Scotland, like a feudal barony, should be partitioned amongst coheiresses, the daughters of David Earl of Huntingdon, younger brother of William the Lion. This provoked a debate about whether Scotland was a kingdom and, if so, whether kingdoms observed the same laws of succession as feudal baronies. Edward judged that Scotland was a kingdom, and was impartible; a judgement based no doubt largely upon common sense, but also perhaps upon a concern to establish a precedent under which if he himself should die leaving only his daughters to succeed him the kingdom of England should not be partitioned amongst their husbands.

The real issue, however, lay, between Robert Bruce and John Balliol, both of whom were descended from the daughters of David Earl of Huntingdon. Bruce was nearer in degree, but Balliol was descended from the senior line. The arguments for each candidate were complex and much debated, with principles from both Roman and feudal law being cited in support; but Edward eventually gave judgement in favour of Balliol. It is unlikely that considerations of political advantage played a large part in his decision. Both Bruce and Balliol had lands in northern England, and both could thus be subjected to some degree of pressure, as Balliol found to his cost during the hearing of his claim. But Bruce was a much older man than Balliol, and not necessarily likely to be less pliable, despite substantial support for his claim amongst other Scottish noble families, which did not greatly diminish after the award to Balliol. In all probability Edward's judgement was founded upon law rather than political expediency, and although it may have solved the immediate problem of the succession it did not succeed in reuniting the Scottish community.

John Balliol did homage to Edward for his kingdom of Scotland at Newcastle in December 1292. In awarding him the kingdom, Edward warned Balliol to govern justly, 'lest the suzerain of Scotland should feel obliged to apply a guiding hand',[19] and it was not long before Balliol and the Scottish community learned how firm Edward's guiding hand might be. Edward now extended to his vassal kingdom of Scotland the same principles of judicial supremacy he had sought to maintain in Wales, using justice as a vehicle for the assertion of his overlordship in a much more intensive manner than the Scots had expected. Almost at once, conflict arose over the hearing of appeals from Scotland in King Edward's court. Edward's right to hear appeals derived from his position as overlord of Scotland; but some of the Scottish nobles, mindful of the clause in the Treaty of Birgham which had laid down that no appeals were to be heard outside Scotland, hoped that Edward would not cite Balliol to appear in court in England. Edward insisted, however, no doubt with right on his side, that the Treaty of Birgham no longer applied, and he proceeded to mete out to Balliol the same kind of treatment that he himself had received from Philip IV of France over appeals from Gascony.[20]

For Scottish nobles discontented with decisions in Balliol's court, the appellate jurisdiction of the English king provided them with an opportunity to have the king of Scots' judgements overturned in England. Matters came to a head in November 1293 when Macduff, the brother of the Earl of Fife, appealed to Edward against a judgement of imprisonment given by Balliol. Balliol attended Edward's court to answer Macduff's appeal, but said that he was 'king of the realm of Scotland and dare not make answer at the suit of Macduff, nor in anything touching his kingdom, without the advice of the people of his realm'.[21] Balliol was evidently under some pressure from the Scottish nobility to resist English jurisdiction; one chronicler perhaps goes too far in suggesting that Balliol was friendless, a lamb among wolves,[22] but there were many nobles and prelates who feared the disintegration of their political community if Balliol allowed himself to be treated merely as an English baron. Edward offered Balliol an adjournment to seek the advice of his people, but Balliol refused the offer, fearing that to agree would imply acceptance of the jurisdiction of the English court. Edward responded by declaring Balliol guilty of contempt of court, and sentenced him to forfeit the castles of Edinburgh, Roxburgh and Stirling. Balliol now submitted, and accepted an adjournment.

At this point, however, the conflict over appeals took second place to the argument over military service from Scotland which erupted on the outbreak of war between England and France in May 1294. Since the Treaty of Paris in 1259, the King of England had held the Duchy of Aquitaine (Gascony) of the King of France by homage and fealty. The feudal relationship between the two kings was particularly sensitive and gave rise to much difficulty. The King of France not only used his judicial supremacy to encourage appeals from Gascons discontented with judgements in the English king's courts, but he might also treat Edward as a disobedient vassal when the interests of the two kings clashed elsewhere, and sentence Edward to loss of the duchy in order to put pressure on him to comply with his wishes. Thus the war of 1294, which began as a private quarrel between sailors, soon became a war for the defence of Gascony. In May 1293 a long-running private feud between the mariners of the Cinque Ports and those of Normandy erupted again. The Cinque Ports fleet defeated the Normans off Cap St Mathieu in Brittany and went on to sack La Rochelle. Philip IV of France decided to take action and required restitution from Edward. Edward argued that incidents at sea should be settled by the international custom of the sea, the law of Oléron, but Philip ordered Edward to appear before him in his court at Paris in January 1294. Edward refused to go, negotiations between Philip and Edward's brother Edmund of Lancaster broke down, and in May 1294 Edward was declared guilty of contempt of court and ordered to forfeit his Duchy of Aquitaine. The parallel with his own treatment of Balliol was close, and ominous.

Edward's response was to prepare for war. He constructed an elaborate network of alliances in the Low Countries, and summoned parliament to meet at Westminster in June 1294. Amongst those who attended was the King of Scotland, who promised aid for the reconquest of Gascony. Later the same month, Balliol together with eight earls, the Steward of Scotland, and twelve Scottish barons were included in Edward's summons to the host for military service in Gascony. Edward's plans were interrupted, however, by the outbreak of a rebellion in Wales led by Madog ap Llywelyn, a Welsh nobleman who had been loyal to Edward in the vain hope that the king would uphold his claim to Merioneth. The rebels seized Caernarvon Castle in October 1294 and killed the sheriff; the king retaliated by assembling a large army for a winter campaign, but the rebels ambushed his baggage train between Conway and Bangor, and he had to abandon the campaign. In the following spring, however, Madog was captured near Montgomery, and when Edward advanced into north Wales in April the revolt collapsed.

Events in Scotland now presented a much more serious threat to Edward's plans. The outbreak of war with France had encouraged Edward to increase his demands on the Scots, and to treat Scotland even more obviously as a subordinate kingdom. At the same time it strengthened the Scottish will to resist and gave rise to a widespread fear that Edward intended to exploit the resources of Scotland to sustain his war against France. In November 1295 the Scots concluded an offensive and defensive alliance with the French, each ally agreeing that the other would not make a separate peace with

England. War between England and Scotland now seemed inevitable: the Scottish host was summoned to meet near Selkirk in March 1296, but not all the nobility answered the call. There were those amongst the Scottish nobility, notably the two Robert Bruces, son and grandson of Robert Bruce the Competitor, who were not prepared to fight for Balliol, and who perhaps hoped to exploit Balliol's difficulties for their own advantage. Bruce the Competitor never did homage to Balliol, but died the year before war broke out, and his son held Carlisle Castle for the English king. Edward was soon to take advantage of the rivalries and dissension within the ranks of the Scottish nobility.

The war which now ensued between England and Scotland was fought with bitterness and brutality on both sides. On 20 March 1296 Edward took Berwick upon Tweed by storm, and massacred the inhabitants: one contemporary chronicler compares their fall to that of autumn leaves,[23] surely far too gentle a simile to convey the butchery that occurred. The Scottish forces took their stand at Dunbar, but on 27 April 1296 Earl Warenne overwhelmed them. The principal castles of the south, Dunbar, Roxburgh and Jedburgh, now capitulated; Edinburgh Castle held out for only a week, and at Stirling the garrison fled in face of Edward's advance. Balliol's rout was virtually complete: only a few members of the Comyn family stood by him, and at Kincardine on 2 July 1296 he was required to surrender his kingdom to Edward. He was sent into imprisonment south of the Trent, and Edward completed the assertion of his lordship with a triumphal march as far as Elgin, meeting no resistance. On his return south he held a parliament at Berwick, at which he received the submission of most of the leading Scottish nobles, prelates, and men of lesser standing, including Robert Bruce the grandson of the Competitor and future leader of resistance to Edward.

After the Berwick parliament Edward must have felt that he had dealt with the Scottish problem as speedily and successfully as he had conquered the Welsh. Indeed, he intended his settlement of Scotland to be just as much a conquest as he had achieved in Wales. Robert Bruce, the Competitor's son, may have hoped that by siding with Edward he would take Balliol's place as a vassal king, but Edward dismissed the idea curtly, saying that he had other things to do than win kingdoms for Bruce.[24] Edward himself assumed the lordship of Scotland, and he set out to destroy the symbols that embodied the Scottish people's sense of identity. The great seal of Scotland was broken up, many relics, plate and jewellery were taken south, and the Stone of Destiny was removed from Scone and sent to Westminster Abbey as a gift to Edward's patron Edward the Confessor. Scotland was now described in documents as a 'land', ruled by the king of England: Scottish kingship had ceased to exist, and Scotland, like Wales, was now a conquered territory of the king of England. Earl Warenne was appointed Keeper of Scotland, and English officials were placed in charge of the administration, though local government remained in Scottish hands. Those Scottish lords who refused to submit to Edward suffered confiscation of their lands, which were granted to English nobles. Edward may have believed that the Scottish kingdom had ceased to exist; yet in imposing this settlement upon Scotland he seriously underestimated the sense of cohesion within the Scottish community and the will to resist that still survived despite the divisions within the ranks of the Scottish nobility and the lengthy and impressive list of submissions to Edward at the Berwick parliament.

The Last Years: War and Political Conflict

Edward now sought to concentrate his attention and resources on the war with France, but in doing so he precipitated a major domestic political crisis and gave the Scots the opportunity to rebel. From the outset, Edward encountered difficulties in raising money, manpower and supplies, and his dealings with the merchants over the taxation of wool exports, with the laity in parliament, and with the clergy in their councils gave rise to protests and to co-operation that was often reluctant. In 1294 Edward first turned his attention to the wool trade, and gave orders for the seizure of all the wool in England, hoping that by exporting it as a monopoly seller he would make a large profit for the crown, while eventually repaying the producers. This scheme met much resistance, and Edward had to abandon it in favour of an export duty of 63s 4d per sack; this too had to be modified, and the customs duty was eventually set at 40s per sack, though this tax too was unpopular with the wool producers. At much the same time Edward seized the money which the church in England had collected to pay a papal crusading tax of one-tenth of the assessed wealth of the clergy, and it is not surprising that Edward's demand for a tax of one-half of the clergy's wealth, which he made later in 1294, received an angry response. Indeed, the Dean of St Paul's is said to have died of apoplexy on discovering what the king had in mind. Edward first sought to persuade the clergy by using the plea of necessity and reminding them of their obligation, along with that of the lay community, to render aid to the king when the safety and welfare of his subjects was in danger. When that argument failed and the clergy offered only two tenths for one year, Edward took an altogether firmer line and threatened them with outlawry if they did not concede the half that he had demanded. This they did, though ominously for Edward one chronicler recorded afterwards that 'If they had first considered the issues more thoroughly and seriously, they would not have ventured to make any concession to the king without consulting the Pope'.[25]

The laity, however, were initially rather more co-operative. Although Edward had to be content with a tax of a tenth and a sixth from the parliament of November 1294, when he had asked for a third and a sixth, parliament raised little objection to further grants of tax on the value of movable goods in the November parliaments of 1295 and 1296.[26] The clergy rather than the laity were the first to oppose the king's growing financial demands. In 1295 the clergy granted a tax of one-tenth, supported by Archbishop Winchelsey with the argument that the king could not defend both himself and the clergy against the enemy without aid from the clergy, and he even promised a further tax next year if there were need for it. In February 1296, however, Edward's difficulties over clerical taxation were exacerbated when Pope Boniface VIII issued the bull *Clericis Laicos*, in which he forbade the clergy to pay taxes to lay rulers. The bull was directed mainly against Edward I and Philip IV, and Boniface may have hoped that pressure of this kind might induce the two kings to make peace; he was also, no doubt, mindful that such a prohibition might make it easier for the papacy to raise taxes on the clergy to finance its own political and diplomatic activities.

The papal bull was received either just before or during the parliament which assembled at Bury St Edmunds in November 1296, in which Edward again asked the clergy for a tax, and led by Archbishop Winchelsey they now refused. Edward responded by outlawing them in January 1297. The way in which royal officials carried out the sentence of outlawry created great bitterness within the Church, for sheriffs were ordered to confiscate both the lands and the goods of the clergy. One contemporary chronicler noted that after the seizure the monks of Christ Church, Canterbury, 'had nothing to eat or drink for several days from their own stores and relied upon the charity of their friends',[27] and it was believed that the outlawry gave licence for laymen to attack and rob clerics. In the face of such a forceful onslaught on their property the clergy did not resist for long, and they submitted in July 1297 with a grant of one-fifth of their incomes.

The problem of clerical taxation might have seemed less serious had it not coincided with a growing reluctance on the part of the lay community to contribute to Edward's wars. The laity showed their hostility not just to Edward's demands for money, but also to his methods of obtaining military service and supplies for his armies. The obligation of subjects to do military service for the crown was well established in custom but was not defined with any precision. The tenants-in-chief of the crown acknowledged their duty to serve when called upon to do so in accordance with their feudal obligation. They did not, however, believe that this obligation required them to serve overseas, yet they showed a marked reluctance to accept payment for service overseas, perhaps believing that to do so was dishonourable and demeaning to their status. In 1295, for instance, the Earl of Arundel and thirteen other barons and knights refused to serve in Gascony at the king's wages, and Edward brought severe financial pressure against them to compel them to go. The feudal summons alone, however, could not provide Edward with the troops he needed, and he attempted to broaden the basis of military obligation by requiring men whose lands reached a certain value to take up knighthood and be ready to serve the king in war. In January 1296 he ordered all £40 landowners to be arrayed for service; in November all £30 landowners were required to take up knighthood, and in the following year he ordered all £20 landowners to muster at London. The order made no mention of payment, and did not say where those summoned were to serve. The Constable and the Marshal (the Earls of Hereford and Norfolk) refused to muster the troops, and Edward dismissed both of them.

Earlier in the year, at the Salisbury parliament in February 1297, the king had clashed with Norfolk and Hereford over plans for the war with France. It seems that Edward intended to lead an expedition to Flanders himself, and attack France from the north, while the two earls were to be sent to Gascony. But according to Guisborough, both earls refused to serve unless the king went with them. The king insisted that they should go to Gascony without him, saying that Norfolk must either go or hang. Norfolk replied that he would neither go nor hang, and he withdrew from parliament, taking various other malcontents with him.[28] According to one source,[29] Norfolk and his friends then held their own assembly in the Forest of Wyre in the Mortimer liberty of Cleobury, where they were joined by the Earl of Hereford. In view of Edward's earlier treatment of the Marcher lords it is not surprising that aristocratic opposition to the king developed in the Marches, and the individual grievances of the Marcher lords played a part in determining their political stance.

Edward's continued exactions were to reveal that discontent was not limited to a group of Marcher lords. The resistance of the Constable and the Marshal had forced him to abandon his plan to mobilize the £20 landowners for service in France, and instead he tried to induce men to serve in Flanders by offering wages, but he received a very poor response. As Professor Prestwich has shown, the troops that eventually accompanied the king to Flanders were mainly household forces: 'not one single earl accompanied the king'.[30] At the same time, opposition was growing to the financial demands of the crown. In March 1297 the king had ordered the seizure of all wool belonging to foreign merchants, intending to export it and use the money thus raised to finance the expedition to Flanders. The seizure was soon extended to the wool of native merchants, but this provoked such an outcry that in June 1297 the king issued a proclamation denying any knowledge of the seizure of native merchants' wool and ordering it to be released. Another seizure was ordered in July but resistance was so strong that little more than a third of the wool the king expected to receive was actually requisitioned.

Of all the grievances against the king's government which were articulated in 1297, however, none was so widely felt as that over the right of prise, the right of the king and his agents to requisition foodstuffs to supply the army and to pay now or (more often) later at below the market price. The king's right to requisition supplies for his household was ancient and accepted, and had generally been local in extent and limited in scope; but between May 1296 and June 1297 the right was enormously extended to provide victuals for the army. The prises of this year provoked hostility on two counts: although men were supposed to be left sufficient foodstuffs for their own immediate needs, the seizures were obviously burdensome, especially if the harvest had been poor; and the behaviour of the royal officials empowered to levy the prises aroused resentment. Above all, men complained that they were not paid for the foodstuffs seized, and that some men were able to secure exemption from the prise by bribing royal officials, thus increasing the burden on their neighbours.

Few if any of these exactions had traditionally been unpopular. Taxation which was occasional in nature and not excessive in scale was acceptable to both clergy and laity, while a modest levy on the export of wool aroused little opposition as long as the trade was not manipulated for financial purposes. The feudal summons for military service for short periods within the realm was traditional and honourable; and the right of prise as an occasional and local burden was borne without undue complaint. But in 1296 and 1297 Edward appeared to be extending these local and occasional burdens into regular, national and permanent obligations, justified by the plea of necessity. It was this revolutionary extension of traditional obligations which aroused such widespread opposition, and the opposition found its leaders in the Earls of Hereford and Norfolk, who had their own private grievances against the king over military service and over the custom of the March.

Opposition came to a head in July 1297. When the Constable and the Marshal refused to co-operate in mustering the forces recruited for service in Flanders they wrote to the king suggesting that he should appoint someone else from his household to hold the muster. The two earls then withdrew from court, and Edward was to leave England without meeting them again. Later in the same month he procured a tax of one-eighth, granted by 'those standing around in his chamber'.[31] Although parliament was in session, the tax was not granted by parliament in the accepted manner, and it appears that the king had persuaded a small group of his military supporters to grant it. The collection of the tax was authorized on 30 July, but the government clearly felt uneasy, for on 8 August royal officials were instructed to 'speak to the people in the most courteous way possible', and to tell them that the earls and barons had consented to the tax.[32]

Edward continued his preparations for the expedition to Flanders, but at the end of July his opponents drew up a document known as the Remonstrances, in which they set out their grievances. The Remonstrances were published in the name of the archbishops, bishops, earls, barons and all the community of the realm. The king's opponents protested that the summons to serve overseas, which did not mention where those summoned were to serve, was too vague, and that since it was believed that the king wished to go to Flanders, the community felt obliged to point out that they did not owe service there. Even if they did owe service there, or anywhere else, they lacked the means to do it 'for they had been worn down too much with divers tallages, aids, and prises'. They complained that the laws and customs of the land were not being upheld, and they also said that they were oppressed by the tax on wool, 'which is too heavy... at 40s on the sack... for the wool of England approaches the value of half of all the land, and the tax which is on it approaches a fifth of the value of all the land'. They concluded by arguing that it was unwise for the king to go to Flanders until he was more assured of the loyalty of the Flemings, and that his departure would be a signal for the Scots to rebel. The document complained of the burden of taxation rather than its constitutional propriety, and by stressing the practical consequences of Edward's demands, its authors expected a sympathetic audience.[33]

The Remonstrances were evidently intended to circulate widely, and they probably reached Edward at Winchelsea in early August. On 12 August Edward issued a manifesto in which he set out his version of events. He declared that he had no knowledge of any articles issued by the earls, though he claimed to have heard rumours of their protest. The manifesto[34] began in a conciliatory manner: the king declared that he greatly regretted the hardships and burdens he had had to impose upon his people, and he promised that he would make amends when he returned from Flanders. He also said that 'the great lords who were recently with him in London' had made him 'a common grant such as he is in great need of at the present time', a reference to the eighth, and he begged the people not to consider this 'gift', as he called it, burdensome. But he warned that anyone disturbing the peace would fall under excommunication by virtue of a bull of Pope Clement IV which the king had in his possession, 'wherefore it behoves each one to take care'. On this minatory note Edward concluded his preparations for embarkation, and sailed from Winchelsea for Flanders on 21 August. On the following day, Hereford and Norfolk went to the Exchequer with a body of armed retainers and forbade the levying of the tax. They wrote to the king saying that the eighth had never been granted by the earls, barons or community of England, and that nothing sooner put men in bondage than to be tallaged arbitrarily. The king replied by ordering the levy to go ahead, but promising that it should not be 'to the prejudice nor to the bondage of any man, nor taken as a precedent in future'.[35]

The country seems to have been moving towards civil war in the summer of 1297. Hereford's and Norfolk's armed demonstration at the Exchequer was an overt challenge to Edward's authority, and castles were put in a state of readiness in various parts of the country. However, the outbreak of rebellion in Scotland made it essential for the English to settle their differences. The rebellion was led by William Wallace, a member of a knightly family from Renfrewshire and a vassal of James Stewart. The Lanercost Chronicle suggests that Stewart and the Bishop of Glasgow advocated rebellion, but persuaded Wallace to lead it because neither of them dared to take part. Wallace enjoyed widespread support. According to Walter of Guisborough, 'the community of the land' followed him, which has sometimes been held to mean the common people, but it may have a wider meaning, and Wallace certainly had some backing from the aristocracy and their dependants, at least as long as he was successful against the English.[36] On 11 September he defeated an English army under the Earl Warenne and Hugh Cressingham, Edward's Treasurer in Scotland, at the battle of Stirling Bridge. Earl Warenne fled to Berwick, and Cressingham was killed in the battle. The Scots flayed him and made souvenirs out of his skin. The whole English position in Scotland collapsed abruptly, revealing how shallowly it was based. Wallace, writing to the merchants of Lübeck and Hamburg, declared that Scotland was now 'recovered by war from the power of the English'.[37]

The reaction of the English government to the defeat in Scotland was to seek a settlement of the political crisis which had erupted during the summer. Tension remained high in the autumn of 1297. The government thought it necessary to issue a proclamation on 16 September forbidding unlawful assemblies, yet some lords evidently mustered their forces. According to Guisborough, Hereford and Norfolk came to parliament in October with sizeable bodies of armed men. But the councillors appointed by the king to act in his absence were anxious to reach agreement, and with Archbishop Winchelsey as mediator the two sides came together. The earls set out their demands in a document, the exact provenance of which is uncertain, known as *De Tallagio non Concedendo*.[38] The emotive use of the word tallage –

a levy usually imposed only on unfree tenants – suggests that the king's opponents were concerned as much with the principle of consent to taxation as with its burdensome effect, for the first clause required that taxes should be levied only with the consent of all free men. The document also required that the maltolt, the 40s export duty on wool, should be abolished, and that prises should be taken only with the consent of the vendor. *De Tallagio* was probably intended as a negotiating position, and the outcome of the discussion was an agreement under which the king promised to confirm Magna Carta and the Charter of the Forest, and to add to the charter certain supplementary articles which went some way towards meeting the barons' grievances. Henceforward no aids, taxes or prises were to be levied without consent; the maltolt was to be abolished and not levied again without consent; and Edward formally remitted his 'rancour and ill will' against Hereford, Norfolk and their supporters. The settlement was sufficient to bring the political crisis to an end, though it did not go as far as the earls might have wished. The new articles were not incorporated in Magna Carta, and thus lacked the special authority that such incorporation would have given them; and the means by which consent to taxes and prises was to be obtained in the future was left vague. Too much depended on Edward's good intentions.

The crisis of 1297 had revealed how widespread was opposition to Edward's exactions, and how little sympathy the plea of necessity aroused. Yet without the leadership of Hereford and Norfolk, for reasons which have as much to do with their personal grievances against the king as with constitutional issues, the opposition to the king could hardly have achieved the success it did. The two nobles took upon themselves, as the chief military officers of the crown, the leadership of the community in resisting Edward's demands. As the crisis developed, the community also showed its concern that the king should observe the law in his dealings with his subjects. Magna Carta not only symbolized the general principle that the king was bound by the law, but it was also capable of being treated as the nucleus of a body of law to which new articles could be added as new problems arose. Although there were clear indications in 1297 that the nobility were prepared to resort to arms if necessary, the main thrust of their policy was to subject the royal prerogative to legal limitation and definition in those areas where its arbitrary exercise had given rise to widespread grievances.

In the last ten years of Edward's reign, however, his need to mobilize the country's resources for war in no way diminished, and he showed little inclination, in face of his continuing necessity, to accept the limitations on his prerogative implicit in the settlement of 1297. The focus of attention now shifted to Scotland. While the regents in

England were dealing with the domestic political crisis, Edward made a truce with Philip IV which effectively marked the end of the war with France. The truce was renewed at intervals until the peace of 1303, by which Edward regained Gascony. Edward had little option but to seek a truce: the Scottish victory at Stirling Bridge made a renewed campaign in Scotland inevitable, and Edward had neither the resources nor the political goodwill to sustain war on two fronts. The war in France had not gone particularly well for Edward: the French had confined English authority in Gascony to a coastal strip, and thus much of the cost of defending the duchy fell upon England. It has been suggested that the cost of defending Gascony was 'about half the estimated total of receipts from all the lay subsidies of Edward I's reign',[39] and it was thus a major reason for the strain on English resources between 1294 and 1297. An expedition to relieve the duchy had set out in January 1296 led by the Earls of Lincoln and Lancaster, but Lancaster died in June, depriving the king of one of his most valued counsellors and lieutenants, and Lincoln could do little but hold the position in Gascony until the truce was concluded.

During the winter of 1297–8 the Scots took the war into England, devastating Northumberland from a base in Rothbury Forest and laying waste much of north Cumberland. According to Guisborough,[40] only the intercession of St Cuthbert stopped them from ravaging Durham as well. The king wrote from Flanders to the Scottish magnates summoning all who remained loyal to him to a parliament at York in January 1298, but none came. On his return to England in March 1298 Edward held another parliament at York, which made preparations for a full-scale campaign in Scotland. In early July the army set out for Edinburgh, hoping to pick up supplies; but contrary winds prevented most of the supplies from getting through. When they finally arrived they turned out to consist mainly of wine.[41] The Welsh contingents in Edward's army promptly got drunk and began to stage anti-English demonstrations, which not surprisingly raised doubts in Edward's mind about their loyalty when it came to battle. Indeed, Edward was faced with the prospect of having to retreat for lack of adequate supplies when he received news that the Scottish army under Wallace was assembled at Falkirk. Had Wallace known that Edward's supply lines had broken down he probably would not have offered battle to the English; but Edward advanced to Falkirk and defeated Wallace's forces on 22 July. Despite the strong resistance offered by the Scottish spearmen drawn up in tight formations known as schiltroms, repeated cavalry charges wore them down and at last destroyed them.

Wallace's position had depended essentially on his continued success in war; after his defeat he fled, eventually reaching France, and Edward advanced to Perth, meeting little resistance. He returned to

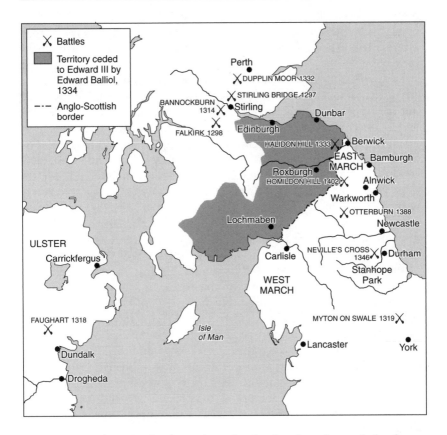

Map 1   Northern England, southern Scotland and north-east Ireland: to
illustrate the Anglo-Scottish wars, 1296–1402

Carlisle via the south-west, and on the way had an acrimonious
encounter with Norfolk and with Hereford's son, who continued his
late father's opposition to the king.[42] The two earls objected to
Edward's grant of the Isle of Arran to an opportunist Irishman called
Thomas Bisset, who hoped to take advantage of Edward's victory to
reassert his family's claim to the island. Edward granted it to him,
perhaps believing that it was scarcely a matter of the greatest importance, but the two earls took exception to the grant, saying that
Edward 'had promised to do nothing new without their advice and
consent'. When the army arrived at Carlisle, Norfolk and Hereford
sought leave to return home, alleging that their troops were tired.
Edward, however, remained at Carlisle, where he held a parliament in
which he made grants to English lords of land confiscated from
rebel Scottish barons, but even after the two earls departed they
could not entirely be ignored. According to Guisborough, Edward

retained Annandale and Galloway in his own hands for the time being, lest by granting them out he should give the two earls ground for believing that they would not receive any share of the spoils.[43]

Edward's success in crushing Wallace's rebellion did not lead to any great diminution in the tension between him and the community, but the opposition now came mainly from the laity. One of Edward's few achievements in 1297 had been his reconciliation with the clergy when Boniface VIII's modification of his opposition to royal taxation of the clergy in the bull *Etsi de Statu* in July 1297 made possible a resolution of the dispute over clerical taxation in England, for the Pope now conceded that secular rulers could levy taxes on the church without papal authorisation in cases of necessity. But the other grievances of 1297 were still unresolved. In the parliament of March 1299 Edward declared that he had considered the Confirmation of the Charters of 1297, and it was now not his will that the Charter of the Forest be observed in all its points. He was especially reluctant to authorize a perambulation of the forest, a survey of the forest boundaries which would probably have led to a reduction in land subject to forest law and a consequent loss of income from forest jurisdiction. Edward also insisted that his concessions of 1297 could not be held to override the rights of the crown and the king's interests. Guisborough tells us that after the statute was published there was an uproar, and the king decided to seek the country air,[44] while the Bury St Edmunds chronicler remarked that 'the earls and barons were exasperated by the king's irritable and empty words and prevarications'.[45]

At the same time, Edward's position in Scotland was proving less secure than he had supposed in the aftermath of Falkirk. Despite the defeat of Wallace, Edward had failed to break the Scottish will to resist and the war had to be continued; only in 1299, 1302 and 1305 was there no campaign in Scotland. Edward had a continuous need for funds, but his dependence on parliament for the money he required allowed the community to press for concessions in return for taxation, and the war itself did not prove popular with the nobility. By 1299, the Scots had developed a form of collective leadership with Bishop Lamberton of St Andrews as chief guardian, supported by Robert Bruce and John Comyn Lord of Badenoch, ' the Red Comyn'. In the autumn of 1299 the triumvirate laid siege to Stirling Castle. Edward resolved upon an expedition to relieve it, but when the army assembled at Berwick the magnates objected to continuing the campaign in winter weather. They also complained that the king was not observing the charters: why should they labour in vain, they argued, if the king did not keep his promises?[46] The king returned home, and Stirling fell to the Scots.

In March 1300 parliament met in London, and Edward once again confirmed the charters, this time with the addition of certain new articles, known as the *Articuli super Cartas*, which were intended to provide remedies for grievances against royal officials, particularly in the administration of prises. The grievances of 1297 remained potent, as royal activity which gave rise to such grievances persisted. The *Articuli*, however, were not such substantial concessions as they seemed, for the last clause contained the statement that 'In all the aforesaid things the king wills...that the right and lordship of his crown be saved'.[47] Edward also refused to accept the findings of the commissioners appointed to perambulate the forest, and parliament insisted that any tax grant should be levied only if the king agreed to accept the commissioners' findings. The king's trustworthiness was now an important issue. Parliament granted a twentieth, but the king refused to levy so derisory a sum under such conditions.

When parliament next met, at Lincoln in January 1301, the community again declined to make a grant until its grievances had been redressed, demonstrating how widespread opposition to the king had become. Although the magnates took the lead, there is little doubt that they had the support of the knightly class in demanding concessions from the king. Edward submitted a document proposing a compromise on the question of the forest which had become for many the 'touchstone of the king's good faith',[48] but it was rejected, and he eventually agreed that the findings of the forest commission should be implemented, even though this meant a large measure of disafforestation. The prelates and magnates then demanded a say in the appointment of the king's ministers: this was directed mainly against Walter Langton, the treasurer and chief minister of the king who was widely believed to be using his position to amass a considerable personal fortune by methods which were none too scrupulous. Their demand provoked a furious reaction from the king, and the prelates and magnates backed down. Of greater significance, however, was the bill presented on behalf of the whole community by Henry Keighley, one of the knights of the shire for Lancashire. In this bill the community sought observance of the charters, completion of the perambulation of the forest, and the appointment of auditors acceptable to the prelates and magnates to hear complaints against royal officials. The substance of the bill was not highly objectionable. Only the last clause met with a firm refusal from the king; but the bill itself indicates the extent to which the king's opponents now saw parliament as an occasion when they could put forward their demands and gain the support of the wider political community, especially the knights who were summoned to parliament whenever a grant of taxes was to be sought. The king's opponents, moreover, had now extended the ground of their opposition to demanding a say in the appointment of the king's ministers and laying down in parliament terms of reference for the conduct of government. It is here, perhaps, that the origins of later movements, such as that of the Ordainers, is to be found. In the development of conflict between crown and nobility in the fourteenth century, the Lincoln parliament is perhaps a more significant landmark than the crisis of 1297.

Despite his political and financial difficulties at home Edward kept up pressure on the Scots, raising money by borrowing and amassing a considerable burden of debt. In the campaign that followed the Lincoln parliament, the English recovered much of southern Scotland, and in February 1303 Edward felt confident enough to write to his justiciar in Ireland saying that he was about to embark on his final conquest. The campaign of 1303 was something of a triumphal progress: Edward marched north via Perth and Aberdeen to Elgin, and returned to winter at Dunfermline. Scottish resistance collapsed, and most of the Scottish magnates submitted to Edward. Wallace, however, who had returned to Scotland and joined in the resistance to Edward in 1303, did not submit. Stirling Castle fell on 24 July 1304 after a siege which Edward intended to be a spectator sport: special siege engines were brought into play – indeed the garrison was forbidden to surrender until they had been used – and a special viewing gallery was constructed so that the ladies of the English court could watch the siege.

After the castle fell, active resistance ceased, and Edward turned his attention to the promulgation of a new system of government for Scotland. At the Lent parliament in 1305 it was agreed that ten representatives of the community of Scotland should join twenty-one Englishmen appointed by the king and draw up an ordinance for the government of Scotland. Edward hoped that these new arrangements would at least appear to have the consent of the Scots, and that Scots would participate in the government of their country. The chief officers in the government were to be English. John of Brittany was appointed the king's Lieutenant in Scotland, and there was to be an English Chancellor and Chamberlain. But the king's council in Scotland was to consist of both English and Scottish notables, and judges, sheriffs and other officials were to be drawn from the men of both countries. The settlement was more generous than that of 1296: the Bishop of St Andrews was appointed deputy to the Lieutenant, and both Robert Bruce the Competitor's grandson and John Comyn were placed on the council. Comyn had a claim to the throne by descent both from Duncan I and Donald Bane on one side, and from David Earl of Huntingdon through John Balliol's sister on the other. The Scottish parliament was to play an important part in the government of the country, and the Scottish nobility and prelates were given a more substantial role in government than they had received in 1296.

Even this settlement, however, revealed Edward's arrogance: the laws of Scotland were to be examined and revised so as to remove anything 'contrary to God and reason'. The similarity to Edward's attitude to Welsh law is striking, though in general the settlement of Scotland was based more closely on the pattern of English rule in Ireland than the 1284 settlement in Wales. Nonetheless, the fact of English domination could not be denied, however much local autonomy Edward was prepared to concede to the Scots. Scottish kingship had ceased to exist, and the symbols of kingship had either been destroyed or taken to England. Towards Wallace Edward proved unforgiving: he gave orders for his capture, and he was eventually brought to London for trial and execution in August 1305. He too had been a symbol of the integrity of the Scottish kingdom, though he had never styled himself as anything more than Guardian of Scotland, and for his resistance to Edward's authority he had to suffer the penalty of treason. Edward's dealings with Scotland, and with Scottish resistance in 1305 suggest, as contemporaries such as Peter Langtoft asserted, that Edward had united the British Isles under his authority, and both the symbols and the manifestations of Scottish and Welsh identity were to have no place in his unified kingdom.[49]

Once again, however, military success and a general acceptance of Edward's overlordship concealed the fundamental weakness of his position in Scotland. The Scottish leadership had collapsed in the face of Edward's invasion in 1303 and this perhaps served to exaggerate the extent and thoroughness of his victory. Irreconcilables still held out in the north and west, and enjoyed some popular support. Edward's supply lines were prone to break down, the northern levies were only too ready to desert, particularly at harvest time, and money could still not be found to pay sufficient troops or purchase sufficient supplies. The divisions amongst the Scottish nobility, and the failure of a leader to emerge to succeed Wallace after 1298, gave Edward the illusion of military superiority, but there was little depth to his position in Scotland. Not merely did he fail to break the Scottish will to resist, but he probably strengthened it by the brutality and arrogance of his behaviour. Furthermore, the Scottish terrain was ideally suited to guerilla warfare: Scottish resistance might melt away in the face of Edward's advances, but it merely reorganized in the inaccessible valleys and islands of the west.

The chronicler Pierre Langtoft maintained that Edward might have consolidated his hold on Scotland if he had shared out the land there amongst his English nobles and thus created a vested interest in English overlordship.[50] Edward, however, had to consider not only the need to reward his own men, but also the demand from those Scots who supported him that they should be confirmed in possession of their estates. Within such constraints, Edward was not notably ungenerous with his land grants in Scotland, however; by 1302 over fifty English lords had been granted lands in Scotland, and even Hereford had benefited with the grant of Annandale. Yet Edward had to ensure that he did not alienate potential supporters in Scotland by over-generous grants of land to his English nobles.[51] As the English hold on much of Scotland proved tenuous, however, the real problem for English grantees was the difficulty they found in taking possession of their Scottish lands and exploiting them. Even if they succeeded, the wealth won from them could not compare with the wealth they gained from their English lands, and Langtoft's suggestion was probably unrealistic. In the event, Edward's settlement of 1305 broke down within four months. In February 1306 Robert Bruce, the grandson of the Competitor, rose in revolt and murdered John Comyn, his principal rival for the Scottish throne, in the Greyfriars church at Dumfries. In 1301–2 Bruce had supported Edward, and his rebellion may have been provoked in part at least by his belief that he had been inadequately rewarded for his loyalty. In the face of his opponents' confusion, he moved with great speed to Scone, where he was installed as king in the following month and soon gathered much support. After a setback in June, when Aymer de Valence surprised and routed Bruce's forces at Ruthven, Bruce took refuge along the western seaboard, whence he descended on Carrick early in 1307. Edward marched north once again, but died at Burgh by Sands near Carlisle in July 1307.

The strains and failures of Edward's last years contrast with his constructive achievements in the first two decades of his reign. Whereas he had managed to carry his nobility with him in his legal reforms and his Welsh campaigns, the years after 1296 were marked by growing conflict between the king and the political community. The Lincoln parliament of 1301 shows how important that body had become as a focus for political conflict. Yet the contrast between the two phases of the reign should not be too sharply drawn. Edward's belief in the ultimate judicial authority of the crown, and his insistence that his prerogative should not be subjected to legal restrictions, are as apparent before 1296 as afterwards. After 1296 a much wider section of the community felt itself aggrieved by Edward's policies, but the principles underlying them did not change substantially: indeed, in the last years of his reign Edward managed to avoid any substantial restrictions on his prerogative. He did so by methods which aroused distrust and provoked political conflict, but in 1305, when he obtained a papal bull absolving him from all the concessions he had made, he probably felt that he had won a significant victory for the principles which underlay his exercise of royal authority throughout his reign. In the following year he persuaded the new Pope, Clement V, to suspend Archbishop Winchelsey, who then went into exile. At the end of the year the Earl of Norfolk died: Edward had now outlived his three leading opponents from the years of emergency.

One reason for the success of Edward's resistance to political pressure was the weakness of his opponents. Baronial recalcitrance and the reluctance of parliament to grant taxes without the assurance of real concessions from the king impeded the war effort in Scotland, but the threat of civil war, which had seemed real in the summer of 1297, diminished thereafter and the nobility failed in the end to make their will prevail or to extract more than the promise of reforms from the king. The forceful leadership which Hereford and Norfolk had offered in 1297 did not endure: Hereford died in 1298, and Norfolk's financial difficulties inhibited his opposition to the king. According to Guisborough, his opposition to Edward in 1297 had been so expensive that he was forced to borrow money from his younger brother John.[52] Furthermore, Edward managed to control the nobility by a mixture of threats and promises, pressure and patronage. The indebtedness of many magnates to the Exchequer was exploited as a means of political pressure: for example the mere threat that the Earl of Arundel's debts would be collected was sufficient to persuade him to overcome his initial reluctance and agree to serve in Gascony. It is noteworthy that whereas Arundel received respite of his debts in 1297, Norfolk did not, despite such severe financial difficulties that he had earlier handed some of his estates over to the king. Respite of debts was regularly granted as a means of showing favour, and as a means of persuading men to serve in the king's wars. The Earl of Lincoln's debts, for instance, were respited on his departure to serve in Gascony in 1294.

Edward was not, however, a generous patron, and his lack of generosity perhaps intensified his difficulties with the nobility. Even his closest associates, who served him loyally over many years, received little reward. William de Valence, who had supported Edward in the barons' wars, had acted for him in Gascony between 1273 and 1279, and had served as commander in Wales in 1282–3, was given the courtesy title earl of Pembroke, by virtue of his marriage, only in 1295. Otto de Grandson, who served Edward in both diplomacy and war throughout his reign, received neither a title nor substantial estates in England. Indeed, Edward's reign saw no increase in the ranks of the titled nobility. Those who successfully used their positions to amass wealth were mainly his ministers, and Walter Langton in particular incurred great unpopularity because of the way in which he exploited his office to benefit himself. The main beneficiaries of Edward's patronage were his own family, and the means by which he went about securing land for them were not above criticism. He married one of his daughters, Joan of Acre, to the Earl of Gloucester, and another, Elizabeth, to the Earl of Hereford, the son of his opponent of 1297. At each of these marriages Edward created an entail under which, in the event of the failure of heirs in the direct line, the inheritances of both earls would revert to the crown. Edward made a similar arrangement with the Earl of Norfolk in 1302, taking advantage of Norfolk's continuing financial difficulties. Norfolk surrendered his estates to the crown and received them back on terms which provided for the lands to revert to the crown in the event of failure of heirs of his body. In return, Edward granted the earl £1,000 worth of land for life. Norfolk was aged sixty in 1302 and had no heirs. Edward clearly got the better of the bargain, and one chronicler took the view that the king forced the agreement on Norfolk in retaliation for his opposition to the king in 1297.[53]

Edward's lordship was demanding rather than generous, and as his demands became regular and national in scale in the last years of his reign his conflict with the community deepened. His preference for dealing with the nobility by threats and pressure rather than by patronage and diplomacy prevented the emergence of the easy understanding which was to characterize his grandson Edward III's relations with the nobility. At the end of his reign he appeared an isolated, if still awe-inspiring figure: the deaths of his brother Edmund of Lancaster in 1296 and his cousin Edmund of Cornwall in 1300 robbed him of loyal support from within his own family, and apart from Otto de Grandson most of the companions of his early years were dead by the time the crisis of 1297 erupted. It is not surprising, perhaps, that he relied so much on ministers, particularly Walter Langton, in the last years of his reign; but at his death he left behind him not only a massive debt and an unsubdued Scotland, but also a nobility which had had little reason over the past ten years to trust or to co-operate with the king. None of these problems was to prove capable of solution by his son.

2
Edward II and Thomas of Lancaster, 1307–1322

Edward II and Gaveston

In the introduction to his edition of the *Vita Edwardi Secundi*, which is probably the most satisfactory contemporary account of Edward II's reign, Noel Denholm-Young said that 'Edward II sat down to the game of kingship with a remarkably poor hand and he played it very badly'.[1] There can be little doubt that Edward II was one of the most incompetent of England's medieval kings: he lurched from one political crisis to another; he seemed incapable of learning from his mistakes; and he finally lost his throne, being damned by his opponents as 'not sufficient to govern'. The disasters of his reign flowed in large part from his own folly, particularly his tendency to allow himself to be dominated by favourites; but he inherited a difficult situation. The problems which had given rise to conflict in his father's reign did not simply go away in 1307, and he had to deal with a political opponent, his cousin Thomas Earl of Lancaster, whose family's wealth and territorial power derived very largely from the munificence of Henry III and Edward I.

Edward's personality, so different from that of his father, had given rise to tensions between father and son in the last years of the old king's reign. Prince Edward had acted as one of the regents during his father's absence in Flanders in 1297 and 1298, and he had served, though apparently without much distinction, in the Scottish campaigns of the last years of his father's reign. It was the prince's personal friends, however, and in particular his relationship with a Gascon knight, Piers Gaveston, which caused Edward most concern. Guisborough told the story that in 1307 the king was so incensed by his son's request that Gaveston should be granted the County of Ponthieu, that he summoned him to his presence and had a blazing row with him. The row supposedly culminated in the king tearing out handfuls of his son's hair.[2] The story may not be true, but nonetheless in 1307 the king sent Gaveston into exile. The relationship between Prince Edward and Gaveston was not yet of any great political significance, for the prince took little part in government, but his unrestrained generosity towards his friend could not but arouse anxiety. At the same time, the king appeared to regard his nephew Thomas of Lancaster in a more favourable light than his son. Lancaster was knighted in 1297, when he was only nineteen, whereas the prince had to wait until he was twenty-two in 1306, and Lancaster enjoyed the king's favour and patronage in the last years of the reign. It is possible that Edward I 'saw in Lancaster the image of his eldest son as he would have liked him to have been',[3] though relations between Lancaster and the prince do not seem to have been affected by the king's favour to one who by virtue of his rank and nearness to the king in blood might in any case expect to enjoy the king's patronage.

The nature of Edward's relationship with Gaveston has given rise to some debate. There was certainly a strong emotional charge to the relationship, and some modern historians have argued that it was homosexual in nature. Contemporary writers, however, were more circumspect. The author of the *Vita* compared Edward and Gaveston with David and Jonathan, and Achilles and Patroclus, which might be taken as a sufficient hint about the relationship, but neither the author of the *Vita* nor other annalists explicitly described the relationship as homosexual. Such reticence may reflect the contemporary hostility to homosexuality, and the dishonour that would befall a kingdom if its king was an acknowledged homosexual; yet it is possible that the relationship was that of adoptive brothers rather than lovers. Such a relationship may have been established by a formal compact in or about 1300, and once Edward succeeded to the throne Gaveston became in effect a junior partner in kingship. The Pauline Annalist gives some credence to this possibility, though for most contemporaries it was Gaveston's closeness to the king, rather than the question of whether the two were lovers or adoptive brothers, that was the real issue.[4]

Edward II's accession in July 1307 was widely welcomed. The author of the *Vita*, looking back from less happy times, said that 'at the beginning of his reign he was rich, with a populous land and the goodwill of his people'.[5] A group of young nobles who were of the new king's own generation and who had not been involved in the crises of 1297 and 1301, men such as Thomas of Lancaster and the Earls of Hereford, Warwick, Arundel and Surrey, may have hoped for much from a new king of twenty-four, 'fair of body and great of strength'. Even Edward's first significant actions as king, the recall of Gaveston from exile and the grant to him of the earldom of Corn-wall, were apparently done with the approval of some of the magnates, notably Henry de Lacy Earl of Lincoln.

In other respects too Edward seems to have been intent upon emphasizing the break with the past which his accession represented. Anthony Bek, Bishop of Durham, who had been deprived of his see by Edward I in a dispute about the liberties of his bishopric, was restored. Edward I's unpopular minister Walter Langton, who had many enemies at court, was dismissed and was soon to be subjected to a long, inconclusive trial. Edward himself had good reason to rid himself of Langton, who had urged Edward I to exile Gaveston and had tried to keep the prince's household expenses under control. He was briefly imprisoned, but released and restored to favour in 1308. In December 1307 the new king wrote to the Pope asking him to reinstate Archbishop Winchelsey, whom his father had driven into exile in 1306, and he returned in triumph. His political views had not greatly changed, however, and he soon gave his support to those who were to demand the banishment of Gaveston. In Scotland Edward appeared to favour a less aggressive stance, and he abandoned the campaign which his father had hoped to launch, though he made arrangements for the defence of the border during the forthcoming winter. Bruce meanwhile took advantage of the breathing space to wage a short but successful war against his aristocratic rivals in Scot-land. Edward made the situation worse for himself by failing to offer any help to those in Scotland who still supported him and had no wish to see Bruce prosper. Edward's hasty abandonment of the Scottish campaign was in itself a cause of tension with some of the nobles, such as Pembroke and Hereford, whose Scottish lands were thereby placed in jeopardy.

The domestic harmony which marked the new king's accession did not long endure, however, and Gaveston's position at court provides the main explanation for the breach which soon developed between Edward and many of his nobility. The *Vita* suggests that Gaveston was unpopular with many magnates from the opening of the reign: 'The magnates of the land hated him, because he alone found favour in the king's eyes and lorded it over them like a second king, to whom all were subject and none equal.'[6] At a tournament held in December 1307, Gaveston's party 'had the upper hand and carried off the spoils', and his success roused 'the earls and barons to still greater hatred of Piers'.[7] Their dislike can only have been intensified by Edward's appointment of him as Keeper of the Realm after Christmas 1307, when the king went to France to marry Isabella, the daughter of Philip IV. During the king's absence Gaveston had the freedom to dispense the king's patronage, and the favours he bestowed on his own friends and kinsmen were a further affront to the nobility. The lavish rewards which Gaveston himself enjoyed and which he obtained for his followers were drawn from the royal Treasury and compounded the financial problem which Edward had inherited from his father. Although parliament in October 1307 granted the king a fifteenth and a twentieth in the atmosphere of goodwill which marked the start of the reign, it was not long before complaints about the burden of taxation and the impoverishment of the people were once again being heard.

The first sign of open opposition to the king appeared in January 1308, when the Bishop of Durham, together with the Earls of Lincoln, Warenne, Pembroke and Hereford, and five barons, drew up letters patent at Boulogne in which they declared their loyalty to the king and their willingness to do all they could to uphold and maintain the honour and rights of the crown; but they added that they would reform 'those things which have been done before this time against the king's honour and the rights of the crown, and the oppressions which have been done and which are still daily being done to his people'.[8] The authors of the Boulogne document made no specific complaint against the king, but they presumably had Gaveston's position in the forefront of their minds, and they were also concerned about fiscal and administrative abuses that went back to Edward I's reign. The document was couched in very general terms, but the principles underlying it were clear enough and show a marked similarity to the arguments put forward by the baronial opponents of Henry III. The barons cast themselves as the king's loyal subjects, and by virtue of their fealty to him they believed they had a duty to protect the rights of the crown and the king's honour against the consequences of his own misjudgements. The barons' right, indeed their duty, to act in this way had not been so clearly stated since *The Song of Lewes*. Although the issues in 1308 might be new, the principles on which the barons justified their political actions were not, and, as will be suggested later, Thomas of Lancaster appears to have regarded Simon de Montfort as a model on which to base his own political actions.

Gaveston had aroused such hostility in the early months of the reign that according to the Pauline Annalist the magnates threatened to prevent the king from being crowned until he agreed to banish his favourite.[9] Whether this is true or not, Gaveston's behaviour at the coronation on 25 February 1308 did nothing to allay anger and jealousy. The Pauline Annalist described him as 'so arrayed that he looked more like the god Mars than an ordinary mortal', dressed in a purple robe embroidered with precious stones. His carrying of the crown at the ceremony itself, and his conduct at the coronation banquet where he upstaged the queen, were unforgivable indiscretions, and his treatment of the queen gave offence to her uncles, one of whom had to be dissuaded from an open confrontation with Gaveston. The Pauline Annalist said that Edward gave Gaveston the wedding presents which he had received from his father-in-law Philip IV, and Philip evidently suspected that Gaveston lay behind the lengthy delay in assigning the queen's dower of 20,000 *livres tournois* which had been promised at the time of the marriage.[10]

Gaveston's flamboyant behaviour ensured him the limelight at the coronation; but of equal, if not greater, significance was the new clause inserted in the king's coronation oath. The three promises, to maintain the laws and customs granted by former kings, to maintain the peace, and to do justice, had been made by all his immediate ancestors at their coronations; but Edward made another promise, to keep 'the rightful laws and customs which the community of your realm shall have chosen'. This fourth clause in the oath has attracted much controversy. It has been described as imprecise, yet the intention seems clear enough, to bind the king as to his future conduct. The motives behind its inclusion are more difficult to assess. It may have been intended to prevent Edward II going back on his word in the way his father had done after 1297, or it may have been drafted with the problem of Gaveston chiefly in mind, and intended to give the nobility some leverage over the king in future.[11]

The immediate problem facing the nobility after the coronation, however, was how to make their will prevail and ensure the removal of Gaveston. According to the Pauline Annalist, the new queen's friends had returned to France complaining that Edward loved Gaveston more than her. (They may well have been right.) The Earl of Lincoln, who at the outset of the reign had agreed to Gaveston's return, now assumed the leadership of the group of earls determined to remove him. The author of the *Vita* suggests that Lincoln had now become Gaveston's 'greatest enemy and persecutor',[12] and Edward's failure to retain the confidence of one who had supported him at the beginning of the reign and who had a record of outstanding and faithful service to his father is a measure of the damage his obsession with Gaveston had caused. The Earls of Warwick, Hereford, Pembroke and Warenne joined Lincoln in opposing the king, but Edward does not yet seem to have lost the loyalty of Thomas of Lancaster. Indeed, Edward used his powers of patronage to see that Lancaster was well rewarded and that favours were procured for his clients and dependants.

The country appeared to be moving towards civil war in the spring of 1308. The *Vita* said that 'the seditious quarrel between the lord king and the barons spread far and wide through England, and the whole land was much desolated by such a tumult ... Ordinary peaceful men, lovers of peace, greatly feared war and the destruction of peace',[13] while in a letter probably written in early April the writer warned that both the king and the earls were arming, and that the situation was very dangerous.[14] Open civil war was averted, however, because Lincoln felt that he could not reverse his lifetime's stance of loyalty and take up arms against his king; but several of the earls came armed to the parliament of April 1308 and put forward a series of articles known as the Declaration of 1308. The Declaration began by maintaining that homage and allegiance were due to the crown rather than to the person of the king, and went on to reassert and elaborate the principles contained in the Boulogne agreement of the previous January. If the king, as the holder of the crown, did not conduct himself reasonably, his subjects were bound by their oath to the crown to provide a remedy. If such a remedy could not be provided by law, which might well be the case since all the judges were appointed by the king, force might be used. Although couched in general terms, the articles were evidently designed to deal with the problem of Gaveston, and the earls followed the Declaration with a demand for Gaveston's banishment. Gaveston, it could be argued, had encouraged the king to behave unreasonably and had thus weakened the authority of the crown by accroaching royal power and appropriating royal property. The barons, by virtue of their oath of fealty, were bound to act to support and maintain the crown and deal with anyone who accroached its authority; the king for his part was required by virtue of the fourth clause in his coronation oath to accept the barons' judgement. There was, perhaps, little that was new in the Declaration, though the doctrine of capacities was set out more precisely than before, and was deployed to deal with an urgent political problem. It also allowed Lincoln to argue that loyalty lay to the crown rather than to the unsatisfactory wearer of it, and thus make his opposition to Edward easier to reconcile with his sense of loyalty to the crown.

In their demand for the banishment of Gaveston, Edward's opponents received support from an unexpected source, Philip IV of France. Philip's dealings with the Templars in his own realm showed how he reacted to the mere suggestion of homosexual relationships, and the disparagement of his daughter implicit in Edward's affection for Gaveston, together with the delay in assigning her dower, created tension between the French king and his son-in-law. The Pauline Annalist even suggested that Philip's brothers had supported the English earls in trying to have the coronation postponed, and a newsletter written in the spring of 1308 declared that the French king would 'pursue as his mortal enemy all who supported Gaveston'.[15] Philip and his sister Margaret, Edward I's widow, were also said to have given the Earls of Lincoln and Pembroke £10,000 sterling for their expenses during the April parliament. The French royal family were evidently prepared to place both military and financial resources at the disposal of Gaveston's opponents, but their motive was probably to avenge the insults suffered by the young queen. As later events were to show, Philip had little sympathy with the political ideas which underlay the Declaration of 1308.

Faced with the threat of force from the English earls, a threat made all the more real by the possibility of financial and even military support from France, Edward gave way and on 16 June 1308 appointed Gaveston Lieutenant in Ireland, and provided him with substantial grants in England and Gascony to support his position. The Lanercost Chronicler went so far as to say that Gaveston took a supply of charters, blank but already sealed, with him to Ireland, and the *Vita* said that 'now that Piers was in Ireland, he converted to his own use and devoured, with the king's express consent, all the revenues of the land which pertained to the king of England'.[16] For the time being, however, Gaveston's departure took much of the force out of the opposition to Edward. To many of the nobility, Gaveston had been the only reason for their stand against the king, and however sophisticated the arguments employed in the Declaration of 1308 to justify opposition to the king, it is probable that at this stage the earls themselves had no wider aim than the removal of Gaveston. The king used his powers of patronage to win back the support of lords such as Lincoln and Pembroke, and it is significant that on 9 May 1308 Edward at last recognized Thomas of Lancaster's claim to the office of Steward of England, which de Montfort had held as appurtenant to the Honour of Leicester.

Edward's purpose in thus rewarding these nobles was to ensure sufficient support for the recall of Gaveston. In March 1309 Pembroke, whose support for Edward had been encouraged by favour at the Exchequer and by the grant of the lordship of Haverfordwest, went to the papal court at Avignon with the Earl of Richmond and the Bishops of Worcester and Norwich to persuade the Pope to issue a bull lifting the sentence of excommunication which Archbishop Winchelsey had pronounced on Gaveston should he return. The Pope duly complied, to Winchelsey's displeasure, and the archbishop was reluctant to publish the bull in England. The Pope's action, engineered perhaps by bishops who were compliant to the royal will, encouraged Winchelsey to give his support to those lords who opposed the king and Gaveston. By late June 1309, however, Edward felt secure enough to recall Gaveston, and he journeyed to Chester to meet him. The author of the *Vita* remarked that 'the Earl of Lincoln, who the year before had been the foremost of the barons in bringing about Piers's exile, now became a friendly go-between and mediator', and Earl Warenne became Gaveston's 'inseparable friend and faithful helper'. Well might the same author comment that 'the love of magnates is as a game of dice'.[17]

Gaveston's restoration, however, was not accomplished merely by the divisions of his opponents. The king also had to make some formal concessions in return for Gaveston's recovery of his lands and honours, and these concessions, embodied in the Statute of Stamford of July 1309, suggest that whereas Gaveston had been the issue on which the king's opponents had so readily united in the previous year, the community had other grievances which, though overshadowed by the Gaveston problem, were none the less serious and, unlike the question of Gaveston, had their origins in the financial and administrative problems of Edward I's last years. The statute was based on a petition submitted by the community of the realm in the April parliament of 1309. The abuses for which this petition sought remedy bear a remarkable similarity to those which the community had complained about in 1300 and which had supposedly been remedied in the *Articuli super Cartas*. The parallel with 1300 can be pressed even further: on both occasions a grant of tax was made conditional upon reforms being implemented, and on both occasions the community asked that government should be carried on in accordance with the Great Charter. The importance which the king's opponents attached to Magna Carta as a criterion of good government had not been diminished by Edward I's successful struggle to maintain the royal prerogative, nor had the accession of a new king diminished the desire of the community for reform in those aspects of royal government which had given rise to discontent in the last years of Edward I's reign.

For Edward, the acceptance of the community's demands in the Statute of Stamford amounted in practice to very little and was no doubt a price worth paying to secure Gaveston's restoration. Gaveston's behaviour now became even more offensive to the earls. One source says that he invented abusive nicknames for them, though the only one which is recorded is 'Black Dog of Arden' applied to the Earl of Warwick. Another source relates that Gaveston began to treat the earls like servants and to sow discord between them and the king. Meanwhile, as the author of the *Vita* says, 'the lord king himself was overjoyed at Piers's presence, and, as one who receives a friend returning from a long pilgrimage, passed pleasant days with him'.[18] The king's continuing infatuation with Gaveston strengthened the hand of those barons who had opposed his return and were unhappy about the agreement at Stamford. With Lincoln reconciled to the king the leadership of these opponents seems to have passed to the Earl of Lancaster, though it is not entirely clear when or how Edward lost Lancaster's support. The author of the *Vita* suggests that it was the result of Gaveston's dismissal from office of a member of Lancaster's household; another chronicler states that Lancaster was chosen as the leader of those opposed to Gaveston when Lincoln had agreed to allow him to return. Dr Maddicott has tentatively suggested that Lancaster may have taken the initiative at the Dunstable tournament in the spring of 1309 and tried to gain a wide basis of support by discussing with the other earls and the knights at the tournament the articles which were to be presented in the April parliament.[19] If this is so, it suggests that Lancaster was motivated as much by a desire to reform government as to prevent Gaveston's return, and indeed as later events were to show Lancaster came to see himself as the political as well as the territorial heir of Simon de Montfort, not least in his concern to win the support of the knightly class.

The Gaveston issue continued to occupy centre stage over the autumn and winter of 1309–10. In October 1309 the Earls of Lancaster, Lincoln, Warwick, Oxford and Arundel refused to attend a council at York 'because of Piers'.[20] Early in the new year the barons declared that they would not attend the parliament summoned to meet on 8 February 1310, for 'as long as their chief enemy, who had set the baronage and the realm in an uproar, was lurking in the king's chamber, their approach would be unsafe', and they threatened to come in arms if they came at all.[21] Edward sent writs to Lancaster, Pembroke, Hereford and Warwick forbidding them to come armed to parliament, but at the same time he persuaded Gaveston to depart discreetly to a 'very safe place', and the magnates eventually agreed to attend parliament. The threat of civil war was once again in the air, however, and Walter of Guisborough said that the earls came to parliament in military array, despite the king's prohibition.[22]

When the parliament met, the lords put before the king a statement of their grievances, which amounted to an indictment of the king's conduct over the previous three years.[23] They complained that the king had been led by evil counsel, and had become so impoverished that he could neither defend the realm nor maintain his household, but had to live by extortion. He had taken prises for which no payment was made; he had all but lost his land of Scotland which, together with England and Ireland, his father had left him 'in good peace', as they somewhat misleadingly put it; and by evil counsel he had been encouraged to waste the taxes granted for the war in Scotland. The lords asked that the Great Charter should be kept and maintained in force, and that the grievances they had put forward should be remedied 'by ordinance of your baronage', for the baronage had a duty to assist in the reform of the realm when the actions of the king's evil counsellors brought it into danger. The rewards which Edward had bestowed on Gaveston and his friends since the beginning of the reign gave colour to these arguments, though the lords chose to ignore the debt of about £200,000 left to Edward II by his father, and they misrepresented the state of Scotland at Edward's accession so as to throw the blame for the disasters of the reign firmly on the king's evil counsellors. There was some substance to the charges, however. The taking of prises was as much a grievance in these years as it had been in the last years of Edward I's reign, for the English had to supply their garrisons in Scotland, and Edward twice prepared campaigns and ordered the necessary prises to be taken though in the event he did not lead a campaign there until September 1310. One chronicler goes so far as to suggest that the taking of prises without proper payment was the main reason for the presentation of the earls' petition.[24]

In Scotland the English position had steadily deteriorated as Bruce consolidated his hold on the country. Edward had held councils to discuss how to deal with Bruce, but, as the author of the *Vita* put it, 'the effects of these were not clear nor did they issue in action'.[25] By his negligence and his preoccupation with Gaveston Edward allowed Bruce to establish his authority to such an extent that the divisions within the ranks of the Scottish nobility which a more effective English king might have exploited to his own advantage had all but disappeared. In that sense, he had 'lost the land'.

The king's immediate reaction to the earls' petition was to prevaricate. But according to the author of the *Vita* 'the united barons held strongly to their plan...saying that unless the king granted their demands they would not have him for king, nor keep the fealty they had sworn to him'.[26] The threat was enough to persuade Edward to give way, but it also gave him a weapon against the earls, for he was able to argue later that he had been coerced into accepting the appointment of a commission to reform the realm. On 16 March 1310, therefore, Edward agreed to the appointment of twenty-one Lords Ordainers, who were given power to reform the household and the realm. The composition of the Ordainers shows how wide was the opposition which Edward had created: only two earls, Warenne and Oxford, were not members, and earls such as Gloucester and Lincoln, whose loyalty to the king had been greatly strained by their dislike of Gaveston, made common cause with Lancaster and Warwick, who seem to have had a more thoroughgoing attitude to the question of reform. But the Ordainers were a far from united body. Gloucester, Lincoln and Arundel continued to serve the king even after their appointment as Ordainers, while Pembroke, Lancaster, Hereford and Warwick seem to have taken the lead in drafting measures of reform. The Gaveston issue had united almost all the earls in opposition to the king, but there remained many divisions amongst them about the extent to which reform should be imposed upon the king.

Now, however, Edward began preparations for a Scottish campaign. By doing so he may have hoped to distract the Ordainers from their work of reform and to draw the sting from at least one of the charges against him while at the same time demonstrating to the remaining pro-English nobles in Scotland that he was at last prepared to make some effort to recover the English position there. He issued writs of summons for an expedition to meet at Berwick on 8 September 1310, but Pembroke, Arundel, Hereford and Lancaster refused to serve in person, though they sent token forces to represent their tenurial obligations. Their excuse for refusing to serve was the pressure of business in London as the work of the Ordainers got under way; but almost certainly their real reason was their dislike of Gaveston, who was to accompany the king on the campaign. The Earl of Lincoln was appointed Keeper of the Realm during the king's absence, and in the event only Gloucester amongst the Ordaining earls went with the king to Scotland. The campaign achieved nothing. The Lanercost Chronicler said that Bruce 'in his customary manner fled and dare not encounter' [27] the English army, and instead harassed the English troops and launched guerrilla attacks on their supply lines. Edward returned to Berwick in December and remained in the north until July 1311, perhaps hoping by his absence from London to disrupt the work of the Ordainers. In October 1310 the king had ordered the Exchequer and the law courts to move to York, ostensibly because of the campaign in Scotland but more probably to hinder the Ordainers' task of reform. The king's action is said to have 'much disturbed and enraged' the Ordainers. Edward also tried to frustrate the work of the Ordainers by delaying the summons of a parliament until after Michaelmas 1311 when their powers were due to expire. A letter written from Alnwick in April 1311 stated that 'the king is in no mood yet for a parliament', [28] and he tried to gather what financial resources he needed without recourse to parliament. The whole episode has many similarities to Richard II's attempt to impede the work of a commission of reform imposed on him in 1386 by leaving London and embarking on a 'gyration' around the midlands.

Edward could not, however, procrastinate indefinitely. The Ordainers themselves were disunited, and a feud between Gloucester and Lancaster, which seems to have originated in a dispute between some of their retainers and which threatened to erupt into open violence in April 1311, exposed their disunity for all to see, though the king was unable to exploit such feuds and divisions effectively. The king suffered a serious blow in February 1311 when the Earl of Lincoln, one of the more moderate of the earls, died, and his inheritance passed to his son-in-law the Earl of Lancaster. Lincoln's death greatly strengthened Lancaster's position, for it brought him the Honours of Pontefract, Bolingbroke, Holt and Clitheroe together with the lordship of Denbigh and smaller estates in nine English counties, worth in all about 10,000 marks a year. Lancaster's estates in Lancashire, the West Riding of Yorkshire and Lincolnshire were very substantially consolidated by the Lincoln inheritance, and Pontefract and Bolingbroke were to become two of the principal Lancaster residences in the future. Lincoln may also have hoped that Lancaster would inherit his political values. On his deathbed, according to two contemporary chroniclers, Lincoln urged Lancaster to revere Edward, to seek to remove evil counsellors from his court, and to listen to the advice of the Earl of Warwick, 'the wisest of the peers'.[29] Lincoln had striven to combine loyalty to Edward himself with opposition to those who monopolized his counsel, a political position which was increasingly difficult to sustain in the face of Edward's stubbornness, and it is not clear that Lancaster took much notice of the first of his dying father-in-law's injunctions. Lancaster's own political ideas seem to owe more to de Montfort than to the Earl of Lincoln, and after Lincoln's death it was Gloucester rather than Lancaster who filled his political place; indeed, Edward appointed Gloucester, though a man of only nineteen, as Keeper of the Realm in succession to Lincoln.

In the end it was probably shortage of money that compelled Edward to give in and summon parliament for 8 August 1311. The king hoped at first to save Gaveston by agreeing to all the other measures of reform which the Ordainers intended to put forward provided Gaveston was allowed to stay. The earls refused to give way, however, and warned the king that he was risking civil war. According to the author of the *Vita*, the king's advisers reminded him of the civil war in the time of his grandfather Henry III, pointing out that 'civil war never yet had an acceptable end, of which the Battle of Lewes is a manifest example, and the Battle of Evesham an everlasting reminder, where the noble man Simon Earl of Leicester laid down his life in the cause of justice'.[30] Once again the threat of violence made the king yield, and he consented to the publication of the Ordinances, first in parliament on 30 September 1311 and then five days later throughout the country.

To some contemporaries, the most important feature of the Ordinances was the decree against Gaveston. The Pauline Annalist thought it was the only clause in the Ordinances worth recording, and the author of the *Vita* said that 'the Ordinance which expelled Piers Gaveston from England was more welcome to many than the rest, for when people examined the Ordinances they at once turned to it, although it did not come at the head of the list'.[31] The indictment of Gaveston was lengthy and comprehensive:[32] it accused him of misleading the king and giving him evil counsel; embezzling the royal treasure and taking it out of the realm; accroaching the royal power and dignity; forcing the king to alienate crown lands; encouraging the king to make war without the consent of the barons; and persuading the king to remove officials and replace them with members of his own following. The indictment goes on to recall earlier sentences of banishment against him, and to allege that his return was never universally approved. The judgement of the Ordainers was that he must leave the realm by 1 November 1311 and should be treated as an outlaw if he returned.

No doubt the chroniclers reflected public opinion accurately enough in giving such prominence to the Gaveston affair, and some of the Ordainers themselves may have shared the chroniclers' views. But the Ordinances amounted to more than just an attack on the king's favourite: they attempted to remedy grievances which had their origins in the war finance of Edward I's last years. Complaints about the abuse of the right of prise and the excessive use of pardons to persuade men to serve in the army, the demand for the abolition of new customs duties levied since Edward I's coronation (the maltolt), and the objection to the payment of customs revenue to Italian merchants echo the complaints of Edward I's opponents in 1297 and 1300; while some of the administrative reforms that the Ordainers proposed were similar to those that Edward I's ministers had attempted to introduce. On the other hand, the attempt to control the king's patronage was a new departure, reflecting the nobility's concern at the king's lavishness, particularly towards Gaveston. Grants made since the Ordainers began their work were to be cancelled, and until the king's debts were paid all future grants required the consent of the baronage.

The measures the earls took to ensure the enforcement of the Ordinances show some similarity to de Montfort's plans in 1258 and 1264 and some awareness of the importance of parliament as a focus for opposition to the king, though the Ordainers went further than before in defining the range of matters which required parliamentary consent. It was the barons' intention that they, as the king's natural counsellors, should exercise some degree of control over him, and the Ordainers proposed that in every parliament a bishop, two earls and two barons should be assigned to hear complaints about contraventions of the Ordinances by the king's ministers. All the chief officers of state were to be chosen with the consent of the baronage in parliament, and parliament was to meet at least once a year. In parliament the magnates might expect to enjoy the support of the commons, and in 1310 and 1311 they successfully exploited the grievances of the commons to gain their support for measures to restrain royal power. The initiative in seeking reform and restraint lay with the magnates, however; the commons readily co-operated as long as their grievances were redressed, but they had not yet come to see themselves as a body standing apart from, and possibly opposed to, the lords.[33]

The Ordainers wished, therefore, to rid the king of evil counsellors, and in the eyes of many of their supporters this may indeed have been the central issue. They also wished to ensure that no new favourite came to occupy the position that Gaveston had held, and to prevent the king from using his patronage to shower gifts on his favourites. To that extent, the Gaveston issue provided the framework for the Ordainers' proposals; but their concern over the conduct of royal officials and ministers, their criticism of the maltolt and prises can be understood only in the more general context of discontent over royal demands since 1296. The strength of the Ordainers' position lay not just in the military force which the Ordainers themselves could in the last resort deploy against the king, but also in the widespread support they could command both for their stand on the specific issue of Gaveston and for their wider measures of reform. The weakness of the Ordinances, however, like that of other baronial attempts at reform both before and after 1311, lay in the provisions for their enforcement. The nobility did not aspire to detailed and specific control over every department of government, but hoped by influencing the appointment of ministers and providing for periodic review of their conduct in parliament to ensure that the principles laid down in the Ordinances were upheld. Responsibility for the day-to-day conduct of government still rested, however, with the king, and, as the events of the following year were to make clear, he could manipulate the officers of state, the institutions of government, and those of the nobility who were susceptible to his patronage, curbed though it might be, in such a way as to make the idea of annual parliamentary review of the conduct of government an ineffective remedy. In the end, only chronic shortage of money or the threat of imminent civil war could force the king to come to terms with parliament.

The question of the authorship of the Ordinances can never be satisfactorily solved. It has been suggested that Archbishop Winchelsey provided the Lords Ordainers 'with brains and policy', but there is no contemporary evidence for this assumption, and apart from the reassertion of the liberty of the Church there is little sign of any specifically ecclesiastical interest at work in the drafting of the Ordinances. The author of the *Vita* thought that the Earl of Warwick framed the document, 'and other earls did many things only after taking his opinion', but another chronicler describes the measures as the 'Ordinances of the Earl of Lancaster'.[34] The widening of the programme of Edward's opponents to embrace measures of reform which went well beyond the ousting of Gaveston seems to coincide with the growth of Lancaster's influence over the earls after the Dunstable tournament, and it is perhaps not unreasonable to assume that Lancaster and Warwick played a leading part in what may have been essentially a collective effort.[35]

The promulgation of the Ordinances was not, however, the end of the matter. The Ordainers continued to meet, even though their powers had lapsed at Michaelmas 1311, and they issued a second set of Ordinances in the November parliament of 1311, a document which lacked legal validity and which was concerned chiefly to enforce changes in the personnel of the royal household and the administration. This so exasperated the king that he complained he was being treated like an idiot, and he retired to Windsor for Christmas. He now concentrated his attention on trying to overthrow the Ordainers and bring back Gaveston. Gaveston had left the country on 3 November, but by the end of the month rumours were circulating that he was back in England, and he evidently spent Christmas with the king. In the new year Edward made a series of grants by which Gaveston was entirely restored to his old position; Walter Langton was appointed Treasurer and given his property back, and a commission was set up to negotiate with the Ordainers for the revision of clauses in the Ordinances which were prejudicial to the king.

Such an open challenge to the Ordainers could not go unanswered, and tension between the king and the earls rapidly increased. In January the king moved to York with Gaveston and apparently told an assembly of the Yorkshire gentry that he had revoked the Ordinances. Gaveston's return provoked Archbishop Winchelsey to excommunicate him, and five earls, Lancaster, Pembroke, Hereford, Arundel and Warwick, bound themselves by oath to bring about his capture. Lancaster appears to have been chosen as the leader of the five. Edward's intrigues had by now deprived him of the support of even the more moderate earls. Gloucester 'promised that he would ratify whatever the earls did',[36] and Henry Percy of Alnwick and Robert Clifford agreed to bar the escape route into Scotland. The author of the *Vita* suggests that Edward was even prepared to concede the kingdom of Scotland to Bruce if he would allow Gaveston to take refuge there, but Bruce scorned Edward's advances, saying, 'How shall the king of England keep faith with me, since he does not observe the sworn promises made to his liegemen?'[37] The king moved to Newcastle in April, but Lancaster pursued him there and the king and Gaveston escaped to Scarborough by sea. Edward then left Gaveston at Scarborough and moved westwards to Knaresborough; Lancaster interposed his forces between them, and Pembroke laid siege to Scarborough Castle. Had the king remained at Scarborough it would have been more difficult for Pembroke to sustain a siege against his lord, but Edward was unable to march to the relief of the castle and Gaveston surrendered on 19 May 1312.

Pembroke took Gaveston south, probably intending to lodge him in Wallingford Castle, but Warwick intercepted them and captured Gaveston, taking him to Warwick Castle, where Warwick, Lancaster, Arundel and Hereford debated his fate. There was evidently much concern that whatever was done should have the appearance of legality, and he was eventually sentenced to death for treason on the authority of the Ordinances. The Bridlington Annalist observed that news of the revocation of the Ordinances had not yet reached Warwickshire.[38] The sentence was of doubtful legality, but it was carried out on 19 June 1312.

Gaveston's death destroyed the unity of his opponents, and however much Edward felt it as a personal loss it nonetheless brought him political gains. Such moral advantages as the king's opponents had enjoyed were destroyed by the execution, and Pembroke, incensed by Warwick's seizure of his prisoner, went over to the king's side. The dissolution of the unity of the Ordainers was accompanied, however, by even greater hatred between the king and Lancaster. From then onwards, wrote Henry Knighton, the king and Lancaster never had any love for each other,[39] and the bitterness following Gaveston's death seemed likely to lead to civil war. Both sides were in arms in the summer of 1312, and Pembroke, Hugh Despenser, and the remnants of Gaveston's following encouraged the king to attack Lancaster. According to the *Vita*, Lancaster had 2,500 men under arms and Hereford raised a large retinue in his Marcher lordships.[40] The barons, however, held back from immediate confrontation, and this pause gave the Earl of Gloucester a chance to mediate. Gloucester faced substantial difficulties: the earls were adamant that the Ordinances should be reimposed, and they even tried to suggest that the next parliament should make the grant of a tax for the Scottish war conditional upon their reimposition. The king, encouraged by the arguments against the Ordinances put forward by two French lawyers and by the indication that now Gaveston was dead the French king would abandon his support for the earls, was anxious to destroy the Ordinances and to avoid having to give the murderers of Gaveston a pardon.

The negotiations between the two sides dragged on in an atmosphere of armed truce. The *Vita* suggests that it was the king who prevaricated,[41] but the earls seem to have been equally unwilling to yield on any substantial point. Eventually, Edward seems to have worn down the barons, and his willingness to give way on the question of a pardon produced a compromise settlement. In October 1313 the lords publicly apologized to the king for the murder of Gaveston, and the king formally pardoned them. The settlement contained no reference to the Ordinances, but by acknowledging their guilt over Gaveston's death the earls implicitly accepted that they were not in force when he was killed. The settlement was in all essentials a victory for the king. By his refusal to accept the Ordinances he successfully resisted the imposition of restrictions on his freedom of action, and he had once again shown his ability to profit from the divisions of his opponents.

In reflecting on the first six years of the king's reign, the author of the *Vita* said that he had 'achieved nothing praiseworthy or memorable';[42] he had devoted himself to Gaveston with a single-mindedness worthy of a better cause, and by doing so he had three times brought his realm to the verge of civil war. Yet despite the strength of the nobles' opposition to Gaveston and the widespread support they could command, they too had achieved little in the way of reform or restraint upon the crown. The death of Gaveston removed the most potent and unifying of the reasons for hostility to the king, and after the settlement of 1313 the problem of Scotland became uppermost in the minds of both the king and the earls.

While Edward and the earls had been preoccupied with the struggle for the Ordinances and the negotiations after Gaveston's death, Bruce had consolidated his authority over Scotland, and had begun to launch raids into northern England. In January 1313 the Scots recaptured Perth, the last English-held castle north of the Forth; in the south-west, Lochmaben, which commanded the main route from Carlisle into Scotland, fell at about the same time, together with other castles in Dumfriesshire and Galloway. In May 1313 Bruce retook the Isle of Man, an important base for naval operations in north-western waters. English authority was now limited to Stirling Castle and an arc of fortresses in Lothian and the Borders stretching from Linlithgow to Dunbar, Berwick and Roxburgh. Here English rule had hitherto had some appearance of solidarity, not merely because of their possession of all the major castles but also because few of the men of Lothian seem to have joined Bruce. They probably took their cue from the leading magnate of the region, Patrick Earl of March. March, who was lord of Dunbar Castle, had extensive estates in Northumberland and had been the most consistent of all the Scottish nobles in support of the English cause. But even in Lothian and the Borders, the English position began to weaken by the autumn of 1313. Linlithgow, Edinburgh and Roxburgh fell between September 1313 and March 1314, leaving the English-held castles on the south-east coast even more vulnerable to attack.

In November 1313 Bruce gave his opponents in Scotland one year in which to make their peace with him, or suffer permanent forfeiture of their lands. Faced with the imminent disintegration of the pro-English faction in Scotland, Edward began to plan a large-scale expedition to Scotland, and the campaign was given added urgency by Edward Bruce's siege of Stirling, which began in April 1313. He made a compact with the English commander of the castle that if it were not relieved by 24 June 1314, the garrison would surrender. Edward now assembled a substantial army, comparable to the largest of Edward I's reign; John Barbour, author of the Scottish national poem 'The Bruce', suggests that there were nearly 200,000 men in Edward's army.[43] This is certainly an exaggeration, for Barbour had an interest in overestimating the size of the opposition to Bruce, and it is more likely that the army numbered some 20,000. But Edward still could not command the united support of the earls. Lancaster, Warwick, Arundel and Warenne refused to serve on the ground that the military summons had not been agreed in parliament as the Ordinances required, though one source suggests that their refusal sprang from fears for their own safety if they joined the king's army.[44] Moderate Ordainers such as Gloucester, Pembroke and Hereford seem to have had no such scruples or fears, and others who had supported Lancaster in 1312, such as Henry Percy and Robert Clifford, did not hesitate to serve with the king. There were few who shared Lancaster's single-minded determination to enforce the Ordinances before all else.

It is doubtful whether the refusal of the four earls to serve greatly weakened Edward's army or was in itself a cause of the defeat the English suffered at Bannockburn on 24 June 1314. The Bannockburn campaign has been analysed by many historians,[45] but the main reason for the English defeat seems to have been the Scots' ability to choose and hold their ground successfully, and the lack of discipline in the English forces: the chronicler Geoffrey le Baker criticized the English forces for arrogance and overconfidence, and reported that they spent the night before the main engagement drinking heavily.[46] Edward himself showed little competence or authority as a military commander. He proved unable to resolve an argument between Gloucester and Hereford over who should lead the vanguard of the army, and Gloucester, 'seeking the glory of the first encounter', as the *Vita* put it,[47] charged headlong into the enemy ranks and was killed. The crucial factor, however, seems to have been the Scottish choice of ground. Bruce forced the English to fight on boggy soil and on too narrow a front to allow them to deploy their heavy cavalry effectively. The tightly packed infantry formations of the Scottish army, the schiltroms, held firm against repeated English charges, and the English forces were eventually broken up. The king himself escaped to safety, but Gloucester was only the most distinguished of a long list of English noble casualties. Gloucester's death was a serious blow to Edward. Despite his youth – he was only twenty-three when he was killed – he had proved himself a skilful mediator in the negotiations after Gaveston's death, and although an Ordainer in 1310 he showed no sign of sharing either the animosity to the king or the overriding commitment to the Ordinances that characterized Lancaster and his immediate associates. In his attempt to combine personal loyalty to the king with moderation in opposition he was perhaps the real successor to the Earl of Lincoln, and Edward could ill afford to lose such a man. Furthermore, Gloucester died leaving no heirs of his body, and his inheritance was divided between his three sisters. The disputes which this division engendered were to form an important element in the political conflicts of the early 1320s.[48]

The Rule of Thomas of Lancaster

Edward's defeat at Bannockburn placed him in Lancaster's hands. After his flight from the battlefield he lodged at Berwick and then moved to York, where, according to the *Vita*, he 'took counsel with the Earl of Lancaster and the other magnates and sought a remedy for his misfortunes. The earls said that the Ordinances had not been observed, and for that reason events had turned out badly for the king.'[49] The king promised to observe the Ordinances, and the earls insisted that they could only be enforced effectively if the administration was purged. The king agreed to this too. The Chancellor, Treasurer, and many household officials were removed, and most of the sheriffs were replaced. The clause in the Ordinances requiring the resumption of all gifts made by the king since 1310 was now implemented, and even some of the nobles had to disgorge: Warenne had to give up the castle and honour of High Peak, and Henry Beaumont had to surrender the Isle of Man, amongst other grants. The expulsion of the Scots in 1315 from the Isle of Man ensured English control of the Irish Sea and was one of the very few successes against the Scots in the aftermath of Bannockburn.

This reversal of the royal patronage of the previous five years was likely to create resentment amongst those who had lost lands, but for the time being Lancaster enjoyed unchallenged supremacy and used his power to ensure that the Ordinances were enforced. At the Lincoln parliament of 1316 his position was formally recognized when he was asked to become chief of the king's council, though he agreed only to be 'of the king's council'. Nothing that concerned the realm was to be done without the advice of the council, and any member who gave 'evil counsel' was liable to removal in parliament.[50] The enforcement of the Ordinances through the exercise of his personal supremacy in government seems, however, to have been the limit of Lancaster's political imagination, and the dominating position he achieved in the Lincoln parliament served to disguise his political isolation. The Earl of Warwick, who was probably Lancaster's closest political ally and was described by the *Vita* as a man without equal in wisdom and council,[51] died in August 1315, while Lancaster's feud with Warenne, which was occasioned by Warenne's abduction of Lancaster's wife in 1317, allegedly at the instigation of a group of courtiers, erupted into open war between the two earls in the winter of 1317–18.

The king for his part now sought to rebuild his strength by recruiting a new party. New favourites appeared at court, notably Hugh

Audley, Roger Damory and William Montague. All three had started their careers as knights in the royal household, and by 1317 Damory in particular had gained such influence over the king that some saw him as a second Gaveston. He and Audley sought to use their position at court to damage relations between the king and Lancaster, and Lancaster regarded Damory as one of his most dangerous opponents.[52] Associated with Damory, Audley and Montague, and also rising in favour at court, were the two Hugh Despensers, father and son. Hugh Despenser senior was the son of Hugh Despenser who had been nominated by the barons as justiciar of England in 1260, and had died fighting for de Montfort at Evesham. Hugh senior had been allowed to inherit his father's forfeited lands when he came of age, and had served both Edward I and Edward II with conspicuous loyalty. He took part in the expedition to Flanders in 1297 and the Scottish campaigns of Edward I's last years. Alone amongst the nobility he sided with the king in 1308 in the conflict over Gaveston, while his son supported the barons. The younger Despenser had married the eldest sister and coheiress of the Earl of Gloucester in 1306 but in 1317 Edward granted the marriage of the other two coheiresses to Audley and Damory, and as the younger Despenser rose to a position of dominance over the king, disputes about the division of the Gloucester inheritance alienated Damory and Audley from the court, even though Damory probably stood higher in favour than either of the Despensers in 1317 and 1318.

The king also used his powers of patronage to win over a number of more important lords. Pembroke agreed to serve the king in peace and war in return for 1,000 marks a year in time of peace and 2,000 marks in time of war and 500 marks' worth of land, while Hereford was retained to serve with 100 men for which he was to receive 1,000 marks a year. Other lords were bound to the king in similar terms. Such actions, however, inevitably aroused Lancaster's suspicions; he ceased to co-operate with the king, and by April 1317 had stopped attending meetings of the council. The result was a political stalemate. As the *Vita* put it, 'whatever pleases the lord king the earl's servants try to upset; and 'whatever pleases the earl the king's servants call treachery'.[53]

This political stalemate took place against the background of invasion and natural disaster. The north of England had suffered sporadic raiding by the Scots since 1296, but after his victory at Bannockburn Bruce carried the war into England almost every year, and some of his raids penetrated much more deeply than the earlier incursions. In 1316, for example, the raiders reached as far south as Wensleydale, returning by Furness and the Cumberland coast. Two years later the Scots reached Airedale and Wharfedale, and then plundered Amounderness and north Lancashire, and in 1319 the West Riding was again under attack. A two-year truce from December 1319 to December 1321 gave the north some respite, but in 1322 raids resumed and reached both the Ribble valley and the East Riding. Much damage was sustained, especially by the lowland agricultural communities, and in the bishopric of Durham in particular local communities sought to protect themselves, their crops and livestock by purchasing immunity from the Scots. The extortion of money in this way may have been one motive for the raids, but Bruce's main purpose was to force Edward II to negotiate an end to the war. He may also have been trying to strengthen his hand in any negotiations by imposing what amounted to a military occupation on parts of Northumberland, perhaps hoping to regain possession of Tynedale, which had been held by the Scottish kings of the kings of England before the war. Edward's response was feeble: he was prepared neither to negotiate nor to provide any effective defence for the communities of the north, difficult though it would have been to mount effective opposition to the highly mobile, lightly armed Scottish raiding parties. Defence was left largely to the local nobility and gentry, and it is not surprising that by 1322 many of the northern nobility and gentry wanted a settlement with the Scots.[54]

At the same time, Robert Bruce's brother Edward opened a second front in the war by invading Ireland. He landed in Ulster in May 1315, and over the next three years he and his army based themselves there and launched raids that penetrated into Meath and, in 1317, into north-west Munster. His motives for his campaigns in Ireland have been much debated. Personal aggrandizement may have played a part, but it is likely that he hoped to cut off the flow of food supplies from eastern Ireland which helped to victual Edward's armies, and also to build up political support amongst the Gaelic Irish, which might in turn encourage the Anglo-Irish to seek military assistance from England, thus diverting Edward's attention from the northern border. Edward Bruce's campaigns in Ireland were, like those of his brother in northern England, widely destructive of lowland agricultural communities, and this in itself may explain why he did not receive the support he expected. Edward II's response, however, was dilatory and limited, as it was in northern England. Eventually a force under Roger Mortimer of Wigmore, who was lord of Trim in Meath, landed at Youghal in April 1317, and the Scots retreated from the country round Limerick northwards to Ulster. In the following year, the Scots moved south again, but were defeated by a large Anglo-Irish force at Faughart near Dundalk on 14 October 1318. Edward Bruce was killed, and for a time the Scottish threat to Ireland was lifted.[55]

The suffering of the northern communities, and of eastern Ireland, in these years was intensified by the famines and livestock diseases which affected much of western Europe between 1315 and 1322. In

1315 severe and prolonged rainfall led to a disastrous harvest. The price of wheat and other food grains trebled over the next twelve months, and other food seems to have been just as scarce. The harvest of 1316 proved just as bad, and not until 1318 did the weather, and the harvests, return to something resembling normality. However, livestock disease proved almost as serious: sheep murrain was widespread in 1315 and 1316, and an epidemic disease affecting cattle and oxen (essential for ploughing) spread through most parts of England between 1319 and 1321. The extent of human mortality in these years of famine and disease is difficult to estimate, not least because it varied from one community to another. It is likely, however, that as much as 10% of the population perished, and that the famine years brought an end to the upward growth of the English population. The government, and especially its fiscal machinery, showed some resilience, however, in the face of these natural disasters. The yield from the taxes granted by parliament in 1315 and 1316 differed little from the yield in pre-famine years, and in the north of England the communities that successfully sought relief from taxation did so mainly on the ground of damage inflicted by the Scottish raiders. The export trade in wool suffered, of course, from the consequences of the widespread sheep murrain, and revenue from the customs fell to unprecedentedly low levels.[56]

Throughout these difficult years the political stand-off between the king and Lancaster continued, seemingly little affected by invasion and famine. Its resolution by peaceful means in 1318 owed much to the efforts of the Earl of Pembroke, who, together with Hereford, Bartholomew Badlesmere, and various bishops and officials, sought to bring about some measure of reconciliation between the two. This political group has traditionally been known as the middle party, and in the sense that their political inclinations were moderate, in the manner of the Earls of Lincoln and Gloucester, there is some substance in the description. But as the author of a study of the Earl of Pembroke has pointed out, 'They certainly did not occupy a middle ground between the king and Lancaster'.[57] They had sympathized with Lancaster only briefly in 1310–11, and they now hoped to use their influence over the king to gain some power for themselves and restore sufficient stability in government to allow a renewed effort against the Scots, which had become more urgent with the Scottish recapture of Berwick in March 1318.

Their negotiations bore fruit in the Treaty of Leake, concluded in August 1318, under which it was agreed that the Ordinances should be maintained and a standing council set up which was to contain none of Lancaster's close political allies and on which he was to be represented only by a banneret. Audley, Damory and Montague were to be removed from court, royal grants were to be examined, and a committee was to be set up to reform the household. Lancaster gained little by the agreement apart from the removal of the three favourites; it is best represented as a modest victory for the king and his associates, for Lancaster now had little influence over the direction of patronage or the conduct of the administration. Despite the substantial military power he could deploy, his political isolation had placed him in a weak negotiating position, and although the Treaty of Leake contained a formal commitment to maintain the Ordinances, there was little that Lancaster could do to ensure that the commitment was honoured. Pembroke and his supporters were not so much a counterpoise between Lancaster and the king as a group whose fundamental loyalty was to the king and who wished to reach an agreement which ensured some measure of stability while giving as little influence as possible to Lancaster. It was Lancaster, not the king, who lacked political support by 1318.

The most pressing task facing the king in the aftermath of the Treaty of Leake was, once again, to deal with the Scots. After the fall of Berwick a major campaign was imperative, and in the nearest approach to a united military effort which he had so far managed to achieve Edward took a large army north in July 1319. He was accompanied by Lancaster, Warenne, Pembroke, Hereford, Arundel and the younger Despenser. The army laid siege to Berwick, but Bruce, aware of the risks of a pitched battle and the rewards to be gained from the highly mobile warfare that his lieutenants had practised against northern England over the previous four years, sent Sir James Douglas to invade England. Douglas reached as far south as Yorkshire and defeated a force hastily assembled by the Archbishop of York at Myton-on-Swale on 20 September 1319. Victory in battle had not been Bruce's main aim in launching the raid: its purpose had been so to alarm those English lords at the siege of Berwick who had lands in Yorkshire that they would break off the siege and return south to protect their property. Bruce's tactic worked: Edward's council debated whether to lift the siege or to remain until the town and castle fell, but Lancaster seems to have decided to leave anyway, and faced with the departure of the Lancastrian forces, which amounted to perhaps one-fifth of the entire army, Edward decided to withdraw, and a two-year truce was agreed, to run from 21 December 1319. According to the *Vita*, Lancaster was widely blamed for the failure of the siege, and rumours once again circulated that he was in secret negotiation with Bruce. The *Vita* reported that 'the earl had received forty thousand pounds from Robert Bruce to lend secret aid to him and his men'. Lancaster offered to clear his name, and indeed it seems doubtful whether there was any substance to the charges of intrigue with the Scots; but some of the mud stuck, and the *Vita* suggests that the popular support he had enjoyed as the champion of the Ordinances now began to ebb away.[58]

Nearly all the contemporary chroniclers make it clear that the siege of Berwick was marred by bitter quarrels amongst the English magnates. The St Albans Chronicler says that the king 'with his usual stupidity' began to promise offices in the government of the town to his favourites when it fell. Despenser was to be keeper of the castle and Damory captain of the town. The *Vita* records that the king threatened to avenge Gaveston once the siege was over, and that Lancaster, hearing of the threat, was less active at the siege than he might have been. The chronicler likens him, somewhat improbably, to Achilles.[59] Once again Edward's ineptitude as a military leader had been demonstrated, and far from reconciling his quarrelsome barons his misjudgements and misguided promises served only to intensify disagreements. The king agreed to a two-year truce with the Scots, and the hopes of Pembroke and his supporters that domestic harmony might lead to effective measures to deal with the Scottish problem were dashed. Although Lancaster's conduct damaged his standing, the king emerged with no credit either. The author of the *Flores* said that from this time onwards his infamy began to be notorious, together with his torpor, his cowardice, and his indifference to his great inheritance.[60]

Hostility between the king and Lancaster intensified during 1320. The earl refused to attend parliament at York in January, saying that 'it was improper to hold parliament in a closet',[61] by which he presumably meant that the commons, who might still have had some sympathy with his cause, were not summoned, and that the assembly consisted mainly of the king's supporters. More substantial, perhaps, was his objection to the Scottish truce on the ground that it had been made without proper consent because it had not been agreed either by parliament or by a large assembly of the magnates. The policy of moderation, however, still had some life left in it, and throughout the summer and autumn of 1320 relations between the king and Pembroke remained cordial. Pembroke was appointed Keeper of the Realm when the king went to France to do homage for Aquitaine to Philip V, and it may have been at Pembroke's insistence that Edward declared after the end of parliament in October that he wished the Ordinances to be observed. The conduct of government in these months shows some regard for the provision of the Ordinances, not least in the matter of royal grants. At the same time, perhaps again at Pembroke's prompting, the Pope wrote to both the king and Lancaster urging them to settle their differences and end the discord between them. But Pembroke's position depended upon the maintenance of his influence with the king, and although the king evidently liked and trusted him, the emergence of a new favourite to a position of prominence at court undermined Pembroke's position and led to the final collapse of the 1318 settlement.

The Rise of the Despensers

Within the group of courtiers which Edward had built up around him after Bannockburn, Hugh Despenser the younger had become the dominant figure by the beginning of 1321. Despenser was ambitious and greedy; the phrase he himself coined, 'that Despenser may be rich and may attain his ends',[62] succinctly summed up his intentions, and after a period of association with the king's opponents he came to the conclusion that his ambitions would best be served by seeking the favour of the king. His appointment as Chamberlain in 1318 and a substantial number of grants to him from 1319 onwards show how successfully he had gained the king's affections. He was married to the eldest of the Gloucester coheiresses, and in right of his wife he acquired the lordship of Glamorgan. He wished, however, to acquire all the Gloucester lands in Wales, together with the title of earl, and he set about using his influence over the king to procure these lands, despite the fact that by doing so he would come into conflict with Audley and Damory, the husbands of the other two coheiresses and themselves close associates of the king. By a campaign of harassment he forced Audley to surrender to him the lordship of Gwynllwg with its castle of Newport in exchange for lands in south-east England; he was granted Dryslwyn and Cantref Mawr in Carmarthenshire for life by the king, and he gained control of Newcastle Emlyn. He also persuaded the king to confiscate the lordship of Gower from John Mowbray on the ground that Mowbray had taken possession of it without royal licence at the death of his father-in-law William de Braose. The question of the right to alienate land without royal licence, which was the issue involved in the Gower affair, raised the principle of Marcher privilege and brought the resentment against Despenser to a head. A coalition of Marcher lords determined to stop Despenser's rise was formed, led by the Earl of Hereford and Roger Mortimer of Wigmore and supported by Audley and Damory and other Marcher lords who felt themselves threatened by Despenser's acquisitiveness.

Despenser's aggrandisement in south Wales was possible only because of the influence which he and his associates exercised over the king, and their dominant position at court was in itself objectionable. According to Geoffrey le Baker,[63] no one could approach the king without their consent, they answered petitions on the king's behalf, and the king took advice only from them. Their monopoly of access to the king was as great as Gaveston's had been (the comparison did not escape contemporaries), and equally effective in alienating the more moderate of the barons. At this stage, however, Hereford rather than Lancaster seems to have been the leader of the anti-Despenser coalition. As Lord of Kidwelly Lancaster might well have felt his own interests threatened by Despenser's rise, but though he responded sympathetically to Hereford's appeal for support he seemed reluctant to throw in his lot immediately with the anti-Despenser coalition; perhaps he could not stomach the thought of working with Audley and Damory, whose removal from court he had sought in 1318. Lancaster undoubtedly shared their object of removing Despenser from power; indeed, this rather than the Ordinances now seems to have been uppermost in his mind, but his strategy seems to have been to form an association of northern lords against Despenser. To rally support, he held a series of assemblies on his Yorkshire lands, the most important of which was the meeting at Sherburn-in-Elmet in June 1321. The outcome of this meeting was an agreement, known as the Sherburn Indenture, under which some sixty magnates pledged themselves to secure the downfall of Despenser. But even now Lancaster could not command the united support of the baronage. It is possible that some of the border magnates refused to set their seals to the Sherburn Indenture, perhaps because they still suspected Lancaster of intrigue with the Scots, and two of the more important Marcher lords, Pembroke and Arundel, still held back from the growing anti-Despenser ranks.

The anti-Despenser coalition adopted the same strategy as Gaveston's opponents earlier in the reign. At the parliament of July 1321 they demanded the banishment of the favourite. The king at first refused to listen to them, and was only brought round, according to the *Vita*,[64] by the threat that the barons 'would utterly renounce their homage and set up another ruler to do justice to all and humble the pride of the guilty and stiff-necked'. Once again Pembroke appears to have acted as a mediator and to have persuaded the king to give way rather than lose his kingdom. The Despensers were banished, but after parliament had dispersed it became obvious that there were no means short of force by which the barons could compel the king to keep his word. Within two months the younger Despenser was back at the king's side, and according to one chronicler he and the king now set about planning their revenge on the barons.[65]

Edward's strategy was to pick off his opponents piecemeal, and he started with Bartholomew Badlesmere, whose castle at Leeds in Kent made him easy prey. Badlesmere had been in favour at court before the rise of the Despensers, but he had been alienated by the younger Despenser's prominence and had associated himself with Despenser's opponents: On the pretext that he had insulted the queen by refusing to offer her hospitality at Leeds on her way to Canterbury, Edward gathered an army, and with the support of Pembroke, Norfolk and Richmond besieged the castle. It surrendered on 23 October 1321, and in an act of judicial violence which foreshadowed the bloodbath of the next decade, Edward ordered all the garrison to be executed. Badlesmere himself, who had not been in residence during the siege, escaped and Edward issued orders for his arrest. Hereford and Mortimer had raised an army to relieve Leeds, but Pembroke, together with the Archbishop of Canterbury and the Bishop of London, met the army at Kingston and tried to persuade it to go no further. Hereford and Mortimer also received a letter from Lancaster suggesting that they should not help Badlesmere. Lancaster had a feud with Badlesmere which seems to have arisen from Lancaster's resentment at Badlesmere's appointment by the king as Steward of the Household, an appointment which Lancaster, as Steward of England, thought he was entitled to make. Hereford and Mortimer withdrew, and once again the divisions amongst his opponents had played into Edward's hands.

After the fall of Leeds civil war was even more probable, and Lancaster summoned an assembly to meet at Doncaster on 29 November 1321. The assembly was an attempt to rally forces that had hitherto been reluctant to support him: men lacked confidence that Lancaster's cause would prevail, and were unwilling to throw in their lot with him. The king issued a writ forbidding attendance at the assembly, and from the list of persons named in the writ, many of whom were known to be staunch supporters of the king, it is evident that Lancaster had hoped to gain support from as wide a section of northern society as possible. The main work of the assembly was to draft a petition [66] against the Despensers which stated that despite the sentence of banishment pronounced against them in the parliament of 1321, the younger Despenser was still being maintained by the king. The petition accused the Despensers of persuading the king to seize castles and lands 'from peers of the land' without lawful judgement and contrary to Magna Carta, and robbing and preying on the people. The authors asked the king to provide a remedy, but warned that if he did not do so they would redress the evil government of the realm, as they were bound to do by their oath to maintain and safeguard the estate of the realm and the crown. Such an argument was, of course, very similar to that employed by the king's opponents at the beginning of the reign to deal with the problem of Gaveston.

It is unlikely that Lancaster now had the support of any groups other than his own retainers and the Marcher lords, but once again there is some possibility that he was seeking support from the Scots. In a series of letters which the Pauline Annalist believed to be forgeries but which modern historians have held to be genuine,[67] the Scots agreed to help the baronial cause, in return for which the barons agreed not to join any campaign launched by Edward II against the Scots and to seek a settlement between the two realms when the civil war was over. Lancaster's negotiations with the Scots robbed him of the last vestiges of the moral authority he had enjoyed as the champion of a programme of reform, and the king's publication of his correspondence with the Scots, which came to him in the form of transcripts from loyalists in the north, gave him a valuable propaganda victory. Already, even before war broke out, Lancaster's cause was waning. Few nobles apart from Hereford supported him: Pembroke was active on the king's side, and may have had much to do with planning the royal campaign; Arundel and Warenne sided with the king; and so did the king's half-brothers the Earls of Kent and Norfolk.

Edward began preparations for war in November 1321, and his initial intention was to strike at the Marcher lords in the west. After some early successes, the Marcher lords had found their support melting away, and the Welsh tenants of the Marcher lordships were ready to intervene on the king's side against their magnate overlords. Edward had sought from the outset of his reign to build up support amongst the Welsh, especially in the lands of the Principality. Now, in early November 1321, he sent writs to two Welsh lords, Gruffydd Llwyd in north Wales and Rhys ap Gruffydd in the south, ordering them to levy the Welsh and prepare them for war. By the end of January 1322 the king had all but eliminated his opponents in south Wales. Mortimer of Wigmore surrendered on 22 January, while Hereford, Mowbray and Clifford fled to join Lancaster, who had failed to provide the expected help from the north.

Edward now turned his attention to the north, where Lancaster had laid siege to Tickhill Castle, a royalist stronghold no more than twenty-five miles from Lancaster's headquarters at Pontefract. Lancaster's attempts to raise troops in the north were largely vain, and one of his chief retainers, Robert Holand, who had been trying to recruit forces in Derbyshire, defected to the king. The king seized Lancaster's castle of Tutbury in south Derbyshire, and Lancaster fled north, perhaps hoping to reach his northernmost stronghold at Dunstanburgh in Northumberland. He found the crossing of the Ure blocked at Boroughbridge on 16 March 1322 by Andrew Harclay and the Cumberland levies, who had marched south-east at the queen's orders to cut off the rebels. Lancaster tried to persuade Harclay to desert to him, but it was from Lancaster's army that desertions occurred, and the earl had to stand and fight. Hereford was killed in the battle, and Lancaster himself was captured the next day. He was taken to Pontefract, where he was indicted as a traitor and a rebel and sentenced to death. He was executed on 22 March 1322.

The sudden collapse of the rebellion exposed the weaknesses and divisions of the king's opponents, and does not suggest any widespread popular support for the king or the Despensers. Indeed, the Despensers had been generally unpopular: the younger Despenser had revealed in a letter to his sheriff of Glamorgan that he was well aware of his unpopularity and conscious of the insecurity which dependence on royal favour produced.[68] Yet his opponents could not combine effectively against him. Of all the earls, only Hereford and Lancaster were consistent in opposition. Warenne had little reason to like or trust Lancaster, and he, together with Pembroke and Arundel, remained loyal to the king despite their dislike of the younger Despenser. Neither the Marcher lords nor Lancaster found it easy to rally support for their cause. The king skilfully exploited the hostility of the Welsh for the Marcher overlords, and in the north Lancaster's efforts at recruitment met with little enthusiasm. Although the Despensers were widely unpopular because of their monopoly of the king's presence, a war against them perhaps had no general appeal. The most intense hostility to them came from a group of Marcher lords whose own interests were threatened by the younger Despenser's aggrandizement, and the opposition lacked the basis in widespread popular grievances that had given force to the opposition of 1310–11. The truce with Scotland between December 1319 and December 1321 meant a lessening of the pressures of taxation and prises, and some relief from attacks on northern England, while the worst effects of the famines, though not of livestock disease, were spent. It is, perhaps, significant that Lancaster's opposition after 1318 was no longer grounded in his commitment to the Ordinances, but seems rather to have been based simply on dislike of the Despensers. His negotiation with the Scots, a major error which cost him much support in the north, indicates how opportunist his opposition had become.

In any assessment of the course of opposition to the crown between 1308 and its failure at Boroughbridge, Lancaster is the most significant figure. Even before he inherited the Lincoln lands, he was probably the wealthiest and most powerful of the earls, and the Lacy inheritance served to strengthen his position still further. His estates provided him with an income of over £11,000 a year, a range of castles and a substantial body of armed men. At the siege of Berwick, for instance, perhaps one-fifth of the English army had been Lancaster's men. His military power was more formidable than that of any of the leaders of the opposition to Edward I, though ironically Edward I and Henry III had been the originators of it by their patronage of Lancaster's father. Yet despite the resources at his command he proved himself an ineffective military leader. At Boroughbridge Hereford's conduct was the more valiant and distinguished, and as the desertions from Lancaster's ranks show, he had difficulty in commanding the loyalty of his men. His political judgement, too, was flawed. He showed a degree of inflexibility which won him few friends amongst the other earls, and this served to intensify that sense of grievance against both the king and the other magnates which became so marked a feature of his attitude by 1316. He allowed his political judgement to be influenced by personal feuds, and he seems to have failed to appreciate the need for united action by the barons in the war against the Despensers.

For all that, however, Lancaster enjoyed a remarkable posthumous reputation. Within six weeks of his death news of miracles allegedly being wrought at his tomb was brought to the king at York. An office for the dead earl was devised in which his death was likened to that of Thomas of Canterbury and his power to work miracles was extolled: 'The pouring out of prayers to Thomas restores the sick to health; the pious earl comes immediately to the aid of those who are feeble.' In 1327 parliament was petitioned to seek the canonization of both Lancaster and Archbishop Winchelsey.[69] Both were revered for their devotion to the cause of reform, and the petition shows how much popular support there had been for the Ordinances, and the extent to which Lancaster was identified with them in the popular mind. Two contemporary chroniclers saw Lancaster as a martyr for the cause of justice in Church and kingdom, and even the author of the *Vita*, whose judgements on Lancaster are harsher, saw the murder of Gaveston as his real political mistake, for which his own death was deserved retribution.[70] In the martyrology of opposition to oppressive kings, Lancaster took his place alongside Thomas Becket and Simon de Montfort.

For the king, however, Boroughbridge was a substantial victory over those who had sought to enforce restraint on his exercise of royal power. The whole course of opposition to the king since 1308 had shown how difficult it was for his opponents to enforce their will upon him. In the face of financial difficulties, defeat in Scotland or the threat of violence, the king might be forced to make concessions to his opponents and to give promises about his future behaviour, but there was no institutional machinery which could ensure that the king kept his word. Indeed, the use of coercion simply served to strengthen the king's moral position, particularly in the eyes of the papacy and the French monarchy. The threat of deposition made in 1310, and of course the act of deposition in 1327, were paradoxically evidence of the strength rather than the weakness of the monarchy: if the king remained recalcitrant, what alternative did his opponents have in the last analysis other than to replace him by another?

Another source of strength which the king exploited was the dis-unity of his opponents. Little apart from the Gaveston issue proved capable of uniting the magnates against him, and even in 1310-11 there were divisions within the ranks of the earls about the importance and the extent of the programme of reform. For many of the magnates, loyalty to the king was a deep-seated, almost instinctive feeling which only Gaveston's dominance or overwhelming military defeat at Bannockburn might weaken. Loyalty, however, was reinforced by the king's exercise of his powers of patronage, which his opponents were never able successfully to control, which they could not match and which the king used with some skill to attract men to his side.

It is doubtful, too, how far the cause of the king's opponents after 1318 enjoyed popular support. The programme of the Ordainers had been widely welcomed, for it seemed to offer some relief from oppressive taxation and the arbitrary conduct of royal officials which had been such a potent source of grievance since the last years of Edward I's reign. The Ordainers had used parliament as a means of articulating this general sympathy for their ideals, and parliament had an important place in their programme: they sought to present themselves as the leaders of a community united in opposition to harsh and oppressive government. In the years after Bannockburn, however, during which the magnates effectively controlled the government, this unity was fractured. The commons in parliament now had to consider demands for taxation from a government dominated by Lancaster. Between 1313 and 1319 taxation was heavier than at any time since 1294–7; heavy taxation was accompanied by prises for the campaign in Scotland, and coincided with famine and, in the north, with raids by the Scots. The grievances of the commons thus had to be put to a government controlled by the magnates, and it is not therefore surprising that the commons came to see themselves, rather than the magnates, as representing the community of the realm. A petition presented by the commons in 1320 was described as being 'from the whole community of the land', and the *Modus Tenendi Parliamentum*,[71] a tract probably written in the early 1320s, stated that 'the proctors of the clergy, the knights of the shire, the citizens and burgesses...represent the whole community of England, and not the magnates because each of these is at parliament for his own individual person, and for no one else'. Although the author of the *Modus* did not claim a large role for parliament in matters of state, he argued that the presence and participation of the commons was essential to the transaction of the business that was placed before the assembly. This was especially true when taxation was under discussion. Although the author said that 'for the granting of such aids it is necessary that all the peers of parliament consent', he made the more significant observation that 'it must be understood that two knights who come to parliament for the shire, have a greater voice in granting and denying than the greatest earl in England'.

The commons' sense of themselves as the representatives of the community of the realm was perhaps strengthened after 1322 by the lack of effective leadership from the magnates. The execution of Lancaster, the death in battle of the earl of Hereford, and the imprisonment or exile of other opponents of the king diminished the effectiveness of aristocratic opposition to the king, as it was intended to do, and the commons in parliament could no longer look to the great nobles for support and leadership in pressing their demands on the king.[72]

The *Modus* implied that the lay nobility, 'the earls and barons and their peers', were a group apart, the 'peers of parliament', who represented only themselves. In the petition against the Despensers the magnates referred to themselves as the 'peers of the land', and it seems that the growth of the idea of peerage was the counterpart to the development of the belief that the commons represented the community of the realm. The peers were summoned to parliament by individual writ, and the basis of summons was territorial importance: the *Modus* argued that no peer should receive an individual summons unless he held a barony, which was reckoned at 400 marks' worth of land, or unless his presence 'is for other causes useful and necessary to parliament'. As K. B. McFarlane put it, the list of those summoned allowed 'something for an ancestor's renown or ancient settlement'.[73] The list did not harden into rigidity until the end of the fourteenth century, but in Edward II's reign there were clear signs of a hereditary peerage in the making, distinguished from the knights of the shire in the commons. In the longer run, this was to be one of the more significant political developments of Edward's reign.[74]

3
The Abasement and Revival of the Monarchy, 1322–1337

The Rule of the Despensers

Although divided by the deposition of Edward II, the years from 1322 to 1330 possess a certain unity. Throughout these years the powers of monarchy were exercised mainly for the advantage of magnate factions who enjoyed supremacy at court but who aroused widespread hostility in the country. The ascendancy of the Despensers which followed Edward II's victory at Boroughbridge was brought to an end by a coup led by queen Isabella and Roger Mortimer of Wigmore which brought about not only the downfall of the Despensers but also the deposition of the king himself. The ascendancy of Mortimer and Isabella was ended only by the resolute action of the young Edward III himself in another coup, which restored the authority of the monarchy and freed the king from domination by faction. These years were also marked by judicial executions, and by forfeiture of lands on a scale unknown, perhaps, since the Conquest, and the relations between the crown and nobility for the rest of the century were to be influenced by these upheavals and by the precedent which was set when the king himself was deposed.

Edward II's triumph at Boroughbridge was followed by a blood-bath which was unprecedented both in its scale and in the unease it aroused amongst contemporaries. Lancaster himself, of course, was the most significant of those who were executed: it was the first time that a man of such high rank had been put to death for rebellion against the king. Although he had been convicted on the king's own record of his treason, a device used by Edward I against his Scottish enemies, many contemporaries thought that the judgement was of dubious legality. The Lanercost Chronicler, for example, argued that he had been executed 'without parliament and without consideration of weighty and wise advice'.[1] Lancaster had not been allowed to say anything in his defence, but was dealt with according to martial law, under which the mere recognition of his offence by the king was sufficient to ensure his condemnation.

The unease which contemporaries felt about the execution of Lancaster perhaps arose from a wider uncertainty about the lengths to which it was acceptable to go in resisting the authority of the king. The author of the *Vita* had no trouble with resistance to the king by constitutional methods, even if they were backed by the barely veiled threat of force, because he believed those who opposed the king were working for the common good of the kingdom, but to appear in arms against the king in person amounted to treason, and deserved the extreme penalty. The Lanercost Chronicler agreed with this point of view, and both argued that Lancaster's execution was just retribution for his part in Gaveston's death. Both writers were, however, as Wendy Childs has pointed out, making a moral rather than a legal judgement, and not all contemporary authors accepted that Lancaster had been guilty of treason. The act of making war against the king, as distinct from encompassing his death, would not have been regarded as treason before Edward I's reign: Wallace's execution had, from the English point of view at least, set a precedent for regarding armed resistance to the king as treason. Lancaster's trial and execution reinforced that precedent, as did the executions for political crimes between 1326 and 1330, and the need for clarification of the law of treason was one reason for the 1352 statute, which laid down a narrower definition of treason than was becoming current after 1305.[2]

After Lancaster's execution, many of his followers were despatched. Six of his retainers were put to death at York on the day of his own execution, together with another eleven rebels, including Roger Clifford and John Mowbray, whose claim to the lordship of Gower had been set aside by the king in 1319. Bartholomew Badlesmere was captured and hanged at Canterbury; others, including Roger Mortimer of Wigmore, Roger Mortimer of Chirk, and Hugh Audley, were imprisoned, while some who escaped capture fled to France. The property of the executed and imprisoned rebels was distributed amongst the victors: the Despensers, as might have been expected, were the chief beneficiaries. The elder Despenser was rewarded with the lordship of Denbigh, and the younger Despenser received substantial grants not just of Lancaster's possessions but also the Bohun lordships of Brecon, Hay and Huntington, Mortimer of Chirk's lordship of Blaenllyfni, and the Welsh lands of Roger Clifford. The effect of these grants was to place most of south Wales under Despenser's influence; only the Earl of Arundel, who was given the lordship of Chirk, could rival him in the Marches. In June of the following year Despenser was pardoned all his debts at the Exchequer: he might indeed believe that he had become rich and had attained his ends.

Six weeks after Lancaster's execution, on 2 May 1322, parliament assembled at York to set the seal on the royalist victory. The sentences against the rebels were confirmed, and a statute passed which formally annulled the Ordinances and sought to ensure that no such accroachment of royal power could ever again be lawful. The statute laid down that measures 'for the estate of our lord the king and his heirs and for the estate of the realm and of the people'[3] should be granted only by the king in parliament, the implication being no doubt that such measures should not be forced upon the king by his subjects or drawn up by non-parliamentary assemblies. The intention was to place a legal obstacle in the way of anyone seeking to imitate the Ordainers, but the Statute of York should not be taken to mean that the king and his supporters had a high view of the function of parliament. Until 1321, parliament had been used by the king's opponents as an occasion when pressure might be brought to bear upon him; to the king, parliament was an inescapable necessity when taxes had to be raised but otherwise was of little significance. Political life revolved around the court, and not around the occasional meetings of parliament. Indeed, after 1322 Edward made little use of parliament. The *Vita* commented that 'parliaments, colloquies and councils decide nothing these days. For the nobles of the realm, terrified by threats and the penalties inflicted on others, let the king's will have free play'. The author of the *Vita* may have exaggerated, however: the nobles had been cowed, but Edward still encountered some resistance from the commons in parliament. Although the truce with Scotland in 1323 lessened the need for taxation, he was unable to obtain any grant of taxation from either parliament or convocation after November 1322. He had to turn to other sources of revenue, especially his feudal rights, which he exploited systematically, and the reform of the Exchequer, for which the Despensers have sometimes been given credit but which was probably the work of the chancellor, Robert Baldock and the treasurer, Walter Stapledon, was also probably motivated by the need to maximize the ordinary revenue of the crown. Both the reluctance of the commons to grant taxes and the more hostile tone of the *Vita* suggest that any goodwill the king and the Despensers might have enjoyed in 1322 did not take long to evaporate as the Despensers consolidated their grip on power.[4]

Apparently secure in their influence over the king, the Despensers' ambition and greed reached new heights. The flow of patronage towards them continued unabated, and some of their household expenses were financed by the king. The most enduring memorial to the younger Despenser's wealth is the extensive building work he undertook at Caerphilly Castle in Glamorgan, where he rebuilt the hall and the private chambers and the western gatehouse of the middle ward. When the castle fell to the queen's forces in 1327 they found there £1,000 in coin belonging to Despenser, together with royal treasure of £13,000 in coin in twenty-six barrels and over 600 pieces of plate and jewellery. The Despensers also enriched themselves by harassing the widows and heiresses of great landowners. Lancaster's widow was pressured into surrendering parts of the Lacy inheritance, and when Pembroke died in 1324 his coheiresses were subjected to unscrupulous treatment to persuade them to surrender portions of their inheritance to the Despensers. It is not, perhaps, surprising that the younger Despenser feared his opponents were using unorthodox methods to get rid of him. In 1324 he wrote to the Pope complaining that he was in danger from magic and occult practices, and the Pope replied by advising him to turn to God with a whole and contrite heart.[5]

The restoration of royal finances, from which the Despensers benefited, arose not just from the efficient exploitation of royal resources and the reform of the financial machinery, but also from the ending of the Scottish war by the truce of 1323. The truce of 1319 had expired at Christmas 1321, and after the parliament at York had been dissolved on 19 May 1322 Edward began to prepare a new invasion of Scotland. Bruce, however, laid waste the country ahead of the English forces, who were unable to live off the land. Their supply ships were held up by contrary winds, and Edward was faced with no alternative but an inglorious retreat to England. Bruce meanwhile had launched a lightning raid into north-west England, and after burning Lancaster he crossed into the North Riding of Yorkshire and almost succeeded in capturing Edward himself near Byland Abbey. This humiliation of the king proved too much for Andrew Harclay, whose support had been of crucial importance at Boroughbridge and who had been raised to the earldom of Carlisle a few days after the battle. Supported by many in the north who had had enough of war, Harclay entered into secret negotiations with Bruce for a peace settlement that recognized Bruce's title to the Scottish crown and the separate status of the Scottish kingdom. Harclay's motives were entirely understandable, but his action was technically treasonable for he was 'a private person to whom it in no way pertained to ordain such things'.[6] Edward II ordered his arrest, and he was convicted of treason in February 1323 and executed. His execution was probably a mistake, for it deprived the north of its only effective military leader, and left Edward little option but to take over the same policy and conclude a truce. Almost immediately after Harclay's execution Edward himself began negotiations with the Scots and a thirteen-year truce was agreed in March 1323.

The truce with the Scots was unpopular with some of the northern nobility, whose personal interest lay in continuing the war, and it could be argued that Edward had been forced into it by another military humiliation and a political misjudgement. But the truce does not seem to have aroused general opposition in England; perhaps more serious in their implications for the regime were the disorders at Pontefract in the summer of 1323, when a mob killed two officials guarding Lancaster's tomb to prevent offerings being made there. Some of Lancaster's supporters who had escaped justice in 1322 were at large committing acts of banditry in the north-west, and a more general change of sentiment perhaps lay behind the petitions in the parliament of February 1324 that the rotting corpses of the rebels who had been hanged should he taken down and given decent burial.

There was little sign yet, however, of any organized opposition to the king and the Despensers. The heirs of the executed and forfeited rebels lacked the means and the backing to use force to regain what their fathers had lost, and the enemies Edward had made in the extreme north by concluding a truce with the Scots were in no position to make their influence felt. When the challenge to the court came, it was not from the heirs of the rebels or from the discontented northerners, but from the queen. Her alienation from the court was one of the most significant, though least obvious, consequences of the Despensers' ascendancy. In 1324 war broke out between England and France over the destruction by the Seneschal of Gascony of the fortress of Saint Sardos on the border between Gascony and the Agenais, the building of which had been authorized by Charles IV of France in the previous year. Edward's officials ignored Charles's summons to make reparations, and Charles accordingly declared Gascony confiscated. When the war broke out the queen, who was Charles's sister, was treated with some suspicion: her lands were seized and her servants sent to various religious houses throughout the country. Edward had neither the money nor the enthusiasm for the war, however, and he sent the queen to France to negotiate peace with her brother. In the spring of 1325 Isabella reached an agreement with Charles under which Gascony was to be occupied by the French until Edward did homage to Charles, when the duchy would be restored to him. Such terms were scarcely to Edward's liking, but he confirmed the treaty on 13 June, and in a fatal misjudgement, for which the Despensers may have been in part responsible, Edward agreed to allow his son Prince Edward, now aged eleven, to go to France in his place to do homage. Isabella was now in a position of great strength. With the heir to the throne in her hands, she wrote to Edward saying that she and her son would not return to England until Edward had dismissed the Despensers from court.[7]

On her arrival in France, Isabella seems to have associated with some of the exiles who had fled there after Boroughbridge, amongst whom was Roger Mortimer of Wigmore, who had escaped from the Tower while under sentence of death. In France Mortimer became Isabella's lover, and the two of them gained the support of other English lords who had travelled to France on diplomatic business and had then defected. The most notable of these defectors were the king's half-brother the Earl of Kent, the Earl of Richmond and the Bishops of Hereford, Winchester and Norwich. Richmond and Kent, who had been amongst the most consistently loyal of the earls in the earlier part of the reign, had probably been alienated by the arrogance and dominance of the Despensers. The Bishop of Hereford was an associate of Mortimer and had been brought before parliament in 1324 to face charges that members of his retinue had helped Mortimer to escape from the Tower. He was found guilty and sentenced to the loss of his goods and lands. John Stratford, the Bishop of Winchester, had not been the king's candidate for the see and had had to buy the king's goodwill for £1,000, which was then paid over to the younger Despenser; and the Bishop of Norwich had been the victim of the king's annoyance about the treaty with Charles IV in 1325, which the bishop had helped to negotiate. The king had refused to grant him his temporalities and he sought exile in France. There is no reason, however, to suppose that Isabella had deliberately tried to build up a party amongst the bishops. Those who joined her in France had their individual grievances against the court, and the bishops in their various ways had either suffered financially at the hands of the king or had been prevented from properly exercising their episcopal authority.

Mortimer and Isabella also had allies on the continent. The Count of Hainault, who was ruler of Holland and Zeeland, had grievances against Edward II over the harassment of Dutch shipping and was willing to help Isabella as a reprisal against England. In France itself the Valois family had good dynastic reasons for wishing to see Isabella removed from France and embroiled in English domestic politics: Charles IV was the last of the Capetians in the direct male line, and the question of Isabella's title to the throne, or her right to pass the title to her son, might soon arise. Philip Count of Valois, however, was the nearest male heir to the last Capetian, and it was very much in his interests for Isabella to leave France and become involved in an English political upheaval. Indeed, as the price of Valois support Isabella may have offered to renounce her son's claim to the French crown. Philip of Valois was the Count of Hainault's brother-in-law, and it was probably the Valois family who prompted the betrothal of Prince Edward to the count's daughter Philippa. It is a measure of Edward II's loss of control of his family that a matter as important as his heir's marriage could be arranged without his prior knowledge or consent.

Isabella and Mortimer began to plan an invasion of England in July 1326, and the Count of Hainault placed shipping and men at their disposal. News of their intentions soon reached England, but seems to have provoked little immediate panic. There was no evidence yet that Isabella enjoyed widespread support in England, and Edward no doubt felt he could count on the loyalty of the nobles to whom he committed responsibility for the defence of the south coast. In this he was to be sadly mistaken, and the collapse of his position in the face of what was initially little more than a *putsch* organized by the queen shows how shallowly based his authority was, resting on fear and coercion rather than genuine loyalty. The ascendancy of the Despensers had alienated many men from their natural loyalty to their king. The numerous victims of their rapacity and greed had no reason to risk their necks for the king and his favourites; nobles such as the king's half-brother the Earl of Norfolk, who might have expected to enjoy some influence at court, hated the Despensers for their monopoly of the king's presence; and the heirs of the victims of 1322 had everything to gain from the overthrow of Edward's regime.

The Ascendancy of Mortimer and Isabella

The queen landed at Orwell in Suffolk on 24 September 1326 with an army of about 1,500 men, of whom almost half were Hainaulters. Even before she landed the lack of enthusiasm for Edward's regime had become apparent, for the fleet which Edward ordered to muster to oppose her landing refused to do so 'because of the great wrath they [i.e. the sailors] had towards Hugh Despenser'.[8] Soon other signs of unwillingness to fight appeared: the Earl of Norfolk, the king's half-brother, who had been placed in charge of the defence of East Anglia, defected to the queen, and Henry of Lancaster, Earl Thomas's brother and heir, who had been ordered to raise troops in the midlands, also went over to Isabella. Such a move on his part was entirely understandable, and it was perhaps unwise of Edward to have entrusted any military authority to one who had so much to gain by his downfall. More serious still for Edward was his loss of London. He had been unpopular in the city since an inquiry in 1321 which led to the curbing of the city's liberties; the citizens had probably helped Mortimer to escape from the Tower, and Froissart, who was a Hainaulter himself and may have written on good authority, said that even before Isabella landed she had received secret assurances of support from them.[9] The king tried to rally the city to his defence, but failed to do so and withdrew westwards with the Despensers and a few remaining friends. The city mob took Edward's flight as the signal for an orgy of destruction in which the unpopular Treasurer, Walter Stapleda Bishop of Exeter, was lynched and the tablet commemorating the Ordinances which had been removed from St Paul's on the king's orders in 1322 was replaced. A Mortimer partisan was elected Lord Mayor, and with that the city's adherence to the queen's cause was assured.

Edward and the younger Despenser fled to Wales, perhaps hoping to rally forces and make a last stand in the lands of the principality. Although Edward's support in England had evaporated, he had built up ties of loyalty and service in the royal lands in Wales ever since his father had granted them to him in 1301; Welshmen had served in the royal household, and although Despenser had made himself unpopular with the Welsh in his lordship of Glamorgan, so too had Mortimer in his lordships, and Edward perhaps believed that he might find a refuge in the one part of his realm where he might still have some support.[10] His hopes, however, soon proved misplaced. The elder Despenser had been left in charge at Bristol, but on the approach of the queen's forces, who had now been joined by a group of northern magnates led by Henry Percy of Alnwick and Thomas Wake of Liddel, he surrendered and was tried and sentenced to death. Isabella then sent Henry of Lancaster to the lordship of Glamorgan to hunt down the king and the younger Despenser. He found them at Neath Abbey, and the king was taken to Kenilworth Castle while Isabella and Mortimer proceeded to wreak their vengeance on his supporters. The younger Despenser was brought before a 'tribunal of judges', as one chronicler put it. He was charged with accroaching royal power and procuring the deaths of the Earl of Lancaster and other nobles, acquiring many lands that belonged to the crown, and disobeying the judgement of banishment pronounced against him in 1321. 'The good men of the realm, great and small, rich and poor, by common assent' found him guilty and sentenced him to death. The sentence was carried out with great brutality, and his head was placed on London Bridge amidst general rejoicing. The Chancellor, Robert Baldock, was imprisoned and died soon after; the Earl of Arundel, who was the younger Despenser's brother-in-law and the only earl to remain loyal to the bitter end, was executed. The Pauline Annalist reported a rumour that Arundel confessed to having plotted the death of the queen,[11] but it is more likely that Mortimer saw him as a territorial rival in the Marches of Wales, where he had held the lordship of Chirk since the confiscations after Boroughbridge.

After this bloodletting, there remained the question of what to do with the king. On 26 October the queen and her supporters had issued a proclamation at Bristol declaring that since the king had deserted the realm, presumably by fleeing to Glamorgan, Prince

Edward was to be Keeper of the Realm, and the prince issued writs in his father's name summoning parliament for 14 December. When the Great Seal was recovered with the capture of the chancellor, Robert Baldock, new writs in the king's name were issued on 3 December postponing the parliament until 7 January 1327. Although both the king and the chancellor were in prison, the fiction was still maintained that the king was responsible for government, and writs still ran in his name. Whatever Isabella's private intentions may have been, the deposition of the king had so far formed no part of her publicly declared programme, which amounted to little more than the removal of the Despensers. It is impossible to discover when and by whom the decision to depose the king was taken, but when parliament assembled, Mortimer and his supporters embarked on a carefully orchestrated campaign to win support for the removal of the king. According to the Lanercost Chronicle,[12] the Bishops of Winchester and Hereford were sent to Kenilworth to ask the king to come to parliament, but on 12 January they returned to Westminster and it was announced that the king refused to do so. On the following day[13] the Bishop of Hereford preached a sermon on the text, 'A foolish king shall ruin his people', and popular clamour for the removal of the king was encouraged. Mortimer then told the assembly that at some earlier date the magnates had agreed that Edward should be deposed. On the same day a series of articles against the king were presented to parliament.

The articles opened with the comprehensively damning statement that the king 'is not sufficient to govern' because throughout his reign he had been led and governed by others who had given him evil counsel, to the dishonour of himself and the destruction of Holy Church and his people, and he had refused to provide any remedy, or to allow one to be made, when he was asked to do so by the great and wise men of his realm. He was also accused of having lost Scotland, of allowing many great and noble men to go to a shameful death or to be imprisoned, exiled and disinherited, and of breaking his coronation oath to do right to all. The indictment concluded by declaring that he had been found 'incorrigible without hope of amendment'. In what appears to have been a carefully stage-managed cry of unanimity, it was agreed that Edward should never rule over them again, and the Bishop of Hereford took a delegation which was headed by William Trussell to Kenilworth to inform Edward of the assembly's decision. According to Geoffrey le Baker,[14] the bishop first of all called upon Edward to abdicate, and in an emotional scene he agreed to do so. On the following day Trussell renounced homage 'on behalf of the whole kingdom', and the delegation returned to London to announce the abdication. The Bishop of Winchester then stated that the peers had unanimously agreed that Prince Edward should become king 'if the people would accept this decision of the prelates and magnates'. The people did so, and the Archbishop of Canterbury then addressed the assembly on the theme 'the voice of the people is the voice of God', saying that by the unanimous consent of all the magnates Edward had been deprived of the government of his kingdom because of his inadequacy and his offences against Church and kingdom. The people replied by crying three times, 'Let it be done.'

There was no precedent in post-Conquest England for the removal of a crowned and anointed king, nor was there any clear guidance in civil or canon law about the means by which a king might be deposed. Indeed, it has been argued that no 'actual sentence of deposition, in the legal sense of the term' was pronounced against Edward. Canon law, however, gave grounds for supposing that an incompetent king, 'rex inutilis', could be required to abdicate, and the articles against the king, which may have been drawn up by the Bishop of Winchester, allege that his 'uselessness' had brought damage and destruction to the Church, people and realm of England. The populist, not to say demagogic, tone of the deposition proceedings themselves implies that the consent of the whole people was deemed sufficient to remove a king and replace him by another, though the sending of a delegation to Kenilworth to obtain the king's abdication suggests some uncertainty about the principle of popular consent.[15]

In April 1327 Edward was moved from Kenilworth to Berkeley Castle. Two attempts to rescue him failed, but in July his former confessor Thomas Dunheved led a band which succeeded in freeing him. There is no specific evidence for his recapture, but it was announced in parliament in the autumn that he had died at Berkeley on 21 September. Later sources had it that the king was murdered: Geoffrey le Baker, writing thirty years after the event, provides the vivid details of the brutal and degrading way in which he is supposed to have met his death, but Dr Cuttino and Dr Lyman have suggested that the story of his escape to Ireland and then via France to Cologne where he ended up as a hermit may not be wholly imaginary.[16] When Mortimer fell in 1330 he and his associates were accused of procuring the king's death, and throughout the reigns of his son and great-grandson he is referred to as King Edward 'who lies at Gloucester' but it remains a mystery as to whether the body which rests in the tomb there is his or not.

Edward's downfall had been sudden and complete; yet its instigators, the queen and Mortimer, had never been popular in England and had enjoyed little if any overt support there until they landed in September 1326. The most striking feature of the revolution of 1326–7 is the unwillingness of anyone apart from Edward's immediate circle of friends to stand by him or to fight for him. Few were even prepared to try to mediate, none to risk anything for the king and the

Despensers. The king did not lack military resources, but they were useless if the men who were placed in command of them defected to the enemy. The Despensers themselves had insufficient military power to underpin their ascendancy. They had some support amongst officials at court, but they had not troubled to build up support amongst the magnates or the lesser landowners. Their power lacked the firm basis in widespread territorial possessions and lordship over men that had made Lancaster such a formidable opponent of the king; they were essentially courtiers, who depended for their influence on royal favour. The incompetence of the king, and the arrogance and greed of the Despensers, had so alienated men from the court that none except the few who profited from the king's favour would fight for him. Even the Despensers' own retainers showed little loyalty at the end, and of those whom the king and the Despensers had appointed as constables of castles only one proved willing to resist Mortimer and Isabella.[17]

Edward was condemned as a 'foolish king', who had proved incapable of redemption. His foolishness consisted in his military ineptitude, his refusal to listen to wise counsel, and the undue influence which he allowed his favourites to exercise over him. The concentration of favour and rewards first upon Gaveston and then on the younger Despenser alienated those who did not share the benefits of intimacy with the king, and it could be represented, more disinterestedly, as a waste of royal resources. The manner in which Gaveston and Despenser monopolized access to the king was deeply resented: when the king's personal decision counted for so much, access to the king was the way to obtain grants and favours for a magnate and for his dependants. If a noble was excluded from favour at court, his dependants might look elsewhere for a patron, and the noble's following would thus be weakened. The monopoly of the king's presence by a particular favourite thus had serious implications for the position of other magnates, which helps to explain the bitterness of their hostility to both Gaveston and the Despensers. Access to the king, however, implied more than just access to the fount of patronage; it also implied the right to give advice on the business of the kingdom. The magnates saw themselves as the natural counsellors of the king, and argued in the Boulogne agreement and in the petition against the Despensers that they had a duty to act to protect the realm if the king was being led by unwise counsel. It should not be assumed that such an argument was merely a cloak for self-interest and greed. The honour and status of the realm were matters of concern to the nobility, and they argued that they had the right to constrain the king for the sake of the common good of the realm. Edward's military humiliations in Scotland were as much an affront to them as his lavishness towards Gaveston and the Despensers.

The deposition of the king was followed by a reversal of the forfeitures of 1322 and an annulment of the grants that the victors of Boroughbridge had made to themselves and their supporters. Henry of Lancaster, Earl Thomas's brother and heir who had successfully petitioned for the restoration of the earldom of Leicester in 1324, now sought a reversal of the sentence on his brother and the restoration of his other lands and honours. Rather surprisingly, perhaps, this petition was not granted in full. Henry was allowed to assume the title of Earl of Lancaster and to receive a great part of the Lancaster inheritance, but the Lacy earldom of Lincoln, which Earl Thomas had held in right of his wife, was not fully recovered until 1348. The Earl of Hereford's son was granted livery of his father's inheritance, the Clifford family was restored, and the Mowbray inheritance was placed in wardship with the Countess of Warenne until John Mowbray's heir came of age.

Any expectations that the removal of Edward II would hold out some hope of better government were soon, however, disappointed. In acquisitiveness and greed there was little to choose between the victors and the vanquished in 1327. Isabella recovered her lands, which were augmented by additional grants worth about £9,000, including Despenser's lordship of Glamorgan; she also obtained the younger Despenser's movables, plate and jewels. Mortimer not only procured a reversal of the judgement against his father, but also very substantial portions of the forfeited Despenser lands, including the lordship of Denbigh, and property in Shropshire which the Earl of Arundel had forfeited. For the moment, the revolution of 1327 seemed to amount to little more than the replacement of one greedy and unscrupulous faction by another. A regency council headed by Henry of Lancaster was set up to administer the realm, but Mortimer remained outside it, or perhaps more accurately above it, occupying a quasi-royal position as Queen Isabella's lover. He now proceeded to use his position to advance his interests still further. In 1328 he obtained the office of justice of North and South Wales for life, and Chief Keeper of the Peace in Shropshire, Worcestershire and Herefordshire. He successfully petitioned parliament to reverse the judgement of 1322 against his cousin Mortimer of Chirk, but declared himself his heir and expropriated his lands despite the fact that he had a son and grandson living. He also obtained the custody, and thus the control, of the lands of the heirs to the Audley and Pembroke inheritances. He had created an empire in the March with all the speed and rapacity of his supplanted rival the younger Despenser, and from this base he ruled England. In the September parliament of 1328 he received the title Earl of March, an honour which was amply justified in terms of his wealth and territorial power but which aroused some hostility amongst the other earls.[18]

Mortimer and Isabella tried to cultivate support for their regime by grants to the deposed king's half-brothers the Earls of Norfolk and Kent: Kent, for example, was granted Despenser's forfeited lands in Leicestershire. Two of the northern lords who had supported the revolution, Henry Beaumont and Wake of Liddel, were well rewarded, and Mortimer tried to buttress his position in Ireland by conferring the earldom of Ormond on the leading Anglo-Irish magnate of Munster, James Butler. The regime perhaps had little choice but to win support by making grants of land which might otherwise have gone to augment royal resources, and Mortimer and Isabella rapidly ran through the treasure inherited from Edward II, who had built up substantial wealth in the years after Boroughbridge. Over £60,000 was in the king's Treasury in November 1326, but some of this was spent paying off the force of Hainault mercenaries which Isabella had recruited for her invasion in 1326; some of it was simply appropriated by Mortimer and Isabella for their personal use, and some of it had to be used to finance the war against the Scots which was renewed in the summer of 1327.[19]

The political turmoil in England following the deposition of Edward II was too good an opportunity for Bruce to miss, even though the truce of 1323 still had nine years to run. On 1 February 1327 a Scottish force made an unsuccessful attempt to seize Norham Castle, and a little over two months later Bruce himself landed in Ulster. Not all the Anglo-Irish lords had welcomed Mortimer's coup: he was himself an Irish landowner in right of his wife, and he had served as Edward II's lieutenant in Ireland in 1317. Some of the Anglo-Irish lords had opposed him then, and Robert Bruce may have hoped in 1327 to take advantage of the animosity towards Mortimer in Ireland to obtain support for an invasion of Wales and thence of England. Although Bruce was persuaded to withdraw from Ireland in face of a general recognition of Edward III as lord of Ireland by the spring of 1327, his lieutenants were raising an army to invade England over the land border. The English response to these manoeuvres was to raise a large army for the invasion of Scotland. Rather surprisingly, perhaps, the war seems to have been popular: Murimuth says there were more volunteers than conscripts in the army's ranks, and Sir Thomas Gray of Heton, the author of the Scalacronica, recorded that there was no lack of enthusiasm for service even amongst the northerners.[20]

The campaign which Mortimer now led turned out, however, to be an ignominious fiasco. The mercenary captain John of Hainault brought a force of 500 men-at-arms from the Low Countries, and at York they became involved in a violent affray with a band of archers from Lincolnshire, which culminated in the deaths of a sizeable number of the Lincolnshire men. The command of the army on the border was entrusted jointly to the Earls of Kent and Lancaster, but the two evidently found it difficult to work together, for after three weeks Lancaster was named as sole captain of the force. English supply ships once more failed to keep up with the advance of the troops, and the Scots pursued their usual diversionary tactic of raiding into England, eluding the English force which reached Durham while the Scots outflanked them to the west. The Scots encamped in Stanhope Park in Weardale on 20 July, and it took the English eleven days to discover where they were. They planned an attack on the encampment, but were dissuaded and the only military action was a surprise move by Sir James Douglas against the English camp. The Scots were allowed to escape, and Sir Thomas Gray of Heton portrayed the young Edward III in tears after such a humiliating failure. Murimuth recorded that Edward returned south with grief and without honour, and it is not surprising that rumours of treachery were rife. Murimuth, who observed that the English army outnumbered the Scots by three to one, believed that the decision not to attack was urged by some of the magnates who were in league with the Scots.[21] Treachery is unlikely, but the decision not to attack the Scottish camp, and not to pursue the Scots when they broke camp, suggests at the very least a lack of confidence and judgement amongst the English commanders, and there is some evidence of disagreement amongst them about the tactics they should adopt.

After the failure of the Stanhope Park campaign Mortimer and Isabella determined upon a negotiated peace with Scotland. They could not afford another campaign: they had run through the treasure inherited from Edward II so quickly that they could not even pay their Hainault mercenaries, and they had to borrow both from the Florentine banking house of Bardi and from English merchants. In the welter of recriminations that followed the Stanhope Park campaign, it is doubtful whether there was enough political will and unity amongst the magnates to launch another invasion of Scotland. Discussions with Bruce were initiated immediately after the Lincoln parliament of September 1327, and the English seem to have been prepared to accept most of Bruce's proposals. On 1 March 1328 Edward III issued letters patent embodying the terms of a settlement, which was then ratified at the parliament of Northampton in May.[22] The treaty conceded most of what Bruce had been fighting for. Edward III agreed that the realm of Scotland 'shall remain for ever to the eminent prince Lord Robert, by the grace of God the illustrious king of Scots', and he renounced any right he might have in the realm of Scotland. There was to be a 'true, final and perpetual peace' between the two kings, and the peace was to be symbolized by the marriage between Edward's sister Joan and Bruce's son David, later David II of Scotland.

The King of Scotland for his part undertook to pay the King of England £20,000 over three years in three instalments, a concession which Mortimer and Isabella must have been especially anxious to procure in view of their financial difficulties, and which Bruce hoped perhaps would sweeten the agreement for the English. The indemnity was described simply as a payment 'for making peace', but it has been pointed out that the sum of £20,000 is close to the amount thought to have been extorted by the Scots from the northern counties of England over the years since Bannockburn, and the payment may have been seen as compensation for the destruction wrought in the north. There was no mention in the treaty, however, either of the estates in Scotland granted to English lords by Edward I and lost as Bruce gained control of the country, or of the Scottish lands held by Anglo-Scottish lords such as the Earl of Angus and forfeited when they adhered to the English cause. In a private agreement made a few months after the treaty was concluded, Bruce restored Henry Percy's Scottish lands and he is said to have promised to restore the lands of Henry Beaumont and Thomas Wake of Liddel. But even if such a promise was made it was not carried out, and the 'disinherited' were soon to form a powerful group at Edward's court seeking the renewal of the Scottish war. Ireland was also included in the treaty. It had become almost as important a front in the Anglo-Scottish war as the land border between the two countries, and Robert Bruce now undertook not to give any assistance to the king's enemies in Ireland.[23]

The peace was widely condemned in England. Murimuth called it 'turpis pax', the shameful peace, and the king himself showed his disapproval by refusing to attend his sister's wedding. The government, nervous about the nobility's reaction to the agreement, issued an order banning tournaments. It was believed that the treaty had been made simply for private gain, and this view was given substance by Isabella's appropriation of much of the £20,000 payment from Bruce. Sir Thomas Gray of Heton said that the peace was not in accordance with the king's will and that the queen and Mortimer had used the opportunity of the king's minority to arrange the whole thing.[24] This argument reflects the official view disseminated after the war had begun again that Edward had been coerced into accepting the treaty while he was under the tutelage of Mortimer and Isabella and that therefore he could not be bound by it.

The peace with Scotland brought opposition to the regime of Mortimer and Isabella into the open, and, perhaps more significantly, marked the beginning of a breach, not as yet overt, between them and the young king, who was now sixteen years old. The first challenge to the regime came from the Earl of Lancaster who perhaps felt that Mortimer had denied him the authority which was his due as chief councillor to the king. He refused to attend the Salisbury parliament in October 1328, but stayed nearby at Winchester with a group of his followers. Lancaster sent 'certain knights' to parliament to explain his absence, but his excuses were not accepted, and the Bishop of Winchester then declared that Lancaster had not come 'because of the quarrel between himself and Lord Mortimer'.[25] Mortimer swore that he intended no harm to Lancaster, and the Bishops of Winchester and London were sent to persuade him to attend after all. But Lancaster replied by attacking the government for extravagance and oppressively burdening the people, saying that he would come armed to parliament and seek to remedy these matters unless the king granted him a safe-conduct. The king and the earls could not agree to the form of the safe-conduct, and Lancaster stayed away. It is not clear whether Lancaster's men were in arms or not, but Mortimer regarded his absence as a sufficient threat to raise a force in the king's name, and on the way back to London from Salisbury in the company of the king this force encountered Lancaster's men near Winchester. The engagement which followed was hardly even a skirmish, but it had been directed against the king, and in December, after Lancaster had moved to the midlands to gather reinforcements, the king wrote to the City of London complaining that Lancaster intended to attack him. The king believed that although Lancaster and his followers claimed to be acting in the king's name they would in fact create disorder and in any case 'it was not their duty to act as judge and do justice'.[26]

Lancaster was now joined by the king's uncles the Earls of Kent and Norfolk and a group of lords who had lost lands in Scotland, chief amongst whom were Henry Beaumont, Thomas Wake of Liddel and David of Strathbogie, claimant to the earldom of Atholl. Norfolk's and Kent's adherence to Lancaster was motivated by little more than expediency, and when it looked as though he was not going to win after all they defected to Mortimer. The disinherited, on the other hand, were opposed to the peace with Scotland, and the propaganda published by the Lancastrian faction condemned the court for giving up the king's right in Scotland and for inflicting the humiliation of Stanhope Park on the king. Lancaster's objections to the regime, however, were concerned just as much with domestic affairs: he criticized the queen for her greed and acquisitiveness, singling out for special mention her appropriation of the lordship of Pontefract which had been held by Earl Thomas in right of his wife. He complained that the treasure left by Edward II had been 'wastede and born away withouten the wille of Kyng Edwarde his sone, in destruccioun of him and of his folc', and proposed that Mortimer 'shouldd dwelle oppon his owen londes'.[27] In early December Lancaster attempted to negotiate with the court by sending Ralph Basset and William de Clinton with proposals for a settlement, but they were met with a firm refusal by Edward, who told Lancaster that he should not attempt to bargain with his king. Both sides were now preparing for war, but Norfolk and Kent made another attempt at mediation in mid-December when they wrote to all the prelates asking them to attend an assembly in London to discuss the king's failure to abide by his coronation oath and Magna Carta. Arising out of this the Archbishop of Canterbury sought a solution by asking the king to avoid the use of force and to summon a parliament to consider the grievances of the Lancastrian party. The king, however, replied that he intended to proceed against the rebels but offered a pardon to anyone who submitted before 7 January 1329, except Henry Beaumont, Thomas Roscelin, William Trussell and Thomas Wyther, all of whom fled to France. The archbishop hoped that this offer would be sufficient to restore peace, and Lancaster together with Wake and others swore a solemn oath that they had not done anything against the estate of the king or to the dishonour of his royal lordship.

Lancaster's oath, however, was not enough to satisfy the court, and Mortimer launched a punitive raid lasting eight days on Lancaster's lands in Leicestershire. Kent and Norfolk now deserted Lancaster and accused him of sedition, and the king ordered the confiscation of all his property and the property of his supporters until they submitted unconditionally. Lancaster meanwhile was encamped near Bedford, and seeing his support ebb away he made another offer of submission. This time the terms imposed upon him and his followers were much more humiliating: they had to 'give such surety as it shall please to our lord the king' that they would make no further trouble. Lancaster himself had to enter into a recognizance of £30,000 and similar large sums were required from his most important followers. His protest against the court had come to nothing.

Lancaster's action in the winter of 1328–9 scarcely deserves the name of rebellion. There is no evidence that he attempted to start an armed rising against Mortimer and the king, and even after his submission Mortimer made no move to have him condemned for treason. Perhaps neither side was prepared for open civil war once again, with its probable aftermath of executions and forfeitures. For his part, Lancaster had evidently hoped for the support of the king, but Edward firmly refused to have anything to do with his protest. It was not in the king's interest to associate himself with a movement which at most would merely ensure the removal from power of one magnate clique and its replacement by another.

Even though the king himself offered Lancaster no support, Mortimer had grounds for doubting the loyalty of some of the magnates, especially the earls of Kent and Norfolk. Norfolk survived unscathed, perhaps because his son was married to Mortimer's daughter; but in March 1330 Kent was arrested on a charge of treason. It was alleged at his trial that he was involved in a conspiracy with the Archbishop of York, the Bishop of London, Henry Beaumont and other exiles in Paris, and even some former associates of the Despensers, to put Edward II back on the throne with the support of a Scottish army. Kent's supposed allies appear little more than an improbable amalgam of all those who might be opposed to the regime of Mortimer and Isabella, and it is hard to believe that the conspiracy had such wideranging support. The conspirators apparently believed that Edward II was still alive, for Kent had been arrested after visiting Corfe Castle where the deposed king was supposed to be hiding. Kent was found guilty and executed, but all the other conspirators except the Archbishop of York were either imprisoned or released after entering into recognizances for their good behaviour. The case against the archbishop was adjourned, however, and abandoned when the regime fell in October 1330.

After Kent's execution the regime probably felt confident that it had overcome its enemies. Lancaster's opposition had received little determined support, and Kent's conspiracy, if conspiracy it really was, had come to nothing. The recognizances which had been required from several of the most powerful nobles gave the regime an effective hold over them, and none of the movements against Mortimer had gained the support of the king himself. The only serious threat appeared to come from a small group of exiles in Paris, chief amongst whom was Henry Beaumont, who had gathered together exiles from Lancaster's rebellion and some of the nobles who had lost lands in Scotland. These men were in touch with Edward Balliol, the heir of the Scottish king dispossessed by Edward I, and they may have been planning some move to recover their position in either England or Scotland. They were forestalled, however, by the coup which the king and a group of trusted household servants carried out on 19 October 1330.

The Reassertion of Royal Authority

As early as March or April 1330 Edward III was attempting to assert his independence of the regime at court and to build up a body of supporters loyal to him rather than to Mortimer and Isabella. One of his associates was the noted bibliophile Richard de Bury, later Bishop of Durham, and it was he who informed the Pope, in response to a message conveyed verbally, that requests which the king himself really wished to be carried out would bear the words *Pater Sancte* in his own hand.[28] Edward sought papal approval for the coup he was planning and as his intermediary in the negotiations he relied on Sir William Montague, a knight of the household whose family had served Edward I and Edward II in the Scottish and Welsh wars.

Montague's father had been a prominent supporter of Edward II, and had been described by one chronicler as 'worse than Piers Gaveston'.[29] In the autumn of 1330 Mortimer got wind of a plot being hatched in the king's immediate circle and he interrogated Montague and others. Montague managed to convince Mortimer of his innocence, but his narrow escape did not discourage the king, and when the coup came it had all the appearance of being carefully planned. The king held a council at Nottingham from 14 to 19 October 1330, and on 19 October he and a small band of followers made their way by a subterranean passage into Nottingham Castle, where Mortimer and Isabella were lodged. They were discovered by Sir Hugh Trumpington, who raised the alarm, but one of Montague's men seized a mace 'and smote the same Hughe oppon the hevede, that the brayn barst out and felle on the Ground'. They then entered Isabella's chamber, where they found her together with Mortimer and the Bishop of Lincoln. Isabella's plea to Edward to 'have pity on gentle Mortimer' was brushed aside, and Edward ordered him to be arrested and placed in safe custody.[30] On the following day his supporters who had come to Nottingham with him were arrested as well.

Mortimer and Isabella were hurried off to London and arraigned before parliament in November. Mortimer was accused of accroaching the royal power and the government of the realm, and removing Edward II from Kenilworth Castle to Berkeley and there murdering him. He was also charged with forcing the king to bestow the earldom of March upon him in the Salisbury parliament of 1328 and then leading an armed band against the Earl of Lancaster, with procuring the death of the Earl of Kent, fomenting discord between Edward II and Isabella, and other offences which together amounted to a comprehensive indictment of his rule since 1326.[31] The earls, barons and other magnates of the realm were asked to give their judgement on these charges and they declared that they were notorious and manifest to all. Sentence then followed: Mortimer was condemned to death and to forfeiture of all his lands and honours. Isabella was sentenced to lose all her lands, but was given an allowance of £3,000 a year to maintain her estate. Knighton suggests that she too came close to being condemned to death, but was spared because of the king's natural tenderness towards his mother.[32]

Mortimer's estates were taken into the king's hands, but, in contrast to his father in 1322 and Mortimer himself in 1327, Edward did not immediately use the confiscated lands to underpin the power of another group of favourites. Indeed, although parts of the inheritance were granted out, the lords successfully petitioned in the parliament of September 1331 for the restoration to Mortimer's son Edmund of the family's lands in mid-Wales, including Wigmore, Maelienydd, Caedewen and Cwmwd Deuddwr. After Mortimer's condemnation

Edward granted pardon and restitution to the families which had suffered at his hands in 1329 and 1330. The fines imposed upon the Earl of Lancaster and his followers were remitted, and Lancaster received confirmation of his right to Pontefract, Tutbury and Leicester, which he had not been able to recover after the revolution of 1327, though he had to lease Pontefract for £1,000 a year from queen Philippa, who had been granted it after Isabella had been deprived of it in 1330. Wake and Beaumont were restored to their English lands, and this aroused hope that they might receive some support in trying to recover their estates in Scotland as well. The judgement on the Earl of Kent was annulled, and his son, a minor, was granted the right to succeed to his father's title and lands. The Earl of Arundel's heir was restored to his inheritance and granted the lordship of Chirk, forfeited by Mortimer, despite a petition from the grandson of Roger Mortimer of Chirk seeking to recover the lordship. The family of Mortimer of Chirk were one of the very few permanent victims of the political upheavals between 1322 and 1330: they abandoned the attempt to recover Chirk, and settled in Kent.[33] Finally, Edward rewarded the group of household knights who had helped him to overthrow Mortimer and Isabella. Sir William Montague, who was the king's chief supporter and evidently the leader of the group, was granted £1,000 worth of land because he 'had nobly laboured'[34] in arresting Mortimer; the £1,000 included the Mortimer lordship of Denbigh. Edward Bohun, a younger brother of the Earl of Hereford, received 400 marks' worth of land and was granted the office of Constable in view of the infirmity of the earl himself; John Neville of Hornby and Robert Ufford, a knight of Suffolk who had served in Gascony in 1324–5 with the Earl of Kent, were given 200 marks for 'helping in the same enterprise'.[35]

The *Brut* suggests that others who were not rewarded in this way also supported the coup, including the younger Bohun brothers Humphrey and William, together with Ralph de Stafford and William de Clinton.[36] Clinton and Neville of Hornby seem to have been followers of the Earl of Lancaster; Neville had been taken prisoner at Boroughbridge but was pardoned in return for a fine of £500, of which he paid only £50. Clinton on the other hand had fought for the king at Boroughbridge, but after the coup of 1327 he established links with the new earl of Lancaster: he was one of the two lords whom Lancaster appointed to take his proposals for a settlement to the king in late November 1328. Clinton had also been a member of the group of knights sent to Hainault in 1327 to escort the count and his daughter Philippa to the English court prior to Philippa's marriage with Edward III. Clinton and Neville thus had links both with the court and with Lancaster, and these links perhaps helped to ensure the tacit support of the Lancaster affinity for Edward's coup. Thus although Edward's closest supporters were well rewarded, his coup did not lead to the displays of favouritism of the kind which had followed Edward II's victory in 1322 or the triumph of Mortimer and Isabella in 1327, and there was no immediate and general reversal of the judgements of 1326–7. Despenser's heir was released from prison in July 1331, but had to wait until 1337 before receiving any of his father's inheritance. The reabsorption into landed society of those families who had suffered in the upheavals of the past decade was to be a slow process, and was to give rise to fresh disputes over lands claimed by families who had been on opposite sides, but Edward showed over the next twenty years that loyalty and service would receive their due reward.

The significance of the coup of 19 October 1330 should not be underestimated. By successfully conspiring to remove Mortimer and Isabella from power Edward re-established the personal authority of the monarchy, though he still had to win the support of the nobility and show that he could rule in a manner different from that of his father. His support came from a small group of household knights who were to be well rewarded for their work, but he was not indebted to any great noble for his position. He had rightly judged that it would have been unwise for him to associate himself with the movement of the Earl of Lancaster or with Kent's conspiracy. If he was to rule as well as reign he himself had to overthrow Mortimer and Isabella and to do so in a way which would not enhance the power of the magnates. In his first independent act as king he established his authority on a sure foundation and revealed both a sound political judgement and a determination not to allow himself to be dependent upon a small group of powerful nobles. Both characteristics were to distinguish his rule over the next forty years.

Sir Thomas Gray of Heton suggested that the atmosphere at court after the coup of 1330 was one of harmony and tranquillity. 'For a long time,' he said, 'the king acted on the advice of William of Montague, who always encouraged him to excellence, honour, and love of arms: and so they led their young lives in pleasant fashion, until there came a more serious time with more serious matters.' Other chroniclers convey the same impression, recording that the king and the young knights at court passed their time in 'jousts, tournaments and the chase, feasting and court ceremonies'.[37] The king took the lead in the creation of a court which exemplified the values of chivalry and which proved attractive to the nobility. In doing so, Edward developed strong ties of sympathy and affection with the nobles, and the contrast with the court of Edward II could scarcely have been more marked. This was especially true in Edward's encouragement of tournaments. Edward II had tried to suppress tournaments, because he feared that they might be used as occasions to form political conspiracies against the court, but his son now encouraged them as occasions when king and nobles could together demonstrate their knightly prowess. From the start of his personal rule Edward showed the qualities of leadership, affability and sympathy with the aspirations of the nobility which were to characterize his reign until its last decade, and which underlay the domestic political harmony of the ensuing years.

'So this king,' wrote Sir Thomas Gray, 'led a gay life in jousts and tourneys and entertaining ladies, until the lords who had been disinherited in Scotland for the cause of himself and his predecessors made supplication to him that he would restore to them their inheritances which they had lost on his account and allow them to take their own measures.'[38] These lords viewed Edward III's seizure of power with enthusiasm, believing not only that Edward might wish to wipe out the stain of the Stanhope Park campaign and the shameful peace, but also that they themselves might reap some political reward for their opposition to Mortimer in 1328. Their hopes were raised still further by the death of Robert Bruce in 1329 and the accession of his son David II who was only five years old. In December 1330 Edward wrote to David asking him to give effect to his father's promise and restore Wake and Beaumont to their Scottish lands; but the Scots prevaricated, and in the autumn of 1331 Edward's policy towards Scotland hardened, influenced no doubt by the fact that the final payment of Bruce's indemnity had been received at midsummer. Beaumont meanwhile, despairing of any settlement by diplomatic means, began to seek support amongst those disinherited lords whose claims Bruce had ignored in 1328, and he brought to England Edward Balliol, whose father had lost not only his kingdom but also his family estates in both Scotland and England. Balliol appears to have had his eye on his English lands rather than his Scottish inheritance, but his claim to the Scottish crown was encouraged by the disinherited lords who now paid court to him. In the early months of 1332 these lords began to organize an invasion of Scotland to recover their lands and place Balliol on the Scottish throne. Edward reacted cautiously to the conspiracy of the disinherited. He saw the advantages that England might gain from a successful coup in Scotland by them, which would take their political pressure off him at home. Yet he was not at this stage prepared to risk open war on their behalf; although he disliked the peace of 1328 he had neither the resources nor the general political support for a renewal of the Scottish war. It was likely that both the leading magnates and the commons in parliament would see a war on behalf of the disinherited as merely a factional struggle in which neither the honour nor the safety of the community was at stake, and which therefore did not merit support.

In public, therefore, Edward gave the impression that he was opposed to any plans to invade Scotland. In March 1332, for instance, he ordered the sheriffs of five northern counties to forbid the assemblies of men-at-arms preparing to invade Scotland, and to arrest anyone found infringing the peace between the realms. In private, however, Edward was quite content, as the Earl of Moray put it, to let 'le pellot aler', the ball roll.[39] He gave Beaumont and David of Strathbogie some limited help in raising the money they needed to launch the invasion, and some time before the expedition left for Scotland he received Edward Balliol's homage for the kingdom he hoped to conquer. In face of Edward's formal prohibition of an invasion, the disinherited could not mount an attack by land from England, and they therefore sailed from the Humber on 31 July 1332. On 6 August they landed near Kinghorn in Fife.

They achieved an immediate success. Although greatly outnumbered they engaged the Scottish forces at Dupplin Moor south of Perth on 11 August 1332 and routed them. Balliol was crowned king at Scone six weeks later and then marched to Galloway to rally the support which the men of that region had traditionally shown to the Balliol family. He spent November at Roxburgh, where he issued letters patent in which he recognized Edward III as lord superior of Scotland and declared that he had already done homage to Edward, in return for which Edward had agreed to maintain and protect him and his heirs in the kingdom. Balliol also agreed to repay Edward for the help he had given in preparing the expedition by handing over to him land worth £2,000 a year to be selected from those parts of Scotland adjacent to England: in effect, the southern counties of Scotland were to be permanently ceded to England. His willingness to dismember the kingdom he had just won is indicative of the underlying weakness of Balliol's position. Despite the rout at Dupplin Moor David II still enjoyed much support in Scotland and Balliol realized he could only hold his gains with English assistance. The cession of the south was not so much payment for help already given, but a concession designed to ensure future support and give Edward III a vested interest in the endurance of Balliol's rule.

Balliol's hold on his kingdom proved even more tenuous than he feared: in December 1332 he moved to Annan, where he was surprised by Sir Archibald Douglas and the Earl of Moray, both partisans of David II, and forced to flee to Carlisle, whence he sent an appeal for support to Edward III. Edward, however, was still reluctant to commit himself wholeheartedly to Balliol's cause. Balliol's letters patent acknowledging the English king's overlordship of Scotland were discussed when parliament met at York in December 1332. Edward made his own views clear by stating that he regarded the 1328 treaty as invalid because it had been made when he was a minor and under the tutelage of others and that his title to the overlordship of Scotland should be reasserted. He asked parliament whether he should proceed to assert his own authority over Scotland, or seek to persuade one side or the other there to acknowledge English superiority. Edward's enthusiasm for war was not shared by the community: the response of the prelates, magnates and commons was notably cautious and they declined to support either alternative.[40] Edward indicated that he was not committed to Balliol's cause, and the arrival of Balliol at Carlisle as a fugitive must have made both king and parliament have second thoughts about his value as an ally. Parliament reconvened at York in late January 1333, and once again declined to offer Edward any positive support for action in Scotland: his income from taxation was no more than the fifteenth and tenth granted by parliament in the previous September. There was little enthusiasm amongst the English nobility for a renewal of war, and the triumphant campaign that now ensued was prepared by the king himself and a small group of his military supporters, notably Henry Percy of Alnwick and William de Clinton.

In the spring of 1333, Edward assembled an army in which those who had helped him to overthrow Mortimer and Isabella took a prominent part.[41] Amongst those who served were Edward Bohun, William de Montague, Robert Ufford, Hugh Audley and John Neville of Hornby, together with the 'disinherited' and the northern magnates. Even they, however, had to be encouraged to serve by gifts of money from the subsidy granted by the September parliament of 1332. The king marched north to besiege Berwick, and by the end of June 1333 the defenders, exhausted by the English assaults, agreed to surrender if no relieving force arrived by 11 July. The Scots thus faced the same challenge that Edward II had faced in 1314, and the outcome was the same. The Scottish army marched to relieve Berwick and encountered the English forces drawn up on Halidon Hill, which lies about two miles north-west of the town and commands all approaches to it from the north. The English had the advantage of a dominating position and they subjected the Scots to a devastating hail of arrows as they struggled up the slope to engage the English forces. The Scots were put to flight with heavy casualties, and Berwick surrendered. Balliol was re-established as king; the disinherited lords received their inheritances, and more besides; and an English administration was established to govern the southern counties which Balliol formally ceded to Edward shortly before he did homage for his kingdom at Newcastle on 17 June 1334. Edward III left for the south feeling well satisfied with the outcome. Once again a single victory had given the English king the illusion of conquest in Scotland, but, like his grandfather Edward I, he was soon to discover how little support there really was in Scotland for his settlement.

In 1326 Scotland and France had concluded a new alliance, the Treaty of Corbeil, under which the French, while not being required to take military action on behalf of the Scots in any future conflict with England, agreed to give them diplomatic support, while the French obtained from the Scots an agreement to attack England in the event of war between the French and the English. The treaty imposed more onerous obligations on the Scots than on the French, but in the spring of 1334 Philip VI invited David II to seek refuge in France, and Philip now began to step up the diplomatic pressure on Edward III. At the same time, Balliol's position in southern Scotland began to crumble. The disinherited fell out over the distribution of some of the fruits of their victory: Beaumont was captured at the siege of Dunlarg Castle and had to raise loans, including one from Edward III, to pay his ransom, while in September 1334 David II's supporters reoccupied much of the land ceded to Edward III, forcing the English administration to retreat to Berwick.

Faced for the second time with the collapse of Balliol's rule, Edward once again mobilized an army, this time for a winter campaign which proved unpopular with the troops and which was abandoned under pressure from Philip VI to conclude a truce, which was to last from Easter to midsummer 1335. The truce gave Edward a useful breathing space in which to organize a much more substantial force, and in July 1335 a two-pronged invasion of Scotland began, led from Carlisle by the king himself with over 13,000 men and from Berwick by Edward Balliol. The campaign was reminiscent of those of Edward I's reign: the armies reached Perth without meeting serious resistance, and Edward obtained the submissions of a number of David II's supporters. He returned south, believing that what little resistance remained would soon be mopped up. But in November 1335 a small band of troops under Sir Andrew Moray defeated and killed David of Strathbogie at Culblean in Aberdeenshire, and from then onwards, as the chronicler Fordun remarked, the fortunes of war favoured the Scots.[42]

The disinherited's adventure had collapsed. The English held the principal castles, especially in the south-east, but they could not control the countryside, and by May 1337 David II's partisans had succeeded, by guerilla warfare rather than by organized campaigns, in limiting English power to Lothian, the Borders and Dumfriesshire. The disinherited lords themselves were ruined by Edward Balliol's failure to hold his kingdom: Gilbert de Umfraville, for example, titular Earl of Angus, lost his lands in Scotland and he never recovered from the collapse of his cause. Eventually, most of his estates in Northumberland were entailed upon the Percy family, who may have advanced him some of the money he needed for the invasion of Scotland in 1332. The war did not prove particularly popular with the

English nobility, who served when called upon to do so but gained little from it. Although the victory at Halidon Hill gave Edward a temporary and illusory supremacy, the war otherwise did little to enhance Edward III's military reputation. The chroniclers report the campaigns in muted terms, and give little impression of a will to war amongst either the nobility or the community generally.[43]

The campaigns in Scotland were accompanied by the familiar grievances of the community over taxation and prises. As early as January 1333 the commons petitioned for new restrictions on the activities of royal purveyors, and the king agreed, in an unprecedented move, to set up 'justices of purveyors' to hear complaints against them.[44] Complaints about the grievous burden of purveyance reappeared the following year, and the Meaux Chronicler complained about the outrageous burden of taxation imposed for the campaign of 1335.[45] Extensive prises were levied in 1336 and 1337 to supply the English armies in Scotland and the garrisons of English-held castles there, and the new method of levying the lay subsidy, first adopted in 1334, yielded larger sums than before and increased the fiscal pressure on the poorer sections of the population by imposing tax quotas on communities rather than assessing individuals whose wealth exceeded a minimum level.

The military demands of the crown also aroused opposition, both to the methods of arraying men for service and to the levying of money to pay their wages and provide their equipment. Opposition came, however, mainly from the commons in parliament, and it is perhaps indicative of the degree of political harmony and stability Edward had managed to achieve since 1330 that the nobility did not seek to exploit the grievances of the community over taxation, purveyance and military service in order to impose measures of restraint upon the king. Despite the increasing difficulties which Edward faced in financing his wars in Scotland, the parliaments of these years did not seek to bring forward any wide-ranging measures of reform, though as the events of 1340–1 were to show, the strains of war were still capable of generating a political crisis. Edward III enjoyed better relations with his nobility than his father had managed to achieve, and he had succeeded in restoring the personal authority of the monarch in government, but the grievances of the community in face of the crown's demands upon it soon resurfaced when he embarked on even greater military endeavours in 1337.

4
The War with France, 1337–1364

The Opening Phase, 1337–1341

Towards the end of October 1337 Henry Burghersh Bishop of Lincoln arrived in Paris with a letter from Edward III addressed to 'Philip of Valois who calls himself king of France'. The letter contained a renunciation of Edward's homage to Philip and a declaration of war. The war which Edward thus inaugurated was to endure, with many intervals of truce and several attempts at a final peace, until the expulsion of the English from Aquitaine in 1453. Although there had been brief conflicts between England and France in the reigns of Edward I and Edward II, the reasons for war were now more substantial than they had been in 1294 or 1324, and the will to war on the part of the king, if not yet on the part of most of the nobility, was much more apparent. The opening phase of the war, however, produced domestic difficulties and grievances not dissimilar to those experienced by Edward's father and grandfather; and it was only with the military successes and material gains of the 1340s that a change in attitude to war amongst both the nobility and the commons became apparent.

Philip of Valois ruled a kingdom which was both wealthier and more populous than England. The population of France was perhaps as high as 20 million, compared with England's 4.5 million,[1] and the extent of the lands over which the French king claimed suzerainty, together with the richness of their agricultural resources, made France potentially the wealthiest kingdom in western Europe. Eventually these advantages were to tell against England in the war, but in its early phases such disparity was of less account, and the ability of the two kings to mobilize the financial resources of their realms and to command the support of the nobility was to be of greater consequence. Here, for much of the fourteenth century, the advantage lay with England.

The immediate reason for the outbreak of war was the French king's confiscation of the Duchy of Aquitaine on the ground that Edward was harbouring Robert of Artois, a rebellious vassal of the French king who had fled to England in 1336 after being condemned as a traitor. Edward's sheltering of Robert of Artois, however, was a symptom rather than a cause of his deteriorating relationship with Philip VI. Of greater importance was Philip's support for David II of Scotland and Edward's fear that Philip might launch an invasion of England on behalf of his Scottish ally. The alarm that such a prospect generated in England was real: in March 1336 Philip VI ordered the French fleet which had been assembling in the Mediterranean for a crusade to transfer to the mouth of the Seine, and Edward felt convinced that Philip was planning a large-scale invasion of England. In a manifesto issued in August 1337[2] Edward accused Philip of aiding the Scots and committing acts of war in support of England's enemies, and a pre-emptive strike against France seemed the most effective way of preventing the Franco-Scottish alliance from growing into an ever more serious threat to England. Philip VI, however, was not acting simply in support of his Scottish ally. He had grounds of his own for concern at Edward's policies, particularly in the Low Countries where Edward's marriage with Philippa of Hainault had led to the development of close diplomatic ties between England and Hainault, Holland and Zeeland. In Flanders, where the count was loyal to Philip VI and perhaps alarmed at the expansionist tendencies of Hainault, Edward pursued a policy of exploiting the social and political tensions between the Flemish-speaking industrial towns and the French-speaking nobility of the countryside.

In the manifesto which Edward published in August 1337, however, he hinted at another issue. He maintained that Philip was trying to keep him at war in Scotland so that he might not 'pursue his rights elsewhere'. This expression might have been intended to refer to his rights in Aquitaine; it might also, or alternatively, have been intended to refer to his claim to the French crown. Both were to be important issues in the war, and shortly before Edward renounced his homage to Philip VI in October 1337 he formally asserted his right to the French throne.

When Charles IV of France died in 1328, the direct male line of the House of Capet came to an end.[3] Charles's sister Isabella, Edward II's queen, was still alive, and his two predecessors, Louis X who died in 1316, and Philip V who died in 1321, had daughters – Philip had five. The nearest heir in the male line was Charles's cousin, Philip of Valois; the nearest male heir in the direct line was Isabella's son Edward III. The issue of principle in 1328 was whether women were excluded from ruling, and, if so, whether they were also excluded from transmitting to their sons the title to rule. If both these exclusions were accepted, the throne was Philip's; if it were allowed that a woman could transmit a right but not exercise it, the throne was Edward's. The argument was not without precedent: in 1316 Louis X's daughter Jeanne had been passed over in favour of his brother Philip V, and Philip's own daughters had been excluded in 1321 in favour of his youngest brother, Charles IV. These precedents encouraged lawyers to talk of the immemorial law of the Salian Franks under which women were excluded from the succession. Lawyers' history, however, had little basis in reality and the exclusion of women was by no means settled practice before the fourteenth century in the great fiefs of France; indeed, Edward III's title to Aquitaine derived from a woman, Eleanor, wife of Henry II. Philip of Valois's claim, however, had the virtues of clarity and logic, whereas Edward's claim, as French lawyers pointed out at the time and French historians have not hesitated to remark since, rested on the unsatisfactory assumption that a woman could transmit a right which she could not exercise. His mother the dowager Queen Isabella survived until 1358 and if she could transmit title to Edward III, why could not Jeanne of Navarre, Louis X's daughter, or any of the daughters of Philip V do likewise? Indeed, Charles of Navarre, Jeanne's son born in 1332, was as close as Edward III to the last Capetians, and he did not hesitate to point this out in the 1350s when it suited him. Perhaps therefore Edward's claim was not as strong in principle as has sometimes been suggested, and if accepted in 1328 it might eventually have been subject to challenge by sons born to other Capetian females.

In practice, of course, there was little chance of Edward III successfully asserting his claim in 1328. It is even possible that Isabella had renounced her son's claim in 1326 in return for Valois help in preparing her invasion of England,[4] and in any case Isabella was scarcely more popular in France than in England: the last thing the French nobles wanted was Mortimer, Isabella and their cronies installed in Paris. Furthermore, the French nobility did not relish the prospect of a foreign ruler, whether or not he was the grandson of Philip IV. One lawyer at the French court observed that it had 'never been seen or known for the kingdom of France to be subjected to the government of the king of England'.[5] Perhaps the clinching argument for Philip, however, was that he was already in possession: he had been appointed as Regent at Charles IV's death and the royal administration was full of Valois clients. Philip was accordingly proclaimed king in an assembly of French nobles summoned so hastily that Edward III had no time to send envoys to press his own claim. Philip's coronation quickly followed, and the new king received proof of divine approval when he routed the Flemish rebels at Cassel within two months of succeeding. Edward made a formal protest, but he was in no position to do more, and in the following year he went to Amiens and did simple homage to Philip VI for Aquitaine: if he wished to prevent a French invasion of the duchy he had little alternative. Philip VI kept up his pressure on Edward, however: in 1330 he insisted that Edward should perform liege homage or face confiscation of the duchy, and in 1331 Edward agreed that he owed liege homage, though he never actually performed it.[6]

After the agreement of 1331, Edward appeared to have tacitly abandoned his claim to the French crown. Contemporaries believed that Edward was persuaded to revive it in 1337 by Robert of Artois who, according to a story which may well be apocryphal and which has attracted widely differing interpretations, placed a heron before the king at a banquet. This bird was the symbol of cowardice, and Robert's action was taken to imply that it was a suitable dish for a king who did not dare to claim his lawful inheritance. It is doubtful, however, whether Edward embarked on war in 1337 specifically in pursuit of his claim to the French throne. His claim gave him a useful propaganda weapon, some bargaining power in negotiations, and a basis on which to appeal to discontented French vassals; it was also a convenient argument with which to counter Philip's confiscation of Aquitaine. As later events were to show, the Valois monarchy had its weaknesses and the successful assertion of Edward's claim might not be beyond the bounds of possibility.

Almost certainly, the underlying cause of the war was the problem of Aquitaine. The Treaty of Paris in 1259 had defined the relationship between Aquitaine and the French crown: the English king, as Duke of Aquitaine, agreed to perform liege homage to the French king for the duchy, and the English king was recognized as a peer of France. But the relationship thus defined was fraught with all manner of difficulties. It ill became the English king, who was sovereign in his own country, to behave as a vassal towards his French suzerain, and the French king had great difficulty in controlling the behaviour of a vassal who was also a sovereign. Furthermore, as the French kings developed and extended their legal powers they increasingly intervened in the affairs of the duchy, and cases arising in the duchy might be taken on appeal to Paris, thus undermining the authority of the duke. The uncertain boundaries of the duchy gave rise to numerous disputes, any one of which might flare up into a major conflict, as the war of Saint Sardos demonstrated. The tension on the border encouraged both sides to maintain themselves in a state of armed readiness and this made conflict even more likely. Neither the last Capetians nor Philip VI wished to deprive the English kings of their French fief, but they intended to maintain their rights as overlords and in particular to hear appeals from the duchy in their own court.

The English kings, however, were unlikely to be willing to relinquish a part of their inheritance which brought them revenue in the

early fourteenth century of about £13,000 a year, and whose subjects
accepted English rule. For Aquitaine was the King of England's
inheritance, not his conquest; the Gascons saw the maintenance of
the English connection as vital to the preservation of their liberties
and customs, and the mercantile community of Bordeaux, together
with the wine producers of the Bordelais, regarded the link with
England as vital to their prosperity. The Gascons did not consider
themselves French; their language was barely intelligible to those who
spoke the *langue d'oil* of the north, and their culture and society had
more in common with Languedoc than with northern France. But
although it was the King of England's inheritance, it was an alien land
to the English nobility. They had no estates of any size there, and
although the king's representative in Bordeaux and a number of high
officials were English, the government of the duchy was in the hands
of the Gascons and places in the Church were filled by Gascon
prelates. In supporting the king's right to Aquitaine, the nobility
were seeking to maintain his honour and his inheritance, but they
had no personal interests there to safeguard, and it was the feudal
relationship between the two kings which was the main source of
difficulty.

In the 1330s, the problems created by this relationship became even
more acute. The policy of centralization and definition of royal rights
adopted by the last Capetians exposed the incompatibility between
the French insistence on the full rights of suzerainty and the English
king's desire for freedom of action for himself and his officials in the
duchy. Like his predecessors, Philip VI used the obligations of liege
homage, and the threat of confiscation of the duchy if Edward
defaulted on these obligations, as a means of putting pressure on the
English king when his policies appeared to threaten French interests.
Yet Philip, perhaps anxious to demonstrate that he could be just as
firm as his Capetian predecessors with the English king, seems deliberately to have increased pressure on Aquitaine, to the point where
Edward began to feel that Philip was making his position as duke of
Aquitaine impossible. By 1336 war over Aquitaine was coming very
close.[7] For Edward, the solution to the problems presented by the
obligations of liege homage and by Philip's assertion of his jurisdictional rights over Aquitaine was to hold Aquitaine in full sovereignty;
but the French would concede this only in the face of overwhelming
defeat, and no settlement based on such a concession could endure.
The problem of Aquitaine underlies the whole of the war, and its
solution by the expulsion of the English in 1453 marks the end of the
conflict.

In preparing to go to war in 1337, ostensibly in defence of his rights
in Aquitaine, it was essential for Edward to gain the support both of
the nobility and of the wider political community. War in France had

not hitherto been popular: in the thirteenth century it had been said that the English knights 'did not give a bean for all of France',[8] and resistance to service in France had been an important element in the political crisis of 1297. There had been little enthusiasm for the renewal of war in Scotland in 1332, and apart from his victory at Halidon Hill Edward had scarcely distinguished himself on his Scottish campaigns. The ground had therefore to be carefully prepared; the nobility had to be encouraged to rally to his cause, and the commons had to be persuaded to support it with grants of money.

Archbishop Stratford maintained in 1341 that in March 1337 the king obtained the assent of parliament to go to war against Philip of France.[9] The record of this parliament is incomplete, but the recollection of contemporaries seems unequivocal, and in later, more difficult, circumstances parliament was to be reminded more than once that it had given its assent to the war. The parliament of 1337 culminated in a series of festivities in which Edward honoured many of the nobles who were to be his companions in arms. His eldest son, Prince Edward, was made Duke of Cornwall, the first time a dukedom had been conferred in England, and six new earls were created. Four of them, William Montague Earl of Salisbury, William de Clinton Earl of Huntingdon, Robert Ufford Earl of Suffolk and William Bohun Earl of Northampton had supported Edward's coup in 1330, and Edward understandably still felt gratitude towards them. The earldom of Derby was conferred on Henry of Grosmont, son and heir of the Earl of Lancaster, and Hugh Audley, the old rival of the Despensers, received the earldom of Gloucester, to which he had a claim by virtue of his marriage to the second of the coheiresses of Gilbert de Clare Earl of Gloucester who fell at Bannockburn. In their patents of creation,[10] Edward explained the principles behind his bestowal of the honours:

> Among the marks of royalty we consider it to be the chief that, through a due distribution of positions, dignities and offices, it is buttressed by wise counsels and fortified by mighty powers. Yet because many hereditary ranks have come into the hands of the king, partly by hereditary descent to coheirs and coparceners according to our laws and partly through failure of issue and other events this realm has long suffered a serious decline in names, honours, and ranks of dignity.

To a king about to embark on war, the support of wise counsels and mighty powers was indeed essential, and the men honoured in 1337 repaid the king's generosity by loyal support for him in the forthcoming campaigns. These new powers, however, were buttressed by substantial grants of land, which led one chronicler to remark that the resources of the crown had been dissipated and a modern historian to comment that 'hereditary offices and jurisdictions were scattered in a way hardly compatible either with the interests of the crown, or with sound finance'.[11] The distribution of titles, however, was very much in the interests of a king who was about to lead his nobility in war, and in any case the king intended to finance the war out of the proceeds of taxation rather than the income from royal estates. The titles were granted in parliament with the consent of the community: there was no question of the new earls being created merely by the royal will. Edward's generosity extended beyond the creation of earls. According to Murimuth,[12] the bestowal of titles on the six earls was followed by the dubbing of twenty-four new knights, and other nobles were rewarded at the same time. The Earl of Arundel was made justice of North Wales for life, and in a gesture of reconciliation towards the Despenser family, Hugh Despenser, the heir to Edward II's favourite, was restored to some of his father's lands. On the eve of war it was desirable to heal some of the wounds that still remained from the convulsions of the 1320s.

Once parliament had given its assent to the war and Edward's prospective companions in arms had been singled out for honours, Edward set about mobilizing the financial support he needed. In July 1337, after a series of negotiations with the wool merchants, the king obtained an agreement under which a select group of wealthy merchants would be empowered to buy up and export 30,000 sacks of wool. This syndicate of merchants would in effect become monopoly purchasers and exporters of wool; in return they would lend the king £200,000 immediately and pay him half the proceeds from the sale of the wool. The scheme had been widely approved: now as always Edward was careful not to proceed without consent, and had the scheme worked it would have proved highly lucrative. In the next parliament, which assembled in September 1337, the commons granted a tenth and a fifteenth to be levied each year for the next three years. This grant was unprecedented in extent; it represented a significant political victory for Edward, and suggests that at this stage there was a considerable degree of support for the war amongst the knights. In view of the king's highly expensive schemes for securing allies in the Low Countries, however, even so substantial a grant was likely to prove insufficient. By the end of 1337 Edward had committed himself to spending £124,000 on his allies, and his parliamentary grants would bring in only about £38,000 a year.

In July 1338 Edward crossed to Brabant and established himself at Antwerp. There was no organized campaigning throughout that year, and Sir Thomas Gray, who took a dim view of the conduct of the war, complained that Edward did nothing at Antwerp except 'jousting and leading a jolly life'.[13] The real problem was the mobilization of resources: Edward experienced difficulty in collecting revenue in

England, and relations between the king's advisers in Brabant, chief amongst whom were the Earl of Salisbury and the Earl of Northampton, and the council in England, dominated by the clerical ministers of state, gradually deteriorated. Not until September 1339 did Edward feel able to move. He took his forces into the Cambrésis, but they failed to take Cambrai and although the French and English armies confronted one another at Buironfosse neither would engage in battle. Edward retreated to Brussels, but in the winter of 1339–40 he achieved an important diplomatic success in Flanders when he persuaded James van Artevelde to enter into an alliance with him under which Artevelde recognized his title to the French throne and agreed to give him military aid. Artevelde was a wealthy burgess of Ghent who became the champion of the economic interests of the Flemish weaving cities, whose prosperity depended upon supplies of wool from England. He assumed the leadership of the Flemish-speaking urban proletariat of Ghent, Bruges and Ypres who were sympathetic to the English interest both from economic necessity and as an expression of their hostility to the French-speaking nobility of Flanders.

To lend substance to this agreement with the Flemings, Edward now formally assumed the title and arms of King of France, to be borne by his successors until 1802. In a proclamation issued at Ghent on 8 February 1340, Edward declared that Philip of Valois had 'intruded himself by force into the kingdom while we were yet of tender years, and holds that kingdom against God and justice'. He went on, 'Lest we should seem to neglect our right and the gift of heavenly grace or be unwilling to conform the impulse of our will to the divine pleasure, we have recognized our right to the kingdom and have undertaken the burden of the rule of that kingdom, as we ought to do.'[14] Edward's formal assumption of his title to the French crown introduced a new element into the conflict. Once assumed, the title could only be renounced in return for the most substantial concessions, and as long as Edward called himself King of France he could pose, with some success, as a potential alternative to the Valois monarchy.

Edward's diplomatic achievement in Flanders was substantial, but it did little immediately to improve his position. He still faced financial and administrative difficulties at home, and English convoys in the Channel were harassed by French privateers. In the summer of 1340 a substantial French fleet assembled in the estuary of the Zwijn, near Sluys, intent on preventing English forces from landing in Flanders. The French fleet was crowded together in a confined space, and on Midsummer Day 1340 the English fleet crashed into the French ships, which were unable to deploy in so cramped a position. The English archers poured a deadly hail of arrows into the French troops, and the English men-at-arms finished them off in hand-to-hand combat. The victory at Sluys enhanced Edward's military prestige, but he was unable to follow it up. The English forces laid siege to Tournai, but Edward withdrew and agreed to the Truce of Esplechin on 25 September 1340. Edward's allies in the Low Countries proved unwilling to fight, and he was unable to pay them the promised subsidies in full. Philip himself had avoided giving battle to the English, and a lengthy campaign of sieges was beyond Edward's means. The opening campaign of the war had achieved little except the Flemish alliance and the destruction of the French fleet, and Edward returned home on 30 November to face a domestic political crisis.

Despite Edward's concern to obtain a wide measure of support for the war and consent for the financial exactions it necessitated, the measures the government took to raise money and supplies in 1338 and 1339 gave rise to grievances which resemble those which underlay the conflicts of Edward I's last years. The financial measures which led to the crisis of 1340–1 and the grievances that the commons laid before parliament in 1339 and 1340, have been analysed in great detail. The significance of the crisis remains obscure, however, and the extent to which the nobility aligned themselves with the commons in seeking concessions in return for grants of taxation is especially difficult to assess. Between 1336 and 1341 the burden of taxation was unprecedentedly heavy, and the oppressive conduct of the royal officials appointed to levy taxes and prises gave rise to widespread complaints. The king provoked hostility by seeking to use his prerogative rights to raise money, and by requiring the payment of debts, many of which had been respited for many years. More seriously, Edward's scheme to create a monopoly in the export of wool broke down in the early months of 1338. The syndicate which had been established as a monopoly purchaser of wool could not enforce its monopoly. There was much smuggling and evasion, and the syndicate found difficulty in selling the wool, for Edward had imposed an embargo on trade with Flanders and had instructed the merchants to sell their wool at Dordrecht in Brabant to please his ally the Duke of Brabant. The king eventually agreed to purchase the wool from the merchants, but to pay them in the so-called Dordrecht Bonds, promissory notes offering the merchants relief from future payments of tax. The holders eventually disposed of most of the bonds at a ruinous discount. When the king's agents bought the wool it fetched much less than the expected price and the scheme collapsed, leaving resentment amongst the producers, the lesser merchants who had not participated in the scheme, and those who had been paid in Dordrecht Bonds.

It was not the affair of the Dordrecht Bonds, however, but the traditional grievances over prises and taxation which formed the burden of the commons' complaints in the February parliament of

1339. The commons presented a series of articles in which they objected to the levying of prises and insisted that 'no free man should be assessed or taxed without the common assent of parliament'. The commons also complained about the burden of military service, saying that the cost of wages and equipment for the troops was especially hard to bear because the 'land was much grieved and charged by many taxes and other burdens'. The king's concession that the cost of troops should fall on the rich and powerful rather than the poor of the community was insufficient to placate the commons, and in the October parliament of the same year they presented a petition in which they called for the abolition of the maltolt, the punishment of purveyors who took prises without making payment, and pardon for debts. The petition was accompanied by one from the magnates, who also sought the withdrawal of the tax on wool: it appears that for the first time since the Ordinances of 1310–11 the commons and the magnates were joining together to seek concessions and measures of reform from the king. The principal concern of Edward's ministers, as always, was to raise money for the war, and they hoped by making concessions to receive the grants the king needed; but the concession of pardon for all debts of £10 or less was insufficient, and the commons insisted that they dare not grant a tax without consulting their communities.[15]

In the spring parliament of 1340 the commons offered a grant of tax subject to conditions which now went much further than the concessions they had sought in the previous year and which were reminiscent of the concerns of the Ordainers in 1310–11. The king, who had returned from Flanders in February and was present in person, was asked to agree to confirm and observe the charters; to agree that no taxes should be levied without the assent of parliament, and to appoint a council which would supervise the expenditure of money raised for the war and exercise jurisdiction over ministers. This proposal to establish a council which would in effect supervise the government of the realm while the king was overseas was the clearest echo of the Ordinances, though with the crucial difference that it was to function only as long as the king was out of the realm: it was not the intention of the commons to subject the king permanently to conciliar restraint. The king agreed to most of the measures demanded by the commons, and a council was set up with Archbishop Stratford and the Earl of Huntingdon acting as chief councillors, assisted by the Earls of Lancaster and Warenne. In return the king was granted the tax he sought, a ninth of corn, wool and sheep, which was to be used exclusively for the war.

The concessions in the spring parliament of 1340 did not, however, allay the discontent in the countryside. Indeed, it has been suggested that a rising against the oppressive behaviour of royal officials might easily have occurred.[16] The difficulties the administration encountered in enforcing the collection of taxes made it impossible for it to maintain a flow of funds to the king in Flanders, and Edward was now suffering severe financial embarrassment. He had to borrow to pay his troops, and he even had to require the Earls of Derby, Northampton and Warwick to submit to imprisonment in Malines as sureties for the debts the king owed there. It is not surprising that those around the king developed hostile feelings towards those responsible for government in England, particularly Archbishop Stratford, whose support for the war had always been lukewarm. At the same time the council in England believed that the king's *familiares* were exercising undue influence over him: the unity which Edward had been at such pains to build up in 1337 was on the point of fracturing.

In November 1340 Edward returned to England, furious at what he regarded as the mismanagement of government during his absence. He ordered the dismissal of the Chancellor and Treasurer, and the arrest of four judges and two of the merchants most heavily involved in the wool monopoly, William de la Pole and Reginald Conduit. Special commissions of inquiry into maladministration were set up, but Edward reserved his special venom for Archbishop Stratford, who was sent to Brabant as surety for the king's debts. The king seemed to regard Stratford's conduct of government as tantamount to treachery, and the king's supporters issued a statement, the *Libellus Famosus*, denouncing his conduct of government during the king's absence and declaring that the delay in providing money for the army in Flanders had arisen from the fault, or the neglect, or even the malice of the archbishop. Such a public attack was unprecedented, and created some sympathy for Stratford, whose position was fraught with difficulty. In the face of royal financial demands he had to bear in mind the interests of the clergy as well as his duty to the king, and he was subject to some pressure from the Pope to urge the king to pay heed to papal diplomatic overtures aimed at bringing an end to the war.

The conflict between the king and the archbishop came to a head in the parliament of April 1341. Edward began by attempting to exclude Stratford from the assembly, but failed in the face of support for the archbishop from the Earl of Arundel, Earl Warenne, and other lay magnates who shared their suspicion of those round the king. Both Arundel and Warenne asserted that it was the right of the magnates to advise and support the king in the great affairs of the realm, and that the charges the king had made against Stratford should be heard by his peers. The king agreed to this, but then had to face petitions for further concessions from both magnates and the commons, who demanded that the charters should be observed, the laws and statutes maintained and the concessions of 1340 upheld. They also demanded that the king should appoint the great officers of state in parliament with the advice of the magnates, and that the ministers of the crown should be answerable in parliament for their conduct. This attempt to assert baronial control of the king's officers, reminiscent both of the Provisions of Oxford and the Ordinances, was the most far-reaching of all the demands made during the crisis of 1339–41. Both Geoffrey le Baker and Murimuth are clear that this was the crucial issue under discussion in the parliament, and both record that the king refused to agree to such a proposal.[17] The most he would concede was that positions should be filled by the advice of the lords and the council around the king, and that officers should take an oath in parliament to act justly. The king agreed to parliament's other requests, however, and was rewarded with a grant of 10,000 sacks of wool. Both lords and commons had won some important concessions. The king had agreed that peers should be tried only in parliament and before their equals, and that accusations against ministers should be heard by the peers in parliament. The commons had gained a paper declaration upholding the charters and franchises, and the concessions embodied in the statute of 1340. The proceedings against Stratford were referred to a committee of two bishops and four earls, including Arundel and Salisbury, and nothing more was heard of them until 1343, when the king ordered the charges to be annulled.

The commons played a more substantial and a more independent part in this political crisis than they had done in the conflicts of Edward I's last years and Edward II's reign, and they showed some awareness of their power to demand concessions in return for agreeing to the king's financial demands. Edward for his part had to accommodate himself to political and financial realities, and was prepared to compromise with the commons in return for taxes, though he would not give way on the fundamental issue of the right to choose his own councillors. His approach, however, was more flexible than that of his father and grandfather; except perhaps in his clash with Archbishop Stratford he showed a surer political touch, and by his readiness to make concessions on many of the issues raised by the commons he prevented the political crisis from escalating into a full-scale assault on royal government in the manner of 1310–11. The crisis revealed, however, that the king's war no longer had the whole-hearted support of the community, and more ominously, that some members of the nobility were prepared to associate themselves with the commons' demands for concessions and reforms. The crisis cannot, however, be interpreted solely in terms of independent action by the commons; the magnates too petitioned for reforms, and a group of them vigorously supported Archbishop Stratford in 1341. They were never united in their opposition to the king, and they never found a leader comparable to Hereford and Norfolk in 1297 or

Map 2   France: to illustrate the Hundred Years War, 1337–1389

Thomas of Lancaster in 1310–11; but their opposition reveals the fragility of the political settlement Edward had achieved after 1330, and the danger that his close associates who had helped him to power might now be seen as a new court clique, the king's *familiares*. Some of the magnates were motivated by personal or local considerations: the northern lords, Wake, Neville and Percy, were concerned at the neglect of the defence of the northern border as Edward's continental campaigns swallowed up all the available resources; but Arundel, Warenne and Huntingdon do not seem to have had personal grievances against the king: perhaps they were unhappy about the king's handling of the war with France.[18]

Suspicion of the king lingered on after the conclusion of the parliament of 1341, and was probably intensified by his solemn revocation of the concessions he had made in that parliament at a council attended by all the magnates in early October 1341. The expedition which the king led to Scotland in the winter of 1341–2 was unpopular: according to Murimuth he was attended only 'by a few knights', and Arundel, Huntingdon, and five other earls declined the invitation to serve. Only the Earl of Derby and the northern lords accompanied the king. Restoration of political harmony was essential, however, if Edward was to continue the war in France, and in re-establishing good relations between the king and the nobility the Earl of Derby seems to have played an important role. In late October 1341 the king and Archbishop Stratford were solemnly and publicly reconciled, and a record of the occasion describes Derby as 'mediator in the settlement'.[19] On his return from Scotland, Edward held a tournament at Dunstable at which he no doubt hoped to revive the jollity and jousting of earlier years. Murimuth remarks, significantly, that almost all the young knights of England came, together with all the young earls, Derby, Warwick, Northampton, Pembroke, Oxford and Suffolk. The author of the *Brut* commented on the youth of those who attended, and Gloucester, Arundel, Devon, Warenne and Huntingdon excused themselves on grounds of age and infirmity.[20] The absence of Arundel and Huntingdon is especially interesting since both were only in their thirties and neither showed any signs of infirmity in their subsequent military careers. In all probability they were not yet reconciled with the king.

Victory and Profit, 1341–1364

The young earls who attended the Dunstable tournament were now to take a leading part in Edward's wars, and with a new generation of earls came a new strategy. The first phase of the war had brought Edward little apart from the victory at Sluys and the Flemish alliance. There had been no major engagements in the field and the sieges that the king had undertaken had been abandoned. These failures arose not only from Edward's lack of adequate financial resources, but also from the effectiveness of Philip VI's resistance and the reluctance of the English to take on the French in pitched battle, as the stand-off at Buironfosse showed. But in the 1340s Edward sought to exploit the growing opposition within France to Philip VI by deploying two or three armies at the same time in provinces where the English cause might expect to receive support. In this context, Edward's assumption of the title and arms of King of France at Ghent in 1340 is significant, for it allowed him to pose as an alternative government in France and attract the loyalty of those who for whatever reason were discontented with Valois rule. This is not to say that even at this stage Edward's principal war aim was the throne of France, but rather that the most effective way of bringing pressure to bear on Philip was to subvert the provinces and establish English military bases there.

Edward had won over the industrial towns of Flanders in 1340, and the maintenance of the English position there was to be a basic strategic principle until its decisive failure in 1385. Neither Count Louis de Nevers, who died in 1346 fighting on the French side at Crécy, nor his successor Louis de Mâle supported the towns in their negotiations with Edward, and both remained loyal to their French suzerain despite the pressures which Edward brought to bear on Flanders. In 1341, the opportunity presented itself to intervene in Brittany, where a succession dispute developed when Duke John III died without leaving a direct heir. The two claimants were John de Montfort, younger half-brother of John III, and Charles of Blois who was married to John III's niece Joan of Penthièvre. Charles of Blois. Charles of Blois was the candidate favoured by Philip VI, and Edward accordingly supported Montfort, offering him not only military assistance but also the earldom of Richmond, with which the Breton ducal family had a connection going back to the Norman Conquest. Froissart suggests that Edward intervened in Brittany merely to distract Philip, and there may be something in this; but it was also important for him to protect the sea route from England to Aquitaine around the Finistère peninsula, and above all the allegiance of the Duke of Brittany would be a great prize in Edward's campaign to undermine Philip VI's authority in France. By the end of 1341 Charles of Blois's forces had overrun most of the duchy and accordingly in 1342 Edward sent three expeditions to help his ally de Montfort. The first, in March, was led by Sir Walter Manny, a Hainaulter and companion of the queen. In July the Earls of Northampton, Oxford, Pembroke and Devon together with Sir Hugh Despenser, Sir Richard Talbot and Sir Richard Stafford took an army to the duchy and put Charles of Blois to flight at the battle of Morlaix on 30 September, while in October the king himself embarked for Brittany, aware that part of the duchy had already been regained for the Montfort cause. Arundel, Huntingdon and Warenne still declined to go with the king, though in November they acceded to his plea for reinforcements and agreed to send troops. The English laid siege to Vannes, Rennes and Nantes, but the English troops were greatly outnumbered by French forces in the duchy, and in January 1343 Edward agreed to the truce of Malestroit, which stabilized the position and left John de Montfort in control of about half the duchy. Edward's intervention had at least saved de Montfort's cause from complete collapse. The campaigns were not only successful politically, but they also became famous for the deeds of prowess and valour done by the leaders of the English forces and the booty and ransoms they won.

While Edward had been preoccupied in northern France, the English position in Aquitaine had deteriorated. Philip VI's armies had taken key English positions along the Garonne, and Philip had been promising grants and pensions to those Gascons who would enter his obedience. Edward's first move in restoring the situation was to counter any possible threat to Aquitaine from the south and from the sea. He sent Henry Earl of Derby to Castile in October 1341 to undermine French influence there that threatened to bring Castile's navy into play against English shipping in the Bay of Biscay. Derby handled the complex politics of the Castilian court with considerable insight and deftness, and when war between England and France was resumed in 1345 Castile remained neutral.

The English position in Aquitaine remained insecure, however, and the government in Bordeaux was rapidly running out of money. Direct English military intervention was now necessary if the duchy were not to collapse into chaos. In the spring and summer of 1345, therefore, Edward denounced the truce of Malestroit and began the planning of a three-pronged attack on France. The first expedition, under the king himself, was to sail to Flanders; the second, under the Earl of Northampton, was to go to Brittany; and the third and largest was despatched to Aquitaine under the command of the Earl of Derby, who succeeded his father as Earl of Lancaster in that year. Lancaster's campaigns in Aquitaine in 1345-7 were highly successful; the area under English control was greatly extended, the prestige of the English government was restored and reforms were undertaken in the government and finance of the duchy. It became clear in the course of the campaigns, however, that the duchy could no longer finance its own defence, and henceforward the costs of campaigning there had to be subsidized by the English Exchequer. Lancaster proved himself one of the most outstanding of Edward's commanders, and he and his men not only covered themselves with glory but also substantially enriched themselves. Northampton's campaign in Brittany also produced some notable successes: the expedition remained in the duchy for two years, and in 1347 Northampton's lieutenant Sir Thomas Dagworth captured Charles of Blois at La Roche-Derrien. The king's own achievements were the least substantial, and the murder of James van Artevelde by his enemies in Ghent weakened the English position there.

In the spring of 1346, however, Edward's attention was directed towards Normandy. A Norman baron, Geoffrey de Harcourt, Lord of Saint-Sauveur-le-Vicomte in the Cotentin, fled to Edward's court in England and sought to persuade him to invade Normandy. Harcourt's reasons for fleeing Normandy are not entirely clear: he was at odds with the Comte of Tancarville over the office of Chamberlain of Normandy, and he appears to have had personal grievances against Philip VI. More significantly, perhaps, he revealed to Edward that there was much opposition in Normandy to the fiscal oppression of the Valois administration and the centralizing policies which seemed to threaten the provincial liberties of the duchy. For Edward, the prospect of gaining Saint-Sauveur-le-Vicomte was attractive in itself. It was the key to the Cotentin and western Normandy, and would be a strongly defended and well-placed military base for the English. But Edward had a more substantial motive for planning an invasion of Normandy: his strategy was to take the pressure off Lancaster in Aquitaine by providing a diversion in Normandy and another in Flanders, where Sir Hugh Hastings had been appointed Lieutenant and given the command of Flemish troops who would advance from the north against Philip.

A very substantial force, perhaps numbering 15,000 men, assembled at Portsmouth in July 1346. Their destination was kept secret, and many assumed that the expedition would sail for Aquitaine; but on 12 July Edward landed at Saint-Vaast-la-Hougue in the Cotentin. The expedition acquired the character of a vast plundering raid. Burning and looting the countryside as he went, Edward took Caen and subjected it to a brutal sacking. He was only restrained from burning it to the ground by Harcourt, who urged him to 'be a little less impetuous and content yourself with what you have done'.[21] The English had every reason to be content with what they had done, and great quantities of loot were shipped back to England. Edward now moved north-east, but heard that Philip was at Rouen with a large force. He advanced to the Seine, slipped across it at Poissy and, with Philip's army hard on his heels, he crossed the Somme at Blanche-Taque by a ford which was revealed to the king in the nick of time, possibly by a prisoner to whom Edward offered enough money to buy the vital information. At Crécy, in the English-held County of Ponthieu, Edward decided to stand and fight. The English established themselves in a strong defensive position and on the evening of 26 August the French approached. Disregarding an order to halt, the knights advanced on the English and as they did so they drove their Genoese crossbowmen before them. They were halted by a hail of arrows from the English; they failed to break the English positions and each advancing wave of cavalry bore down on those who had gone before, leading to utter confusion and heavy losses. Edward himself watched the battle from a windmill to the south-west of the English positions, and Northampton, Arundel, and king's eldest son, Edward Prince of Wales, now aged sixteen, bore the main burden of the day. According to Froissart, the prince and those fighting with him, faced with a fierce attack from the French, sent word to the king asking him to send them reinforcements. But the king replied, 'Tell them not to send for me again today as long as my son is alive. Give them my command to let the boy win his spurs, for if God has so ordained it, I wish the day to be his and the honour to go to him and to those in whose charge I have placed him.'[22] Shortly before midnight, the French retreated in disarray, leaving the field to the English. The French suffered heavy casualties, including King John of Bohemia, the Duke of Lorraine and the Counts of Blois and Flanders, and Froissart suggests that only Edward's decision not to pursue the remnants of the French forces saved them from even more serious losses. Contemporaries believed that the English archers played a decisive part in the victory, but poor leadership and indiscipline in the French forces also contributed to their downfall.

After his victory Edward rallied his troops and marched north to lay siege to Calais. The strategic significance of Calais was obvious, and its possession would mean that Edward no longer had to rely on Flanders as a bridgehead for invasion. The siege lasted almost a year; Philip VI put in an appearance with a relieving army at the beginning of August 1347 but he came to the conclusion that the English could not be dislodged and went away again. His departure was, understandably, followed immediately by the surrender of the town, which Edward proceeded to turn into an English base.

Edward's absence from England at the siege of Calais gave the Scots an opportunity to assist their French ally by invading the northern counties. In October 1346 a Scottish army under David II moved into Cumberland and extorted money from the inhabitants; they then moved east, and on 17 October were confronted at Neville's Cross, near Durham, by an English force led by the Archbishop of York. The English archers broke up the Scottish positions and the Earl of Dunbar and Robert the Steward fled with their troops. David himself, however, was wounded in the face and taken prisoner by a Northumbrian knight, John of Copeland: he was to remain a prisoner in England for eleven years. The defeat was a disaster for the Scots. The losses sustained by the Scottish nobility left something of a vacuum at the centre of Scottish politics, and the king, in captivity in England, lacked the means to make his will felt in government. In the following summer the English reoccupied the border counties and Dumfriesshire, and for the next ten years the principal concern of the Scots became the recovery of their king and their lost territory.

The victories at Crécy and Neville's Cross and the fall of Calais were greeted with euphoria in England. When parliament heard the news of Crécy the commons 'thanked God for the great victory He had given their king and they said that all their money had been well spent'.[23] But the campaigns of the 1340s have a wider significance, for they mark the beginning of a change in attitude to foreign war amongst the English nobility. This change arose from a realization that war provided opportunities for the nobles not only to increase their honour and their prestige but also to enrich themselves. The campaigns in Brittany had offered a foretaste of what might be gained in loot and ransoms, but the expeditions to Aquitaine and Normandy were of much greater importance in demonstrating how much wealth might be won from war. At the surrender of Bergerac in August 1345, for instance, Lancaster is said to have 'carried off in triumph...a whole barrel full of gold, besides other treasures beyond number'.[24] After his victory at Auberoche, prisoners were taken whose ransoms were said to be worth over £50,000, and in 1346, according to Froissart, Lancaster's army returned from a raid into Poitou so laden with riches that they had difficulty in transporting all their gains. In Normandy, the army under the command of the Earl of Warwick sacked Carentan and carried off huge quantities of plunder, while Froissart observed that after the sack of Caen the English 'won an amazing quantity of wealth for themselves', and 'sent boats and barges laden with their gains – clothes, jewellery, gold and silver plate and many other valuable things – down the river to Ouistreham where their main fleet lay'.[25] Well might Walsingham remark that there was scarcely a woman in England who did not have some household possession from the sack of Caen, the seizure of Calais and other English successes in France.[26] Even in Brittany, which was a much less wealthy province than Normandy, there were rewards to be won: Sir Thomas Dagworth, for instance, was paid 25,000 gold écus as a reward for his capture of Charles of Blois, and the English garrisons in Brittany plundered the surrounding countryside. Eventually they devised a support system based on levying charges in enemy territory: each fortress had a number of parishes attached to it, and these parishes were obliged to pay a levy to the commander of the garrison. This system was extended to Normandy in 1350 and to other English-occupied parts of France after the victory at Poitiers in 1356.

The profits of war were not to be found only in France: a grateful king rewarded his commanders with grants at home, and the wounds of 1341 seem to have been healed by success in war. In 1348 the king restored the Earl of Lancaster's title to the honour and castle of Pontefract, which he had hitherto held on lease from the queen, 'having regard to the good service and great honour which our... cousin has done us in Gascony'.[27] This amounted in effect to a grant of £1,000 a year, the annual amount of the lease which was now extinguished. Lancaster also received some lesser grants in England, and some small estates in Gascony. The Earl of Warwick was made Sheriff of Warwickshire and Leicestershire for life, and Arundel Sheriff of Shropshire for life, a sign that his reconciliation with the king was now complete. These grants, however, were not lavish, and the crown's resources were not greatly diminished by Edward's patronage. Just as important in binding the nobility to the crown was Edward's development of a court life which embodied the military ethos and chivalric ideals of aristocratic society. Tournaments were a regular feature of noble life in these years, and in 1344 at an especially magnificent tournament held at Windsor the king took an oath to establish an Order of Knights of the Round Table as it had existed in the days of King Arthur. According to Murimuth the Earls of Derby, Salisbury, Warwick, Arundel, Pembroke and Suffolk 'and many other barons and knights' took the same oath.[28] A building to house the round table was begun, but otherwise nothing came of the idea.

At some time in 1348 or 1349, however, Edward did establish an order of chivalry, the Order of the Garter, which was to be a fellow-ship of twenty-six knights bound together by oath as companions to help one another and their king. Once again, Arthurian legend under-lay the idea of the Order, but the adoption of the garter as its symbol was said in later years to have occurred when, at a ball at Calais in 1348, the Countess of Salisbury dropped her garter and the king, who was rumoured to have been in love with her, picked it up and in the face of derisive cries from the onlookers put it on his own knee with the remark, 'Honi soit qui mal y pense' – 'shame upon him who thinks ill of it'. There is, however, no contemporary evidence for this roman-tic story, and the precise date and circumstances of the establishment of the Order remain uncertain. Most of the founder-members had served at Crécy, but it was not brought into existence specifically to commemorate the battle.[29] With the soldier-martyr St George at its patron, the Order served to strengthen the bonds between the king and the nobility: chivalric honour was as acceptable a mark of royal favour as grants of land and office. It may be hard to reconcile the ideals of chivalry at Edward's court with the burning, looting and killing which were so much a part of the campaigns the nobles fought in France, and difficult to argue that the idea of chivalry had any substantially mitigating effect on the horrors of war. But the nobles fought for both profit and honour, and they gained renown at home by their prowess on the battlefield as well as by the material success they enjoyed. It is not surprising that the nobles' traditional attitude of hostility to foreign war gave way to growing enthusiasm for contin-ental campaigns that brought them both riches and renown.

The capture of Calais and the foundation of the Order of the Garter mark the high point of Edward's military and chivalric reputation, and for seven years after 1348 the war languished. In the summer and autumn of 1348 the Black Death swept through France and southern England, and moved steadily northwards and westwards to reach Scotland and Ireland by the following year. In England, the mortality from the plague has been variously estimated at between 20 per cent and 35 per cent of the population, and it may be that the higher figure is the more accurate. Contemporary chroniclers vividly convey the sense of shock induced by such great mortality, and the dislocation caused to almost every aspect of daily life. Henry Knighton records the reaction of the Scots, who assembled an army to invade England

and take advantage of what they called 'the foul death of England', but nemesis overtook them when they too were struck down with the plague and abandoned their attack.[30]

The sudden loss of perhaps a third of the population was bound to have a serious effect upon government as well as upon relationships between lords and tenants in the countryside, but just as the government, and especially the fiscal machinery, had held up well during the famines of 1315–18, so now, in face of a much more far-reaching disaster, the system of government proved resilient. Some disruption was inevitable: no parliament met between April 1348 and February 1351, and Geoffrey le Baker noted that the sessions of the king's bench and common pleas ceased while the plague was at its height. Many government officials perished, as did some members of the royal household. The Archbishop of Canterbury Thomas Bradwardine, died of the plague in August 1349, but none of the chief officers of state succumbed, and amongst the titled nobility only the death of the Earl of Pembroke in August 1348 may possibly have been caused by the plague. Indeed le Baker observed that 'few nobles died'.[31]

Nonetheless, the government continued to collect the proceeds of the three-year lay subsidy granted in the parliament of March 1348. The yield was less than might have been expected in normal circumstances, and the crown's income from customs duties fell in the immediate aftermath of the plague, but by the early 1350s both direct and indirect taxation had recovered, and the yield was back to pre-plague levels. As far as direct taxation is concerned, the crown was able to maintain the pre-plague assessments, so that communities which had lost at least a third of their population were still expected to contribute the quotas of tax revenue that had been assessed in 1334. Edward III's ability to maintain both the flow of revenue and the pre-plague tax base underlay the military successes of the 1350s.[32]

In the immediate aftermath of the plague, neither combatant was anxious to resume the war, and both were willing to listen to Pope Innocent VI when he attempted to mediate between them and bring about a lasting peace. By 1355, however, some stability had returned after the Black Death and two new protagonists had appeared on the scene, each in his different way determined to enhance his prestige through war. On the English side the king's eldest son, the Black Prince, had grown to manhood anxious to win his share of the glory and profits of war, of which he had had a taste at Crécy. The Black Prince was to show that he was a man of considerable military flair but rather less political sensitivity than his father, and that he was capable of adopting a harsh and inflexible approach in government which would have augured ill had he ever become king. On the French side the Black Prince's principal opponent was King John II, who succeeded his father Philip VI in 1350 and who was to allow his enthusiasm for chivalric deeds to outrun his political and military judgement.

In 1355 Edward III appointed the Black Prince his Lieutenant in Aquitaine, and the prince took a small force there in the autumn of that year. He found no French to fight, but kept his troops happy looting and destroying in Languedoc. Edward III's intention was that the Black Prince's campaign in Aquitaine should be accompanied by an expedition to Brittany under Lancaster and an invasion of Normandy led by Charles of Navarre, king of the small Pyrenean kingdom lying between Aquitaine and Castile. Charles was the grandson of Louis X of France, and had a claim to the French throne which was arguably as good as Edward III's. His chief importance to Edward was that he was a substantial landowner in Normandy and was at odds with John II over the succession to the counties of Angoulême and Mortain. He was potentially a useful ally and one with whom Edward needed to keep on good terms, if only because of his claim to the French throne; but he proved unreliable and the expedition to Normandy was aborted when he suddenly came to terms with John II. Lancaster's expedition to Brittany also had to be postponed, probably because of the need to recover Berwick, which had fallen to the Scots in October 1355.

Edward had had to defer rather than abandon his plans, however, and in 1356 he sent Lancaster to Normandy with a small force of no more than 1,000 archers and 1,400 men-at-arms, which included supporting contingents from Normandy and from the Breton garrisons. It was a highly successful *chevauchée*: Lancaster relieved Pont Audemer, captured Verneuil, took a large number of prisoners and carried off much booty. But there may have been a broader strategic plan behind the expedition. In August, the Black Prince led a raid northwards from Bergerac towards Bourges. He described his intention in only the vaguest of terms, saying that 'it was our purpose to ride forth against the enemies in the parts of France',[33] but it is likely that he and Lancaster hoped to join forces. Lancaster moved towards the Loire in August, but he found his advance blocked by the French, who destroyed the bridge at Angers. He retreated, leaving English garrisons in a string of fortresses in Anjou and Maine. The Black Prince reached Tours in early September, but King John barred his way northwards, and he accordingly turned south, planning to retreat to Bordeaux. The French pursued him, however, and although it is doubtful whether the prince intended to force them to fight it became clear that a battle could not be avoided.

The encounter took place near Poitiers on 19 September 1356. Once again, as at Crécy, the English were outnumbered, but the prince, imitating his father's tactics at Crécy, drew up his forces in a strong defensive position in hilly, wooded country. The French cavalry charge which opened the battle was halted by the English archers; the main body of the French army then advanced on foot, but was halted by the English and after bitter fighting withdrew. The Duke of Orléans left the field with his contingent, perhaps objecting to King John's novel decision that his army should advance dismounted, and the king then moved forward on foot with his troops. The Black Prince led a cavalry charge against them and forced them back towards the River Moisson. The king himself was captured, and the remnants of the French force fled. The English haul of booty and prisoners was enormous: the list of those captured was headed by the king himself, together with his son Philip, the Archbishop of Sens, the Comte of Tancarville, the Comte of Sancerre, the Vicomte of Narbonne, the Seneschal of Poitou and the Comte of Ventadour. Geoffrey le Baker lists in all thirty-five noble Frenchmen who were captured. The Black Prince, acting on behalf of the king, bought fourteen of these noblemen from their captors for £66,000 and shipped them back to England. On the battlefield the English took vast plunder. Froissart says that the English found 'plate and gold and silver belts and precious jewels in chests crammed full of them as well as excellent cloaks',[34] and the Black Prince made off with King John's own jewels.

The king, of course, was the chief prize of Poitiers, and Edward intended that the price of his release should be not only a substantial ransom but also a definitive peace with France: the gains of battle needed to be consolidated by a diplomatic success. The French had little room for manoeuvre, and in May 1358 a treaty known as the 'First Treaty of London' was drawn up, under which Edward was to have a Greater Aquitaine in full sovereignty, together with Calais, Ponthieu and Guînes. King John was to be ransomed for 4 million écus to be paid within six months. The treaty was never implemented, however, perhaps because the French could not raise the first instalment of the ransom in the six months specified, and in May 1359 the 'Second Treaty of London' was concluded. This drove a much harder bargain and, it has been suggested, represents the moment at which Edward overplayed his hand. Under this treaty, a vast area from Calais in the north to Aquitaine in the south was to be ceded to Edward to hold in full sovereignty. Edward was not only to regain the Angevin inheritance in France, but also the coast of Picardy, the Counties of Guînes and Boulogne, and suzerainty over Brittany. The whole western seaboard of France and all the western provinces would thus fall into English hands. The ransom was set at 4 million écus once again, but this time the French were given four months to raise three-quarters of it, which was clearly impossible. In return for all this, Edward agreed to drop his claim to the French throne. King

John may have been willing to agree to anything, even the dismemberment of his kingdom, in order to ensure that he did not die in prison;
but, as Professor Fowler remarked, the treaty was 'so preposterous
that it is difficult to believe that it was ever intended seriously'.[35] It
was totally unacceptable to the Dauphin Charles and his court, and
the Estates-General rejected it out of hand.

Perhaps Edward expected no other outcome, and indeed preparations for another campaign in France were well in hand when the
treaty was concluded. Evidently Edward's purpose now was to inflict
a final blow on the Valois monarchy by marching to Rheims and
having himself crowned King of France. He assembled a large army –
12,000 men – and laid siege to the city on 4 December 1359. With
France in chaos, its king a prisoner, Navarrese forces in control in
Normandy and English garrisons established not just in Brittany and
Aquitaine but also in Anjou, Maine and Touraine, it must have
appeared to Edward that his ultimate triumph was in sight, and it is
arguable that now, after the failure of the Second Treaty of London,
Edward's aim was nothing less than the crown. Indeed, the intention
of the English negotiators when the Second Treaty of London was
drawn up may well have been to make the French an offer they would
be bound to refuse. But Rheims closed its gates to him; its Captain,
Gauchier de Châtillon, conducted an effective defence, and on 11
January 1360, after a siege lasting only five weeks, Edward withdrew.
His supplies had run short, the army was dispirited by the uncomfort-
able winter conditions, and the king himself proved reluctant to take
the city by storm. Despite all the obvious practical difficulties that
Edward encountered in maintaining the siege, its abandonment after
so short a time must raise questions about the extent of his commitment, even at this stage of the war, to the French throne.

The setback before Rheims weakened Edward's position, and
shortly after Easter Edward and the Dauphin agreed to resume negotiations. At Brétigny, on 8 May 1360, a treaty was concluded under
which Edward was to receive much less than had been envisaged in
the second Treaty of London. He was to hold an enlarged Aquitaine
in full sovereignty, together with Calais, Ponthieu and Guînes; but
there was no question of transferring the rest of western France to
him, and King John's ransom was reduced from 4 to 3 million écus.
Edward in return undertook to renounce his claim to the French
throne. This treaty was ratified at Calais on 24 October 1360, with
one important modification. The clauses under which Edward renounced his claim to the French throne and John renounced sovereignty
over Aquitaine were excised from the treaty and embodied in a
separate document which laid down that the renunciations were to
be carried out no later than 1 November 1361, and were to be
conditional upon the transfers of territory agreed in the treaty being

implemented by June 1361. Edward's hopes of the crown had vanished before the gates of Rheims, but he was still in a strong enough
position, with King John as his prisoner, to insist on a final solution to
the problem of Aquitaine. The Treaty of Brétigny provided for this,
and a treaty which the French appeared for the moment willing
to accept was a much more substantial victory for Edward than
one which gave him a vast area on paper but which the French
would be bound to resist. Edward probably realized, after the failure
of the Rheims campaign, that he lacked the resources to mount
the kind of campaign that would be necessary to compel the French
to accept the second Treaty of London. His campaigns in Aquitaine,
Normandy and Brittany in the 1340s and 1350s had been essentially
plundering raids which had brought a substantial return for a modest
outlay and had therefore enjoyed the support of the nobility and
the commons. The sudden and catastrophic nature of the French
defeat at Poitiers placed Edward in a powerful negotiating position,
but did little to remove the difficulties he would face in financing and
sustaining the campaigns that would be necessary if negotiations with
the French broke down.

It was not long, however, before problems began to arise. King John
was released on the understanding that his ransom would he paid,
and Edward retained some noble hostages as sureties for the payment.
One of these, the king's younger son Louis Duke of Anjou, broke his
word and returned to France, at which King John, showing a misplaced sense of honour, returned voluntarily to captivity in England
and died at the Savoy in April 1364. The exclusion of the renunciation
clauses weakened the force of the treaty; it gave both sides the
opportunity to prevaricate and, in the event, the renunciations were
never carried out. The Dauphin's interest in delaying the transfer of
territory and renunciation of sovereignty is obvious, but it has been
suggested that Edward too might have been glad of an excuse to
resume the war if he wanted to. Such a suggestion should, however,
be treated with caution. Edward stopped using the title and arms of
France for eight years, and only resumed them when war began again
after Charles V had taken advantage of the failure to carry out the
renunciation clauses and heard appeals in his court from discontented
subjects of the Black Prince in Aquitaine.

Although the Treaty of Brétigny represented a retreat from the
terms Edward had offered in 1359, it was the culmination of a period
of outstandingly successful warfare. Edward had captured his adversaries of France and Scotland; he had gained, on paper at least, the
sovereign lordship of Aquitaine and had turned Calais into the
most substantial military town the English kings had possessed in
France since 1204; while his companions in arms had enriched themselves and won renown in battle. Even though the ultimate prize had

eluded him, his prestige, and the military reputation of his country-men, was at its height in 1360.

The Sinews of War: Manpower and Money

Edward III's victories at Crécy and Poitiers did much in themselves to generate enthusiasm for the war, and the profits both from these victories and from the *chevauchées* in Aquitaine, Normandy and Brittany helped to ensure the support of the nobility for the war. The successful prosecution of the war, however, required not just aristocratic support but also the plentiful, and as far as possible the willing, supply of manpower and money. In the 1290s and again in the 1330s the pressure of taxation and resistance to the crown's recruiting methods led to political crises which undermined the king's ability to wage war successfully. Yet the campaigns of the 1340s and 1350s do not seem to have generated such political tension at home: victory and profit undoubtedly provide part of the explanation, but so too do changes in the methods of military recruitment and a concil-iatory approach on the part of the king to the question of taxation.

Both Edward I and Edward II had made substantial use of the traditional feudal levy for raising an army, summoning all tenants-in-chief of the crown to serve unpaid with a set quota of men for forty days. The feudal summons had some attractive features from the nobility's point of view: service without pay by virtue of tenure and according to their oath of homage was considered an honourable obligation; and whenever a feudal muster was ordered the tenants-in-chief were entitled to levy scutage on their own tenants. The crown too stood to gain financially from fines paid by those tenants-in-chief who were unable or unwilling to serve in person. At best, however, the feudal summons could produce a cavalry force of little over 500 men, and even in Edward I's reign it had obviously been insufficient in itself as a means of raising an army. Since there was no requirement to attend in person, there was no way of knowing how many men were likely to appear in arms. To raise the cavalry force needed in his French and Scottish wars, Edward I sought to extend the principle of military obligation to all members of the knightly class and others who held land worth either £40 a year or, if the need were especially pressing, £20. In effect the king was seeking to make wealth rather than feudal tenure the basis of military obligations, but he met much resistance, and for the final campaigns of his reign he relied upon appeals for voluntary paid service from all except those summoned personally by virtue of their tenure. His armies in his last years were partly feudal and partly mercenary, and his attempt to establish the principle of compulsory unpaid service had been defeated.

The infantry of Edward I's armies were recruited by commissioners of array who were required to select men from each shire for service in the army. The methods by which men were chosen remain obscure; it was probably left to the village assembly to decide who should serve, and no doubt much bribery and corruption attended the process. The local communities had to pay for the equipment of the men selected and their expenses until they reached the county boundary, after which they served at the king's wages. Faced with mounting debt, Edward II tried to shift the burden of support back on to the local communities. In 1310, for example, he demanded one foot soldier from each vill for service in his projected campaign in Scotland, and the vill was to pay the soldier's wages for seven weeks by means of a special aid levied on each vill by the sheriff. The campaign proved abortive, however, and Edward did not try to revive this method of payment for those who served in the army which was defeated at Bannockburn. At the Lincoln parliament of 1316, with Lancaster at the head of the council, a campaign in Scotland was planned and the proposal to levy one man from each vill was revived, with the vill responsible for wages for sixty days' service. At the same time all £50 landowners were summoned to serve without pay. The opposition to these measures provides one reason for the failure of the campaign and the growth of hostility within the community to Lancaster's rule. After Edward's triumph at Boroughbridge in 1322 he once again sought to levy one man from each vill for service in Scotland, with the vill this time paying the wages for forty days. The *Brut* blames the Despensers for this measure, but the king was able to raise almost 7,000 men who served for four weeks at their vills' expense.[36]

After the revolution of 1327 the commons in parliament sought statutory protection against the measures Edward II had taken. It was enacted that the vill should not be required to pay the cost of service beyond the county boundary, that the equipment required of troops should not go beyond that laid down in the Statute of Winchester, and that service overseas should not be required as an obligation of tenure. However, this legislation did not put an end to complaints about military obligation. In his wars in Scotland in the 1330s, Edward III made great use of hobelars and mounted archers who were paid more and required more expensive equipment than foot soldiers. Local communities thus had to find more money to fulfil even their admitted obligations under the statute of 1327, and the regular wearing of military uniform, which began in the 1330s, added to their burden since it too had to he paid for by the community. The crown's failure to observe in every instance the legislation of 1327 led to renewed complaints from the commons about the burden borne by the local communities in providing wages and equipment for the troops.

The feudal summons, the summons of the £40 or £20 landowners, and the use of commissions of array thus supplied troops for armies led by the king, while the royal household provided the administrative machinery by which wages were paid. From Edward I's reign onwards, however, it became increasingly common for the crown to use contract armies on campaigns where the king and the household were not present and to defend castles and towns in enemy territory. A magnate would engage to serve with a specified number of men for a particular time in return for wages which were agreed in advance and paid by the Exchequer. Lancaster and Lincoln served on this basis in Gascony in 1294 and 1298; and in Edward II's reign contract armies became more common as a means of defending the northern border in the absence of the king. A precedent was set in 1337 when the commanders of an army going to Scotland were engaged by contract, but their troops were raised by array. The ready response on this occasion no doubt did much to establish the contract system as the principal method of raising armies during the war with France. The feudal levy now fell into disuse: it was summoned in 1327, and then for the last time, and probably for financial reasons, in 1385. Commissions of array continued to be used for major expeditions led by the king or the Prince of Wales and administered by the Wardrobe, such as those of 1346 and 1359, but with these exceptions the armies which fought in France came increasingly to consist of volunteers rather than conscripts; and this in itself goes some way towards explaining popular support for the war.

The contract army had a number of advantages for the crown.[37] By placing responsibility for recruitment in the hands of the military captains themselves and their subordinates, the crown and its officials avoided arousing the grievances, and the complaints in parliament, that accompanied selection for compulsory service by means of the array. There was no limitation on the period of service overseas that a man could agree to undertake, and the crown was relieved of the burden of administration: recruiting, mustering and paying the troops were carried out by the officials of the magnates who made the contracts. The size of the army and the period of time for which it would serve were established when the contracts were made, and thus the costs were known in advance, and the system could, in theory at least, be kept under control by the practice of muster and review. The system allowed the nobility much more initiative in war than they had enjoyed under Edward I and Edward II, and their wishes and inter-ests, together with their willingness and ability to raise troops, had to be taken into account in planning a campaign. The war thus became very much a joint concern, with the nobility playing as important a part as the king in recruiting and commanding armies and conducting campaigns. The captains who contracted with the king to provide troops were not, however, directly responsible for recruiting all the troops they agreed to provide. They made extensive use of subcontractors, some of whom might agree to bring as few as a dozen men-at-arms and archers to the force. The contract army thus extended responsibility for military recruitment very widely through society, and the many knights who brought a handful of men-at-arms and archers were as important an element in the make-up of the contract army as the retainers of the magnate himself.

The recruitment of contract armies was no doubt helped by the general popularity of the war. Although men who were retained for life by a great magnate had an obligation to serve him in peace and war, and although there is little evidence about how the sub-contractors recruited their troops, neither the magnate captains nor their subcontractors seem to have encountered much difficulty in persuading men to serve. The most important reason was, of course, financial. The wages themselves were good: a mounted archer was paid 6d a day, the wage a skilled craftsman might expect to earn in civilian life, and a man-at-arms received 1s a day. It was also customary to add to the men's wages a bonus payment or 'reward' (regardum) paid quarterly to the leader of each group, usually at the rate of 100 marks per quarter for every thirty men engaged, and, until the 1370s, to pay compensation for the loss of war-horses.[38] The first instalment of wages was generally paid over by the Exchequer in advance of the campaign, but subsequent instalments were often delayed until after the campaign was over, sometimes long after. Captains had therefore to use their own resources to pay their men and bargain as best they could with the Exchequer. From the crown's point of view the mobilization of magnate financial resources was another advantage of the contract system, but the consequent indebtedness of the crown to magnates had the potential to exacerbate political tensions. Thomas of Woodstock's difficulty in obtaining payment for the expenses he incurred on his expedition to Brittany in 1380, for example, provided one reason amongst many for his opposition to Richard II between 1386 and 1388. Other magnates had to bargain with the Exchequer, and their debts to the crown were offset against the sums they were owed by the crown. In 1386, for instance, the earl of Northumberland reached agreement with the Exchequer whereby in return for £700 he discharged the king of all debts owing to the earl 'from any time past until the making of this indenture', and the earl was discharged of all the debts he incurred when he held the office of Admiral.[39]

The prospect of booty was probably more important than wages in persuading men to serve. Some of the gains made by the nobility in the campaigns of the 1340s and 1350s have already been discussed, but the opportunities for enrichment were open to men of all ranks.

Knights as well as nobles took prisoners at Poitiers, and the Black Prince granted lands, offices and annuities to many yeomen and bachelors who served him on his campaigns in Gascony between 1355 and 1357. On the earlier campaigns of Edward III's reign it was usual for a man to pay to his captain, and for the captain to pay to the crown, one-half of his profits of war. In the last decade of Edward's reign, however, the portion to be handed over was reduced to one-third, though at the same time the practice of paying compensation for the loss of one war-horse was abandoned.[40] The 'rule of thirds' became the standard method of division from the 1370s onwards, but other arrangements were sometimes made which might reflect the contractor's view of the likely profits to be won from a particular campaign. The careful and precise manner in which these financial arrangements were laid down suggests that many who served saw the war as essentially a business enterprise holding out the promise of substantial rewards for those who were fortunate or who distinguished themselves in the field. Some individuals enjoyed spectacular success: Sir Robert Salle, for example, who was a bondsman from Norfolk, rose through his gains of war to become a landowner in East Anglia. John of Copeland, a Northumbrian knight of modest means who was fortunate enough to capture David II of Scotland at the battle of Neville's Cross in 1346, was rewarded by the king with an annuity of £500. Robert Knolles, whose origins were said to be very humble, made a fortune out of war service in the 1350s and 1360s, and may be taken as typical of the successful captains with no inherited wealth who raised themselves by their military skills. Sir John Chandos and Sir Hugh Calveley were men of a similar kind, while on the French side Bertrand du Guesclin's career showed that the hereditary nobility had no monopoly of skill and prowess in war.

The extent to which the nobility enriched themselves through war is difficult to assess. Lancaster and the Black Prince brought back substantial plunder from their campaigns in France, and the earl of Northampton profited from the ransoms of prisoners taken in Brittany. On the other hand the great wealth of the earl of Arundel cannot be shown to have been derived from the profits of war. Arundel was wealthy enough to lend both to the king and to his fellow noblemen such as John of Gaunt. At his death in 1376 he apparently had £29,987 in a chest in the tower of Arundel Castle and another £30,253 elsewhere. By lending to the crown Arundel was using his personal wealth to underpin the war effort, and it is likely that he profited both in financial terms and in terms of patronage from his influence with the king.[41]

There is, of course, another side to the story. Soldiers who were captured by the enemy had to seek redemption where they could, and the cost of their ransom might be ruinous. Luke de Warton, who was captured by the Scots in the early 1320s, had to mortgage his lands to the Captain of Berwick Castle to raise the money to redeem himself, and he ended his days living on the charity of a religious house in York. Walter Ferrefort, a soldier serving with the Earl of March in Brittany in 1375, was held in the gaol of St Brieuc as surety for a debt. He wrote a pathetic letter to his lord, describing his condition in prison where he lay bound with fetters of iron and beseeching aid from the Earl of March to secure his deliverance.[42] The careers of John of Copeland and Sir Robert Knolles on the one hand, and Luke de Warton and Walter Ferrefort on the other represent the extremes of success and failure. More typical, perhaps, were the modest gains of a group of Cheshire archers who divided £8 12s 6d amongst them as their share of the proceeds of a silver ship belonging to the King of France and seized at Poitiers. Such small gains were incentive enough for many.

The prospect of good wages and modest gains provided ample inducement to serve; but there were no doubt other motives as well. Professor Saul's study of the Gloucestershire gentry showed that many of those from the knightly class who served were young men, whose elders carried the burden of local administration.[43] The disproportion-ately large numbers of recruits from Cheshire, and the martial reputation that the men from that county acquired, may have had something to do with the successful recruiting drives organized by the Black Prince, who was Earl of Chester as well as Prince of Wales; but it also, perhaps, reflected the problems of underemployment in a predominantly pastoral society. Many young men were attracted to the profession of arms for its own sake, and the excitement and glory of successful war were reasons in themselves for service, but some at least of those who engaged with a captain may have been responding to pressures at home and in the local economy rather than to the material incentives that war offered.

From the political point of view, the successful development of the contract army had important implications. The frequency with which campaigns were organized in the 1340s, 1350s and 1370s and the need to provide substantial forces for the defence of English-held castles and towns encouraged the nobility to maintain permanent forces which might be augmented by the use of sub-contractors when necessary. The crown alone still had the power to compel military service, especially for defence against invasion. The array did not fall completely into disuse, and the crown still relied on the sheriffs to call out the *posse comitatus* to deal with local disturbances. But none of this could disguise the fact that the great nobles had substantial bodies of experienced soldiers at their disposal. This was nowhere more true than on the northern border, where the nobles who held office as Wardens of the Marches, a system that had reached full development by the end of Edward III's reign, were in effect allowed to maintain permanent standing armies at the Exchequer's expense. The ambitions of the northern nobility were to play a crucial role in national politics at the end of the century.

The successful use of contract armies also enhanced the prestige of the nobility. Almost all the great noble families served Edward III abroad, and the freedom of action they enjoyed allowed them to win glory and renown for themselves, as Lancaster succeeded in doing in Aquitaine between 1343 and 1345, Northampton in Brittany in the 1340s and the Black Prince in Languedoc in 1355. The triumphs of war were a source of pride to them, and strengthened their loyalty to the crown. But the successes of the 1340s and 1350s created expectations which were not fulfilled when war was renewed in 1369. A new generation of nobles who were not to taste the sweetness of military success and knew only at second hand of the prestige and profits gained in the 1340s and 1350s led the opposition to the court in the last years of Edward III's reign and during the reign of Richard II. In so far as the political stability of mid-century depended upon the success of the king's cause in France, it was shallowly based.

The use of contract armies to fight the war depended, of course, not just upon the readiness of men to serve but also upon the willingness of parliament to vote taxes to pay for the war. Under Edward I and Edward II, and in the early years of Edward III, grants of money had generally been made with reluctance, and had been accompanied by many complaints about the conduct of royal financial officials. The commons had shown themselves increasingly adept at procuring political concessions in return for grants of taxes, and although they were at their most effective when they enjoyed the support of at least some sections of the nobility, they had gained substantially in experience and cohesion by the time the crisis of 1340–1 arose. Yet after that crisis Edward's political skills, together with the popularity of the war, enabled the king to maintain the flow of funds for the war without provoking opposition of the kind that had arisen in 1297 or 1339–41.

The opening campaign of the war, in 1338–41, taught Edward some important financial lessons. The construction of a network of alliances in the Low Countries had been enormously expensive and brought the king little real diplomatic or military support. The problems of financing and supplying expeditions to the continent provoked political opposition which had a wide popular basis and in which some of the nobility allied themselves with the commons in seeking redress for the grievances of the community. Edward's manipulation of the wool trade for his financial advantage intensified the divisions between the small group of wealthy merchants who stood to benefit from Edward's schemes and the lesser merchants who eventually made common cause with the producers in opposing the monopolistic structure that Edward tried to create.

After 1341, however, the costs of war fell sharply from the levels they had reached between 1338 and 1341, and not until the 1370s did they begin once again to approach those levels. It is important to realize in explaining Edward's success in handling the commons in the 1340s and 1350s that successful war was being fought comparatively cheaply. Even the Crécy–Calais campaign cost only £150,000, and the expeditions to Normandy and Brittany were significantly shorter and less expensive than the campaigns of the opening phase of the war. It has been estimated that, even allowing for Lancaster's expenses in Aquitaine, the campaigns between 1344 and 1347 cost only about two-thirds of the amount spent between 1338 and 1341. The burden of war was thus more manageable, but large sums still had to be raised by parliamentary grants and the commons were seldom disposed to make such grants unconditionally. The grievances of the commons have a familiar air: in 1344, for instance, they offered a grant of two tenths and fifteenths, and presented a series of petitions in which they complained about purveyance and other administrative abuses. They granted the second subsidy only on condition that the king himself went abroad to try to bring an end to the war. After the fall of Calais, when war ceased for some years, the king had to persuade the commons that direct taxes should continue in order to finance the defence of English positions abroad, notably Calais itself, and to maintain English forces in a state of readiness in case the enemy broke the truce and resumed the war. The commons accepted these arguments, and direct taxation became in effect a regular impost, levied both in time of war and time of truce. The king was thus able to mobilize substantial wealth through the taxation system: Professor Ormrod has estimated that in the whole course of the reign direct taxation on the laity yielded at least £1,120,000.[44]

For some years direct taxation ceased to be contentious, and arguments in the 1340s arose over the taxation of wool and the king's manipulation of the wool trade to raise money for the war.[45] Between 1337 and 1353 the tax on wool formed part of a series of schemes under which the king attempted to establish a body of powerful and wealthy merchants who would be granted a monopoly in the purchase and export of wool in return for making loans to the king which would be repaid from the maltolt, the export tax on wool. Borrowing and taxation were inseparably linked in these schemes, and the merchants would use their monopolistic powers to enrich themselves and ensure that sufficient cash was available to satisfy the king's need for loans. From the king's point of view these schemes had many attractive features, but in practice they did not work. The monopolistic merchants found that they had insufficient capital to advance the loans required; there was much evasion of the monopolies; and the export trade itself was disrupted by the crown's impressment of merchant shipping for war, and its political pressures on Flanders. The commons, too, objected to the king's manipulation of the wool trade. In 1336, as on earlier occasions, a tax of 20s a sack had been agreed by an assembly of merchants, and in 1338 the merchants agreed to increase it to 40s. Since the tax was paid out of the financial resources of the merchants it was quite proper to seek consent from them rather than from parliament, but the merchants were suspected, no doubt with some justification, of seeking to pass the real burden of the tax on to the producers. The tax thus came to be seen as an impost on the whole community, to which the general assent of the community was required.

In 1340 the king conceded that parliament should have the right to grant the maltolt, which it proceeded to do for a period of fifteen months. The commons granted it again from 1343 to 1346, from 1348 to 1351, 1353 to 1356, and in 1356 for a period of six years. The willingness of the commons to grant the maltolt in these years should dispose of the argument that they wished to see the tax abolished. Their object was to control it themselves and to use their control over it as a means of persuading the king to abolish the monopolistic cartels which exploited the trade. Thus in 1343 the commons granted the maltolt in return for a concession that the minimum price for wool should be increased and that no one should be allowed to purchase wool below that price. In 1348 they demanded free trade in wool, and in 1351, when they petitioned that the maltolt should be granted only in parliament and that all merchants should be permitted to deal in wool 'without being restricted by those merchants who call themselves the king's merchants' they secured their own control over the tax, and control of the trade by monopolists came to an end.[46] The destruction of the monopolistic purchasing cartels, which was the commons' real object, ensured that the tax would no longer be passed on to the producer in the form of lower prices, and the establishment of the Company of the Staple as a selling cartel enabled the real burden of the tax to be imposed upon the purchasers, the cloth manufacturers of Flanders. The maltolt too thus became a regular impost, though the commons were not prepared to grant it for more than a year or two at a time for fear of losing control over it and to prevent the king from reviving the monopolistic schemes for exploiting the producers which they had struggled against between 1336 and 1351.

Both king and commons had an interest in compromise rather than conflict on the question of taxation in the 1340s and 1350s. In their struggle to gain control of the wool tax the commons arguably gained more by agreeing to grant the tax and receiving in return concessions on free trade in wool than they would have achieved by seeking to abolish the tax. The king ensured that vital funds continued to flow, and was in any case disposed to make concessions on the question of cartels because many of the monopolistic companies had gone bankrupt and were useless to him. The assembly of merchants had become of little value as a tax-granting body not just because of the hostility of the commons but also because Edward's monopolistic schemes had so divided the mercantile community that it could no longer speak with one voice. Edward's handling of the commons on matters of taxation showed his pragmatism and political skills at their best. Support for the war was readily given, and the heavy burdens of the Crécy–Calais campaign and the Rheims campaign of 1359–60 produced few political problems. The concessions Edward made on matters such as purveyance and unparliamentary taxation went a long way towards meeting the grievances of the commons, and the king was able to mobilize the resources he required for war.

The part played by the nobility in the debates about taxation in these years has never been satisfactorily analysed, but it appears that the initiative lay almost entirely with the commons. From at least 1340 it was accepted that the lords in parliament could impose taxation only upon themselves, and although they might make proposals about taxation to the Commons, the granting of a tax was essentially a matter for the representative element in parliament. Indeed, Professor Roskell has argued that the nobility could not be relied upon to attend parliament in the 1350s and 1360s even when they were present in England, and that these parliaments amounted to little more than tax bargaining sessions between the king and the commons.[47] There is undoubtedly some truth in this; the nobility frequently sent proxies to parliament in these years; they were too preoccupied with war to have any reason for opposing the king in parliament, and their independent campaigns on the continent took some of them away from England for several years at a time.

It would be wrong, however, to suggest that the commons ensured the flow of funds for the war simply in return for concessions on their most persistent grievances. They also responded to the king's skilful use of propaganda to generate support for the war. Throughout the 1340s and 1350s the king played on the commons' fear of a French invasion of England: the threat that the French might 'destroy the English tongue and occupy the realm of England' was used more than once to persuade the commons to grant money for the war, and the discovery at the sack of Caen of a French plan for the invasion of England in 1339 was a gift to royal propaganda. It was read out in parliament to persuade the commons in the euphoric aftermath of Crécy to grant two subsidies and publicly proclaimed at St Paul's to arouse popular enthusiasm for the war. Edward's rhetoric was not, however, wholly defensive. In assuming the title and arms of King of France in 1340, he laid much stress on his God-given duty to recover his right, and in the speeches made by the Chancellor at the opening of parliament in the 1340s and 1350s the commons were asked to grant aids 'in pursuit of the king's quarrel to recover his rights', or in consideration of 'the pursuit of our right'. The offensive and defensive aims of the war were skilfully linked in the argument deployed in 1352 that the security of England was threatened by the French king's denial of Edward's right.[48] In case such arguments failed, the king also reminded the commons frequently that the war had been undertaken with their consent and that this consent had from time to time been renewed, as Sir William Thorp pointed out in the parliament of January 1348.

Edward's war propaganda was designed to reach a wider audience than the commons in parliament. Bishops were ordered to ensure that prayers were said in every church for the success of the king's expeditions to France, and news of the victory of Crécy was proclaimed throughout the realm. Newsletters were circulated giving details of campaigns, and some of these, such as those sent by Bartholomew Burghersh to the Archbishop of Canterbury in 1346, were carefully phrased so as to generate public support for the invasion of Normandy. Such propaganda could only be successful, however, if it corresponded to some genuine feeling both amongst the commons and in the country generally that the king's cause was just and worthy of support. There seems little doubt that such feeling existed, especially in the 1340s and 1350s. Popular verses echoed the sentiments of royal propaganda, and a crude xenophobia appeared in lampoons about the French and the Scots. *An Invective against France*, probably written around 1347, opened with these words: 'France! effeminate, pharisaical, shadow of vigour, Lynx, viper, foxy, wolvish, Medea, Sly, siren, heartless, repulsive, proud.'[49] As Dr Barnie pointed out, such lampoons show how ancient and persistent are national stereotypes: the English accused the French of sexual promiscuity, while the French assiduously propagated the idea that the English were violent and gluttonous drunkards, and that they all had tails.

Criticism of the war seems to have been confined to a few individuals. Complaints about the burden of taxation, the oppressive behaviour of royal officials and the costs of the army did not develop into outright opposition to the war on principle. The king's willingness to remedy such grievances helped to allay the disquiet of the commons and public opinion outside parliament. As John of Reading observed in 1362 (perhaps rather too optimistically), the passage of a statute in that year dealing with the problem of purveyance put an end to discontent amongst the common people.[50] More fundamental doubts about the war were expressed by Richard de Bury Bishop of Durham in his *Philobiblion,* where he said that 'war, wanting discretion of reason, furiously attacks whatever falls in its way, and not being under the guidance of reason it destroys the vessels of reason', and he beseeched 'the ruler of Olympus and the most high Dispenser of all the world, that he may abolish war, establish peace, and bring about tranquil times under his own special protection'.[51]

Only some Lollards seem to have elaborated a pacifist doctrine founded upon the Biblical injunction against killing: the tenth of the twelve Lollard conclusions published in 1395 declared that 'manslaute be batayle or pretense lawe of rythwysnesse for temperal cause or spirituel withouten special revelaciun is expres contrarious to the newe testament, the qwiche is a lawe of grace and ful of mercy'.[52] Pacifism, however, was not a doctrine widely held amongst the Lollards. Wycliffe himself adhered (though with some doubts and reservations) to the doctrine of the just war, and several of the knights at Richard II's court who were suspected of being Lollards had enjoyed military careers. With these limited exceptions, therefore, the belief that the war was just did not come under serious challenge in the fourteenth century. The English, of course, could well afford such sentiments, for they largely escaped the horrors of war. Even in the northern counties, Scottish raids were never as frequent or as deeply penetrating as they had been in Edward II's reign, and although the inhabitants of those counties made the most of their plight in petitions for relief from taxation, the raids in the years after 1332 did little long-term damage to the region's economy. The southern coastal counties of England were at risk from seaborne invasion, but here too the raids were spasmodic and localized. Neither the extreme north of England nor the south coast had to endure the kind of onslaught that brought a plaintive cry from the Prior of St Thibaut-des-Brûles, south-east of Paris, describing how an English force had burnt his village and ransomed the inhabitants and asking those who dwelt in towns and castles whether their suffering was anything like his. His letter was written 'behind our grange, for I dare not write anywhere else'.[53] Nor did England ever approach the state of social and political collapse which France faced after Poitiers. A successful and popular war was not only one which brought victory and profit, but also one which was fought well away from home.

The King and the Nobles

Edward III's orchestration of support for the war was skilful and successful, yet fundamentally he depended on the co-operation of the nobility, who recruited and led the contract armies that became increasingly important as the war continued. Victory and profit, together with the king's affable personality and chivalric reputation, ensured that this co-operation, once offered, would not lightly be withdrawn; but in dealing with the nobility Edward showed a degree of political skill and a sensitivity to their interests which went beyond simply sharing in a glorious and profitable enterprise abroad.

Although the principal activity of many of the nobles in Edward III's reign was war, their fundamental concern was always their inheritance, the lands and rights which formed the basis of their wealth and power and which they expected to hand on to their heirs.[54] Edward III's attitude towards questions of tenure and inheritance suggests that he sympathized with the outlook of his peers and was prepared to encourage their aspirations even at the expense of the rights of the crown. The oligarchic tendency within the nobility which had shown itself in Edward II's reign was intensified by the practice of granting new earldoms, and regranting old ones, in tail male. This encouraged the growth of a clearly defined body of hereditary peers, for it eliminated the risks that an earldom would pass into other hands by marriage, that the lands would become separate from the title, or that they would be divided up amongst coheiresses. The earldoms granted by Edward III in 1337 were all granted in tail male, and in the course of the century the earldoms of Oxford, Warwick, Arundel and Surrey were surrendered to the king and regranted in tail male. Such grants had some advantages from the crown's point of view, for in the event of the failure of direct heirs the lands and title would revert to the crown and would augment the resources of royal patronage, as happened with the Audley, Clinton and Ufford inheritances; but the underlying reason for limiting descent to heirs male was the wish of the nobility to preserve the integrity of their inheritances and to ensure that the title descended with the land. Edward was also generous in granting licences to entail, under which lands would not revert to the crown if the male line failed, and this too helped to preserve the integrity of great estates.

The nobles' freedom to do what they wished with their lands was enhanced by the development of the legal device known as the 'use'. The idea was similar to that of a trust. Lands were granted to a group of men known as feoffees, who became the legal owners of the land, while the grantor enjoyed the use of the lands – in other words, all the rights and profits arising from them. But because the feoffees were the legal owners, the lands could not be taken into wardship if the grantor died leaving an heir under age, nor could the crown require the payment of a relief when the heir entered upon his inheritance, and lands held in trust in this way could not be forfeited for treason. The device also enabled the lord to mitigate the rigour of primogeniture and make provision for younger sons, for daughters, and for the endowment of Masses for his soul and the souls of members of his family. The development of the use enhanced the landowner's freedom of action, while the crown's rights of wardship, escheat and relief were lost. Edward III, however, seems to have made little effort to safeguard these rights. He readily granted licences for enfeoffment to uses, and although Chancery officials made some effort to track down unlicensed or fraudulent uses, such cases 'form a very small minority of all those tenants in chief who had conveyed land to uses'.[55] These devices protected the integrity of the inheritance, and both the patronage of the crown and the wealth won from war enabled many inheritances to grow larger in the course of Edward III's reign. The concentration of extensive territorial power in the hands of a small number of great nobles became more marked than ever. For example, between 1338 and 1376 the Earl of Arundel bought over twenty manors in Sussex and Surrey. His purchases cost him in all over £4,000, and those who sold property to him were mainly small landowners, widows and heiresses. Lancaster too augmented his inheritance with purchases from lesser men, particularly in Lancashire and Cheshire, where a number of members of the knightly class conveyed manors to him. Both landowners were also granted legal rights, the most significant of which was the establishment in March 1351 of Lancashire as a county palatine, in which royal powers were in effect devolved to Henry of Lancaster, now raised to ducal status.

None of these measures to protect and augment the inheritance, however, were proof against the greatest misfortunes that could befall a noble family in the fourteenth century: failure of heirs and political miscalculation. Two of the earldoms that Edward created in 1337, those of Gloucester and Huntingdon, died with their first holder, and a third, the Ufford earldom of Suffolk, survived for only two generations. None of these earls had male heirs, and the lands and titles reverted to the crown. When Earl Warenne died in 1347 he left no direct heir. The inheritance had earlier been surrendered to the king and regranted in tail male, with reversion to the king if the male line failed. But in 1348 the Earl of Arundel, who was Warenne's sister's husband and sole legitimate heir, petitioned the king to revoke this agreement, for it would 'disinherit the petitioner of his right to premises which should descend to him in the event of the death of the earl... without lawful heir.'[56] The king gave way, and much of the Warenne inheritance eventually passed to Arundel.

Failure of heirs, or the survival only of heiresses, was exploited by the king himself for the benefit of his own sons, who expected endowments and titles as befitted their rank and who by virtue of their birth played a leading part in aristocratic society. Indeed, the politics of the last thirty years of the century cannot properly be understood without reference to the wealth and ambition of the members of the king's own family. When the last de Burgh Earl of Ulster died in 1333 he left only a daughter, Elizabeth Countess of Ulster in her own right, whom the king married to his second son, Lionel of Antwerp, created Duke of Clarence in 1362. Edward no doubt hoped that part of the Clare inheritance and a substantial Irish patrimony would thus provide for Clarence and his heirs, but he died aged thirty in 1368, leaving as the only child of his marriage a daughter, Philippa. The king married Philippa to Edmund Mortimer Earl of March in 1368, and thus the earl came to possess not only the Mortimer family lands in the Welsh March which had been restored to his father in 1354, but also the Clare lordship of Usk, the Clare lands in Dorset, Somerset and East Anglia, and the de Burgh earldom of Ulster. The earl became the largest landowner in Ireland, and second only to the Duke of Lancaster in England, while his descendants had royal blood in their veins. The revival in the fortunes of the Mortimer family is an important example of the working of Edward III's patronage, first in setting aside the forfeiture of 1330 and then in permitting Edmund Mortimer to marry his granddaughter.

Royal patronage and unexpected death also laid the foundation of the power of Edward's third son, John of Gaunt. Henry of Grosmont, whose earldom of Lancaster had been raised to a duchy in 1351, died of the plague on 23 March 1361, leaving two daughters as his coheiresses. The elder, Maud, was married to the Count of Holland and Zeeland, while the younger, Blanche, had been married in 1359 to John of Gaunt in the expectation that he would eventually receive half the Lancaster inheritance. Under a statute passed in 1351, any children of Maud's marriage would have been entitled to inherit in England, even though they had been born outside the allegiance; but Maud died childless in April 1362, little more than a year after her father, and thus the inheritance was unexpectedly reunited in Gaunt's hands. In practice, however, Gaunt would have been able to exercise substantial influence over Maud's share even if she had survived. This did not, however, discourage Henry Knighton from suggesting that he had poisoned his sister-in-law in order to gain possession of the whole of the inheritance.[57]

Edward took advantage of the failure of another earldom, that of Hereford, to endow his youngest son, Thomas of Woodstock. Humphrey Bohun Earl of Hereford died at the age of thirty in 1373 leaving, like Lancaster, two coheiresses, though both were under age when their father died. The elder sister, Eleanor, was married to Thomas in 1374, and Thomas received her share of the inheritance when she came of age in 1380. The other sister, Mary, was four years younger than Eleanor, and Froissart tells the story that Thomas took responsibility for educating Mary in the hope of persuading her to go into a nunnery, so that he would receive the entire Bohun inheritance. Froissart goes on to relate that while Thomas was abroad in 1380, ladies of Mary's family removed her from Pleshey, and soon afterwards she was married to Gaunt's son, Henry Bolingbroke, later Henry IV. It is hard to say how much of the story is true. Mary's marriage to Henry had certainly taken place by February 1381, and Thomas might well have done what he could to prevent her marrying, but Froissart casts Thomas as a villain in his account of English politics in Richard II's reign, and not every detail in the story should necessarily be accepted at face value.

In his concern to endow his sons adequately, Edward behaved in much the same way as other members of landowning society, and although he exploited the marriage market for the benefit of his own family he did not monopolize it: both the Earl of Arundel and the Earl of March gained substantially from the king's bestowal upon them of wealthy heiresses. No small group of favourites emerged to monopolize access to the king or royal patronage: even the Hainaulters at court attracted little of the obloquy that surrounded the Savoyards at Henry III's court, and the families which had suffered forfeiture in the political violence between 1322 and 1330 were gradually restored. The political stability of Edward's reign thus removed, for a time, the threat that political miscalculation and the penalty for treason presented to the integrity of the aristocratic inheritance. The Statute of Treasons, passed in 1352, set out a limited definition of the crime, and implicitly excluded from its scope political offences of the kind that had brought so many families to destruction between 1322 and 1330. This was not, in all probability, the intent of the statute: it seems to have arisen from concern expressed by the commons in parliament at the tendency of the judges in the 1340s to construe as usurpation of royal power, and thus treason, such offences as riot and highway robbery. The statute defined treason as an act intended to encompass the death of the king, the Chancellor, the Treasurer or the judges; the violation of the queen, the king's eldest daughter or the wife of the heir to the throne; making war against the king in his kingdom; and bringing false money into the realm. The narrowness of the definition gave the nobility some security against the construction of political offences as treason, even if this had not been Edward's original intention.[58]

Edward's achievement in the years between 1341 and 1369 was substantial. He built up popular support for a war which, in its opening phase, had given rise to a political crisis similar to those that had broken over his father and grandfather. He succeeded in harnessing national resources for war on a basis of regular national taxation and with a degree of consent and co-operation which had eluded his predecessors. Above all, he established a rapport between himself and the leading noblemen, his companions in arms, which formed the basis of the longest period of political stability the country had known since the early years of Edward I. These achievements, however, had their price. Money flowed to pay for the war, but control of taxation lay firmly with the commons in parliament. The nobility readily supported the king's 'just quarrel', but at the same time their military importance was greatly enhanced, and both the profits of war and the generosity of the crown enabled them to extend and safeguard their inheritances. The king and his nobles understood one another, shared common interests and ideals, and enjoyed the glory, prestige and profit that success in the common enterprise in France brought them. But when victory gave way to stalemate and defeat, when the king's early vigour gave way to senility, and when he was succeeded by a king with a very different personality, the limitations of his achievement became apparent.

5
Military Stalemate and Political Conflict, 1364–1389

The Renewal of the War

In June 1364, shortly after the accession of Charles V to the French throne, a spy of the Black Prince wrote to his master reporting a conversation between Charles of Navarre and the Count of Foix, in which the count had claimed intimate knowledge of the new king's intentions.[1] Charles was determined to string Edward III along with fine words until he had recovered the hostages from England and settled accounts with the Duke of Brittany and with Charles of Navarre. He then proposed to gather an army to use against Aquitaine, to secure his alliance with Scotland, establish an alliance with Castile, foment rebellion within Aquitaine, recover what had been lost to the English and then attack and destroy England. This was a formidable programme for a king whose father had been defeated and captured by the English only eight years earlier, and who had agreed to a treaty which conceded a Greater Aquitaine in full sovereignty to Edward III; but in the sixteen years of his reign Charles achieved each one of these objects except the last, and even though he did not attack and destroy England, French and Castilian naval raids along the south coast induced a sense of panic and defensiveness unknown in England since the very earliest months of the war.

Charles V was a ruler of a very different calibre from his father, John II. He was determined to regain what his father had lost, and raise the French monarchy from its abasement after Poitiers; but his methods were to be diplomacy, subversion, and limited campaigns rather than a great battle in which, as he appreciated, the French were liable to be defeated yet again. At the beginning of his reign, Charles V had such pressing problems within his kingdom that an early renewal of the war with England was scarcely conceivable. The most serious immediate threat to Charles came from Charles of Navarre, who held several castles on the border between Normandy and the Ile-de-France and who was thus in a position to threaten Paris. In the last months of John II's reign Charles of Navarre had raised a rebellion over the succession to Burgundy, which Navarre claimed by virtue of descent from the great-aunt of the last Capetian duke, Philip of Rouvres. Charles V, showing that good judgement of men which was to stand him in good stead throughout his reign, chose Bertrand du Guesclin to command his forces, and du Guesclin defeated Navarre at the battle of Cocherel in May 1364. Navarre lost his castles and was lucky not to lose his life; he was to attempt further intrigues with the English, but his double-dealing made the English wary of him. In 1370 he negotiated an alliance with Edward III, but the Black Prince would have none of it, and in the following year Navarre made his peace with Charles V in the Treaty of Vernon, though even this did not mark the end of the Anglo-Navarrese relationship. In 1365 the succession dispute in Brittany was settled by an agreement, the Treaty of Guérande, under which John de Montfort, son of the John de Montfort who had allied with Edward III in 1341, was recognized as duke by Charles V and agreed to do homage to him, though many Englishmen remained in the ducal household, and some English captains who owed their fortunes to war, such as Robert Knolles, stayed on in the duchy.

Of even greater importance than the settlement of the Breton succession or the defeat of Charles of Navarre was Charles V's skilful and successful handling of the question of the Flemish succession. The Count of Flanders, Louis de Mâle, had only one child, his daughter Margaret, whose marriage was eagerly sought by both protagonists in the war, for with her went not only the County of Flanders itself with its substantial revenues but also Artois, Nevers, Rethel and the County of Burgundy. The count himself appears to have been anxious for an English husband for his daughter, and negotiations opened for her marriage to Edward III's fourth son, Edmund Langley. The effect of such a marriage, had it ever taken place, would have been to create a substantial English-dominated fief on France's northern and eastern borders which would have been a northern equivalent of Aquitaine. Charles V's policy was to prevent this at all costs, and his candidate for Margaret's hand was his brother Philip, who had been created Duke of Burgundy in 1364. Margaret's marriage to either candidate required a papal dispensation, for both were within the forbidden degrees, and Charles put pressure on the Pope to refuse a dispensation for Margaret to marry Edmund Langley. Charles's diplomacy eventually bore fruit, and on 19 June 1369 Margaret was married to Philip at Ghent. Although Margaret's father lived on until 1384, English interests in Flanders were now gradually eclipsed. Bruges was closed to English vessels, and Calais became more vulnerable.

A few months before Margaret's marriage to Philip of Burgundy Charles V had also gained an important victory in the Iberian peninsula. In 1362 the Black Prince had concluded an alliance with Pedro I of Castile. Under this alliance the Black Prince agreed to give Pedro help against his enemies, and the enemy whom Pedro had chiefly in mind was his illegitimate half- brother Enrique of Trastámara, who was in exile at the French court and was seeking French support for his designs upon the Castilian crown. In February 1366 du Guesclin took a force consisting mainly of members of the Free Companies into Castile. Within a few weeks they had put Pedro to flight and Enrique was crowned king. The Black Prince, however, raised an army in Aquitaine and marched into Castile in support of his deposed ally. At Nájera on 3 April 1367 he routed Enrique's forces and restored Pedro to the throne. Pedro, however, was, an unreliable ally: he was unpopular with many of the Castilian nobles, and with their connivance Enrique of Trastámara had him murdered in March 1369. Pedro's heiress was his eldest surviving daughter Constanza, who married John of Gaunt in September 1371. By this marriage Gaunt acquired a claim to the throne of Castile which, if successfully asserted, might reverse the most important consequence of Pedro's murder, the movement of Castile into the French orbit. On the other hand, as long as John of Gaunt remained titular head of the rival faction in Castile, the Trastámara dynasty would look to France to maintain its hold on the crown. The price the French exacted for their support was the deployment of the Castilian fleet against England. The Castilian fleet, based in the Cantabrian coast ports, was perhaps the most professional and well-organized navy in western Europe in the 1360s and 1370s, and it was well placed both to attack English shipping on the route between England and Bordeaux and to harry the south coast of England. Castilian admirals also gave the French advice on re-establishing their own navy in the Clos de Gallées at Rouen, and the combined power of the French and Castilian navies presented a formidable threat to England in the 1370s.

None of these military and diplomatic successes for Charles V was in itself a reason for the renewal of war in 1369, though they strengthened his hand and were an important preparation for the war which Charles believed would eventually reopen. The immediate reason for war was, once again, the French king's confiscation of Aquitaine. The duchy had been elevated to the status of a principality and placed in the Black Prince's hands in 1362. He established his court at Bordeaux, but his administration was not popular with his Gascon subjects. Pedro of Castile had promised to pay the wages of the troops the Black Prince took to Spain, but he reneged on his obligation, and the prince had to tax his Gascon subjects heavily to raise the money he needed. A hearth tax agreed in the autumn of 1367 aroused particularly bitter opposition, and two Gascon lords refused to levy the tax in their domains. The Black Prince insisted, and the lords, realizing that the renunciation clauses in the Treaty of Brétigny had never been carried out, appealed to the King of France as their suzerain. Charles kept the appellants waiting, bribing them from time to time to stop them becoming too impatient; meanwhile his younger brother Louis Duke of Anjou concentrated on building up a party in Aquitaine, winning over many of the nobility of Périgord, Rouergue, Quercy and the Agenais by a judicious mixture of bribes and promises. In January 1369 Charles summoned the Black Prince to appear before the *parlement* of Paris. The prince said he would do so only at the head of an army of 60,000 men; the *parlement* pronounced him a contumacious vassal, and sentenced him to loss of the duchy.

The English were poorly prepared for the renewal of the war, and indeed Edward III urged the Black Prince to adopt a more conciliatory stance towards his Gascon subjects. France's diplomatic successes had made little impact on English opinion, and English military leadership was markedly weaker than it had been during the first phase of the war. Above all, the king himself was a different man. Both his mental and his physical powers seemed to weaken in the 1370s: he became increasingly preoccupied with his mistress, Alice Perrers, and could no longer offer the leadership which had united the nobility behind him in the 1340s and 1350s. The chroniclers were kind to Edward in these years, aiming much of their criticism at his mistress, at those around him at court, and in 1376–7 at John of Gaunt; but his loss of touch does much to explain the growing political factionalism in England in these years.

The Black Prince might have been expected to step into his father's shoes and fulfil the promise he had shown at Crécy and Poitiers; but he developed an illness in Spain in 1367 which never entirely left him. His spirit was as warlike as ever, but he could no longer offer effective military leadership. Chandos Herald, the Black Prince's biographer, makes the prince reply to Charles V's letter citing him to appear before the *parlement* of Paris by saying, 'Lords, by my faith it seems to me that the French think I am dead; but if God gives me comfort, and I can get up from this bed, I will do them a great deal of harm even now, for God knows that they lack a good case, and they will have real cause to complain of me'.[2] In September 1370 the prince, together with Gaunt, Langley, Pembroke and one of the leading Gascon noblemen, Jean de Grailly, Captal de Buch, took Limoges by storm and ruthlessly sacked it. Its destruction marred the prince's reputation, and it marked the end of his military career. According to Froissart he had to be carried to Limoges on a litter;[3] his health deteriorated still further over the winter of 1370, and in January 1371 he returned to England. He never fully recovered, and died in June 1376. His eldest son Edward had died in 1370, and his heir was now his younger son Richard, born at Bordeaux in 1367. After the prince returned to England it must have seemed increasingly unlikely that he would live to inherit the throne, and the prospect of Richard's succession as a child served only to increase uncertainty.

Edward's other sons could not offer the leadership that the king and the Black Prince had once provided. His second son, Lionel Duke of Clarence, had died in 1368, and his third son, John of Gaunt Duke of Lancaster, spent much time abroad in the early 1370s. He only came to the forefront as 'governor and ruler of the kingdom', to use Walsingham's words,[4] after the Good Parliament of 1376. Gaunt showed consistent loyalty to his father and, after 1377, to his young nephew Richard II, but he lacked the charismatic authority of his father and eldest brother, and he was widely if unfairly blamed for the misfortunes that befell England in the last years of his father's reign. Edward's two youngest sons played an insignificant part in politics in these years. Edmund Langley, born in 1342 and created Earl of Cambridge in 1362, was granted part of the Warenne inheritance to maintain his estate, but his marriage to Isabella, youngest daughter of Pedro I of Castile, was used to further Gaunt's diplomatic schemes rather than to provide him with an adequate endowment. Thomas of Woodstock, Edward's youngest son, was born in 1355 and was thus only just of age when his father died. He had to wait until the coronation of Richard II before receiving an earldom, and his endowment with part of the Bohun inheritance was scarcely sufficient for one of his rank. Edward's treatment of his youngest sons was markedly lacking in generosity, and noted by contemporaries: in a political sermon delivered during the crisis of 1376 Thomas Brinton Bishop of Rochester argued that the king should place his sons above the servants, for it was not right and just that servants should become lords and lords beggars.[5]

Edward's sons-in-law, on the other hand, received generous treatment. His youngest daughter Margaret married John Hastings Earl of Pembroke in 1359, and although she died two years later, Pembroke remained high in favour at court and, with royal encouragement, embarked on a plan to reunite the inheritance of his ancestor William Marshal, which had twice been partitioned in the previous century and a half. The king's eldest daughter, Isabella, long remained unmarried but in the early 1360s she met and fell in love with Enguerrand de Coucy, a French nobleman who came to England in 1360 as a hostage for the payment of John II's ransom. Coucy soon rose high in favour at court: in 1363 Edward granted him lands in north Lancashire, Cumberland and Westmorland to which he had some claim by inheritance; two years later he married Isabella, and in 1366 the king created him Earl of Bedford with an endowment of 1,000 marks a year. Lands to the value of 300 marks were found for him in England, but half the endowment was found by persuading Guy de Blois, another French hostage, to surrender to Edward the county of Soissons, worth 500 marks a year, which Edward then granted to the new Earl of Bedford. Bedford's position as a landowner in both countries became difficult to sustain after the renewal of the war in 1369, and his allegiance to England rested essentially on his friendship with the king. After Edward III's death he resigned his allegiance and his title, and returned to France, leaving his wife in England. After she died in 1379 some of the Bedford inheritance found its way to his son-in-law Robert de Vere, Richard II's arch-favourite.

Bedford was the only new earl created by Edward III after his family settlement in 1362, and his patronage of the nobility was less generous than it had been in the first two decades of his reign. His companions in arms, the nobles who had shared the glory and profits of victory in France in the 1340s and 1350s, were a vanishing generation by the 1370s. William Bohun Earl of Northampton died in 1360; Henry of Grosmont Duke of Lancaster in 1361; the Earls of Warwick and Suffolk in 1369; the Earl of Hereford in 1373; and the Earl of Arundel in 1376. The significance of the weakening of the royal family and the ranks of the nobility through death and illness in the 1360s, and especially in 1368 and 1369, those two years when English fortunes seemed suddenly to be reversed, should not be underestimated. In the years after 1369 the king more and more sought the company of his *privata familia*, a small group of his personal followers, some of whom were suspected, perhaps rightly, of using their position to enrich themselves.[6] The most important members of this courtier group were the king's mistress Alice Perrers, William Latimer and John Lord Neville of Raby. Alice Perrers's intimacy with the king began in the 1360s, and she received lavish gifts of jewellery and clothes, together with enough property to establish her as a substantial landowner in her own right. She also exercised much informal influence at court and procured favours for her husband William of Windsor, though when she was accused of corruption in 1376 the king declared that he did not even know she was married, let alone that Windsor was her husband.

William Latimer, who became Chamberlain in 1371, was a figure of rather more political consequence and seems to have been regarded as the leader of the group around the king. He had enjoyed a distinguished military career: he fought with the Black Prince at Crécy when he was only sixteen, and served in Brittany between 1360 and 1367. He was appointed Keeper of Bécherel in 1368 and of Saint Sauveur-le-Vicomte in 1370. He was a wealthy man, and although some of his wealth may have come from the profits of war, he benefited substantially from Edward's patronage. His son-in-law, John Lord Neville, became Steward of the Household in 1371, and he too enjoyed the profits of royal patronage, though he was a man of substantial inherited wealth from his estates in Durham and York-shire. Both Latimer and Neville were soldiers and diplomats. They played a leading part in the organization of the war after 1369; they both had considerable experience of Breton affairs, and their influence at court may be one reason for the important position occupied by Brittany in English strategy from 1372 to 1375. Latimer and Neville were probably the dominant figures at court between 1369 and 1376, and their influence over the king may well have been greater than that of John of Gaunt and his brothers. Closely associated with Latimer and Neville was a small group of chamber knights, who also benefited substantially from Edward's patronage, and a London merchant, Richard Lyons, who became a member of the king's council, an unusual distinction for one of his status. He lent considerable sums to the crown, perhaps as much as £50,000 between 1373 and 1376. This group's unsuccessful conduct of the war incurred them much unpopularity, and discontent at their domination of the king, together with rumours of corruption, self-seeking and extortion, underlay the commons' attack upon them in the Good Parliament of 1376.

When the war reopened in 1369 Charles V was in a position of some strength. The need to raise money for John II's ransom had led to the levying of a salt tax and taxes on merchandise throughout the kingdom, and by 1367 these taxes had come to acquire a look of permanence. Charles was thus able to mobilize French resources for war more effectively than his predecessors, and to pay his troops more regularly. He could also count on the co-operation of his brothers, Louis Duke of Anjou and Philip Duke of Burgundy, and in Bertrand du Guesclin he had perhaps the ablest commander on either side in this phase of the war. The opening campaigns of the war went well for the French. In Aquitaine many towns in the Lot and Garonne valleys went over to them, and by the autumn of 1370 most of the eastern part of the duchy was in French hands. The English response was ineffective: campaigns of the 1340s and 1350s had been essentially plundering raids, launched into enemy territory from secure bases; but after 1369 England was thrown on to the defensive in Aquitaine, and she had little idea how to fight a defensive war. Her response was to revive the tactics of earlier campaigns with *chevauchées* which might lead to the capture of strongpoints in northern France and put pressure on Paris itself. In 1369, for instance, John of Gaunt took an army from Calais to Harfleur, and devastated the Pays de Caux, while in the following year Sir Robert Knolles led an army from

Calais which did much damage in the Ile-de-France; but Charles V refused to give battle and neither *chevauchée* achieved anything. The tactics adopted by both sides produced stalemate. Charles's avoidance of battle denied the English their chance of victory, but he could not succeed in driving the English out of their strongholds around Calais and Bordeaux which they had the will and the resources to defend. And Charles's tactics were damaging to his own subjects: the peasant who declared that he dare not get out of bed in the morning for fear of the English spoke for many of his compatriots,[7] and the unchallenged presence of English armies on French soil not only caused substantial physical hardship to the population but also lowered Charles's prestige.

The Good Parliament

The first signs of political discontent in England over the conduct of the war surfaced in the parliament of February 1371, when the commons refused to grant a subsidy until the king's clerical ministers of state had been replaced by laymen who, unlike their clerical counterparts, would be liable to answer for their misdeeds in the royal courts. The king gave way; William of Wykeham Bishop of Winchester was removed from the office of Chancellor and Thomas Brantingham Bishop of Exeter was removed from the Exchequer. The commons then agreed to a subsidy of £50,000 which was to be raised by the novel expedient of imposing a levy on each parish in England. Unfortunately, however, the government overestimated the number of parishes in the country, and the tax brought in much less than had been expected. The attack upon the clerical ministers in the parliament of 1371 has sometimes been compared with the similar attack in 1340–1. Both crises arose from discontent over the financing of the war, and it is possible that some part in the attack on the king's ministers was played by a group of lay nobles, amongst whom was the warlike young Earl of Pembroke.[8] Pembroke was well placed to speak for those who wanted a more vigorous and successful war: he had a special place in the king's affections, and he had acquitted himself well in Aquitaine. In April 1372 he was appointed Lieutenant in Aquitaine and assembled a fleet to take money and reinforcements to the garrisons there, which were hard pressed by the French. But in June Pembroke's fleet was defeated by the Castilian navy off La Rochelle and Pembroke himself was captured. The defeat deprived the garrisons in Aquitaine of the reinforcements they needed, and less than a month after the destruction of Pembroke's fleet du Guesclin entered Poitiers. By the autumn little more than Gascony itself remained to the English. Pembroke himself spent three years in

captivity, and although he was ransomed in 1375 he died soon afterwards of an illness worsened by the rigours of his imprisonment. His
closeness to the king and his enthusiasm for the war would have
ensured him a place as a leader of the younger generation of nobles,
and his death was yet another misfortune for the king.

After the defeat off La Rochelle, the English government seems to
have lost interest in the defence of Aquitaine. For the next three years
little more than £1,000 was sent to Bordeaux for the defence of the
duchy, and Edward concentrated his attention on Brittany. In July
1372 Duke John IV of Brittany renewed his alliance with England. He
had been under pressure from Edward III to do so for some time, but
he seems also to have feared that Charles V's forces, which were
advancing into the duchy, might revive the rivalries of the civil war
period. Edward undertook to place a force of 600 men at the duke's
disposal and to grant him the earldom of Richmond, to which his
family had an ancient claim and which John of Gaunt relinquished for
the purpose. Duke John for his part promised military support to
Edward if he came to France. An English army under John Lord
Neville landed in Brittany in October 1372, but its arrival sparked
off a reaction against the duke by many of his subjects. Edward
promised further help, and a force of almost 5,000 men under the
Earl of Salisbury was mustered in March 1373; but du Guesclin
invaded the duchy and subjected much of it to a French military
occupation. At the end of April Duke John, left with only a handful
of fortresses, fled to England.

The collapse of Duke John's position made an English response
inevitable. A force was assembled under John of Gaunt which was to
sail for Brittany in May, but its departure was held up until July, and
when it eventually set out it made for Calais instead of Brittany. From
Calais Gaunt took his force on a long march southwards, pillaging
some of the richest country in France. His army eventually arrived in
Bordeaux, but it achieved little, and Gaunt lost almost half his men as
they marched over the Massif Central in winter. Froissart remarked
that 'the greatest and the grandest among them sometimes went for
six days without tasting bread', and Walsingham observed that 'a
great part of his army perished of hunger and disease and almost all
their horses died'. The author of the Anonimalle Chronicle, however,
who evidently had some admiration for Gaunt's achievement,
believed that the army only began to suffer in this way when it
wintered in Gascony.[9] If the purpose of the march was to force the
French to battle it failed; Charles's council debated whether to go on
the offensive against Gaunt's army, but in the event their belief in the
military superiority of the English was still sufficiently strong to
inhibit them from offering an open challenge, and they agreed to
pursue the usual defensive tactics. Some French troops had to be

withdrawn from Brittany to pursue and harry Gaunt's forces, but the diversion of the expedition from its original destination served to embitter relations between Duke John and Gaunt, which were in any case strained after a quarrel between them over the wages due to their troops, and the English garrisons at Brest, Bécherel (a fortress some twenty miles south of St Malo), and Saint-Sauveur-le-Vicomte were still hard pressed by du Guesclin's forces.

Preparations for another expedition to Brittany were under discussion in May 1374, and in August Duke John, together with Edmund Langley Earl of Cambridge, the Earl of March and Edward Despenser agreed to take 4,000 men to the duchy for a year. The leaders were to receive wages for their men for six months, and for the rest of the year they were to pay the troops out of the ransoms they expected to take. But the expedition was held up all through the winter, and Bécherel fell to the French on 1 November. Not until April 1375 did the army land in Brittany. At the same time, the English government responded favourably to peace overtures from Pope Gregory XI, who was anxious on the one hand to unite the rulers of western Christendom in a crusade, and on the other to tax the western churches so as to fund both this endeavour and his political and diplomatic schemes in Italy. The papal mediator, the Archbishop of Ravenna, accordingly proposed a meeting between English and French negotiators at Bruges in March 1375. In effect, the English government was pursuing two policies at once. It may be that the Breton expedition was intended to keep up pressure on the French to make the sort of concessions the English would feel able to accept, but it is equally possible that the confused direction of English policy reflected conflicting influences at court. Latimer and Neville had substantial experience of campaigning in Brittany, and Latimer had some personal interests there to protect. Gaunt, on the other hand, lent his weight to the policy of negotiating a settlement with France, perhaps in the hope that a peace or lengthy truce would reduce the financial pressure which was politically damaging to the crown.[10]

Both policies went ahead successfully. Duke John and the Earl of Cambridge laid siege to Quimperlé, probably on 23 June, and after a heavy English assault the garrison agreed that if they were not relieved within a week they would surrender. Meanwhile at Bruges a truce for one year was agreed on 26 May. Under the terms of the truce and the modifications agreed to it on 27 June, the siege of Quimperlé would be lifted, Duke John would withdraw his army from Brittany, Saint-Sauveur-le-Vicomte would be handed over to papal mediators who would deliver it to the King of France when the truce expired, and the English would receive 40,000 francs in compensation. The truce also provided for the continuation of discussions about a permanent peace between the two realms. To many in England the truce of Bruges seemed literally a sell-out: the French forced the garrison at Saint Sauveur to hand the fortress over to them directly in return for 53,000 francs. Some of this money was pocketed by the English captain there, Thomas Catterton, who was regarded as an accomplice to the deal and was subsequently accused of treason. Meanwhile Cambridge and March were ordered to raise the siege of Quimperlé and return home at once. They had engaged soldiers for a year, but had been deprived by the truce of most of the ransoms which were to pay the troops' wages for the second half of the year.

The response in England to the agreement reached at Bruges was hostile. Walsingham wrote that the English broke off the siege of Quimperlé and returned home sadly and slowly.[11] Rumours of treachery and corruption soon began to circulate. Anger at the court's conduct of the war burst into the open at the meeting of parliament in April 1376. Ever since its own time this parliament has been known as the 'Good Parliament'; it has been thoroughly analysed by modern historians,[12] and the Anonimalle Chronicle of St Mary's Abbey, York, preserves an account of the deliberations amongst the commons which surpasses in its detail any other surviving account of the debates in a fourteenth-century parliament.[13]

The parliament opened on 28 April with the usual request for a subsidy. Two days later, according to the Anonimalle Chronicle, the commons assembled in the Chapter House of Westminster Abbey, and a knight from the south country opened the debate on the subsidy with an attack on the government for mis-spending earlier subsidies. He suggested that the king should finance the war out of his own resources, and he hinted at corruption at court. Another knight, perhaps emboldened by his companion's hints, argued that the removal of the wool staple from Calais, where it had helped to pay part of the cost of defending the town, had been for the private profit of Lord Latimer, Richard Lyons and others. But a third knight made the significant point that the commons were not likely to progress far without the agreement of the lords, and suggested that they should ask the king to appoint a group of prelates and magnates to help them in their deliberations. All agreed to this, and then another knight, Sir Peter de la Mare, who was the Earl of March's steward, summed up the debate so skilfully that he was chosen by the commons to speak on their behalf before the lords. This was the first recorded occasion on which one member of the commons was chosen to act as a spokesman for them all. The Anonimalle Chronicle's account of de la Mare's selection does not give the impression that it was usual to choose a speaker, though it is possible that the small groups which had appeared before the lords on behalf of the commons in earlier parliaments had chosen one of their number to speak on their behalf. De la Mare's connections probably did as much as his eloquence to ensure his choice as speaker. The Earl of March had substantial grievances of his own against the court, and if the complaints of the commons and the hostility of some of the nobility were to be effectively co-ordinated, de la Mare's influence would be crucial. De la Mare asked for the Earl of March to be appointed to the advisory group, together with the Earls of Warwick, Stafford and Suffolk. Henry Percy, Guy Brian, Henry Scrope and Richard Stafford represented the barons and bannerets, while the Bishops of London, Norwich, Carlisle and St David's were appointed from amongst the prelates.

This committee held a series of meetings with the commons, and the commons, led by de la Mare, appeared before the lords on a number of occasions, with John of Gaunt presiding in place of the king who was too ill to attend. De la Mare made a series of charges against Latimer, Neville, Alice Perrers and Richard Lyons. He also declared that the commons would not proceed with the business of parliament until the king had removed Latimer, Neville and Alice Perrers from court and agreed that a new council consisting of three bishops, three earls and three barons should be named in parliament. The lords agreed to this proposal immediately, and established a new council which consisted of the Archbishop of Canterbury, William of Wykeham Bishop of Winchester, and eight of those who had been appointed to the advisory committee, including March, Arundel and Stafford.

The commons then proceeded with their charges against Latimer and Lyons. The principal charges against Latimer were that he had made improper profits out of the campaign in Brittany and that he was responsible for the loss of Bécherel and Saint-Sauveur. Bécherel had been under the command of one of his retainers, and another had been Constable of Saint-Sauveur, though in all probability he had not been involved in its surrender. This charge against Latimer was almost certainly baseless, though it is more difficult to assess whether he had made undue profits for himself out of the campaign in Brittany. Lyons was charged on his own with two relatively minor financial offences, but much more important were the accusations against Latimer and Lyons jointly. The commons alleged that they had lent the king 20,000 marks at 33 per cent interest, that they had sold licences to export wool to ports other than Calais, and had imposed a charge of 11s per sack for each licence granted. It is doubtful whether these last two charges could properly be regarded as offences, for such licences had frequently been sold in the past, and the surviving evidence does not provide conclusive proof one way or the other about the usurious nature of Latimer's and Lyons's financial dealings. The commons also brought charges of corruption and extortion against Neville and a number of other courtiers and merchants, while Alice Perrers was accused of misappropriating the king's goods and of bribery; but it is clear that Latimer and Lyons were the principal objects of the commons' hostility. The commons acted as a body in putting the charges against Latimer, Lyons and their associates, and they were tried before the lords in parliament. This process, which became known as impeachment, seems to have arisen by accident when de la Mare declared that he and his colleagues would maintain their charges in common.[14] The precedent thus set by the commons became of great significance in later political crises, for it gave the commons a means of dealing with unpopular royal officials and ministers, with the sanction of non-cooperation in the business of parliament if their charges were not heard. Latimer pleaded for time to prepare a defence to the charges against him, but William of Wykeham insisted that he should answer them immediately. He was eventually placed in the custody of the Earl Marshal, the Earl of March, while Lyons was sentenced to imprisonment and all his goods were forfeited. Alice Perrers was removed from the royal household, and Neville was dismissed from the king's council, though he was not imprisoned.

The author of the *Anonimalle Chronicle* had no doubt that the initiative in pressing the charges against the courtiers, and in making political demands on the crown, came from the commons, with de la Mare acting as their spokesman. Yet the successful pressing home of their attack owed something to the advice of the committee of lords established at the beginning of the parliament. The grievances which the commons presented were not just their own but were shared by some amongst the magnates, whose support was important when it came to pressing charges before the lords. The respective roles of the nobility and the commons in the Good Parliament, however, were different from those in earlier political crises. There was no Thomas of Lancaster amongst the nobility in 1376 to give leadership to an aristocratic group seeking to curb the king's power, nor were the courtiers whom the commons attacked men of such power and wealth as the Despensers. The crisis grew out of the commons' hostility to a clique at court whose handling of royal finances aroused suspicions of corruption and who were thought to have advanced their own interests by manipulating the elderly and enfeebled king.

After the downfall of the courtiers, the king's youngest sons benefited from royal patronage. Edmund Langley was appointed Constable of Dover Castle, an office previously held by Latimer, while Woodstock was granted the office of Constable of England, which was hereditary in the Bohun family but had been delegated when necessary to other lords after the death of the last Bohun earl of Hereford, Woodstock's father-in-law. Both men also received annuities of 1,000 marks, which went some considerable way towards endowing them at a level appropriate to their rank. The victories of the court's opponents did not, however, endure for long. John of

Gaunt, who had represented the king throughout the parliament, regarded its proceedings as an unacceptable interference with the royal prerogative. According to Walsingham, whose account of the parliament is admittedly full of malice and prejudice, Gaunt was amazed at the commons attitude: 'Do they think,' he said, 'that they are kings or princes in this land? I think they do not know how powerful I am.'[15]

The death of the Black Prince and the illness of the king meant that Gaunt was in effect ruler of England in Edward's last year, and it was his intention to reverse the acts of the Good Parliament and punish those who had instigated them. His fiercest wrath was reserved for William of Wykeham, because of the part he had played in the impeachment of Latimer, and for Peter de la Mare. Wykeham was arrested, deprived of his temporalities, and accused of corruption when he was Keeper of the Privy Seal and Chancellor before 1371, while de la Mare was arrested and imprisoned in Nottingham Castle. The council of nine ceased to be active, and Latimer and Lyons were released from imprisonment. Furthermore, in a move which Gaunt may well have opposed and which illustrated the limits of his influence over the king even at this time, Alice Perrers was pardoned and reinstated at court. The royalist reaction was complete, and those who had opposed the court were duly punished. Gaunt had used the strength of his position as the representative of the king to break up the opposition and to reassert the authority of the crown. Thomas Walsingham believed that Gaunt was motivated by vindictiveness, and that he himself had designs on the crown once Edward III was dead. Gaunt may have played a part in drawing up the agreement over the succession to the crown which sought to restrict its descent to the male heirs of Edward III, thus making the house of Lancaster the inheritor of the crown if the young Richard Prince of Wales were to die childless. Beyond this, however, there no evidence that Gaunt sought the crown for himself, and indeed throughout his career, Gaunt was conspicuous for his loyalty to the king. Even when Richard II spurned that loyalty for a time, Gaunt did not associate himself with opposition to the court. Wycliffe maintained that Gaunt regarded political instability as one of the greatest evils that could befall a state; and Gaunt's political career suggests that he believed that political stability was best ensured by the maintenance of the prerogatives of the monarchy.[16]

The Good Parliament had refused to grant a subsidy, and accordingly another parliament was summoned for January 1377. Despite Gaunt's reversal of many of the acts of the Good Parliament this parliament proved remarkably compliant. It quashed the sentences imposed on those convicted in the Good Parliament, and, at the suggestion of the commons, agreed to a poll tax of 4d on every lay person over fourteen years of age. Parliament's acquiescence in the reversal of the acts of its predecessor has led to suggestions that Gaunt interfered with the elections to the commons. A smaller than usual proportion of members who had sat in the Good Parliament were re-elected to this parliament, but it is hard to find evidence that the government tried to ensure the election of their own supporters. Indeed, although the commons appointed as Speaker Sir Thomas Hungerford, who was Gaunt's Steward of South Parts, they were not quite as docile as has sometimes been supposed. They demanded the release of de la Mare and submitted a petition protesting against the annulment of statutes except by parliament. They seem, however, to have had little support amongst the lords, and the opposition which undoubtedly existed to Gaunt's reversal of the acts of the Good Parliament lacked leadership and co-ordination.

The ease and speed with which the acts of the Good Parliament were set aside revealed the strength of the court in the face of opposition from the commons and a group of discontented nobles. But although Gaunt's defence of the royal prerogative, and particularly the royal right to choose ministers freely, was vigorous and effective, he drew upon himself much unpopularity. Thomas Walsingham, who stood in the St Albans tradition of recording history from the baronial point of view wrote a ferociously hostile attack on him which may well reflect popular feeling.[17] Gaunt aroused the opposition of the Church by his attack upon William of Wykeham and his refusal to include Wykeham in the general pardon offered in honour of the king's golden jubilee. This so incensed William Courtenay, the Bishop of London, that he summoned John Wycliffe, whom Gaunt had used to stir up public opinion against Wykeham, to St Paul's to answer for his erroneous teachings. Gaunt was determined to defend Wycliffe, and he ordered the new Marshal, Henry Percy, to arrest anyone who opposed his heterodox protégé. This was taken by the Londoners as a threat to extend the Marshal's jurisdiction to the City itself, and intensified rumours that Gaunt was intent upon curtailing the City's liberties and replacing the Lord Mayor with a captain appointed by the crown. The mob rose and attacked Gaunt's palace of the Savoy, hanging his coat of arms upside down as the sign of a traitor. Rumours that Gaunt had designs on the crown were flying about, and it was alleged that he was a changeling, a butcher's son, substituted for the queen's own son who had been smothered at birth.

Court and Councils, 1377–1385

The summer of 1377, however, was an inopportune moment for the renewal of political conflict. The king was close to death, and the truce with France was due to expire on 24 June. The imminence of these two events concentrated the minds of the protagonists and induced them to patch up their differences. Princess Joan, the Black Prince's widow, successfully mediated between Gaunt and the Londoners, and at her request Gaunt authorized the restoration of William of Wykeham's temporalities on 18 June. Three days later the king died, deserted, so Walsingham said, by his courtiers and attended only by a priest who administered the last rites.[18] If Walsingham's story is true, the courtiers were no doubt anxious to establish their positions around the new king, Richard II, who was ten years of age at his accession.

The new reign started with a series of gestures deliberately intended to mark a break with the immediate past and to offer hope of a fresh start. John of Gaunt and the citizens of London were publicly reconciled, Wykeham and Gaunt formally resolved their quarrel, and, in a gesture to the commons, Peter de la Mare was released from prison. The young king's coronation was celebrated with great magnificence, and four new earls were created: the king's uncle Thomas of Woodstock was created Earl of Buckingham, John Mowbray of Axholme became Earl of Nottingham, Henry Percy, the wealthiest and most powerful of the northern lords, became Earl of Northumberland, and the earldom of Huntingdon was bestowed upon the king's tutor, the Poitevin nobleman Guichard d'Angle. The French attacks on the south coast, in the course of which Rye was seized and burnt, detracted only a little from the hopeful atmosphere in which the reign began.

In the arrangements that now had to be made for the government of the country during the king's minority the political conflicts of the previous year could not be so easily forgotten. Of all the kings since the Conquest, only Henry III had succeeded as a minor, and during his minority William Marshal had been entrusted with royal authority and the title *Rector regis et regni*. There was a precedent in France for a regency by the king's mother, Blanche of Castile, during the minority of Louis IX, though there had been resistance to her regency on the grounds that she was a woman and a foreigner. But in 1377 none of these precedents was followed; no regent or protector was appointed, and instead the pretence was made that the king himself was fully competent to govern. All business was transacted in his name, and a continual council was established which had responsibility for the conduct of routine business but which had no control over the king himself or those who surrounded him at court. John of Gaunt would have been the obvious candidate for the office of regent or protector by virtue of his kinship with the king and his pre-eminent wealth and status; but his unpopularity with the Church, the Londoners and the commons as a result of the events of 1376 would probably have ensured a revival of political conflict had he been in control of the government when it sought another subsidy from the commons. The king's mother, Princess Joan, had shown her skill as a mediator in the last weeks of Edward's life, and she seems to have been widely popular. Her influence over Richard must have been substantial in these years, but she had no formal role in government, perhaps because she was a woman and thus inexperienced in politics, and perhaps because, though popular, it is not clear how widely she was respected or how far her colourful past, magnified by rumour, counted against her.

The three continual councils which held office from July 1377 until January 1380 have been unjustly denigrated by historians. Their membership was designed to ensure a balance amongst the various estates of prelates, magnates, barons and bannerets, and knights bachelor. The king's uncles, Lancaster, Cambridge and Buckingham, were not included on any of the councils, though they were given power to deal with councillors suspected of using their position for their personal advantage. The Earl of Arundel sat on the first and third councils, March on the first and second, Stafford on the second, and Suffolk on the third, but it is difficult to interpret their appointments as representing the supremacy of any particular faction. Indeed, representation of the various estates was perhaps more important than the representation of various political factions which historians have tried to identify in analysing the membership of the continual councils. The belief that such bodies should have members drawn from each of the estates of prelates, magnates, barons and bannerets, and knights bachelor, seems to appear for the first time in the Good Parliament. The distinction of status within the ranks of the nobility was becoming more precise and rigid, and the barons in parliament, who by 1377 had become a group distinguished from the other landowners by the regularity of their summons to parliament, had now attained the status of a minor nobility. The omission of Gaunt and his two younger brothers is striking, and although Gaunt in particular had ample opportunity, by virtue of his status and his nearness in blood to the young king, to make his influence felt behind the scenes, his power had evidently ebbed since its high tide in the early months of 1377, despite Walsingham's assertion that he manipulated the council indirectly.[19]

In the early years of the reign the government's principal preoccupation was the war. Because of the king's youth no new initiative in negotiation could be expected, and military leadership necessarily devolved upon his uncles and other adult nobles, especially the Earls of Arundel and Buckingham. The government's strategy between 1377 and 1383 was to maintain pressure on France by launching *chevauchées* and by acquiring, or trying to acquire, a ring of fortresses along the French coast. In 1378 the English took leases on Brest and Cherbourg, but English attempts to seize other strongpoints failed completely; Gaunt besieged St Malo for five months before giving up and returning home; Arundel's attempt to take Harfleur was repulsed; an attempt to seize Nantes in the winter of 1379–80 failed, and in the following year Buckingham led a march through north-west France and spent the autumn and winter unsuccessfully besieging Nantes again. Although these fortresses were described in 1378 as 'fine and noble entries and ports to grieve the enemy',[20] the policy of trying to develop a 'barbican' in France was presented to the commons as essentially a defensive measure, perhaps to reassure the commons that the government was taking some action to combat the French and Castilian naval activity in the Channel which had led to raids on the south coast in 1377 and a French invasion of the Isle of Wight in the same summer.

These expeditions, together with the defence of Calais and Gascony, proved enormously expensive. Over £467,000 was spent in the various theatres of war between 1376 and 1381. The cost of defending Calais, Cherbourg and Brest amounted to £157,000, and the naval operations in these years cost over £100,000.[21] By contrast, less than £45,000 was spent on the defence of Gascony: the government's strategic priorities were northern France and the war at sea. Taxation reached unprecedented heights between 1376 and 1381, but there was little to show for it: naval operations and the maintenance of garrisons in France consumed much of the available resources, and the commons' complaints about the burden of taxation became steadily more vociferous. In the Gloucester parliament of 1378 they went so far as to deny that they had any responsibility to finance foreign war, arguing that they should be taxed only for the defence of the realm. In 1379 they voted another poll tax, which yielded a very substantial proportion of the amount assessed, and in the Northampton parliament of November 1380 they offered three alternatives, another poll tax, a sales tax or a subsidy of the usual kind. The lords encouraged them to agree to another poll tax, at the unprecedentedly high rate of 1s per head. The author of the *Anonimalle Chronicle* did not believe that sufficient thought had been given to the grant of such a tax, and he wrote that 'the subsidies were granted irresponsibly'. The commons did not lay down the principles according to which the tax was to be collected with the same concern for detail that they had shown in 1379, when they had proposed a graduated scale according to wealth, which made the tax 'probably the most equitable of all the direct taxes of the fourteenth century'.[22] This time they contented themselves with the vague exhortation that the rich should help the poor. The tax failed to produce the expected yield, and the government resorted to special commissions of inquiry to investigate evasion of the tax.

The commons' complaints about the burden of taxation were not, however, accompanied by attacks upon individual ministers or officials. Their ostensible reason for seeking an end to the system of continual councils in January 1380 was that the king had now reached the same age as 'his noble grandfather at the time of his coronation',[23] but they also expressed some concern about the state of royal finances and the royal household. No individual was attacked, but the commons successfully petitioned for the appointment of a commission of inquiry, which was duly established, though there is no evidence that it ever met. It is possible that the Earl of Buckingham's influence lay behind the commons' concern over royal finances. The Speaker in this parliament, Sir Thomas Gildesborough, was one of Buckingham's retainers and the subsidy which the commons granted was specifically earmarked for the expedition to Brittany which Buckingham intended to lead in the coming summer. Buckingham's own personal position too was in part dependent on the solvency of the Exchequer: when he was created earl at Richard's coronation he was granted an annuity of £1,000 a year to maintain his estate, and he also had an annuity of £300 to maintain himself and his wife until she came of age. These annuities were assigned upon the revenues from the alien priories, an insecure source and one which depended upon the continuation of the war with France.

The commissions established to inquire into the evasion of the poll tax granted in November 1380 sparked off a series of risings in southeast England and East Anglia which are collectively known as the Peasants' Revolt. The risings, however, were much more than merely a series of protests by social groups who feared that they might be brought permanently within the taxation net. Conflicts arising out of the changes in agrarian society following the Black Death and subsequent outbreaks of plague probably underlay the revolt, though in Kent in particular there was evidence of hostility to the king's ministers and officials. In Kent the revolt was given some coherence and ideological underpinning by preachers who proclaimed the equality of all men at the beginning of the world and perhaps encouraged some of the rebels to believe that a social revolution was within their grasp. The Kentish rebels managed to enter the city of London and make common cause with those in the city who had their own grievances against the mercantile oligarchy of the city. Gaunt's Savoy palace was sacked, and the rebels broke into the Tower and murdered the chancellor and the treasurer. Richard's courage in face of this threat not just to his own authority but to social order is well documented, though whether his offer when he met the rebels from Essex at Mile End to grant them the charters of manumission from serfdom that they demanded was genuine or merely an attempt to disperse the rebels and buy time is debatable. It seems likely that his attitude to the peasants' demands was essentially unsympathetic, and although some modern writers have suggested that he was affected by the apparent respect for his kingly office that the rebels displayed, it is likely that the lesson he eventually drew from the rebellion was authoritarian rather than libertarian, and that subjects owed a duty of obedience to their king.[24]

In the short run, the revolt had important financial consequences for the government. In the November parliament of 1381 the commons expressed the view that it was the oppressive behaviour of officials that had brought about the revolt. They were mainly concerned to avoid another rising, and the possibility of arousing social unrest thus became for the first time an element in their political calculations. Not only did the parliament of November 1381 refuse a subsidy, but two subsequent parliaments, in May 1382 and February 1383, also refused to grant an adequate tax, in spite of considerable pressure from the lords and the council. This unprecedented refusal to provide finance for the war made it impossible for the lords to implement their plans for an expedition to re-establish English influence in Flanders, and explains the commons' willingness to accept the Bishop of Norwich's proposal to lead a crusade in Flanders.[25]

During the November parliament, the commons returned to the attack on the royal household, complaining of the 'outrageous' number of servants in the household, and the ruinous purveyance to which so large a household gave rise. The king agreed to the establishment of a committee to examine 'the estate and governance of the king's person and his household, and to ordain sufficient remedy'. The commons asked the committee to appoint 'good and worthy men' to be around the king, and to ensure that the household was of such a size that the king could 'live honestly of his own'. This committee, unlike its predecessor, began its work promptly, and one result of its activity was that the Earl of Arundel and Michael de la Pole were placed in the household 'to advise and govern' the king.[26]

The commons were concerned not just about the burden the swollen household placed on royal finances but also about the influence being exercised over the king by members of the household. There were some grounds for their concern: within the household the former servants and followers of the Black Prince naturally had an important place, and two of them, Aubrey de Vere and Simon Burley, who held the offices of Chamberlain and Under-Chamberlain, became especially close to the king and took decisions on petitions that were addressed to the king himself. They thus assumed some degree of control over royal patronage, and Aubrey de Vere also took the fateful step of introducing at court his young nephew Robert, Earl of Oxford, who soon became one of Richard's closest associates. As

Richard grew up, he came to place his trust in these men, and to lavish favour and office upon them.

Robert de Vere came of ancient lineage, for the first Earl of Oxford had received his title and the hereditary chamberlainship of England from the Empress Matilda. But by the beginning of the fourteenth century the de Veres had become 'the most insignificant of English earls'. Their only substantial estate was in the Colne valley in Essex, with Castle Hedingham as its centre. Robert de Vere had married well: his bride was Philippa, second daughter and heiress to the English estates of Enguerrand de Coucy Earl of Bedford and Isabella Edward III's eldest daughter. The Bedford estates in England were not extensive, but Richard soon made up for this with substantial grants in Essex, Kent and Devon, and in 1385 the king conferred on him the title of Marquis of Dublin with a grant of palatine powers in the whole of the lordship of Ireland. The title of marquis was hitherto unknown in the English peerage, and when de Vere took his place in parliament between the dukes and the earls Walsingham remarked that the other nobles were furious, for they saw one who was in no way their superior in valour rising above them merely by virtue of royal favour.[27] In 1386 Richard added insult to injury from the nobles' point of view by creating de Vere Duke of Ireland. The nobles' animosity towards de Vere followed him beyond the grave: in 1395, when his body was brought back to England for reburial at Colne Priory, most of the magnates pointedly stayed away from the ceremony 'because they had not yet forgotten the hatred they bore him'.[28]

Second only to de Vere in influence over the king and unpopularity with the nobility was Michael de la Pole, son of Sir William de la Pole, the Hull merchant who had played a prominent part in Edward III's schemes for manipulating the wool trade. Pole may have seen the opportunities for advancement and profit at court when he was placed in the royal household to supervise the king in 1381, and he rose rapidly in royal favour. He was appointed Chancellor in 1383, and played an important part in the conduct of foreign policy until his fall in October 1386. His most significant territorial acquisition was the Ufford earldom of Suffolk, which escheated to the king when William de Ufford died, possibly from a heart attack, after a meeting with the commons in the parliament of September 1382. There was nothing irregular about Pole's acquisition of the Suffolk inheritance, but some of his peers regarded him as a creature of the king, unworthy of the dignity of an earldom. When he was impeached in 1386 Sir Richard Scrope, defending him, felt it necessary to rebut the accusation that he had been 'raised from low estate to this honour of earl',[29] and to point out that he had possessed sufficient means to maintain his estate as a banneret, the rank immediately below that of earl. This defence did not satisfy Walsingham, however, who described Pole as a man 'more suited to commerce than war'.[30]

Both Michael de la Pole and Simon Burley, the Under-Chamberlain and tutor to the king, were former retainers of the Black Prince and both had served him with some distinction in war. Burley did not receive a title from Richard, though it is possible that the king proposed to confer the earldom of Huntingdon on him in 1385 but was balked by parliament. He did, however, receive substantial grants of land, including property which had belonged to the widow of William de Clinton Earl of Huntingdon and which Edward III had intended to use as the endowment for three religious houses.[31] In 1384 Richard appointed Burley Warden of the Cinque Ports and Constable of Dover Castle, a grant which understandably aroused the suspicions of those nobles opposed to Richard's conduct of the war. Burley's rise was remarkably rapid: Knighton said that 'in a few years of service to the king he accumulated a fortune worth 3,000 marks a year', and the Kirkstall Chronicler said that 'no equal of his rank was more glorious in outward apparel; he excelled all lords in the equipment of his horses and worldly show'.[32] None of these courtiers were men of great substance in their own right. In 1387, de Vere sought to protect his own position by recruiting an army in the royal earldom of Chester rather than relying on his own and his friends' retinues; and Michael de la Pole simply fled overseas. Neither they nor Burley possessed the extensive lordship over men which was necessary to buttress their position at court; indeed, their rise had been so rapid that they had scarcely had time to establish such lordship, and like the Despensers in the 1320s the weakness of their position was that it depended ultimately on royal favour.

The first hint of opposition to the court and to the flow of patronage towards favourites and household officials came in 1382 in a dispute over the farming out of the inheritance of the Earl of March during the minority of the heir. Richard had intended to grant the custody of the inheritance piecemeal to members of his household, but the Chancellor refused to seal the grants and was dismissed 'because', said Walsingham, 'he had administered in a praiseworthy and careful manner'.[33] The king eventually had to back down and grant the custody of the inheritance to a group of magnates. Much more substantial grievances against the court, however, surfaced with the failure of the Bishop of Norwich's crusade in Flanders in the following year.

Although the marriage of Margaret of Flanders to Philip of Burgundy in 1369 was a major diplomatic setback for England, English hopes of retaining some influence there revived in 1382 when Philip van Artevelde, grandson of the Flemish leader who had allied with Edward III, led a revolt in Ghent against the Count of Flanders and sought aid from Richard II. Such a prospect was too attractive to miss, and in the spring of 1382 the government began preparations for an expedition to go to the aid of Ghent. At the same time, however, the Count of Flanders appealed for support to his suzerain Charles VI, and the Duke of Burgundy raised an army which defeated the Flemish rebels at Roosebeke on 27 November 1382. Philip van Artevelde was killed, but Ghent still held out and England was determined to support her. To get round the inadequate grants voted by parliament, the Bishop of Norwich, Henry Despenser, offered to lead an army in the guise of a crusade against the French adherents of the anti-Pope and to finance it in part by selling indulgences. This extraordinary proposition was welcomed by the commons, for financial reasons. It was opposed by the nobility on grounds both of expediency and principle, yet it went ahead and the bishop incurred still more aristocratic hostility when he refused to accept the Earl of Arundel as his lay lieutenant. The crusade won some initial successes, meeting little resistance in northern Flanders; but Ypres put up an unexpectedly stubborn defence, and Charles VI took the oriflamme and marched to its relief. Lancaster and Buckingham assembled their retinues and set out for Kent, expecting that the king would join them and that they would all sail to Flanders to help the bishop; but the council, according to the Monk of Westminster, 'produced the reply that it was impossible in so short a time as a week or two for the king to have an army ready... and that the royal treasury did not contain the means to fulfil his aim'.[34] The bishop was left without reinforcements, and had to return to England. Ghent held out for another two years, but English hopes of re-establishing some influence in Flanders had effectively vanished.

The failure of the Bishop of Norwich's crusade was followed by a change of approach in England. Michael de la Pole, who had been appointed Chancellor earlier the same year, believed that the most advantageous course was to reopen peace talks with France, and the government of the young Charles VI, which was perhaps weaker than the English realized, proved willing to negotiate. Envoys of the two sides met in December 1383 and quickly produced a series of articles which were to be examined by both governments. A truce was agreed on 26 January 1384 to last until 1 October, and it was eventually extended until 1 May 1385.

In the parliament of November 1383, however, the Bishop of Norwich came under attack from the lords. According to Westminster, the Chancellor denounced his conduct of the crusade, saying that he had left his undertaking unfulfilled, had drained away the country's treasure, and had 'brought the military situation to virtual ruin'.[35] The bishop was unable to offer any effective defence, and was sentenced to the loss of his temporalities. The failure of the crusade brought aristocratic opposition to the court out into the open. The lords in parliament launched an attack on the king's policies and advisers, complaining that he 'clung to unsound policies and for this reason excluded wholesome guidance from his entourage'. They went on to argue that 'in former times the most illustrious of his royal predecessors had been ruled by the advice of their lords, and for as long as the control of those lords had been accepted the realm of England was a land of plenty and brilliant prosperity'.[36] This starry-eyed view of the benign effects of aristocratic influence in government was understandably unacceptable to Richard, who replied that he was unwilling to be ruled or led exclusively by the advice of the lords, and there the matter rested for the time being.

The king had fended off this criticism with little difficulty; the commons did not support the lords, perhaps because they disagreed with them over the Bishop of Norwich's crusade, and no clear leader of aristocratic discontent with the court had yet emerged. In the next parliament, however, which assembled at Salisbury in April 1384, the Earl of Arundel launched an attack on the king, saying that 'this country, which as you know began long ago through bad government to lose strength, is at present almost in a state of decay', and unless a remedy was promptly applied it would soon suffer 'enormous setbacks and crippling losses'. The king replied with equal vigour, rounding on Arundel and saying that 'If . . . it is supposed to be my fault that there is misgovernment in the kingdom you lie in your teeth. You can go to the devil!' His reply reduced the lords to silence, as well it might, but Gaunt tried to heal the breach and according to Westminster 'delivered a speech in which he skilfully glossed the earl's remarks, so that the king's anger was assuaged'.[37]

Gaunt's mediation, however, could not hide the deterioration in relations between the king and some of the leading nobles, and Gaunt himself now felt the hostility of those round the king. The episode during the Salisbury parliament in 1384 when Gaunt was accused of treason by a mad Carmelite friar was perhaps of less significance than has sometimes been supposed, not least because Richard's reaction to the accusation was less hysterical than one chronicler alleged. It does not seem likely that Richard ordered Gaunt's immediate execution, as the Monk of Westminster supposed, and it is perhaps safer to accept Walsingham's story that he confronted Gaunt with the charge. Gaunt denied it and Richard accepted his word.[38] More serious was the plot to kill Gaunt which was apparently hatched at the conclusion of a tournament held on 13 and 14 February 1385 by some of the nobles round the king, chief amongst whom were the Earls of Nottingham, Oxford and Salisbury. The Monk of Westminster suggested that the plot originated with disagreements in the council about the conduct of the war,[39] but it is also likely that the king's friends resented Gaunt's influence at court and the king's reliance on him for advice and mediation. Gaunt was forewarned of the conspiracy and unobtrusively left the tournament. Ten days later, however, he went armed to the king at Sheen and reproached him 'for having kept such bad counsellors about him for so long'. Gaunt advised the king to 'get rid of them altogether and to cling in future to men of sounder judgement'. He also reminded Richard that it was 'shameful for a king in his own kingdom, where he was lord of all, to avenge himself by means of private murder when he was himself above the law and had the power to vouchsafe life and limb with a nod'.[40] The king mollified Gaunt with promises that he would improve in future; but Richard was left in no doubt how his uncle felt about his choice of friends and advisers. Gaunt's feelings were widely shared amongst the nobility. At a council in March 1385 the prelates and some lay lords 'were bitter in their complaints against those councillors who moved in the king's immediate circle for having induced him to countenance the Duke of Lancaster's being callously murdered in secret'.[41] Gaunt's loyalty to the crown was not in question, but it was placed under some strain by the preponderant influence Richard's friends now enjoyed at court. While not seeking to associate himself with the more public hostility to the court which Arundel for example, had displayed in the previous year, Gaunt's warning to the king of the danger of relying on 'evil counsel' was unequivocal and none the less significant for being delivered in a private interview rather than in parliament or council.

The expiry of the truce in May 1385 and the despatch of a French army to Scotland under Jean de Vienne brought a temporary halt to political conflict. The threat of a Franco-Scottish invasion over the northern border was imminent, and Charles VI was preparing an invasion of England by sea. The government's response was to assemble a large army, with Richard at its head, to invade Scotland. The campaign has something of the character of a formal opening to the young king's military career. He was now eighteen years of age, two years older than Edward III had been on the inglorious Stanhope Park campaign, and ready to lead his first military expedition. On crossing the border into Teviotdale he bestowed new titles on the leaders of his army: the Earl of Buckingham became Duke of Gloucester, the Earl of Cambridge Duke of York, and Michael de la Pole received the earldom of Suffolk. It is possible that Richard granted earldoms to Simon Burley and John Lord Neville, and that parliament subsequently refused to ratify the grants.[42] The army marched to Edinburgh without meeting any resistance, and Richard then insisted on turning back in spite of Gaunt's proposal that they should cross the Firth of Forth and ravage further north. Richard's reasons for turning back were sound, and show some concern for the welfare of his troops: he rounded on Gaunt and declared that 'though you and the other lords here might have plenty of food for yourselves, the rest, the humbler and lowlier members of our army, would certainly not find over there such a wealth of victuals as would prevent their dying of hunger', and he retreated to Newcastle.[43] Meanwhile the French and Scots had invaded Cumberland, and it was left to the local forces led by Northumberland's son Hotspur to put them to flight.

The government issued a feudal summons for the Scottish campaign, the last time in English history that this method of raising an army was used. The reason, however, was financial rather than military: in the previous parliament the commons had granted a subsidy on condition that if the king failed to lead an army to the continent in the summer of 1385 half of the subsidy was to be cancelled. Rather than levy the whole subsidy in defiance of the restriction imposed by parliament, the government proposed to levy scutage for the expedition. But the levy aroused much opposition. In the parliament of October 1385 which followed the king's return from Scotland, the government was forced to abandon it and the king had to face renewed criticism from the commons over his handling of finance. The commons complained that the king's extravagance was impoverishing the crown, that the revenues of the Exchequer could be increased if the king took better advice about his gifts, and that the profits from feudal incidents could be increased if the king took advice about their value instead of granting them out 'hastily'. The king agreed to appoint a committee of nine 'to survey his estate, and inquire into his revenues and diminish his expenses'.[44] Such an investigating committee can hardly have been welcome to him, smacking as it did of earlier attempts to examine and control his powers of patronage; but the Chancellor, Michael de la Pole, ignored the ordinance and the reforms it envisaged were not implemented.

Both the financial problems of the government and the tension between Richard and some of his nobles increased sharply during the following year. In August 1385 the Portuguese had defeated the Castilians at the battle of Aljubarrota, and this offered Gaunt an opportunity to press his claim to the throne of Castile. It is unlikely that Gaunt seriously thought he could conquer Castile; parliament voted a subsidy for his expedition in October 1385, and he supplemented the grant out of his own resources, but his diplomatic preparations were as thorough as his military plans, and he probably hoped by taking a large army to a weakened Castile to extract the best terms he could for a diplomatic settlement there rather than to enforce a military solution.

Gaunt's departure in July 1386, however, provoked Charles VI to prepare a massive invasion of England with the same intention that had lain behind the planned invasion in the previous year: to put pressure on England to resume negotiations for peace. France's ascendancy in Flanders gave her control of a series of ports which could be used to assemble an invasion fleet, and in August 1386 a fleet which contemporary French chroniclers estimated at some 900 ships and 60,000 fighting men assembled in the estuary of the Zwijn. In reality the force may have been substantially smaller than this, but it nonetheless presented the most serious threat that England had faced in the whole course of the war, and provoked widespread panic in southern England. The government levied troops and deployed them along the south coast, while the English fleet kept well out of the way, perhaps intending to hold back until the French had landed and then destroy their ships. Eventually a parliament would have to be summoned to vote money to pay for coastal defence, but the government hoped to postpone it for as long as possible. They required the maritime counties to pay the costs of half the defence force and imposed a forced loan to raise the rest of the money they needed. Most of this expenditure had already been incurred when, early in November, Charles VI called off the invasion. The official reason put forward by his council was bad weather and contrary winds, but it is more likely that the French government could not raise the enormous sums required to keep so large a force in being, and without wages the troops began to desert.

Richard II and the Appellants, 1386–1388

Parliament met on 1 October 1386 with the French encamped at Sluys and their invasion plans well advanced. The threatened invasion was, of course, in the forefront of the minds of the commons, who were determined to call the king's ministers to account. The cost of defence against the invasion was the principal concern of the Chancellor, Michael de la Pole, who sought from the commons the unprecedentedly large grant of four fifteenths and tenths. The commons responded by calling for Pole's dismissal, to which Richard returned his famous reply that he would not dismiss even a scullion from his kitchen at parliament's request. The king declined to meet parliament, preferring to stay at Eltham, and the commons, mindful of the precedent of 1376, refused to proceed with the business of parliament until the king came in person and agreed to dismiss Pole. The king proposed that forty knights should be chosen to come to Eltham and negotiate with him on behalf of the commons, but the commons refused to agree to this and instead sent the Duke of Gloucester and Thomas Arundel Bishop of Ely, the Earl of Arundel's brother, to Eltham to interview the king. The only surviving account of the speech which the two lords made at Eltham is preserved in Henry

Knighton's chronicle, and Knighton's recent editor has suggested that his source might have been Gloucester himself. The two lords maintained that according to statute there should be a parliament every year for the redress of grievances, and that if the king chose to absent himself from parliament for more than forty days without good cause it was automatically dissolved. The king intervened at this point with a characteristically impetuous threat to call in help from the King of France, saying that he would rather submit to him than give way to his subjects. Gloucester and Arundel pointed out the foolishness of such a move, and reminded Richard how much blood and treasure had been poured out in the time of Edward III and the Black Prince to maintain their rights in France. They went on to argue that the realm was being impoverished by evil counsellors, and, in a final thrust, they threatened the king with deposition 'according to an ancient statute and, regrettably, recent example' if he preferred to follow his own stubborn will rather than rule his kingdom according to law and custom and with the wise advice of the lords. This pointed reminder of Edward II's fate brought the king to submission.[45] He agreed to meet parliament and to dismiss Pole together with the Treasurer, John Fordham Bishop of Durham.

The king's reply both to the commons when they demanded Pole's dismissal and to Gloucester and Bishop Arundel at Eltham suggests that he was angry and sensitive both to criticism in general and to attacks on his prerogative. Whether his impetuous responses suggest any more profound reflection on the nature of royal power is debatable, though the two lords put forward a coherent view of the aristocratic obligation to intervene in government to protect the interests of the realm, against which Richard's view of his prerogative right, however crudely expressed, presented a more authoritarian view of government which was to become of greater significance in the last years of Richard's reign.

After Pole's dismissal the commons proceeded to impeach him, on the precedent of 1376.[46] The two most substantial charges against him were that he had failed to convene the commission of inquiry into royal finances established in the parliament of October 1385 and that he had failed to send help to Ghent so that 'by the said Chancellor's negligence the said town was lost'. There was substance to both counts: there could be little doubt that Pole had frustrated the commons' intentions in the previous year, and although Richard had sent John Bourchier to Ghent in November 1384 with 100 men-at-arms and 700 archers, he had failed to offer any help when the men of Ghent were besieged at Damme in August 1385. Ghent had had little alternative but to submit to Philip of Burgundy in December 1385. Pole was convicted and sentenced to imprisonment, though because the charges related to his misdeeds as Chancellor he retained his newly acquired earldom and the lands with which the king had endowed him.

The impeachment of Pole was followed by a far-reaching attempt to impose restraint upon the king. A commission of fourteen prelates and nobles was established which was given the power to examine all royal revenue, to inquire how that revenue had been spent, and to investigate all grants of land made since the coronation. It was also empowered to carry out what reforms it thought fit, and it was given wide powers of supervision over the royal household and the administration. The commission's composition was not to Richard's taste: the newly appointed Chancellor, Thomas Arundel, together with the other two great officers of state, the two archbishops, and three other prelates, were complemented by the Dukes of York and Gloucester, the Earl of Arundel, and three bannerets. The strong clerical representation on the commission suggests that the anti-clericalism of the 1370s had abated, and that the episcopate was still expected to play its part in affairs of state.[47] The Archbishop of Canterbury, William Courtenay, was the younger brother of the Earl of Devon; the Bishop of Norwich was the grandson of the younger Despenser, while Alexander Neville Archbishop of York and Richard Scrope, who became Bishop of Lichfield in 1386, were members of powerful northern families. Despite the traditional reluctance of the episcopate to become directly involved in politics, the family ties of such men may have encouraged a more overt political stance than the episcopate had shown since the last months of Edward II's reign. Bishop Arundel was more openly hostile to the king than any prelate since Archbishop Stratford, and the Archbishop of Canterbury had been involved in a violent incident with the king in the previous year when he had criticized Richard for his apparent connivance at the plot against Gaunt. Gloucester and the Arundel brothers made a formidable trio of opponents of the court, and although York took a more moderate view there was no one on the commission whom Richard could consider favourable to his own point of view. There was little he could do to resist, and he had to content himself with a formal protest that nothing done in the parliament should be taken to prejudice his prerogative, and that the liberties of his crown should be safeguarded.

Once again, as in 1376, the commons acting with the support of a group of powerful lords had been able to make their will prevail; but once again, after parliament dispersed the king was able to reassert his authority with surprising ease, though with less moderation and judgement than Gaunt had shown in 1376. In February 1387 he left London and embarked upon a 'gyration' that took him to the midlands and to his own earldom of Chester. In this way he avoided direct supervision by the commission established in the previous parliament, though he kept in touch with it and received regular sums of money for the expenses of his household. The commission's authority was due to expire on 20 November 1387, and if calmer advice had prevailed Richard might simply have waited until that happened and resumed control of government. But during his 'gyration' he planned a counter-attack, and in the summer of 1387 he began to survey his military resources and inquire into his legal rights. He consulted his judges on two occasions, first at Shrewsbury in early August and then at Nottingham. On 25 August at Nottingham the judges formally set their seals to a document embodying the questions asked and the answers given on both occasions. The judges stated that the commission established in the last parliament infringed the royal prerogative, especially because it was contrary to the king's will; that the judgement against Pole was revocable; that the king could dissolve parliament at will; and that the king alone had authority to determine the business of parliament.[48] There was little thus far in the judges' answers that was new, apart perhaps from the fact that so extensive a statement of the royal prerogative was made at all. They provided a rebuttal of the political arguments put forward by Gloucester and Bishop Arundel at Eltham, but Richard's predecessors would not have seen these statements about the extent of royal authority as anything out of the ordinary. What was novel and potentially danger-ous about the judges' answers, however, was the punishment they proposed for those who had acted against the king's will in the last parliament: they were to be punished 'as traitors'. Their offence was not declared to be treason, but they were to receive the same punishment. In fact, if not strictly in law, this represented a reversion to the belief that accroachment of the royal power was treason, and it amounted to a substantial widening of the definition of treason laid down in the act of 1352.

If Richard was well pleased with the judges' answers, he had less reason to be satisfied when, at about the same time, he asked the sheriffs of the English counties and a deputation of Londoners what support they could give him. Walsingham suggests that the Londoners gave a devious answer, designed to placate the king; but the sheriffs were much blunter. Richard asked them what military support they could command in the shires, and whether it would be possible to influence the next parliamentary elections to ensure that no knight unacceptable to the king was returned. The sheriffs replied that the commons were all on the side of the barons, and that they were unwilling to break the established custom of freely electing the knights of the shire.[49] Some confirmation of the sheriffs' opinion was provided when a royal recruiting agent sent into East Anglia with money to induce men to take up arms on the king's behalf was arrested and thrown into Cambridge gaol. Public opinion in the summer of 1387 seemed to be firmly with the king's opponents.

At the same time the king sent a personal agent, Simon Shiringham, to Charles VI's court, probably to discuss the possibility of a meeting between the two kings with a view to concluding peace. The Monk of Westminster suggests that 'in common with his council' the king 'thought it better to secure a short breathing-space from the tumult of strife' and repeats rumours that the king was willing to give up all his French possessions except Aquitaine, and was prepared to do homage for Aquitaine.[50] There was nothing secret about the king's diplomacy, but the rumours reflect public disquiet at the course it was taking, and it ran counter to the wishes of at least some of the members of the commission, who were pursuing a much more vigorous war policy. In late March the Earl of Arundel put to sea with a sizeable fleet and in the Channel captured fifty French and Flemish ships loaded with wine, which was taken to England and sold cheaply. Arundel's popularity reached new heights. In May Arundel put to sea again and raided the country round Brest, though he failed to force the French to lift the siege they had mounted since 1386. In September, however, the Earl of Northumberland's son led another naval expedition to Brest which fired the French siege towers under cover of darkness and forced the besiegers to retreat. These exploits did much to strengthen public support for the king's opponents, and the successful deployment of English forces at sea provided a welcome boost to morale after the invasion scare in the previous year.

At some date in the autumn of 1387 the Archbishop of Dublin, who had been with the king when the judges were consulted, reported to the Duke of Gloucester all that had been going on in the king's circle during the summer, and especially no doubt the judges' answers. Gloucester and Arundel now seem to have planned a pre-emptive strike. The two lords were joined by the Earl of Warwick, and they assembled their retinues at Harringay Park in north London on 13 November. According to the Monk of Westminster, 'huge numbers of gentry came flocking from all directions to join them'. The king sent eight of the members of the commission to meet the three lords at Waltham Cross on the following day and ask them why they were in arms. They replied that the realm was in danger of being overthrown 'by the traitors who haunted the king's presence', and 'therefore our own loyalty to the king and the realm makes us eager to move as quickly as possible against these creatures so that we can save ourselves – indeed the entire kingdom – from treachery lurking unseen and the snares that spell death'.[51] The argument was essentially the same as that used by Gloucester and Arundel at Eltham in the previous year, and indeed by the opponents of Edward II, that the magnates' oath of loyalty to the king entailed an obligation to save him from evil counsel which endangered the realm. But self-interest and concern for self-preservation were barely concealed in the lords' reply, and they turned the tables on the king by issuing an appeal of treason against de Vere, Pole, the Archbishop of York, Nicholas Brembre and Sir Robert Tresilian.

The lords' animosity against de Vere and Pole was understandable enough, but the other three had not taken so prominent a part in politics over the previous few years. Tresilian was the chief justice of the king's bench and had taken a leading part in formulating the judges' answers in August; Brembre had been Lord Mayor of London in 1387, and had tried to hold the city for the king in the autumn; but Alexander Neville, the Archbishop of York, had been a member of the 1386 commission and had not been closely associated with the court until 1387, when he became a strong partisan of the king. He seems to have made enemies easily, and the lords may have regarded him as a traitor to his duty as a member of the commission and an abettor of the king's defiance of it.

It was not immediately clear how the lords intended to proceed with their appeal. Westminster indicates that they expected the matters alleged in the appeal to be dealt with according to common law, and on 17 November, when the lords met the king at Westminster, they agreed that the appeal should be heard in the next parliament, which was to meet on 3 February 1388. This probably represents something of a victory for the king: it gave him time to rally his forces, and it also provided a breathing space in which two of the accused, Pole and Neville, escaped overseas. Richard now despatched de Vere to Cheshire to raise an army. Gloucester, Arundel and Warwick assembled their forces and were joined by the Earls of Derby and Nottingham, both of whom, but the latter especially, had been alienated by de Vere's intimacy with the king. The Londoners, who had welcomed Richard back in mid-November, declared only a fortnight later that they could provide no military help for him. Sir Ralph Basset no doubt spoke for many when he stated that he had been and always would be loyal to the king, but he was not going to have his head broken for the sake of the Duke of Ireland; and the Earl of Northumberland, trying perhaps to act as a mediator lest civil war in England jeopardize the security of the northern border, tried to persuade the king that the lords ranged against him were indeed loyal but felt themselves unjustly oppressed by the king's favourites.[52]

In the event, Richard could rally military support only from his own earldom of Chester, and de Vere's Cheshire army was defeated by the five Lords Appellant at Radcot Bridge on 20 December 1387. De Vere escaped and fled to the Low Countries, while the victorious lords moved to London and interviewed the king in the Tower on 30 December. According to Westminster, they told him that 'he must of necessity correct his mistakes and henceforward submit himself to the control of the lords';[53] if he refused to do so, he ran the risk of being deposed. Another chronicler suggested that he actually was deposed for two or three days at the end of December, and only reinstated because the lords could not agree upon a successor. There is some supporting evidence for this story, and it may be that Gloucester's ambition extended even to the crown, only to be thwarted by the Earl of Derby, Gaunt's son. If he was indeed deposed for three days, as seems likely, his temporary deposition provided a further reason for his growing concern, in the 1390s, for his regality and his insistence on his subjects' duty of obedience to their king.[54] With the threat, or fact, of deposition Richard's resistance finally collapsed, and on 1 January 1388 the lords appellant carried out a purge of the royal household. They arrested Simon Burley, Sir John Beauchamp of Holt the Steward of the Household, six other chamber knights, the king's secretary and two clerks of the signet office. These men had been responsible for the administration of Richard's personal will over the previous three years, and several of them were suspected of involvement in Richard's negotiations with Charles VI.

When parliament opened on 3 February, the five Lords Appellant entered the assembly 'arm in arm and dressed in cloth of gold'[55] to present their appeal. The appeal contained thirty-nine charges. Some arose out of Richard's defiance of the commission of 1386, some out of the events of 1387, but all were so phrased as to imply that the accused had accroached the royal power and taken advantage of the king's youth to establish their influence over him. Only Brembre, however, was present to face his accusers; Pole, de Vere and Neville had fled overseas and Tresilian was in sanctuary in Westminster Abbey. It immediately became apparent that the Appellants were not going to find it easy to procure the convictions they sought, not least because common law did not allow for the condemnation of defendants in their absence. The king asked his judges and those expert in civil law to advise the lords of parliament how they should proceed. They replied that the appeal was inconsistent with both civil and common law, presumably on the grounds that the alleged offences fell outside the scope of the 1352 Statute of Treasons and that civil law had never been applied in cases of alleged treason within the realm. The lords got round this by saying that cases involving such serious crimes as were alleged in the appeal, perpetrated by peers of the realm, should be heard in parliament and by 'the law and course of parliament'.[56] This was not a far-reaching declaration of parliamentary supremacy: it has, rather, the character of a spur of the moment improvisation to overcome an unforeseen procedural difficulty, though it had been established as early as 1330, when Roger Mortimer was tried in parliament, that parliament was the appropriate venue for the trial of great men of the realm.

The Appellants thus found a way forward which did not conflict with the 1352 statute or the jurisdiction of the common law courts; but they now encountered some difficulty in persuading the lords to convict the accused. Pole, de Vere and Tresilian were readily condemned in their absence to death and forfeiture of their lands, and Neville was sentenced to the loss of his temporalities; but Brembre vigorously defended himself and offered to maintain his defence by combat. According to Westminster, [57] 305 peers, knights and esquires threw down their gauntlets against him, but at this point the Duke of Gloucester and Sir John Cobham created a diversion by dragging Tresilian from sanctuary and bringing him before parliament. The Monk of Westminster hints that Tresilian's capture served to prevent an open breach between the Appellants and other lords over Brembre's fate, but after Tresilian had been condemned and executed the Appellants returned to the case against Brembre and now decided to refer it to a committee made up of two representatives of each of the London craft guilds. This committee declined to express an opinion either way, and finally in desperation the Appellants consulted the Lord Mayor, aldermen and Recorder of the City of London, who declared that on balance he was more likely than not to be guilty. On this flimsy basis he was condemned and executed.

It was already clear that the Appellants lacked the wholehearted support of their peers in parliament, and as the trials proceeded the divisions amongst the lords became even more apparent. The judges who had given their answers at Nottingham were impeached by the commons, but 'the peers of the realm could not agree upon their judgement'.[58] Eventually they were persuaded to find them guilty, but they successfully petitioned that their lives should be spared. On 12 March the commons proceeded to impeach four of the chamber knights, Simon Burley, John Beauchamp, James Berners and John Salesbury. The charges against them were essentially the same as those brought against the five favourites under the appeal, but the use of impeachment rather than appeal suggests that the Appellants had no wish once again to face the procedural difficulties they had encountered earlier in the parliament. The chamber knights were accused of accroaching royal power, taking advantage of the king's tender years, and using their influence over the king for their own private profit. Burley also faced a number of specific charges arising out of his conduct as Constable of Dover and Windsor Castles, and according to Westminster the lords had a special animus against Salesbury because they believed he was guilty of treason both within and without the realm, a reference to his participation in negotiations for an interview between Richard and Charles VI. No one was prepared to fight for the lives of Beauchamp, Berners or Salesbury, but a bitter and prolonged dispute developed over Burley's fate. The Duke of York declared that Burley had been 'in all his dealings loyal to the king and the realm', to which Gloucester replied that Burley had been false to his allegiance. York retorted that his brother was a liar and Gloucester returned the insult: only the king's intervention calmed them down.[59] The bitterest hostility to Burley came from the commons, for reasons which are not entirely clear, and it is possible that Gloucester's determination to have him convicted arose in part at least from his wish to retain his popularity with the commons. Gloucester could not carry his fellow lords with him in seeking Burley's execution: the lords sent York and Cobham to intercede with the commons on Burley's behalf, and the queen and the Earl of Derby tried to persuade Gloucester and the commons to commute his death sentence. Their entreaties were to no avail, however, and on 5 May Burley was executed. A week later, and after much less argument, Beauchamp, Berners and Salesbury followed him to the scaffold.

After this blood-letting, the lords and commons turned to the subject of 'control over the king and the choice of persons to surround him and guide him'. It was agreed that the Bishops of London and Winchester, the Earl of Warwick, Sir John Cobham and Sir Richard Scrope 'should be in constant attendance upon him and that he should do nothing without their consent'.[60] This council now assumed control of policy, but its powers were never precisely defined and there is little evidence that its members met together after the opening of the next parliament on 10 September. The Appellants had rid the kingdom of evil counsellors, and no doubt felt that their work was done; a revival of the 1386 commission was unnecessary. The parliament ended with the king solemnly renewing his coronation oath, and the lords once again swearing allegiance to him.

The parliament well deserved its name 'Merciless': not since the reign of Edward II had there been such a thoroughgoing attack upon the king's favourites. In 1386 Gloucester and bishop Arundel had used the fate of Edward II as a warning to Richard, but the parallels with Edward II's reign should not be pressed too far. Unlike his namesake of Lancaster, Thomas of Woodstock showed little of the concern for reform in government which motivated some at least of the Ordainers in 1310 and 1311; there was some pressure for action to remedy the abuses of royal officials, but it came from outside parliament, and played little or no part in the Appellants' programme. Nor did the Appellants contemplate drawing up a political programme such as the Ordinances. Their aims seem to have been more short-term and specific than their predecessors in 1310–11. They did, however, enjoy substantial popular support. It was brought home to Richard in the summer of 1387 that his government was unpopular, and during the Merciless Parliament the commons readily backed the Appellants. Indeed, the commons were even more hostile to Richard's favourites, especially Burley, than many of the nobility, and Gloucester had little difficulty in persuading the commons to support his own hard line against Burley.

The Appellant coalition had come into being to bring about the destruction of the king's favourites; it had proved disunited even in the pursuit of that object, and it did not survive the summer of 1388. Its most signal failure came in foreign policy. In February 1388 Gaunt concluded the Treaty of Bayonne with King Juan of Castile, Enrique of Trastámara's son, under which Gaunt renounced his claim to the Castilian throne in return for a capital payment of £100,000 and an annual pension of £6,000. Catalina, Gaunt's daughter by Constanza of Castile, was to marry King Juan's heir Don Enrique, and thus the two dynasties were united. The main terms of the treaty had been provisionally agreed in the previous year, but ratification was delayed until the summer of 1388. Gloucester now hoped to enlist Gaunt's support for an elaborate offensive in France. Gloucester and Arundel planned to deploy a joint Anglo-Breton force north of the Loire, while Gaunt, who was created Lieutenant in Aquitaine in August, would lead an army north from Bordeaux. Arundel prepared a naval force to sail to Brittany, but the whole plan collapsed when Gaunt refused to accept Gloucester's authority and made a separate truce with the French, thus in effect withdrawing from the campaign. Gaunt's withdrawal prompted the Duke of Brittany to make his peace with Charles VI and Arundel was left hovering about the coast of Brittany with no campaign to join. He ignored orders to return to England and relieved his frustration by a series of plundering attacks on La Rochelle and its adjacent islands. On 12 June Gloucester made the first move to reverse his strategy by accepting a conciliar decision to reopen negotiations with the Duke of Burgundy, and agreeing to a truce. As it turned out, this marked the end of the war for a generation.[61]

While Gloucester and Arundel were occupied with planning and then halting an offensive against France, the Scots launched an invasion of England, hoping to take advantage of England's domestic crisis. It was a three-pronged attack, planned as a reprisal for the English invasion of 1385. Sir William Douglas of Nithsdale led a naval attack on Carlingford in Ireland, and on his return voyage raided the Isle of Man. The Earl of Fife led a damaging raid into Cumberland and Westmorland, while the Earl of Douglas took his troops over Carter Bar into Northumberland, raiding as far south as the Tyne. The Appellants offered little or no military help to the northern nobles, who were left to provide what defence they could against so substantial a Scottish invasion. Outside the walls of Newcastle, Douglas reputedly challenged Henry Percy (Hotspur) to give battle, and then retreated northwards to Otterburn, where he defeated Percy's forces at Otterburn on 22 August. Douglas was killed in the battle, but Percy was captured and subsequently ransomed. The defeat did nothing to enhance the standing of the Appellants. They had shown themselves neglectful of the defence of the north, and had seen the Scots inflict the first serious reverse on the English since the days of Edward II.[62]

The Appellants' failure in the war against both France and Scotland helps to explain why, when parliament assembled at Cambridge in September 1388, the commons came in a disillusioned mood. They called Arundel's officials to account for the money spent on his naval expedition, and they insisted that the subsidy they granted should be spent on the defence of the north rather that on another expedition to the continent. They also demanded the abolition of the liveried retinues of the lords, alleging that they were used to pervert the course of justice, and they asked that justices of the peace and justices of assize should have the power to investigate and try cases of main-tenance, bribery, and other forms of corruption of juries. The lords vigorously opposed these petitions, offering only to punish offenders if they were discovered. The lords' opposition to the commons' pro-posals gave the king a chance to intervene on the side of the commons by offering to abolish his own livery if the lords would follow suit. This was an astute move: it was a proposal which the lords were unlikely to accept, yet it won him some support from the commons, and his proposal that the whole issue should be considered in the next parliament provided the basis for a compromise which eventually led to a settlement of the matter at a great council in 1390.[63]

The Cambridge parliament marks the beginning of the recovery of Richard's power and influence. The Appellants were discredited in the eyes of the commons, and the king rather than the lords had shown sympathy with their concern over livery and maintenance. From the autumn of 1388 onwards some of the officials removed by the Appel-lants began to reappear at court, and in a council at Westminster on 3 May 1389 the king formally declared himself of age and sought the agreement of the lords to assume full control of government. He disavowed responsibility for the events of the past few years by disingenuously claiming that 'throughout the twelve years since I became king I, and the entire kingdom too, have been under the control of others', and announcing that now he was twenty-two he intended to assume the conduct of affairs.[64] The lords could not but agree to this, and in an immediate demonstration of his authority Richard dismissed the Chancellor, the Treasurer and the Keeper of the Privy Seal and replaced them by the Bishop of Winchester, the Bishop of Exeter, and Edmund Stafford. These new appointments, however, could hardly be regarded as provocative or partisan, and for the next seven years the king avoided the manner of rule which had aroused such hostility in the 1380s. Pole, de Vere and Neville were left to die in exile; no new favourites appeared and the council, now composed of the king's own nominees, exercised some supervision over patronage. Gloucester and Arundel were restored to the council in 1390, and Gaunt returned to England in the autumn of 1389. Over the next nine years he provided Richard's regime with powerful support, expressed symbolically by walking arm-in-arm with the king and by the king wearing the Lancastrian livery.

The opposition which Richard encountered between 1385 and 1388 derived much of its force from the unpopularity of the favourites at court and the widespread suspicion about Richard's policy towards France. Although Richard formally disavowed responsibility for the events of the first twelve years of his reign, it is hard to believe that he was not responsible for the control and direction of policy from 1385 onwards. It is equally hard to believe that his policy in these years was founded on a view of his kingly office which differed substantially from that of his predecessors. Under pressure he retreated to a more categorical statement of his rights and of the penalty for seeking to accroach them than his grandfather would have thought wise, but Richard's purpose was to uphold and defend his inherited prerogative rather than to extend it. His faults were his lack of wisdom in his choice of advisers and friends, especially Robert de Vere, and his espousal of a foreign policy which was not yet acceptable to many of the nobles who had actually fought the war during his minority. Yet his difficulties were not wholly of his own making. The policy of maintaining expensive garrisons in France had been adopted before he was of an age to influence the conduct of the war, and costly naval operations were made necessary by the growing threat from the navies of France and Castile. In purely financial terms there was much to be said for negotiating peace with France but the young king lacked both the prestige that flowed from successful campaigns and the easy rapport with his nobles which might have enabled him to take such an initiative with their support. Gloucester's grievances and ambition were sharpened by the favour Richard showed to the courtiers in the 1380s, but they have their origin in his ungenerous treatment by Edward III and his failure to unite the whole of the Bohun inheritance in his own hands when Gaunt married his son Derby to the younger of the Bohun coheiresses. The uneasy relationship which Gloucester had with both Gaunt and Derby cannot be laid at Richard's door.

In the event, Richard's submission was enforced by the military power which the Appellants deployed against him in December 1387. Richard could offer little resistance to the armed retinues of the magnates; he could rely upon the loyalty of the knights, men-at-arms and archers from his earldom of Chester, but under de Vere's inept generalship they were routed, and he could not count on the sheriffs to mobilize the *posse comitatus* when public opinion so strongly favoured the Appellants' cause. In the years that followed the Merciless Parliament, Richard showed that the defence of his regality would rest not only on theories of kingship but also on the development of his own retinue, the placing of trusted royal officials in positions of influence, and a settlement with France which would end the financial dependence on the commons that continued war entailed.

6

Richard II and Henry of Lancaster, 1389–1413

The End of the French War

The principal concern of the English government between 1389 and 1394 was the negotiation of a final peace with France. Even while the Earl of Arundel was still at sea in June 1388, the Duke of Gloucester had responded to overtures from the Duke of Burgundy and agreed to reopen the peace negotiations which had terminated with the overthrow of Richard's favourites at the end of the previous year. Talks resumed before the end of 1388, and continued for the next five years, in a search for peace which was to be more substantial and purposeful than any of the negotiations which had taken place since the conclusion of the Treaty of Brétigny.

From the French point of view there was little doubt that a settlement with England would be advantageous. The Duke of Burgundy had an interest as ruler of Flanders in a final peace with England which would ensure the flow of wool to the looms of the Flemish weaving cities and remove the temptation for Flemish rebels to look to England for support. The other royal dukes had interests which would be best served by a settlement with England, and transcending their personal interests was the ideal, to which they paid lip-service with varying degrees of sincerity, of a united western crusade against the Turks. Burgundy's ascendancy in French politics was interrupted in 1389, when Charles VI declared himself of age, but was restored in 1392 when the king suffered the first of a recurring series of fits of madness. Burgundy carried his brothers with him in the search for a settlement, and offered support and encouragement to those who believed a crusade was a serious proposition. His son and heir John of Nevers was to be captured and ransomed by the Turks when the crusade which many in the west had worked so hard to achieve was cut to pieces by the Turks at Nicopolis in 1396.

In England, attitudes to peace were more ambiguous. Richard's own views were well summed up by the Monk of Westminster who ascribed Richard's wish to negotiate with Charles in 1387 to a fear that if the war continued 'he would inevitably be compelled to be for ever burdening his people with new imposts, with damaging results for himself'.[1] Just how damaging to the royal position the regular demands for money had become was brought home to Richard in the parliaments of 1385 and 1386, when the commons used the king's request for subsidies to press for reforms in government and restraint upon the king. The ending of the war and the consequent reduction in royal financial demands was an important reason for the political stability of the early 1390s; parliament met infrequently, and the commons voted the taxes needed for the defence of Calais, Gascony, Ireland and the northern border without serious demur. Yet finance may not have been the only consideration inclining Richard to seek peace. He may, as Professor Saul has argued, have had a genuine abhorrence of the shedding of Christian blood, and he may have sympathized to a greater extent than many of his subjects with the French concern to save Christendom from the Turks.[2]

John of Gaunt was to play a leading part in the negotiations for peace: he had a personal interest in their outcome, for he was created duke of Aquitaine for life on 2 March 1390. In all probability, too he shared Richard's belief that constant demands for taxation were damaging to the crown. He had shown consistent loyalty both to Edward III and Richard II: he had defended Edward III's prerogatives in 1376–7, and although his son had been an Appellant in 1387–8 there is no reason to suppose that he himself had any sympathy with the methods that his son and the other Appellants had adopted to remove the king's favourites from power at that time. Gaunt's loyalty and his concern for political stability were not entirely altruistic. As long as Richard remained childless he was the nearest heir in the male line, and although the Earl of March, who was descended through the female line from Gaunt's elder brother Lionel Duke of Clarence, might have been regarded in some quarters as the heir-presumptive, the possibility of the house of Lancaster inheriting the crown cannot have been wholly absent from Gaunt's mind.

Other nobles, however, had reservations about a settlement with France. According to Froissart, Gloucester argued in 1391 that the prosperity of the 'poor knights and esquires of England' depended upon war,[3] while in 1394 he apparently told Robert the Hermit that the French were calling the tune in the negotiations and that no peace between the two countries ought to be concluded until England received all that was due to her under the Treaty of Brétigny. This was perhaps consistent with his emotional appeal to Richard in 1386 not to forget all the blood and treasure that had been poured out in defence of the king's rights in France, but as the negotiations continued Gloucester seems to have blown hot and cold about the prospect of peace. He was not averse to participating in the negotiations in 1392, and two of Froissart's informants believed that Gloucester wanted the negotiations to succeed so that Gaunt might remove himself permanently to Aquitaine; yet according to the Monk of Westminster, Gloucester opposed the proposed settlement in 1394 until Gaunt bought his support with the promise of land in Aquitaine. The Earl of Arundel, on the other hand, took a more directly hostile view of the negotiations. According to Froissart he objected to the resumption of negotiations in 1391, and three years later he appears to have raised objections to the draft treaty.[4] Perhaps he regretted the loss of any further opportunity for personal military glory, and perhaps he thought that the proposed terms constituted a betrayal of all that he and his father had fought for.

There is some evidence that Gloucester and Arundel were not the only nobles who had doubts about the negotiations. Froissart thought in 1391 that many barons shared Gloucester's view that England should hold out for the terms agreed at Brétigny, and the Monk of Westminster suggested that when the proposed peace treaty was discussed in parliament in 1394 lords and commons objected to the grant of Aquitaine to Gaunt. Doubts about the virtues of peace were not confined to members of the nobility who looked to war for profit and prestige. In 1393 rumours of an impending settlement with France led to a rising in Cheshire by men whose employment was war and who feared for their livelihood if peace was agreed. With some tact and skill Gaunt put down the rising and recruited many of the rebels into the army he took to Aquitaine in 1394. The commons welcomed an easing of the pressure for taxation that would come with peace, but they were also anxious that the honour and integrity of the crown should be upheld and that no settlement should be concluded which appeared to disinherit the crown or gratuitously surrender the gains that Edward III had made. To all men in England who had been involved in the war it had become the natural and seemingly permanent state of affairs. It was by no means self-evident that peace was preferable to war, as Sir Thomas Gray had pointed out forty years earlier in his *Scalacronica*,[5] and the effect on their lives, their income and their self-respect if the war came to an end was incalculable.

Opposition to peace thus arose from a wide variety of motives, but it came to focus specifically on the concessions that the English were prepared to make over the status of Aquitaine. If an enduring peace were to emerge from the negotiations the question of Aquitaine would have to be resolved, but although both sides were willing to give ground the English appeared to make the more substantial concessions. The French offered a greatly enlarged duchy, which would include Saintonge south of the Charente, the Agenais, Périgord, Limousin, Quercy, Angoumois, and Rouergue. This was a very substantial part of the territory which was to have been ceded to England under the Treaty of Brétigny. It was much more extensive than any area which the English controlled or could realistically hope to gain by war, and the offer thus had the appearance of generosity. But in return the English negotiators agreed to drop their demand to hold this territory in full sovereignty, and conceded that it should be held of the King of France by liege homage. The French proposed that it should be held not by the English king but by the Duke of Lancaster and Gaunt may well have been sympathetic to this suggestion. In 1393 Lancaster, Gloucester, Burgundy and Berry were able to agree to a provisional settlement which embodied the substance of these proposals, though it did not specifically mention the grant to Gaunt.

This provisional agreement, however, encountered resistance both in England and in Aquitaine. The Gascons welcomed Gaunt as their duke for his lifetime provided that his grant of the duchy did not lead to its permanent separation from the English crown. A series of grants by earlier English kings had established that Aquitaine could be separated from the English crown only temporarily as an appanage for the king's eldest son, and the lack of definition in Richard's grant of the duchy to Gaunt in 1390 aroused their suspicions. In that year the Estates of Bordeaux sought assurances that the grant would not lead to the separation of the duchy from the English crown, and asked the king to promise that this would not happen. The English political community shared the feelings of the Gascons. At a council held at Stamford in May 1392 and attended by the knights from the shires as well as the lords, Gaunt put forward the French proposals for a peace, including the separation of Aquitaine from the crown. 'These terms,' said the Monk of Westminster, 'were not at all to the liking of the English commons, who said that it was absurd, besides being extremely damaging to the king and the Crown, that for the benefit of a single person he should suffer the permanent loss of such extensive and such fair domains.' Nonetheless, the draft articles for peace which had been drawn up in 1393 were presented to parliament in January 1394. Westminster observed that the commons were dissatisfied with many aspects of the proposals, and both lords and commons refused their consent to them. The real stumbling-block seems to have been the question of homage. The parliamentary record suggests that the lords and commons were willing to agree to the proposals subject to the condition that Aquitaine should he held by simple rather than liege homage. Liege homage they saw as meaning, so Westminster reported, that every Englishman 'would pass under the heel of the French king and be kept for the future under the yoke of slavery', and they would not accept it. Westminster, however, believed that Gaunt bought Gloucester's support for the agreement with the promise of land in Aquitaine, and that 'in consequence the Duke of Gloucester from now on lost popular support'.[6] The two dukes returned to France after parliament came to an end and a committee of legal experts attempted to meet parliament's concerns by finding ways in which liege homage could be modified in practice. There was little sign that the French were willing to make substantial concessions, however, and by the early summer of 1394 the negotiations had broken down.

Neither Richard and Gaunt nor Charles VI and his uncles had any wish, however, to renew the war, and in the summer of 1394 Richard felt able to turn his attention to Ireland. In 1385 the Anglo-Irish community had asked Richard to go over in person and rescue the English colony from the verge of extinction, and once he had ceased to be preoccupied with continental affairs he responded to their entreaties. He assembled a substantial force under his own command, administered by the household, in a manner reminiscent of the armies of Edward I's reign and the expeditions led by the king himself in Edward III's reign. The Duke of Gloucester, the Earls of Nottingham, Rutland and Huntingdon, and the heir of the Earl of Kent accompanied him with their retinues. The campaign was a superficial success: a show of force in Leinster brought about the submission of Art Mac Murchadha, the Gaelic Irish king of Leinster, and his subordinates there. Mac Murchadha's submission persuaded the Gaelic Irish rulers elsewhere to submit to Richard: by early 1395 he had achieved an almost universal acceptance of his overlordship by the Gaelic Irish kings and sub-kings. But the settlement which followed this general recognition of his lordship was hasty and took little account of the complexities of the conflict between the Gaelic Irish and the Anglo-Irish lords. The agreement that Mac Murchadha and his subordinates should leave Leinster and find lands elsewhere was unrealistic, and above all the settlement ignored the inherent incompatibility between Richard's obligations as lord of the Gaelic Irish rulers and his obligations to the Anglo-Irish lords whose lands the Irish kings and sub-kings occupied.

The campaign showed that Richard possessed some strategic judgement and military skill, but his attempt at a political settlement revealed little understanding of the realities of the Irish situation. His momentary success in Ireland raised his prestige at home, but few of the nobles who went over with him found the country an attractive prospect. According to Froissart Gloucester remarked that it was a land which could be neither conquered nor exploited, and that what was won there in one year would be lost in the next.[7] Apart from the Earl of March, whose nominal territorial interests in Ireland were far more extensive than those of any other English lord, no English noble showed any enthusiasm for defending his Irish possessions. Richard himself was pressed by parliament in January 1395 to return to England, but he did not hurry back and eventually reached England in April. Walsingham maintained[8] that he was recalled to deal with the Lollards, who published a manifesto during the January 1395 parliament, but it is more likely that he chose to return because he had achieved his main purpose, the submission of the Gaelic Irish rulers, and the detailed implementation of the settlement could be left to his lieutenant the Earl of March.

Perhaps, too, the problem of Gascony necessitated the king's presence in England. In April 1394 the Estates of Gascony swore an oath that they would henceforth be governed only by the king and the crown of England. In the 'Instrument of Union' which the Estates drew up to justify their oath, they refused to accept Gaunt as duke and refused to recognize the authority of Gaunt's officers in the duchy. In November Gaunt took an army 15,000 strong to the duchy, and tried, with some success, to buy off the opposition. The Estates agreed to remit the fundamental issue, that of Gaunt's status in the duchy, to the king for decision. A council held at Eltham in July 1395 considered the problem, and a majority seems to have accepted the view of the king's legal advisers that the grant of the duchy to Gaunt should be revoked, though no final decision was taken. At the same time, the question of the king's re-marriage after queen Anne's death in 1394 led to the reopening of negotiations with the French court. Early in 1395 Richard was considering a marriage with Yolande, daughter of the king of Aragon; but this aroused misgivings in France, and in May Charles VI proposed that Richard should marry his six-year old daughter Isabella.

Both Richard and Charles perhaps saw a marriage alliance as strengthening their commitment to peace, and negotiations for a marriage alliance and a peace treaty opened in July 1395. There was little prospect of a peace treaty being agreed, for the gap between the two sides was probably even greater than it had been in 1394, but on 9 March 1396 the two sides agreed a twenty-eight-year truce. This had the advantage for Richard that it ended the war for a generation but avoided the need to settle the question of homage for Aquitaine, which had been the sticking point for parliament in 1394. The truce was accompanied by an agreement that Richard should marry Isabella, and bring with her a dowry of 800,000 francs. The truce left all the main issues between England and France unresolved, but from Richard's point of view it offered the prospect of a lengthy respite from war taxation and a rapprochement between the two courts which might allow both kings to prepare a crusade against the Turks.

But the very possibility of such a rapprochement aroused suspicions in England, and in the event the negotiations with France not only failed to sustain the political stability of the early 1390s, but led to a revival of political conflict which was to culminate in Richard's loss of his throne.

Richard II's Tyranny and Deposition

While Gloucester and Arundel distanced themselves from the court after 1394, a group of younger noblemen had formed round the king, and these men were to provide him with essential political support when he moved against his former enemies in July 1397. Amongst them were his half-brothers Thomas and John Holand, Earls of Kent and Huntingdon, the Duke of York's son Edward who had been created Earl of Rutland in 1390, and John Beaufort, eldest of Gaunt's children by his mistress and third wife, Katherine Swynford. The Beauforts had been legitimized by act of parliament in February 1397, and John was created earl of Somerset at the same time. John Montague Earl of Salisbury, grandson of Edward III's close associate, and Thomas Lord Despenser, great-grandson of Edward II's favourite, were also associated with this group, while Thomas Mowbray Earl of Nottingham had moved back into favour at court by this time.

Although these noblemen did not attract the same degree of hostility as de Vere and Pole in the 1380s, Richard nonetheless rewarded them well. John Holand Earl of Huntingdon was granted lands and castles in Devon and Cornwall which enabled him to build up a substantial power base there, while Rutland was not only granted a title in his father's lifetime but also the lordship of Oakham and the office of sheriff of Rutland. Two other nobles also rose in favour at court in these years. Sir Thomas Percy, younger brother of the earl of Northumberland, became Steward of the Household in 1393 and was granted offices in south Wales, while Sir William Scrope, son of Richard lord Scrope of Bolton, became Chamberlain of the Household in 1394 and was granted the lordship of the Isle of Man together with offices in Wales and Ireland. Both these men were ennobled in 1397, and both were amongst the closest advisers and supporters of the king until Bolingbroke's invasion in 1399. Not until 1397, however did Richard's court begin to incur the same kind of criticism which it had aroused in the 1380s.

Some of the members of Richard's court in these years had important, literary and theological interests, and some were suspected of heresy. K. B. McFarlane suggested that the 'Lollard knights' formed a cohesive group at Richard II's court, while Dr Wilks has argued that Lollardy was actually a court-centred movement. Wycliffe's preaching, he suggests, was addressed to the 'lords of England, who would make sure that the clergy was being reformed'.[9] In the early years of Richard's reign a number of knights at court do indeed seem to have shown some sympathy with Wycliffite ideas, though they appear to have behaved discreetly, and it is unlikely that they determined the religious outlook of the entire court. Some of them came into the king's service from the households of the Black Prince and Princess Joan, and it may be that the puritanical personal religion of the Black Prince led him to tolerate the presence in his circle of knights whose views were unorthodox. In the 1380s Richard himself took no action against these men, and some continued to serve him in the 1390s, but apart from Sir John Montague, later Earl of Salisbury, there is no reason to associate any of the nobles at court in the 1390s with Lollard beliefs. Indeed, the nobles closest to the king in the 1390s were notable for their patronage of the Carthusians rather than the Lollards, and the court's interest in that religious order is not easy to reconcile with the picture of the court as a centre of Lollardy. Richard's own orthodoxy seems to have been beyond question, and in the later years of his reign, perhaps under the influence of Archbishop Arundel, he became more vigorous in his determination to root out heresy and deal with minor officials in his household who were suspected of Lollard sympathies.[10]

The first sign of rising political tension occurred in the parliament of January 1397. The commons presented a bill which, amongst other things, complained about liveried retainers and criticized the excessive costs of the household. The king reacted angrily to this criticism of his household, which must have reminded him of similar complaints by the commons in the early years of his reign. He insisted that the commons should produce the author of the petition, Thomas Haxey, who was convicted of treason. Some of the issues raised in the petition, such as the request that sheriffs and escheators should be changed annually and the complaint about the giving of liveries, reflected the concerns of the gentry and the clerks in the royal administration rather than the nobility.[11] There is no reason to suppose that any members of the nobility were behind the petition, and the grievances were not novel. Perhaps the most revealing aspect of the episode was the king's reaction. He pardoned Haxey, as a member of the clerical estate, but the commons were required humbly to apologize for their presumption in presenting the petition. The king had shown once again his sensitivity to criticism and, more significantly, his willingness to suggest that such criticism was treasonable.

Five months later, on 10 July, Richard ordered the arrest of the Duke of Gloucester and the Earls of Arundel and Warwick, and in the following September brought them to trial in parliament. Richard's motives for proceeding against the former Appellants were interpreted in sharply conflicting ways by contemporaries and have remained difficult to understand. Thomas Walsingham, writing after 1399 from a strongly anti-Ricardian point of view, suggested that Richard was moved to anger against the three earls when envoys from Germany who came to offer him the imperial crown implied that he was not fit to wear it if he could not control his subjects at home. From that time onwards, Walsingham says, Richard 'began to act as a tyrant and oppress the people'. A French source, the *Chronicle of the Betrayal and Death of Richard II*,[12] maintains that Richard uncovered a conspiracy against him and launched a pre-emptive strike against those who were plotting to kill or imprison him and his followers. Some modern historians, following hints and suggestions in other sources such as the Kirkstall Chronicle, have interpreted Richard's action as revenge for the humiliation he suffered at the hands of the Appellants in 1387-8.

None of these explanations, whether contemporary or modern, is wholly satisfactory. In a proclamation issued at the time of the arrest of the three lords, Richard declared that they had not been arrested for their part in the events of 1387-8 but 'for great number of extortions, oppressions, grievances etc. committed against the king and people and for other offences against the King's majesty which shall be declared in the next parliament'.[13] Yet these new offences were never mentioned again, and when the three lords came to trial in September the indictment against them referred only to their part in the events of 1386-8, giving some substance to the view that Richard's real motive was revenge. The July proclamation might then be interpreted as an attempt to lull the retainers of Gloucester, Arundel and Warwick, who had taken part with their lords in the show of force against the king in the winter of 1387, into a sense of false security and to avoid alarming Derby and Nottingham and the other lords who had been members of the 1386 commission, some of whom now stood high in favour at court. Yet if revenge was Richard's motive it is hard to understand why he waited until July 1397. He was arguably in a stronger position in 1395, when he had just returned from an apparently successful campaign in Ireland and had a substantial army behind him. In 1397 he had to recruit an army from Cheshire to overawe parliament, occupy London, and provide a personal bodyguard. It is difficult to believe that Richard's move against the Appellants was motivated solely by long-held resentment or that it came, as Walsingham implied, out of pique at the suggestion that he could not control his subjects.

On the other hand, the suggestion that there was a plot against the king in the summer of 1397 cannot be accepted at its face value. The author of the *Traison* appears to be relying in part on a confused recollection of the events of 1387 and perhaps in part on his own imagination, for the dramatic unity of his account of the betrayal of an innocent king requires the existence of a threat to Richard's life and rule to justify his arrest of the Appellants. However, apart from the suggestion of new offences in the July proclamation there is no supporting evidence for the *Traison*'s story. The roles the author assigns to particular individuals make the story implausible as it stands, and if there were any truth at all in it Richard would certainly have wished to use it in the charges against the three lords when they came to trial.

It is, however, clear that by early 1397 the political stability of the past eight years was close to breakdown, and Haxey's petition had raised in Richard's mind the possibility that the kind of criticism which had been directed against Richard's court and household in the 1380s was going to be renewed. Richard's reaction to Haxey's petition perhaps served to distract attention from the criticism of his foreign policy, and in particular his rapprochement with Charles VI, which was just as important in raising political tension. The suggestion that Richard and Charles should mount a joint military expedition against Giangaleazzo Visconti, ruler of Milan, was flatly opposed by the commons, who told the king that if he wanted to take an army to Milan he could pay for it himself. Milan had traditionally enjoyed good relations with England and with the English-supported Pope in Rome; an expedition against its ruler could hardly therefore be construed as consistent with English interests. Equally unpopular was the return of Brest to the Duke of Brittany in 1396 under the terms of the twenty-eight-year truce. According to the *Traison*,[14] Gloucester complained bitterly to Richard about the abandonment of Brest, and the author maintains that the surrender of the town was the occasion for the growth of hostility between Gloucester and the king. Rumours that Calais would shortly be given up, and even that the purpose of the Count of St Pol's visit in 1396 was to negotiate its surrender, flew about in the autumn and winter of that year and Gloucester especially seems to have been critical of Richard's attitude to France. If Froissart can be believed, Richard's suspicions of Gloucester grew sharply from 1395 onwards, and he went to some trouble to find out from visitors to Pleshey what Gloucester was thinking. Reports reached the king that Gloucester was hostile to the settlement with France, and, again according to Froissart, Richard's courtiers pressed for action against him.[15] It was, therefore, perhaps an unwise move for Gloucester and Arundel to refuse to attend a council in February 1397 and thereby intensify the king's suspicion of their intentions. Such an action, together with the reports Richard had received about Gloucester's attitude to the truce with France, may have made Richard believe that Gloucester and his associates were planning another move against him. Richard's arrest of the Appellants in July may thus have the character of a pre-emptive strike, while the proceedings against them in parliament in September enabled him formally and definitively to annul the acts of the parliaments of 1386 and 1388: to that extent, revenge was one of his motives, though probably not the most important.

The parliament of September 1397 was a carefully stage-managed event. The earl of Arundel seems to have believed that the elections to the commons had been rigged: 'where are the faithful commons?', he apparently asked at his trial, and at his deposition Richard was accused of appointing his own clients as sheriffs so as to manipulate the elections. This was probably not true, but nonetheless, an unusually large number of members of the commons – 86 out of 203 – had not been elected to any previous parliament, and almost the same number (85), though not necessarily the same persons, can be shown to have had links with the court.[16] Richard did not, however, rely solely upon the inexperience or the curial connections of many of the members to ensure a compliant parliament. His Cheshire archers surrounded Westminster Hall and according to Adam of Usk and the Monk of Evesham they were ready to shoot at the slightest sign of any disturbance.[17] Although there could be little doubt about the persuasive effect of the Cheshire archers, Richard also relied on the effective management of the commons by the Speaker, Sir John Bushy, a retainer of the king and the Duke of Lancaster and an experienced manager of the commons, who was to prove thoroughly loyal to his masters.

The theme which the Chancellor Edmund Stafford Bishop of Exeter took for his sermon at the opening of parliament on 17 September was the text from Ezekiel 'There shall be one king over all', and he went on to stress that for the good governance of the realm the king must enjoy his regalities and prerogatives in full. The sermon was a clear and concise expression of the king's philosophy of government, and three days after the opening, parliament embarked on the business of dealing with those who had violated the royal prerogative between 1386 and 1388. Speaking in the name of the commons, Bushy impeached Thomas Arundel Archbishop of Canterbury of treason, accusing him of usurping royal power through membership of the 1386 commission, and by means of that usurpation putting Burley and Berners to death. The suggestion that membership of the 1386 commission was in itself treasonable had dangerous implications for lords who were now in favour at court, and Richard promptly declared all the other members of that commission except Gloucester and Arundel free of treason. The Duke of York and the Bishop of Winchester had particular reason to be grateful to Richard for this; but the Archbishop was convicted, sentenced to forfeiture of his lands and possessions, and sent into exile.

On the day after Archbishop Arundel's appearance before parliament, the Earls of Rutland, Kent, Huntingdon, Nottingham, Somerset and Salisbury, together with Lord Despenser and Sir William Scrope appealed Gloucester, Arundel and Warwick of treason, in deliberate imitation of the procedure followed in the Merciless Parliament. The charges against them amounted to accroaching the royal power by establishing the commission of government in 1386, assembling and riding against the king in November and December 1387, and usurping the royal power of justice by procuring the deaths of Simon Burley and others in the Merciless Parliament of 1388, all of which were said to be treasonable offences. Arundel was the first to stand trial. He put up a spirited defence, but Bushy, Derby and the king himself all joined in the attack, the king in particular reminding him of his part in Burley's death. His defence was of no avail, however, and Gaunt, who as High Steward of England presided over the trials, condemned him to death. He was executed the same day. Warwick was then brought before parliament, but he broke down and 'like a wretched old woman, he began to weep and sob and wail, declaring that he had indeed, like a traitor, done everything that was alleged in the appeal'.[18] This emotional display was sufficient to gain him his life, and he was sentenced to exile in the Isle of Man where he would be under the watchful eye of Sir William Scrope. When Gloucester was ordered to appear to stand trial, however, it was reported that he was already dead, and a confession was produced before parliament in which he acknowledged his guilt. There is good, but not conclusive, evidence that Gloucester was murdered: after his arrest he had been taken to Calais, and most contemporaries believed that he was murdered there, perhaps with the connivance of the Earl of Nottingham, who was Captain of Calais. It is just possible, however, that since he was apparently a sick man at the time of his arrest he died a natural death, though one hastened by the rigours of his imprisonment. Richard had good reason for wishing him dead: the risk of popular demonstrations in his favour was substantial, and Gaunt might have been unwilling to pronounce sentence upon his own brother.

All three lords were sentenced to forfeiture of their lands and titles, and much of their property was granted to the new Appellants, who were also raised in rank. Rutland, Kent, Huntingdon and Nottingham were granted the dukedoms of Albemarle, Surrey, Exeter and Norfolk, and Gaunt's son was elevated to the dukedom of Hereford. John Beaufort Earl of Somerset became Marquis of Dorset, Sir William Scrope became Earl of Wiltshire, the earldom of Worcester was conferred on Sir Thomas Percy, and Thomas Lord Despenser was created Earl of Gloucester, a title which had eluded his ancestor in Edward II's reign. Despenser also took advantage of the turn of fortune's wheel to petition successfully for the annulment of the 1327 judgement on his ancestors and the return of the lands confiscated then. The creation of so many dukedoms seemed to devalue the title, and Walsingham commented that the newly honoured lords were derisively called 'Duketti' by the common people.[19] Although the commons in parliament, manipulated by Bushy and overawed by Richard's Cheshire army, had acquiesced in the condemnation of the former Appellants, public opinion outside parliament was hostile to the king. Walsingham noted Arundel's noble bearing at his execution, and described how the multitude venerated him as a martyr. Miracles were wrought at his tomb, and Richard was apparently so alarmed that he ordered the tomb to be hidden and the earl's banners to be removed from above it. In Walsingham's eyes Arundel was a martyr to the cause of resistance to a tyrannical king, another Thomas of Lancaster, and Gloucester too was extolled as 'the best of men, who always laboured for the benefit and honour of the king and the advancement of the whole kingdom'.[20] Walsingham wrote in the St Albans tradition of eulogizing those who suffered for their resistance to weak or tyrannical kings; but Adam of Usk also described the popular veneration of Arundel and made it clear that he agreed with the popular view: 'I have no doubt,' he wrote, 'that he has been admitted to the fellowship of the saints' and his body is now 'venerated with great reverence and glory, and people continually make offerings' at his tomb in the house of the Augustinian friars in London.[21]

Parliament adjourned on 29 September, and reconvened at Shrewsbury on 28 January 1398. At Shrewsbury, the king dealt with the lesser men who had supported the Appellants in 1387. Sir John Cobham, who had been a member both of the 1386 commission and of the committee set up to supervise the king at the conclusion of the Merciless Parliament, was sentenced to exile in Jersey, and all those who had 'ridden in arms and risen forcibly against the king'[22] were excluded from the general pardon for past offences which the king now granted. Richard interpreted this exclusion so widely that the representatives of the communities of seventeen counties in the south and east of England were required to admit their complicity in the rising of 1387 and submit themselves to the king's grace. The representatives were required to seal charters on behalf of their counties submitting themselves and their goods to the king's pleasure, giving him carte blanche to do what he wished to them. From this basis in fact grew the legend that Richard extorted 'blank charters' from his subjects. Contemporary chronicles agree that Richard ordered each county to make a payment of either £1,000 or 1,000 marks for their pardon, but if he did, the payments have left no entry in the financial records.[23]

Fear and mistrust were now to be the basis of the relationship between the king and his subjects. In return for the general pardon, the commons agreed to grant Richard the customs revenue for life; if the grant was revoked at any time, the pardon would lapse. This grant, rather than the more famous establishment of the committee to deal with business left over at the end of the Shrewsbury sessions, reveals Richard's true intentions towards parliament. In time of peace, as Richard had shown in the early 1390s, he could manage with only an occasional parliamentary subsidy provided he had the customs revenue and exploited his other sources of income effectively. It was not his intention to eliminate parliament altogether, but it was consistent with his search for security and his fear of criticism and control that he should seek to ensure that its meetings were infrequent and its financial powers diminished. Richard also required each of the lords spiritual and temporal and all the commons assembled at Shrewsbury to swear an oath to uphold the Acts of the 1397 parliament, and this oath was extended in the 'blank charters' to the men of the seventeen south-eastern counties. The imposition of these special oaths shows how little confidence Richard really had in public support for his destruction of the Appellants.

These collective measures were accompanied by pressure on individuals who were suspected of complicity with the Appellants in 1387 or of disloyalty to Richard's settlement of 1397. Men who had been associated with the Appellants in the Radcot Bridge campaign were brought before the council and required to pay a fine before receiving their pardon. If they could not agree with the council about the size of the fine, they were liable to be imprisoned until they did agree. The sessions of the council to which such men were summoned were attended only by the three officers of state and three of Richard's closest supporters, Bushy, William Bagot and Henry Green. These three, together with the Earl of Wiltshire, were the most hated of all Richard's advisers: Usk described Wiltshire, Bushy and Green as 'those most evil counsellors of the king, the chief aiders and abettors of his malevolence'.[24] Wiltshire in particular played a central role in Richard's government, as keeper of castles and justice in Chester and North Wales, justice in Leinster, keeper of confiscated property, member of the inner group of the council responsible for dealing with political offenders and Treasurer from September 1398 until his death. Contemporaries were all too aware of the pervasiveness of his influence, and in 1399 it was rumoured that he was plotting the deaths of several leading noblemen so that he could exploit their property. It is not surprising that his execution in July 1399 was greeted with widespread joy.

The chronicles make it clear that Richard's rule was widely unpopular, but fear did its work and there was little sign of open hostility. The removal of Richard's most prominent aristocratic opponents and his terrorization of their associates gave him for the moment the security he sought. Rebellion could not succeed without aristocratic leadership, and in 1398 it was difficult to see who might provide that leadership. Richard's dealings with a small number of noblemen, however, were to create the circumstances in which successful rebellion became possible. Since 1395 the Earl of March had been the king's representative in Ireland, but Richard summoned him to the Shrewsbury parliament and required him to take the oath to uphold the settlement of 1397. Richard had good grounds for distrusting March. He was suspected of harbouring his illegitimate uncle, Sir Thomas Mortimer, who was wanted in connection with the Appellants' rising in 1387. More significantly, he was the king's heir general and the most powerful magnate in England after the Duke of Lancaster. Usk suggests that Richard's friends were alarmed at the joyous reception March received when he arrived at Shrewsbury and after he returned to Ireland they plotted to destroy him.[25] There may be some truth in the story, for Richard dismissed him from the lieutenancy of Ireland on 27 July 1398 and replaced him by the Duke of Surrey. A few days before this, however, March had been killed in County Kilkenny in an engagement with the Irish, and it is impossible to say what fate Richard had in store for him when he ceased to be Lieutenant in Ireland. The custody of the March inheritance was assigned to Albemarle, Surrey, Exeter, and that ubiquitous agent of the royal will, the Earl of Wiltshire.

On the northern border Richard sought to curb the power of the magnates who traditionally held office there. The Duke of Albemarle was appointed Warden of the West March in February 1398, and Lancaster was given general power as Lieutenant in the Marches for the duration of the truce with Scotland. At the same time Bushy, Green and others were appointed to deal with violators of the truce. These appointments were bound to antagonize the Earl of Northumberland, and to encourage the Earl of Westmorland, Northumberland's rival in the north, to make common cause with him to reduce the influence in the region of Richard's courtiers. Richard's exclusion of the northern magnates from office in the Marches goes far towards explaining their support for Bolingbroke's invasion in the following year.[26]

The king's dealings with the Dukes of Norfolk and Hereford, however, precipitated the events that were to lead to his downfall. On 20 January Hereford came before the king at Great Haywood in Staffordshire and alleged that Norfolk had told him in the previous month of a plot at court against both of them for their part in the events of 1387, and that they should save themselves by flight or counter-plot. Furthermore, he apparently revealed, the conspirators had Gaunt in their sights as well, and intended to have the Act of 1327 restoring the Lancastrian inheritance after the forfeiture of Thomas of Lancaster reversed. Hereford's account of his conversation with Norfolk may well have been true. Anti-Lancastrian sentiment at court would not have been surprising, in view of Gaunt's wealth and his position as Richard's male heir, though there is no reason to suppose that the king himself was party to such feeling. There is, however, some firmer evidence for a conspiracy. Bagot appears to have been implicated in a plot against Gaunt, and some at court seem to have contemplated the possibility of reinstating the sentence of forfeiture on Thomas of Lancaster. The effect of this would be that the whole Lancastrian inheritance would revert to the crown, and no doubt provide rich pickings for the king's friends at court.[27] As a former Appellant, Norfolk had reason to fear for his personal safety, but he perhaps made an error of judgement in unburdening himself to Hereford, on the mistaken assumption that the story would not reach the king or Gaunt. Norfolk seems to have panicked on realizing that it had, and tried to ambush and kill the Duke of Lancaster. At the Shrewsbury parliament Hereford presented an accusation against Norfolk, and the parliamentary committee met twice to consider it. There was insufficient evidence to reach a decision, however, and the committee decided that it should be resolved by trial by battle at Coventry on 16 September 1398. When both combatants were ready in the lists, Richard halted the proceedings and handed down judgement, as martial law entitled him to do. He sentenced Norfolk to exile for life, and Hereford to ten years' banishment. Hereford was, however, given leave to appoint attorneys to receive the Lancaster inheritance if, as seemed likely, his father died before his exile ended. No such favour was extended to Norfolk, though he too could expect a substantial inheritance on the death of his grandmother Margaret Marshal. The more lenient sentence which Hereford received may reflect Richard's view that there was some truth in his story, but equally the king needed to retain Gaunt's support for the settlement of 1397, and he could not be entirely sure of Hereford's loyalty. Richard could not risk either an unduly harsh judgement against Gaunt's son or a triumph for him in single combat.

On 3 February 1399, four months after Hereford had gone into exile, John of Gaunt died. Although Richard can hardly have been surprised by his death, it presented him with an almost insoluble dilemma. If he kept his promise and allowed Hereford to receive his father's inheritance the new Duke of Lancaster in exile would have access to all the financial, personal and military resources of the largest inheritance in the kingdom. If he went back on his word he would cut off Hereford from his sources of support but at the same time would give him a grievance which would command the sympathy of most members of the landowning class. Richard took the latter course, and although it proved disastrous for him it was not such an obvious error of judgement as has sometimes been supposed. The inheritance was not to be permanently confiscated: custody was given to various nobles in favour at court, including the Earl of Wiltshire, but it was presumably Richard's intention that Hereford's son Henry, later Henry V, would receive the inheritance when he came of age.

Henry of Hereford spent his exile in Paris, where Charles VI provided the Hôtel de Clisson for his residence. He gathered around him a small group of fellow exiles, including Thomas Arundel Archbishop of Canterbury and the young heir of the Earl of Arundel. Some of his retainers shared his exile, but there was nothing comparable to the defections to the queen and Prince Edward that had occurred in 1326. Richard had every reason to believe that the Duke of Burgundy would ensure that Henry was kept under supervision, for it was in Burgundy's interests to maintain the truce of 1396 between England and France and preserve the good personal relations between the English and French courts. Richard felt he had little to fear from Henry and his small band of exiles, and in May 1399 he left for Ireland, to salvage what he could of his 1395 settlement there. His departure from the country at a time when his position seemed so insecure has been interpreted as an act of insane misjudgement; yet despite the unpopularity of his rule there was no one in England with sufficient power and authority to lead a rebellion, and Richard had good reason to believe that the Duke of Burgundy would use his influence to prevent Hereford leaving Paris. Richard could not, however, have foreseen that a sudden change in political circumstances in France would give Henry the opportunity he needed. In late May the Duke of Orléans ousted Burgundy from power temporarily and on 17 June Orléans entered into an alliance with Henry, hoping thereby to break the Anglo-French entente, press his claim to lands in Aquitaine and diminish the authority of the Duke of Burgundy. The alliance excluded the Kings of England and France, but Orléans's supremacy gave Henry freedom to organize a force, and despite the formal exclusion of the Kings of England and France from the terms of the alliance it is likely that he gave him some more positive support. Internal French rivalries thus helped to determine the course of events in England.[28]

Towards the end of June 1399 Henry landed at Ravenspur in east Yorkshire, with a small band of followers, probably numbering no more than forty or fifty. He was soon joined by many knights and esquires from the Lancaster lands in Yorkshire and, according to the Kirkstall Chronicle, by 'a great multitude of gentlemen, knights and esquires of Lancashire and Yorkshire, with their men; some of their own free will and others for fear of future events'.[29] At Doncaster in early July the Earls of Northumberland and Westmorland brought their retinues to support Henry, and the military forces they placed at his disposal made his army a formidable threat to the local levies which the English government under the Duke of York sought to muster. The Percies afterwards tried to maintain that Henry swore an oath at Doncaster that he had come only to claim his inheritance and that Richard would be allowed to remain king. It is doubtful whether he committed himself to such an explicit statement of his intentions, but a declaration which was likely to arouse sympathy with his grievance over his disinheritance while not at the same time committing himself specifically to deposing the king might well have served to broaden the basis of his appeal.[30]

The government under the Duke of York had not been inactive in the face of Henry's invasion. Royal spies in Picardy had warned of Henry's movements, but the government expected him to seize Calais and then launch an invasion of Kent; his landing in Yorkshire took them by surprise. York called out the shire levies, and the response was substantial in the southern and eastern counties. Some of the few magnates remaining in England, notably Michael de la Pole Earl of Suffolk, John Beaufort Marquis of Dorset, and the Bishop of Norwich mustered their retinues. But the will to resist crumbled as Henry's ever-growing army moved south; only the Bishop of Norwich engaged Henry's forces, and he was easily beaten off. At Berkeley Castle on 27 July Henry met the Duke of York, and York agreed to join forces with him. He had little alternative, for his force was small and many of his men probably sympathized with Henry. The following day Henry received the surrender of Bristol and, to the delight of his supporters, had Bushy, Green and Wiltshire executed. He then embarked on what amounted to a punitive expedition through the Welsh Marches to Chester, which he entered on 9 August, and three days later he ordered the execution of Peter Legh, keeper of the royal forest of Delamere and a supporter of Richard II, whom Usk described as reputedly 'a great malefactor'.[31] The executions at Bristol and Chester constituted a usurpation of the royal prerogative, however popular they may have been, and the expedition through the Marches gave colour to the belief that he intended to take the realm by conquest. Such actions suggest a substantial hardening of his intention to make himself king.

Meanwhile in Ireland the Duke of Albemarle had advised Richard against a hasty return, and had encouraged him to send the Earl of Salisbury on ahead to north Wales to rally troops there. Albemarle's plan turned out to be such a disastrous misjudgement that he has been suspected of treasonably delaying Richard's departure to allow Henry to consolidate his position. Such an interpretation is certainly possible: Albemarle could not have been in collusion with his father the Duke of York, for his advice was given well before York joined Henry, but the atmosphere of suspicion and disloyalty at Richard's court in the last months of his reign was such that a plot of that kind might well have been devised. On the other hand, Albemarle might merely have decided, wrongly but not treasonably, that Richard would do better to wait in Ireland until he could assemble all his forces at Waterford and then return at the head of a large army. When Salisbury landed in north Wales, however, the troops he had expected to rally melted away, believing that Henry had won and that Richard was dead. Richard himself landed at Haverfordwest, probably about 28 July, only to find that his own army deserted him and that Albemarle and Northumberland's brother the Earl of Worcester, who was Steward of the Household, had gone over to Henry. The disintegration of his army left Richard with no alternative but to go to north Wales and join Salisbury at Conway.

Henry now sent Northumberland and Archbishop Arundel to interview the king at Conway. The story that Richard willingly agreed to renounce the crown is Lancastrian propaganda; more probable is the story which suggests Northumberland swore before Richard that Henry had come only to regain his inheritance, and persuaded Richard to travel to Flint to meet Henry. It is hard to believe that Northumberland was honest, or that he had any doubts at this stage about Henry's intentions. The *Traison* takes the view that Richard was tricked into leaving Conway, and when he arrived at Flint Henry treated him as a captive.[32] Richard was taken from Flint to Chester, and from Chester to London, where he was lodged in the Tower. His downfall had been sudden and complete: in little more than a month, Henry had made himself master of the kingdom without meeting any serious resistance. None of the nobles left in England was prepared to risk his neck for Richard, and there was no sign of any popular support for him outside Cheshire. The nobles who might have tried to hold England for him were with him in Ireland, and even amongst them there were suspicions of disloyalty. Richard's triumph of 1397 had been based upon widespread fear and upon the self-interest of a small group of courtiers who were bound to the king by their share in the profits of the Appellants' downfall. Once Richard's rule was effectively challenged, men ceased to fear it and its shallowness was evident for all to see.

Assured of his victory, Henry now had to work out a political settlement. At some time in the second half of September 1399 he established a council of 'doctors, bishops and others', of whom Adam of Usk was one, to consider 'the question of deposing King Richard and replacing him as king with Henry duke of Lancaster, and of how and for what reasons this might lawfully be done'. After Richard's capture there can have been little doubt about Henry's intentions, but this was the first explicit indication that he intended to make himself king. According to Usk, the council agreed that although Richard was ready himself to yield up the crown, 'it was nevertheless decided that, as a further precaution, he should be·deposed by authority of the clergy and people...for which purpose they were therefore summoned'. The story that Richard had agreed to resign the crown had already become an integral and essential part of the deposition proceeding. Some days after this, according to Usk, the council raised the question of Henry's right to the throne by descent from Edmund of Lancaster who, according to legend, had in reality been the elder son of Henry III but had been set aside by his younger brother Edward I 'because of his imbecility'.[33] Other sources maintained that he had a physical deformity, and was therefore nicknamed Crouchback. However, the council decisively rejected this story, and with it any suggestion that not only Richard II but also the three Edwards had no right to have occupied the throne. More interesting than the council's deliberation on the Crouchback legend was its recommendation that the crimes with which Richard was charged were sufficient reason to depose him and that the decree *Ad Apostolice* provided a legal basis for deposition in such circumstances. The decree was an abridgement of the sentence of deposition passed by Innocent IV in 1245 against Frederick II, and it has been argued that in order to justify a sentence of deposition in 1399 it was necessary, in accordance with canonist tradition, actually to charge the king with grave crimes. The problem of deposition was seen as essentially one to be solved by reference to canon law.[34]

On 30 September 1399 the clergy and people assembled in Westminster Hall. The throne stood vacant, covered with a cloth of gold. The record of this assembly was skilfully drawn up to present an ordered sequence of events, beginning the day before it met with the despatch of a commission to the Tower to interview Richard and remind him of his promise supposedly made at Conway that he would resign the crown. The king asked to see the Duke of Lancaster, who accordingly came to the Tower the same afternoon. The record then suggests that Richard acknowledged his insufficiency to rule, declared that he was willing to abdicate, and absolved his subjects from their allegiance to him. Richard then set his seal to an instrument of abdication, and declared that he wished the Duke of Lancaster to succeed him. The following day, when the assembly met, Richard's instrument of abdication was read to the prelates, magnates and commons, who were asked if they wished to accept it. They unanimously assented, and then, as the council had planned earlier in the month, it was agreed that in order to remove any doubts and uncertainties, Richard's crimes and defects should be set down in writing, to show that he was worthy of deposition. The charges were prefaced by a recital of Richard's coronation oath, and the essence of the indictment was that he had violated his oath to rule in accordance with the laws and customs of the realm, and had sought instead to

rule according to his own will. The charges amounted to an indictment of Richard's rule over the previous two years. They show a
degree of intellectual coherence and a consistent interpretation of
the relationship between the king and the law which suggest careful
preparation and, perhaps, the hand of Archbishop Arundel, who,
with the Duke of Gloucester, had made similar points about the king's
attitude to the law at their interview with him in 1386. Many of the
specific charges against Richard were justified. It could well be argued
that he had abandoned due process of law in his dealings with his
subjects, and that he had acted as though the lives and property of his
subjects were his to dispose of at will because he believed he was
above the law. He may never actually have said that the laws 'were in
his mouth, and also in his breast, and that he alone could establish
and change the laws of the realm',[35] but in his opponents' eyes he had
behaved as if he believed such ideas.

The three estates then declared that these charges were notorious
and sufficient to warrant deposition, having regard to his own admission of his insufficiency to rule, and they agreed to depose him. A
delegation representing the three estates went to the Tower to
announce their decision to Richard on 1 October, and in the only
statement attributed to Richard in the official record which has the
ring of truth, 'he answerd and seyd that he loked not ther after; but he
sayde that after all this he hoped that is cosyn wolde be goode lorde to
hym'.[36] The official record gives the impression that the proceedings
were marked by complete unanimity on the part of the three estates,
but other sources suggest that there was some dissent and that
Richard's role was less passive. The Dieulacres Chronicle portrays a
king resigned to his fate but not in the least disposed to co-operate
with his supplanter, and instead of agreeing that Henry should succeed him he placed his crown on the ground and resigned his right to
God.[37] The author of the *Traison* suggests that the Bishop of Carlisle
spoke out in the assembly on Richard's behalf and argued that he
should not be condemned unheard. Some doubt has been cast on this
story,[38] but the bishop was deprived of his see in December 1399, and
although the story itself may be untrue, the bishop's unwillingness to
throw in his lot with the new regime seems clear. The Dieulacres
Chronicle suggests that Northumberland and his son were unhappy
about Henry's seizure of the throne and that Hotspur refused to
attend Henry's coronation banquet, while in 1403 the Percies were
to claim that they knew at the time that Henry was a perjurer and a
usurper. The façade of unity appears on close examination to have a
few cracks in it, but they were not sufficient to jeopardize Henry's
position, and there is no evidence that anyone sought to promote the
claim of a rival candidate when, after sentence of deposition had been
pronounced, Henry claimed the throne.

The question of Henry's title to the throne, however, presented some difficulties. At one point Henry proposed to claim by right of conquest, but was dissuaded from doing so by Chief Justice William Thirning, who argued that it would place men's title to their property in jeopardy, and that such a claim would come ill from one who had returned to England ostensibly as the champion of the right of inheritance. Claim by descent was a safer alternative, but although Henry had a good hereditary claim it was not unchallengeable once the Crouchback legend had been disposed of. The law of succession to the crown of England had never been precisely defined, and although precedent implied that son should succeed father and that a brother might inherit if the king had no progeny of his own, Richard was the first King of England since 1066 to leave neither children nor brothers and sisters: the direct line of the Plantagenets came to an end with him. In the circumstances, therefore, no one could have an unchallenged hereditary title to the crown.

Henry himself was the heir male, and it had become the custom over the past sixty years to restrict the descent of earldoms to heirs male. More significantly, in late 1376 or early 1377 Edward III had settled the succession on his male descendants,[39] though his settlement was not regarded as definitive, and there are no references to it either during Richard's reign or at the time of his deposition. Henry made no use of it in claiming the throne, and it may be that the settlement was thought to lack the authority it would have had if it had been proclaimed in parliament or embodied in statute, as Henry was to ensure happened in 1406. Furthermore, to limit the descent of the crown to male heirs might, by analogy, invalidate the English kings' claim to the French throne and thus surrender one of the key English positions in the war with France. The heir general was the Earl of March, but he was a boy of seven, and despite later Yorkist claims there is no good contemporary evidence that Richard ever proclaimed him as his heir, though it is possible that in 1385 Richard had declared the earl's father Roger Mortimer who died in 1398 as his heir. Henry's advantage over the Earl of March, however, was not just that he was an adult and in possession but that he was descended from Henry III on both his mother's and his father's side; this may be what he meant by the words 'disendit be right lyne of the blode comyng fro the gude lorde Kyng Henry therde' in his claim to the throne. One narrative of the deposition states that Henry claimed the throne as 'next heir male and most worthy in blood to the good King Henry III',[40] which may perhaps indicate how contemporaries interpreted Henry's words. In a sideways glance at the Earl of March, Archbishop Arundel preached a sermon on the text 'A man shall rule over the people', in which he dwelt on the ills that befall a kingdom which is governed by a child. The clergy and people assented to

Henry's claim, and parliament ratified the new dynasty's possession by recognizing his son as heir to the throne. In reality, of course, Henry had made himself king by force of arms, albeit with the support of a significant body of nobles and the acquiescence of most of Richard's subjects. He did, however, have a hereditary claim to the throne that was as good as anyone else's, and it would be wrong to suppose that the ills that befell the Lancastrian dynasty in the middle of the fifteenth century arose from a defective title to the throne in 1399.

In the end, Richard's cause had commanded virtually no significant support in the face of Henry's invasion; yet there had been much that was of value in Richard's approach to government. He understood the damage that was being done to the position of the crown by constant demands for money to finance an unsuccessful war, and he sought to give the crown more financial freedom by ending the war and by persuading parliament to grant him the customs revenue for life. He sought to counter the territorial and military power of the nobility by placing men he could trust in important positions in local government, by trying to curb the liveried retainers of the great magnates, and, when that failed, by trying to build up his own retinue. The epitaph he composed for himself, which began 'He threw down whomsoever violated the royal prerogative' perhaps epitomized his idea of kingship and the wrongfulness of resistance to royal authority, a theme which runs through his reign, perhaps from the time of the Peasants' Revolt. In the 1390s he used the language of majesty and the symbols of kingship to express his increasingly exalted view of his authority, but this view was rejected by his opponents in 1399, who approached the issue of resistance, and the problem of the relationship between the law and the royal will, from a different standpoint. The success of Bolingbroke's invasion brought about not just the downfall of the king himself but also the rejection of the ideas on which his kingship was founded.[41]

Richard failed, therefore, to establish a popular basis for his concept of royal authority and to carry most of the nobility with him. Those who supported him after 1397 did so mainly out of self-interest and greed, and their intrigues and treachery contributed to his downfall. They were not the men on whom the reassertion of royal authority could easily have been founded. His failure to command the support of the nobility in the manner of his grandfather did not spring simply from his inability, or unwillingness, to offer them leadership, victory and profit in war, though this has much to do with it; it was also a failure of character. He showed himself arrogant and petulant, touchy rather than sensitive and prone to hasty and vengeful judgements. These traits became even more apparent in the last years of his reign when, driven by insecurity, he sought to base his rule on fear. To men of the fourteenth century, a tyrant was a ruler who exploited the realm for his own benefit rather than for the common good, and who dealt with the persons and property of his subjects according to his own will rather than according to due process of law. By 1399, Richard's rule had acquired the characteristics of a tyranny, though he was not formally accused of acting like a tyrant, and Henry Bolingbroke enjoyed much support for his claim that the 'rewme was in poynt to be undone for defaut of governance and undoyng of the gode lawes'.[42]

Rebellions Against the Lancastrian Dynasty

Henry IV, however, had no intention of allowing the traditional prerogatives of the monarchy to be diminished by his seizure of the throne. He had come to end the excesses of Richard's rule, not to sit upon the throne as a crowned magnate. On 6 October the estates who had deposed Richard reassembled as the first parliament of the new reign and Archbishop Arundel preached a sermon in which he declared that the new king wished to be advised and governed by the honourable, wise and discreet persons of his kingdom, and that he did not wish to be governed by his own will but by common advice, council and assent. The archbishop's remarks were designed to contrast the old regime with the new, but they were little more than general expressions of good intentions. The proceedings of the parliament of 1397–8 were annulled and the heirs of its victims restored to their lands and honours. At the same time the acts of the Merciless Parliament were reinstated, though the Earls of Suffolk and Oxford retained the lands they had inherited from their convicted predecessors. The reversal of Richard's 1397 settlement meant that the Dukes of Albemarle, Exeter and Surrey, the Marquis of Dorset, and the Earl of Gloucester had to surrender the lands they had been granted in 1397 and revert to the titles they had held before that parliament. Henry's treatment of Richard's supporters was remarkably lenient: there were no executions, apart from those at Bristol and Chester before he became king, and he even showed some favour to his half-brother John Beaufort, who had had to relinquish his marquisate, by granting him the office of Chamberlain of England. Henry wished to avoid creating a group of disinherited nobles who would have nothing to lose by rising in favour of Richard, and he perhaps recognized that his authority would depend to some extent on his ability to attract the loyalty of many of those who had supported Richard.

Thus Henry confirmed all Richard's judges in office, and reappointed Richard Clifford as keeper of the Privy Seal, while at the lower levels of the household and the administration continuity of personnel was very substantial. On the other hand members of Henry's own affinity, especially those who had shared his exile, figure prominently in the new appointments he made at the outset of his reign. John Norbury, an esquire who had been in Henry's service for at least the previous ten years, was appointed Treasurer in succession to the executed Earl of Wiltshire; another companion of Henry's exile, Sir Thomas Erpingham, was appointed Constable of Dover Castle, and the key positions in Calais were given to Duchy of Lancaster servants. The chief offices in the royal household were entrusted to friends of his exile and Duchy of Lancaster servants, and Henry appointed as his Chancellor John Scarle, who had been chancellor of the palatinate of Lancaster between 1382 and 1394 but who had then become keeper of the rolls of Chancery. He was essentially a career civil servant, and it may be that archbishop Arundel continued, informally at least, with the ceremonial and advisory role which he had had as chancellor under Richard II.

Those who had shared Henry's exile reaped their rewards, but Henry also had to reward those who had joined him after his arrival in England and whose support had made his victory possible. Chief amongst these, of course, were the northern noble families, the Percies and the Nevilles. The Earl of Northumberland and his son received substantial grants. Northumberland was appointed Constable of England for life and Warden of the West March. His son Hotspur became Warden of the East March and Captain of Roxburgh Castle; he received a life grant of Bamburgh Castle, offices and castles in north Wales, and a hereditary grant of the Isle of Man. The earl and his son thus controlled not only the whole northern border, but north Wales as well, where the Percies' clients and dependants set about establishing their influence and enriching themselves. The earl's brother Thomas Percy Earl of Worcester was rewarded for his disloyalty to Richard II by receiving confirmation of all his grants from Richard together with an annuity of 500 marks and the office of Admiral of England. By contrast, Henry's grants to the Neville family, the Percies' rivals in the north, were of less financial or strategic importance. Ralph Neville Earl of Westmorland was appointed Marshal of England and received the Honour of Richmond for life, while his brother Thomas Lord Furnivall was granted Lochmaben Castle and Annandale. Since both were in the hands of the Scots the grant was of little real value. Both Northumberland and Westmorland attended the council regularly in the first months of Henry's reign, and Henry was careful to maintain a balance between them; but the Percies' pre-eminence in the north was unlikely in the long run to prove tolerable to the Nevilles, and their authority in north Wales gave them and their followers influence in a region where other lords close to Henry, notably Reginald Grey of Ruthin and the young

Thomas Earl of Arundel, had interests. The sudden aggrandizement of the Percy family held dangers for Henry, no matter how politically necessary it was in October 1399.

The first challenge to Henry's rule came, however, from Richard's former friends. Kent, Rutland and Huntingdon had not only kept all the estates which they had acquired before 1397, but they also quickly regained the king's confidence and were present at court and on the council in the autumn of 1399. Henry's trust in them soon proved to be misplaced. In December 1399 they joined the Earl of Salisbury and Thomas Lord Despenser in conspiring to kill Henry and restore Richard to the throne. A tournament due to be held at Windsor at Epiphany 1400 was to provide the opportunity to seize the king and his sons, and the revolt took Henry by surprise. He left Windsor, rallied London to his side and gathered a substantial army. The rebels retreated westward from Windsor and Henry advanced to engage them; Kent and Salisbury were eventually cornered at Cirencester, but before they could be handed over to the king they were beheaded by an angry mob. Huntingdon was captured near Shoeburyness and taken to Pleshey, where he was put to death by the men of Essex, while Despenser was lynched by the mob at Bristol. Eighty other rebels were brought to trial before the king at Oxford, and nearly thirty were executed.[43] The revolt was a failure, and the rebels' brutal treatment at the hands of the mob showed how little support their cause had in the country. No other nobles joined the revolt, and the ease with which Henry quelled it suggests that support for Richard's cause was limited to those who might expect to benefit substantially from his restoration. As long as Richard remained alive, however, he presented some danger to Henry's authority and in all probability his death occurred in mid-February 1400, at Pontefract castle. The French put it about that Henry had him murdered by a knight called Sir Piers Exton, who is not otherwise known to have existed; other sources believed that he starved to death, but whether out of despair at the failure of the rebellion or through neglect on the part of his gaolers will never be known. Rumours soon spread that he was alive and well and living in hiding somewhere outside the realm, possibly in Scotland; but these rumours are less convincing than the stories of Edward II's survival, and it is probably safe to conclude that Richard did indeed die in the late winter of 1400.

The estates of the executed rebels were confiscated, and the council which met at Westminster in February 1400 ordered that they should be used to support the royal household. Some of them were granted to members of the household, and others found their way into the hands of other royal servants. Henry did not, however, use these lands to enhance still further the power of those nobles who had helped him to the throne, and his policy towards the forfeited lands perhaps bears out the suggestion that in the early months of his reign he placed greater reliance upon his household servants than upon the nobility who supported him in 1399.

A more serious threat to Henry's rule was the rebellion in Wales which broke out in September 1399 and was led by Owain Glyn Dŵr, a Welsh landowner who was lord of Glyndyfrdwy in the east of Merionethshire. The revolt grew out of a quarrel between Glyn Dŵr and Reginald Grey of Ruthin over the ownership of land between their two estates. Glyn Dŵr attacked Ruthin and other English settlements in north-east Wales, but was beaten back at Welshpool on 24 September 1399 by the local levies under the command of Hugh Burnell. The revolt spread to Caernarvonshire and Anglesey, however, and Henry, who had hurried home from a Scottish campaign which had achieved nothing, made a punitive raid into north Wales which drove the rebels into hiding but did not break the revolt. Although it had begun merely as a dispute between two landowners the revolt soon developed into a rising against oppressive English lords, and it acquired both social and racial overtones, nourished by mythology and prophecy.[44] As long as it was confined to Wales it was no more than an expensive nuisance for Henry, though part of the cost of defence was met by income from the Duchy of Lancaster lordships in south and east Wales. In 1402, however, the revolt suddenly acquired a broader significance. In April of that year Glyn Dŵr captured Reginald Grey, and in June, in an engagement near Radnor, he took prisoner Edmund Mortimer, uncle of the Earl of March. Henry quickly ransomed Grey, but proved more reluctant to purchase Edmund Mortimer's freedom, and Glyn Dŵr exploited the situation to bring Mortimer into his own allegiance. Mortimer married Glyn Dŵr's daughter and each agreed to support the other's political aims, which now extended not just to securing Owain's right in Wales but also to making the Earl of March king. The defection of Mortimer was serious enough, for much of the March inheritance in Wales was now lost to the English cause; but in the following year the Percies rose in revolt with a programme which, like Mortimer's, aimed at deposing Henry IV and replacing him with the Earl of March. The Percies thus completely reversed the position they had taken in 1399, and in seeking to unite their forces with those of Glyn Dŵr they presented Henry with the most serious threat he had faced since taking the throne.

In the manifesto which the Percies issued in July 1403 to justify their rebellion[45] they claimed that they had intended only to help Henry regain his inheritance, that he had violated his oath to them by taking the throne, and that they had wanted the Earl of March and not Henry to succeed Richard in 1399. Northumberland's actions in the summer of 1399 do not suggest that he had many scruples about supporting Henry's seizure of the throne, and his portrayal of Henry as a perjurer making himself king against the wishes of the Percy family cannot stand up to serious examination. Nonetheless, there are signs that the Percies became disillusioned with Henry soon after he became king. Northumberland and his younger brother the Earl of Worcester played a prominent part in the political crisis of 1401, which had something of the character of a magnate reaction against Henry's reliance on a group of household intimates in administration in the first fifteen months of his reign. In February 1401 Northumberland was commissioned 'to hear and determine divers unaccustomed cases and businesses concerning the estate, fame and condition of the king's person and the dignity of the crown'[46] which could not be determined by the Constable or the common law. This appointment suggests a degree of pre-eminence in the king's counsels, and both Northumberland and Worcester were members of the council nominated in the Hilary parliament of 1401.

Between 1401 and 1403, however, relations between Henry and the Percies gradually deteriorated. The author of the continuation of the *Eulogium Historiarum* attributed the origin of the rebellion to a quarrel between Henry and Northumberland in which the king replied to Northumberland's demand for money to defend the border by saying 'I have no money so you shall have no money.'[47] Twice in 1401 Hotspur wrote to Henry complaining about difficulties in obtaining sums due to him as Warden of the East March, and neither he nor his father received all the sums they were owed by the Exchequer between 1399 and 1403. The importance of the Percies' financial grievances should not, however, be exaggerated. Such difficulties were not unusual, and in the early years of Henry's reign the Exchequer seems to have tried as best it could to maintain its payments to the Percies. It is more likely that personal matters embittered relationships: Henry refused the Percies' offer to mediate with Glyn Dŵr; he refused to allow them to ransom the Scottish prisoners captured at the battle of Homildon Hill in 1402; and he appeared to be showing too much favour to their rivals in the north, the Neville family. In March 1402 Henry removed Hotspur from his position as Keeper of Roxburgh Castle, which he had granted him for life in 1399, and gave it to the Earl of Westmorland.

The Percies may also have felt threatened by the influence at court of the Scottish Earl of March, George Dunbar, who had entered the English allegiance in the hope of receiving support against his rival the Earl of Douglas. Dunbar had fought on the English side at Homildon Hill, but his relations with the Percies were delicate. He was the head of an ancient Anglo-Scottish family which had lost its lands in Northumberland during the war of independence. These lands had been granted to the Percies, and the Percies may well have felt that Dunbar had territorial ambitions which could only be achieved at their expense. Dunbar had reason to fear that the English victory at Homildon Hill might open up southern Scotland to Percy ambitions, and Henry's grant to the Percies of most of the estates of the Earl of Douglas, captured at Homildon Hill, gave substance to these fears. It also suggests that Henry was still trying to conciliate the Percies. The author of Giles's Chronicle believed that Dunbar 'desired the death of Henry Percy so that he might dominate more easily in the parts of Northumbria',[48] and the Percies responded by allying themselves with the Earl of Douglas, who was to fight for them at the battle of Shrewsbury. Dunbar's ambitions and his influence at the English court were perhaps just as great a threat to the Percies' domination of the north as Henry's patronage of their Neville rivals.

The decision to revolt may have been prompted by the opportunity Glyn Dŵr's rebellion provided for a more general rising against Henry; but Adam of Usk grasped the underlying reason for their revolt when he said that after the Percies' victory at Homildon Hill 'their house [became] so puffed up with pride that it later fell headlong to its ruin'.[49] They believed that they could use their military power to control the crown and force it to act in accordance with their interests. The influence of Dunbar and Westmorland at court showed that Henry was no longer in their pocket, and they determined to have another attempt at kingmaking.

Hotspur, however, was probably the moving spirit behind the rebellion. In May 1403 he was in direct contact with Owain Glyn Dŵr, while on 17 July Henry heard rumours that Hotspur and the Earl of Worcester were in revolt in Cheshire, playing on pro-Ricardian sympathies by claiming that Richard II was still alive. The Prince of Wales was at Shrewsbury with a small army, and the rebels moved south to capture him. Dunbar now urged Henry to take swift action before Northumberland and Glyn Dŵr joined the rebel forces. Dunbar and the king marched to Shrewsbury, and on 21 July 1403 defeated the rebels in a hard-fought battle. Hotspur was killed, and the Earl of Worcester was executed after the battle. Northumberland submitted to the king, but lost his offices in the West March and his principal castles. The Earl of Westmorland became Warden of the West March, an office he was to hold until 1414, and the king's son John was appointed Warden of the East March. Dunbar was rewarded with a few minor grants, including the custody of the Umfraville inheritance in Lincolnshire which Hotspur had held.

The Percy rebellion was the most serious threat that Henry had had to face since he became king, and only his swift and resolute action crushed it so quickly. But the rebellion did not enjoy widespread support; it was serious because of the substantial military power the Percies could deploy, even though most of the rest of the nobility remained loyal to Henry. The rebellion had its origins in the personal grievances and the ambition of the Percy family, and these did not command much support amongst the rest of the nobility. Neither the rising of the earls in 1400 nor the Percy rebellion suggest that Henry's rule was generally unpopular. In the aftermath of the rebellion neither the king nor the commons showed much desire for vengeance. In the parliament which assembled in January 1404 the commons asked that the Earl of Northumberland should be pardoned and reconciled to both Westmorland and Dunbar. The commons no doubt appreciated that personal rivalries amongst these families had played a part in bringing about the rebellion and they were anxious, in the interests of political stability, to see an end to such feuds. The commons' concern that Northumberland should receive a pardon does not imply any lack of support for the king: there was no sign, in this parliament or later, of any sympathy for the March candidature, and indeed by asking for the renewal of oaths of loyalty to the king and the Prince of Wales parliament was upholding the legitimacy of the Lancastrian dynasty.

The reconciliation of 1404 proved superficial, however, and in the following year Henry had to face renewed dissension, in which the Earl of Northumberland was once again involved. Although there was no sign of any general support for the Earl of March's claim to the throne, Henry thought it wise to keep the earl and his brother under surveillance at Windsor Castle, where they were in the charge of Lady Despenser, the Duke of York's sister. But in February 1405 Lady Despenser took both boys and headed for the Despenser and Mortimer lands in south Wales. They were captured and brought before the council, whereupon Lady Despenser accused the Duke of York of hatching a plot to kill the king the previous Christmas. York was imprisoned in the Tower for a few months, but fully restored the following year. It is impossible to say how much truth there was in Lady Despenser's story, but her flight to south Wales with the March boys was suspicious, and Henry had good reason not to trust York (the erstwhile Rutland, who succeeded his father as Duke of York in 1402).

More serious, however, was news from the north in May 1405 that Northumberland had risen in rebellion again and had been joined by Thomas Mowbray the Earl Marshal, and the Archbishop of York Richard Scrope. Northumberland's rivalry with Neville had continued despite their superficial reconciliation, and in May he and his retainers had tried to capture Neville, though he escaped and alerted the king to Northumberland's insurrection. The Earl Marshal's part in the revolt is difficult to understand. He was only twenty in 1405, and had little political experience. He was married to the Earl of Huntingdon's daughter, and thus may have sympathized with the earls who rebelled in 1400. He may also have been motivated by a belief that Henry IV had been responsible for his father's exile and by a desire to avenge him. The Archbishop of York, however, set out his reasons for rebellion in a series of manifestos. His chief grounds of complaint were the lack of governance in the realm, the burden of taxation, and the inadequate defence of the realm; but one of the manifestos denounced Henry as a usurper and murderer, and sought help to put the 'right heir' on the throne.[50] Some of these arguments are similar to those put forward by the Percies in 1403, though the Scrope family did not have any very close connection with the Percies and the archbishop himself had given no indication of hostility to Henry earlier in the reign. The reappearance of grievances about taxation and defence suggests that Scrope hoped to broaden the base of his rebellion and attract popular support. Northumberland, however, had a much more grandiose scheme in mind. In 1404 Glyn Dŵr's rebellion had flared up again, and Harlech and Aberystwyth had fallen to the rebels. Much of north and west Wales was now in rebel hands, and the Bishops of Bangor and St Asaph's reopened negotiations between Glyn Dŵr and Northumberland. The outcome was the famous 'tripartite indenture' probably made in February 1405 which envisaged a threefold division of Henry's kingdom. Northumberland was to have all northern England together with Lincolnshire, Norfolk, Leicestershire, Warwickshire and Northamptonshire. Glyn Dŵr was to rule Wales and the Marches, including Herefordshire, much of Worcestershire, Staffordshire, Shropshire and Cheshire. Edmund Mortimer was to be king and was to have what was left, which included only a small part of his family's lands. The Earl of March can have had no real part in this proposal: it was obviously to the advantage of Glyn Dŵr, Northumberland and his uncle, though it is difficult to believe that any party seriously envisaged its implementation.

In the event, the revolt collapsed. The Earl of Westmorland, who remained loyal to Henry, moved against the rebels and defeated a small band of Percy retainers at Topcliffe, near Thirsk, and then caught up with the archbishop and the Earl Marshal at Shipton Moor, a few miles north of York, on 27 May. By promising that the king would redress their grievances Westmorland persuaded the rebel leaders to disband their armies, and he then promptly arrested them. They were brought before the king at York, and tried and executed as traitors, despite Archbishop Arundel's plea for his brother archbishop's life. Northumberland, who had the knack of avoiding direct involvement in the rebellions he helped to foment, refused to submit and fled to Scotland. His castles fell to Henry's army, however, and his estates were confiscated. The king's younger son John, later Duke of Bedford, received the principal Percy castles in Northumberland, and Neville was rewarded for his loyalty by the grant of Cockermouth

Castle, and, for a few months, the Isle of Man, though in October 1405 the island was granted to Sir John Stanley, thus beginning that family's long connection with Man.

Henry's preoccupation with the northern rebellion had allowed Glyn Dŵr to make yet more progress in Wales and the Marches. A small force of Frenchmen arrived at Milford Haven in August 1405 to help the Welsh rebels. They took Carmarthen and pressed eastwards to within ten miles of Worcester before falling back, short of supplies. But Glyn Dŵr was not to be easily crushed: after his setback before Worcester, his rebellion became confined to Wales, but Henry did not recapture Harlech and Aberystwyth until 1409 and Glyn Dŵr himself lived on into Henry V's reign. Much of the burden of defence against the rebels was borne by the Duchy of Lancaster castles in Wales, and duchy revenue was used to supplement expenditure by the Exchequer in putting down the rebellion; but the duchy lands and the inheritances of other English lords suffered severely from the destruction done during the rebellion. At the same time, Northumberland continued plotting: he was in touch with Glyn Dŵr again in 1406, and in 1407 he went to France vainly seeking aid from the Duke of Orléans. He launched a final revolt against Henry in 1408 but was killed in a skirmish with the Yorkshire levies at Bramham Moor.

Northumberland's final fling, however, did not present a serious threat to Henry's rule. He was supported only by Lord Bardolf, who had stood by him since 1405, and neither the French nor the Welsh now seemed eager to become involved in Northumberland's ambitions. The rebellions which Henry had to face between 1400 and 1408 may give the impression that his hold on the crown was chronically insecure; but such an impression would be false. The rebellion in Wales commanded support within the principality and the Marches for social and national reasons; but neither the rebellion of the earls in 1400, nor the three rebellions in which Northumberland was involved ever seemed likely to grow into general movements against Henry. Despite the grandiose plans embodied in the tripartite indenture the Welsh rebels failed to make common cause with the Percies and their northern followers, and hardly any of the English nobility wished to be used as vehicles for the enhancement of the power of the Percies. Although, as is suggested below, the commons in parliament were far from uncritical of Henry's rule, such criticisms should not be taken to mean that either the commons or the great majority of the lords had any wish to see the 1399 settlement overturned. Henry avoided the manner of rule which had brought about his predecessor's downfall, and in doing so ensured at least the acquiescence of the community in the revolution of 1399.

In suppressing the northern rebellions, Henry showed an ability to act swiftly and decisively. On all three occasions he retained the loyalty of virtually all the nobility, not just those such as Westmorland who had a personal interest in the Percies' downfall. The Earl Marshal's support for the Scrope rebellion in 1405 is the only exception to this generalization; of the other earls, Warwick, Stafford and Kent fought alongside Henry at Shrewsbury, and Arundel and Warwick participated in the trial of the Archbishop of York and the Earl Marshal after Shipton Moor. Kent's support for Henry is particularly significant: his brother had been one of the leaders of the rebellion in 1400 and had been beheaded by the mob at Cirencester, but Henry allowed him to inherit his brother's lands and title, and he remained loyal to the Lancastrian dynasty. He was on the council from 1405 onwards, and took part in military and naval engagements until his death in 1408. Henry showed no vindictiveness towards the heirs of other nobles who had opposed him: Salisbury's son was restored to his father's lands and title in 1409 and Despenser's heir was allowed to inherit the family lands, though he was not permitted to assume the title of Earl of Gloucester. The Earl of March was treated rather less leniently, since although he was only twelve when the Percies rose in revolt in 1403 his claim to the throne ensured that he would be the figurehead around whom rebels would gather. Henry kept him under surveillance and never granted him livery of his inheritance, although he was twenty-two at the king's death in 1413.

The King's Illness and the Renewal of the French War

In France, Henry IV's seizure of the throne was regarded as a disaster. With Gaunt dead and Richard a prisoner, the French believed that Henry would be a puppet of the commons, and that 'the Commons of England want nothing but war'.[51] But in the event neither side showed itself anxious to rush into war. At a meeting at Westminster in June 1401, the lords showed themselves divided over whether to go to war with France, some fearing that there was insufficient money to finance an expedition, and in the event the truce of 1396 was renewed. The truce remained in force throughout 1402 and most of 1403, but the death of the Duke of Burgundy in 1404 emboldened the Duke of Orléans to increase pressure on Aquitaine. Open war in Aquitaine had been resumed in October 1403, and between then and 1408, when another truce was agreed, the area within the English obedience diminished so much that in 1406 the Archbishop of Bordeaux wrote to Henry that the duchy was in danger of being lost.[52] No major expedition was sent to relieve the duchy, but Henry endeavoured to maintain the flow of funds to the garrisons there.

The commons in parliament, however, proved less bellicose than the French had predicted. Their principal concern in their dealings with the king over finance was to ensure that the burden on the community did not become unreasonable or insupportable. Although the commons were prepared to grant Henry the customs revenue regularly, and to vote direct taxes when necessary, they expected Henry to exploit his resources to the fullest. They were especially concerned that lands which fell to the crown should be retained to augment royal resources instead of being granted out again, and in the Coventry parliament of 1404 the commons insisted on an Act of Resumption which would apply to all grants and leases made since 1366. If the act had been enforced it would have led to an unacceptable upheaval, but it indicated the concern the commons felt over the alienation of royal resources. A more effective proposal was that all who held annuities or grants of profit should surrender the current year's income to the king. The commons also voted a tax described by Walsingham as 'novel and exquisite'[53] of one shilling in the pound on rents and incomes from land exceeding 500 marks per annum. The tax did not bring in much more than a lay subsidy of the traditional kind, but it may have persuaded the commons that the magnates were bearing their fair share of taxation.

The commons' concern over finance should not be taken as evidence of hostility to Henry's regime, and indeed in his conduct of financial affairs he went to some lengths to respect the sensitiveness of the commons. He avoided the extravagance which had characterized Richard's rule in the 1380s and in the last years of his reign. Neither taxation nor borrowing were heavier than they had been in Richard's reign, despite the fact that between 1400 and 1405 he had to make substantial calls on the country's financial resources for external defence and for the suppression of the rebellions against him. In the early years of the reign, too, Henry used the Duchy of Lancaster, whose administration remained separate from the Exchequer, to augment his resources. Duchy offices, lands and revenues were used to reward servants and followers, and duchy income and castles were used in defence of the king's position in Wales. The duchy provided him with a small but serviceable private income, on average about £1,000 a year, but its principal value was as a reservoir of patronage. Nonetheless, the payment of annuities represented a substantial burden on the exchequer, and the commons were critical of this form of expenditure throughout the early years of Henry's reign. Henry, however, needed to ensure widespread support for his regime in the country, and the granting (and regular payment) of annuities was an important means of creating and retaining such support. The political wisdom of his policy was apparent during the rebellions of 1403 and 1405 when most of Henry's annuitants in the northern counties remained loyal to him.[54]

Henry's achievement in the first eight years of his reign had been substantial. He overcame the rebellions against him, retained the loyalty of most of the nobility, and handled parliament with sufficient skill to avoid a major political crisis. Yet after 1408 his grip on affairs weakened, and a struggle for power developed at court, with Henry's half-brothers the Beauforts and his eldest son the Prince of Wales playing a leading part. The underlying reason for Henry's weakness was ill health. He was in all probability slightly older than the king he supplanted, and as early as December 1399 there were indications that he was suffering from some malady, though this may have been nothing more serious than food poisoning. On the very day of Scrope's execution, 8 June 1405, Henry suffered a sudden seizure as he was riding from York to Ripon. Thomas Gascoigne, the only near-contemporary writer to mention this episode, describes it as an attack of leprosy.[55] This perhaps makes a moral rather than a medical point: leprosy was seen as a sign of divine displeasure, which many expected Henry to incur after ordering the execution of an archbishop. The seizure was more likely to have been a coronary episode, and after a week's rest he recovered. During the parliament of 1406 he was once again taken ill, however, and from then onwards his health remained uncertain: he suffered another seizure in June 1408, and he was incapacitated for a lengthy period early in 1409. He evidently believed he was near to death, and on 21 January 1409 he made his will. His illness cannot readily be diagnosed from contemporaries' accounts. Gascoigne, as we have seen, believed that his seizure in 1405 was leprosy; Adam of Usk said that the king was tormented for five years 'with festering of the flesh, dehydration of the eyes, and rupture of the internal organs', and Walsingham described how he lost consciousness for several hours after returning from the north in 1408.[56] Modern writers have discounted the view that he suffered from leprosy, and some have seen his physical collapse as the outward sign of psychological problems, notably a sense of guilt, induced by the circumstances of his seizure of the throne and the subsequent strains and stresses of his reign. The most recent discussion, however, suggests that his illness was indeed physical, possibly heart disease brought on by rheumatic fever, and although it may well be true that Henry had some doubts about the legitimacy of his actions in 1399 there is little hard evidence for any nervous condition sufficient to produce the collapses of 1405, 1406, and 1408–9. A physical rather than a psychological origin for his illness seems most probable.[57]

During the king's illness in the winter of 1408–9 government was carried on by Archbishop Arundel and the council, while the Prince of Wales busied himself with mopping up Glyn Dŵr's rebellion in Wales. With the recapture of Harlech and Aberystwyth the revolt effectively came to an end, and the prince now felt able to devote his time more fully to domestic politics. Closely associated with the prince were the

Beaufort brothers, the children of John of Gaunt by Katherine Swynford. The eldest, John Earl of Somerset, died in 1410, but Thomas and Henry, Bishop of Winchester, seem to have formed an understanding with the Prince of Wales against Archbishop Arundel and, perhaps, the prince's younger brother Thomas, who was created Duke of Clarence in 1412. It is not clear why friction developed between the archbishop and the Beauforts. Arundel may have offended them by insisting on the insertion of a clause excluding them from any claim to the crown when their legitimization was confirmed in 1407,[58] but the prospect that they might succeed to the throne was very remote, since the king had four sons living, and it is more likely that they were merely ambitious: the subsequent career of Bishop (later Cardinal) Beaufort suggests a considerable appetite for power.

In December 1409 Archbishop Arundel resigned the office of Chancellor, and when parliament met in January 1410 the commons, through their Speaker Thomas Chaucer, a cousin of the Beauforts, sought the nomination of a new council in parliament. Not only the archbishop but also several of the knights who had served Henry well since his accession were excluded from the new council, which was headed by the Prince of Wales. Bishop Beaufort was appointed to it, together with the Earls of Arundel and Westmorland, and Thomas Beaufort was made Chancellor. The new council held office for twenty-one months, and the most important issue it had to deal with concerned relations with France. Until his death in 1404 the Duke of Burgundy had retained his ascendancy at the court of the weak and periodically insane Charles VI, and as long as Burgundy lived the truce between France and England had broadly held. Burgundy's death brought the Duke of Orléans to power, however, and he began to increase pressure on Aquitaine. England thus had to make a greater effort to defend the duchy, but Henry was unwilling to commit himself to a more extensive involvement in France. The murder of the Duke of Orléans by agents of the new Duke of Burgundy, John the Fearless, in 1407 transformed the situation, and the struggle for power at the French court reached a new intensity. Open civil war between the Duke of Burgundy and the princes allied with the new Duke of Orléans, amongst whom was Bernard Count of Armagnac (who gave his name to the Orleanist faction) became increasingly probable and England found herself in the unaccustomed position of being courted by both sides. Henry hoped to use the rivalry between the two factions in France to extract from one side or the other a commitment to recognize English sovereignty in the lands ceded under the Treaty of Brétigny. Such a commitment could probably be obtained by negotiation and a limited military involvement which the French princes might in any case be willing to pay for. The Prince of Wales, on the other hand, hoped that negotiations might bring the promise of wider English gains in France, and he was perhaps prepared to risk a more substantial military commitment. The struggle for ascendancy at court in Henry's last three years is thus very much bound up with different appreciations of the benefits to be derived from the struggle for power in France.

Civil war between the Burgundians and the Armagnacs flared up in August 1411, when the Armagnacs occupied Vermandois and threatened several towns close to the border with the Duke of Burgundy's Flemish lands. John the Fearless made overtures to England for an alliance and for military aid against the Armagnacs. He offered his daughter Anne in marriage to the Prince of Wales, but there is no firm evidence for the long-held belief that he also offered to hand over to the English the towns of Gravelines, Dunkerque, Sluys and Dixmude.[59] These negotiations were inconclusive, but Henry began preparations for an expedition to defend Calais from attack by the Armagnac princes who had been raiding in the neighbourhood of Bapaume. Henry intended to lead the expedition himself, but his health gave way and towards the end of September he called off the expedition. Meanwhile an embassy had been despatched to negotiate with John the Fearless at Arras, but John returned a non-committal answer to the embassy's request for Burgundian help in the reconquest of Aquitaine. The English council, led by the Prince of Wales, decided nonetheless to send a force of 800 lances and 2,000 archers under the Earl of Arundel to help the Duke of Burgundy. The English force reached Arras at the beginning of October, but by then Duke John had already reconquered Vermandois and had forced the Armagnac princes back to the Oise valley, from where they tried to encircle Paris. Duke John's response was to head straight for Paris, which he entered in triumph on 22 October with the Earl of Arundel and his English contingent. It was the first time for twenty-six years that an English force had been in arms on French territory.

Henry's failure to lead the proposed expedition to Calais precipitated a political crisis in October and November 1411. In early October the suggestion was apparently made that Henry should abdicate in favour of his son, and that the parliament which was due to assemble on 3 November should be invited to approve the Prince of Wales's accession. The author of Giles's Chronicle[60] states that the suggestion came from the prince himself, and that Henry firmly rejected it, insisting that he would rule as long as he had breath in his body. Other sources suggest that Bishop Beaufort put the proposal to Henry, and fourteen years later, when taxed with having suggested that the king should abdicate, he did not explicitly deny it. Corroborating evidence for the prince's responsibility for the proposal is provided by the arrest on 23 October of six knights, including the steward of the prince's household. All six were sent to the Tower, and were released only after parliament had ended. The record does not suggest any open confrontation in the parliament which met on 3 November but on 30 November the lords who had been appointed to the council in 1410 were thanked for their services and thus presumably discharged from office. Two days after parliament ended, the Chancellor and the Treasurer resigned, Archbishop Arundel was appointed Chancellor again, and a new council was formed from which the Prince of Wales, the Beaufort brothers and the Earls of Warwick and Arundel were omitted. The king had fended off this challenge to his rule with some ease, and it is hard to know how much support the proposal that he should abdicate had commanded. Over the previous three years Prince Henry had formed a group of political friends, chief amongst whom were the Earl of Arundel and the Beauforts, but Arundel was abroad when the crisis developed, and the most likely explanation is that the proposal emanated from the prince himself, frustrated at the element of unpredictability which the king's failing health brought to diplomatic negotiations and military preparations. Once again, however, there was no general disposition to reject the authority of the king or to restrict his prerogative by giving the prince any formal power in government. As long as the king lived, he intended to enjoy his powers to the full.

The king thus recovered his authority, and his return to power was followed in May 1412 by a change in English diplomacy from support of Burgundy to alliance with the Armagnac princes. It has sometimes been supposed that this volte-face was a result of the Prince of Wales's loss of power in November 1411, but such an interpretation is an oversimplification of a complex diplomatic situation. Negotiations between Henry and the Burgundian envoys continued in the winter of 1412: a Burgundian embassy was in England between 1 February and 4 March 1412, and Henry received the Burgundian ambassadors twice, at Coldharbour and at Rochester. Henry also appointed a commission to discuss the terms of a marriage between the Prince of Wales and a Burgundian princess. When the Burgundians left England they evidently believed an agreement was in prospect; but they were on the point of being outbidden by the Armagnacs. In January 1412 the Armagnac princes agreed to send an embassy to Henry, and for some months the king was negotiating with both sides, much to the annoyance of the Emperor Sigismund, who wrote to Henry reprimanding him for doing so and arguing that if Englishmen were to fight on both sides it would only exacerbate the civil war. In the event, the Armagnacs won, and by the Treaty of Bourges, ratified in Westminster on 18 May 1412, they agreed to 'help the King of England in his just quarrels with their lives and all their power'. Among the King of England's just quarrels they agreed to include his 'claim to the duchy of Guienne, which they regard as rightfully his'.[61] In return,

Henry agreed not to enter into any treaties with the Duke of Burgundy, and to help the Armagnac princes to defeat him and bring him to justice. In pursuit of this goal, Henry agreed to send immediately a force of 1,000 men-at-arms and 3,000 archers to fight alongside the Armagnac princes, who would pay their wages.

The Treaty of Bourges was a more solid commitment than anything the Duke of Burgundy had offered, but the Prince of Wales appears to have been unhappy about it. The prince and his three brothers took an oath to uphold the treaty, but on 31 May the prince thought it necessary to write to the Duke of Burgundy saying that although he had hoped to conclude a treaty of alliance and marriage with him, the proposals made by the Armagnac princes appeared to the king his father to be 'too advantageous to be rejected'. The Earl of Arundel also wrote to John the Fearless on the same day, saying that, at the request of the duke's envoys and because of the duke's generosity towards him, he had promised not to favour the duke's adversaries save on the order of the king or the Prince of Wales'.[62] The prince and the earl evidently wanted to keep in touch with the duke and have him believe that the Treaty of Bourges was not of their making. Rumours about the prince's dissatisfaction with the treaty, and about his part in the abortive proposal to persuade his father to abdicate, goaded him into publishing an open letter on 17 June 1412 in which he refuted any suggestion of disloyalty and denied that he had tried to seize the throne. He protested his love and filial devotion to the king, and Walsingham goes on to suggest that he came in person to the king at the end of June and sought the punishment of his detractors. The king seemed to agree, but told him he should wait for the assembly of parliament, so that such people could be punished by the judgement of their peers',[63] an indication, perhaps, that some of those who had spread rumours about the prince's disloyalty were to be found amongst the ranks of the nobility.

The prince took no part in the expedition to France which left England at the beginning of August 1412. Its command was entrusted to the king's second son Thomas, who was created Duke of Clarence and Lieutenant in Aquitaine in July. With Clarence went the Duke of York, the newly created Earl of Dorset Thomas Beaufort, the Earls of Ormond, Oxford and Salisbury, eight barons and twenty-eight knights, with retinues amounting to about 6,500 men-at-arms and archers. The army landed at Saint-Vaast-la-Hougue on 10 August and marched south, hoping to join the Armagnac princes on the Loire. But news of the army's arrival caused consternation at Charles VI's court, and the Burgundians and Armagnacs temporarily resolved their differences. They concluded an agreement on 22 August, the Peace of Auxerre, in which both sides agreed to renounce their alliances with England. By this time Clarence's army was well on its way south, and at Blois on 6 September he heard of the Armagnac volte-face. From Blois Clarence sent a letter to the Armagnac princes saying that he could not understand why they had broken off their alliance with England, and warning them that if they did not respect their obligation to England Anglo-French relations would be gravely compromised. He also pointed out that the Duke of Burgundy had no alliance with England to renounce, since it was not the English habit to support both sides at the same time.

The first reaction of the Armagnac princes was to fight the English, but the Duke of Berry, who was alarmed at the damage a marauding English army might do to his lands in Berry and Poitou, suggested that they might be willing to be bought off. Accordingly on 13 October the Armagnac princes sent an embassy to Clarence to ask him how much he wanted in return for agreeing to leave France. Negotiations lasted for just over a month, and on 14 November in the Treaty of Buzançais the princes agreed to pay Clarence and his fellow captains 150,000 écus, of which two-thirds was to be found by 30 November and the balance by Christmas. Seven hostages would be handed over, including the Count of Angoulême, third son of the Duke of Orléans, and treasure from the Duke of Berry's chapel at Bourges worth 66,375 écus was given as a pledge for the payment. The treasure included one great golden cross which the Duke of York received, and another golden crucifix with three large diamonds in the hands and feet, and a ruby in the wound side, which went to Clarence. Clarence also received a reliquary containing one of the nails with which Christ was fixed to the Cross. This never found its way back to France, and it was thirty years before all the money due was handed over and the Count of Angoulême released. Clarence's expedition was the most profitable that the English had sent to France since the days of Edward III. A new generation of nobles, especially York, Salisbury and Clarence, had had their appetites for gain whetted, and the ease with which the English could march through France had been well demonstrated. On the other hand, although the English had extricated themselves with some honour and profit from a potentially difficult situation, the Prince of Wales may have drawn the conclusion that it was unwise to become too deeply committed to either of the factions in France.[64]

After the conclusion of the Treaty of Buzançais Clarence took his forces south to Bordeaux, and they did not return to England until April 1413. By then the king was dead: his health deteriorated sharply over the winter, and although parliament was summoned for 3 February he was too ill to meet it, and he died on 20 March 1413. The revival of faction at his court in the last years of Henry's reign, as his illness became more acute, should not be allowed to detract from his substantial achievements in the years before his health gave way. He overcame a series of challenges to his rule from disaffected nobles who believed that their ambitions would best be served by a reversal of the revolution of 1399, but he never lost the general support of the nobility. Archbishop Arundel was too kind when he said that Henry was humane and forgiving to his enemies, but he was ready enough to restore the heirs of some of the nobles who opposed him, though he took care not to allow Northumberland's heir or the Earl of March to have livery of their inheritances. His relations with the commons were marked by fractiousness and difficulty over taxation, but he handled them with sufficient skill to ensure that they did not make common cause with disaffected nobles in a fundamental challenge to his rule. As the popular reaction to the rising of the earls in 1400 showed, the revolution of 1399 commanded general support, and Henry's manner of rule ensured that he never lost this support. The factionalism of the king's last years was essentially a struggle to promote the influence of the Prince of Wales and his friends against that of the king himself and Archbishop Arundel; it cannot be interpreted as indicative of the unpopularity of the Lancastrian dynasty. Indeed, the very fact of the king's ill health may have prevented factionalism from becoming too overt. The chroniclers suggest that after 1405 no one expected the king to live long; the outcome could not remain in doubt for many years, and despite the friction between the king and the prince in 1412, and the rumours that Clarence might supplant the prince in the succession, the prince's right to succeed had been confirmed in parliament on more than one occasion.[65] Henry understandably resisted any suggestion that he should abdicate, but when he died Prince Henry succeeded to a united realm, and to a monarchy which had its prerogatives intact and which had defeated challenges to its legitimacy. These were Henry IV's real achievements.

7
Henry V and the Dual Monarchy,
1413–1435

The Agincourt Campaign

It has often been argued that the accession of Henry V in 1413 marks a decisive turning point in the Anglo-French conflict of the later Middle Ages. Henry IV's deteriorating health had prevented him from becoming personally involved in warfare in France, and in his negotiations with both sides in the French civil war he had been concerned to obtain an agreement to an enlarged and sovereign Aquitaine, as envisaged in the Treaty of Brétigny. Henry V's approach, however, was to be very different. He was, of course, young and able-bodied (twenty-six years of age at his accession) and eager to establish his military reputation, but for him the conquest of territory in France and the assertion of his claim to the French throne were the most important motives for going to war: his strategy was much bolder and more grandiose than that of his father. Yet the contrast between father and son can be overdrawn. Henry's contemporary biographers portray him as a man with a mission to complete the task undertaken by his predecessors, and there was nothing novel about seeking by negotiation or war to win sovereign territory in France. The events of Henry IV's last years had demonstrated both the risks and the advantages of negotiating with both sides in the French civil war, and Henry V's diplomacy embodied the same approach; indeed, it was doubtful whether any other policy would have served England's interests. Nor, with one exception, were Henry's methods new: his policy of negotiating with both the Burgundians and the Armagnacs was a continuation of the strategy adopted in 1411, and, in broader terms, it bears comparison with Edward III's negotiations with Brittany, Flanders, and the King of Navarre in the 1340s and 1350s. Indeed, the momentum of Henry's war, and its successful climax in the Treaty of

Troyes, were determined mainly by internal French political rivalries, and although Henry's ultimate goal was the French crown, his approach was essentially opportunistic, seeking whatever concessions he could from the two factions in France while at the same time benefiting militarily from their rivalry.

In one respect, however, Henry's war embodied a novel feature: the conquest and settlement by Englishmen of substantial territory in Normandy. In the fourteenth century the English had garrisoned fortresses in Normandy, Brittany and Anjou, and had exploited the surrounding countryside; but with the exception of Calais no part of France under English control had experienced an influx of English civilian settlers prepared to make their home in conquered territory. Under Henry V, however, Normandy experienced both military occupation and civilian settlement by the English, and the presence of so many English settlers, mainly drawn from the ranks of the lesser landowning class, was to prove a major obstacle when the two protagonists sought to negotiate peace in the 1440s.

Like his great-grandfather Edward III, Henry found much support for his war amongst the nobility and gentry, though it would probably be wrong to suggest that he went to war to distract the nobility's attention from his supposedly insecure claim to the throne. As a modern commentator has remarked, 'Henry renewed the war because he wanted to, not because he was forced to',[1] and the nobility and gentry followed him because they expected to gain from doing so. Their motives in going to war were much the same as those of their ancestors in Edward III's reign: to serve the king, and to win honour, glory and profit. The expedition of 1412 had perhaps shown a generation of nobles unaccustomed to war in France what profits could be won there, and in his opening sermon to the parliament of November 1414 the Chancellor, Bishop Beaufort, had indicated that successful war might lead to a reduction in the burdens on the king's subjects.[2] Henry's armies were mainly contract armies, recruited both by the titled nobility and by numerous knights and esquires. Indeed, such lesser men seem to have played a more important part both in recruiting troops and in lending money to the crown than they had done in Edward III's day. They received their reward in the form of lands and offices in Normandy, and they became essential to the garrisoning and administration of occupied territory. Henry's war made the fortunes of some men of this social rank, and in so doing, created a substantial vested interest in the maintenance of the Lancastrian conquests.

The leadership in war, however, was taken by the king, his brothers, and the titled nobility. In this respect too Henry's war resembled that of Edward III. The king with his companions in arms occupied a preeminent position in the planning and fighting of the war. The king had

had considerable preparation both for government and for war: his celebrated youthful escapades, if authentic, had not filled the whole of his life as Prince of Wales. He had been wounded at the battle of Shrewsbury in 1403 when he was only sixteen, and he gained invaluable experience of hard campaigning in dealing with the Glyn Dŵr rebellion between 1403 and 1408. His campaigns in Wales taught him the virtues of the careful, persistent and systematic approach to subduing a country and the dangers of a quick and superficial victory in the field: both lessons were to stand him in good stead in France. His presence on the council after 1408 brought him into collision with his father and Archbishop Arundel, but his experiences both on campaign and in government allowed him to establish a group of political friends, notably the Earl of Arundel (who died of dysentery at the siege of Harfleur in 1415), the earl of Warwick, and Thomas Beaufort Earl of Dorset, who played a leading part in Henry's campaigns in Normandy. Henry was not just a warrior-king, however; he appears to have been a genuinely religious man, following perhaps in the pious tradition of his great-grandfather Henry Duke of Lancaster, author of *Le livre de saintz medicines*. Like his father and his grandfather his piety was of a strictly conventional and orthodox nature. It is not therefore surprising that he believed in divine support for his cause and considered that by establishing his just claim he was fulfilling the will of God. There was an element of self-righteousness in Henry's character which, combined with a single-minded devotion to the task in hand, whether war or government, made him a ruthless and determined opponent and at the same time an outstandingly effective leader of men, maintaining firm discipline yet enjoying loyalty and respect for his fairness and impartiality.

The characters of Henry's brothers, Thomas Duke of Clarence, John Duke of Bedford and Humphrey Duke of Gloucester, emerge with less clarity. Clarence had identified himself more with his father than his brother in the political conflicts of Henry IV's last years, but all three served Henry V with loyalty and devotion in his campaigns in France. Clarence was killed at the battle of Baugé 1421: had he lived the politics of both England and France during the minority of Henry VI might well have taken a different course. Gloucester, the youngest brother, eventually proved to be a man of poor judgement and only moderate political skill, but Bedford had something of the qualities of the king himself, and proved both an able general and a skilful administrator. His death in 1435 was a serious setback for Lancastrian France. In the long run, however, one of the most significant disservices Henry's brothers did their dynasty was their failure to produce legitimate heirs, either male or female. After the Duke of Gloucester's death in 1447 Henry VI became the sole representative of Henry IV's male progeny.

When Henry V became king in March 1413, the two factions in the French civil war had patched up a precarious peace agreement, the Peace of Auxerre, and the English army which had been bought off by the Treaty of Buzançais was wintering at Bordeaux. At the opening of the new king's first parliament in May, the new Chancellor, Henry Beaufort, reminded parliament that they should provide for the king's estate and the establishment of good governance; but apart from a very general reference to the king's intention to protect his allies and resist his enemies there was no attempt to persuade the commons to grant taxes specifically for war. War, however, was in the forefront of Henry's mind, and preparations for an expedition to France began in June, with the raising of substantial loans from the citizens of London and the clergy. But these warlike plans were accompanied by negotiations. Juvenel des Ursins observed that 'even the English princes were divided by the quarrel between Burgundy and Orléans, for the Dukes of Clarence and Gloucester, the king's brothers, and with them the Duke of York, favoured the Orleanists; while the king and the Duke of Bedford, likewise his brother, were inclined to the Burgundians'.[3] It is doubtful whether Henry was merely reverting to the pro-Burgundian stance he had adopted in 1411. The alliance with the Armagnacs in 1412 had proved a failure, though a profitable failure nonetheless, and John the Fearless's position in Paris had been shaken both by the Cabochien revolt in April 1413 and by the king's support, when he recovered his wits in the following month, for the Armagnac faction. Henry concluded that Burgundy might now be more anxious to court English support, and negotiations went on during May and June 1413.

The Burgundians suggested a military alliance with England in which Burgundy would help the English to conquer the lands of the Counts of Armagnac and Angoulême and the Lord of Albret, while the two powers would jointly conquer the lands of the Dukes of Orléans, Anjou and Bourbon and the Counts of Alençon, Vertus and Eu. The alliance was to be cemented by a marriage between Henry and one of the Duke of Burgundy's daughters. But when the English pressed the Burgundian ambassadors to be more specific about the conduct of the proposed campaign, they were notably evasive and the negotiations came to nothing. In September John the Fearless negotiated a settlement with the Armagnacs, the Treaty of Arras, in which he promised not to make any alliance with Henry; but nevertheless he continued to negotiate with England. There was suspicion and duplicity on both sides, and both Henry and John the Fearless probably hoped to get the other to do much of his work for him without offering anything very substantial in the way of concessions.

At the same time, Henry was negotiating with the Armagnac princes in Paris. So long as they remained in power they could offer real concessions to Henry and had a strong incentive to do so. Henry's ambassadors demanded not merely sovereignty over Aquitaine, but also Normandy, Touraine, Anjou, Maine, Brittany, Flanders and part of Artois, together with half the county of Provence, the arrears of John II's ransom, and a dowry of 2 million écus if a marriage was agreed between Henry and Charles VI's daughter Catherine. The French were prepared to offer an enlarged Aquitaine in full sovereignty, and a dowry of 800,000 écus for Catherine. The English demands were so exorbitant that it is hard to believe that Henry was serious. Although the Armagnacs' hold on power was precarious, they could scarcely have been expected to agree to give Henry half the kingdom. In the event, the terms they offered did not differ substantially from those they had offered Henry IV, and although negotiations dragged on into 1415 there was no prospect of an agreement.

Henry meanwhile continued his preparations for war. It was essential to ensure that the country was united behind him, and like Edward III he took a series of steps to reinforce aristocratic support for the crown, both by the restoration of some of those who had suffered under his father and by bestowing titles on those who would be expected to play a leading part in the war. His two youngest brothers, John and Humphrey, were created Duke of Bedford and Duke of Gloucester in 1414, and the Duke of York's younger brother was created Earl of Cambridge. The Earl of March, now aged twenty-two, was given livery of his lands, as was the brother and heir of the Earl Marshal, Thomas Mowbray, executed in 1405 for his part in the Scrope rebellion. The heir of John Holand Earl of Huntingdon was restored when he came of age in 1417, but the dynasty's animus against Salisbury and Despenser was not yet fully abated.

Salisbury had received his father's earldom and the lands he held in tail in 1409, but he had to wait until 1421 for full restitution, and Despenser's heir was never fully restored. In December 1413 Henry made a symbolic gesture of reconciliation when he had Richard II's body removed from King's Langley, where it had lain since his death in 1400, and ceremonially interred it in Westminster Abbey in the elaborate tomb which Richard had prepared for himself in 1395. Henry was not, however, yet willing to take the more substantial risk of restoring the Percy family. Hotspur's son, the heir to the earldom of Northumberland, was in exile in Scotland, and Henry did not bring him back and grant him his grandfather's lands and title until March 1416 when, in the aftermath of Agincourt, he probably felt even more secure.

Events were to show that Henry's suspicion of the Percy connection in the north was justified; but in 1413 and 1414 the most immediate danger came from the Lollards. In September 1413 Sir John Old-castle was tried and condemned for heresy. Oldcastle was a

Herefordshire knight who had served with Prince Henry in Wales, held office as sheriff of his county, and after 1408 sat in the lords by virtue of his marriage to the widow of John Lord Cobham of Kent. The presence of so committed a heretic in the affinity of the Prince raises questions about the Prince's own attitude towards religious unorthodoxy, though like the so-called Lollard knights of Richard II's reign Oldcastle may not have drawn attention to his beliefs until 1413.[4] Towards the end of October, however, he escaped from imprisonment in the Tower, and fomented a conspiracy to capture the king and his brothers at Christmas 1413, seize the City of London, and execute a number of bishops. But the plot was betrayed to the king, who surprised the rebels at St Giles's Field in January 1414 and arrested them. Oldcastle himself escaped and remained at large until 1417, when he was captured and put to death. Oldcastle's followers were mainly ordinary people from the various Lollard communities in England, and the organization of the rising suggests that there was a substantial measure of underground communication between these various heretical groups. The rebellion enjoyed the support of a number of members of the knightly class, but it attracted no aristocratic sympathy and it never stood any chance of success.

More serious was the conspiracy revealed to Henry as he mustered his troops at Southampton in August 1415 for the invasion of France. Its object was to kill the king and his brothers, and place the Earl of March on the throne. March himself betrayed the plot to Henry, however, and it is difficult to believe that he was deeply involved in it. Once again, his claim to the throne made him a convenient vehicle for the ambition of others. The ringleaders were the Earl of Cambridge, Sir Thomas Grey of Heton in Northumberland, and Henry Lord Scrope of Masham. Cambridge's wife was a member of the Clifford family, which was closely allied with the Percies and looked to them for support against their neighbours and rivals in the north, the Nevilles. Cambridge, however, had (or believed he had) his own grievances against Henry: his earldom was little more than titular, and he had not received from the crown the endowments he perhaps thought he should have had to maintain his estate. Grey was Cambridge's son-in-law, but Scrope was an improbable conspirator. Although he was the nephew of the Archbishop of York executed in 1405, he had been appointed as Treasurer of England in January 1410 and had been dismissed when the Prince of Wales fell from power in December 1411. He had, however, engaged to bring a sizeable retinue to serve with Henry on his forthcoming expedition to France. He had family ties with both Cambridge and March, and March was substantially in debt to him. Perhaps, therefore, Scrope was drawn into the conspiracy because he could not afford to see March suffer forfeiture for treason if the conspiracy was betrayed, though probably the last thing he expected was that March himself would betray the plot. The conspirators hoped that the young Henry Percy, Hotspur's heir, would join them and bring the military power of the Percy affinity to their aid; but they made no attempt to win wider support from the nobility. Cambridge did not even inform his brother the Duke of York; Lord Clifford seems to have known nothing about it, and the Percy connection in the north remained quiet. When March betrayed the plot, the three ringleaders were arrested, tried and executed. The ineffectiveness of the Southampton plot suggests that the cause the conspirators hoped to advance was now discredited. There was no general support for the Earl of March's claim to the throne backed by Percy arms, and March himself had no wish to be involved in the conspirators' plans. Henry's firm response made it clear to any remaining sympathizers with the cause of March and Percy that nothing was to be gained by conspiracy, while his restoration of Hotspur's heir in 1416 demonstrated the rewards that flowed from loyalty to the king and dynasty.[5]

Henry embarked for France on 7 August 1415 with an army of about 10,500 fighting men. Two-thirds of the force consisted of mounted archers or mounted men-at-arms, suggesting that mobility was an essential part of his strategy, but the real purpose of the expedition remains unclear. Until the force landed in Normandy it was not even certain where Henry intended to go: there is some possibility that even an expedition to Aquitaine was not entirely out of the question, and Henry may have wished to keep several options open in case of a sudden development in his negotiations with the French, or, more likely, a sudden change in the French political situation. In the event, however, Henry's decision to attack Harfleur was probably dictated by an appreciation of the advantages which possession of the town would give him in future campaigns. Not only did it command the Seine estuary and thus the route to Rouen, but it also provided a base from which the English could keep some control of the sea. The town fell on 22 September 1415, though not without loss. The Earl of Arundel and Michael de la Pole Earl of Suffolk died during the siege, together with the Bishop of Norwich, who had led the English embassies to France in 1414 and early 1415, and at least eight knights. All seem to have died of dysentery. Henry now set about turning Harfleur into an English base. All the French inhabitants who would not swear fealty to him or who were not worth ransoming were deported and an English garrison was established under the command of Thomas Beaufort Earl of Dorset.

Henry's next move has been the subject of much debate. Despite the lateness of the season and the losses his army had sustained from disease, he determined, against the wishes of some of his advisers, to march through Normandy to Calais, where he would re-embark for

England. K. B. McFarlane suggested that the march was a cunning ruse to lure the French to battle and defeat them; but such a judgement is surely influenced by hindsight.[6] Henry set out from Harfleur with little more than half his original army, and deliberately to lure the French to battle would have seemed foolhardy. It may be that Henry intended the march to be no more than a reconnaissance venture, to find out what he could about the French forces which had so signally failed to come to the relief of Harfleur; but since he did not know where the French were he must have accepted that there was some risk of being forced to battle. He may well have believed, however, that divine aid and the choice of a good defensive position would bring him victory.

When the English reached the Somme they found the crossing at Blanche–Taque, west of Abbeville, blocked by the French, and they had to march over fifty miles south-eastwards to an unguarded ford south of Peronne. The weary English troops were now very close to the French army, and the two forces moved north-westwards along roughly parallel lines, the English probably hoping to reach Calais without having to fight. But on 24 October the French took up their position across the line of English advance near the village of Agincourt. Henry's escape route to Calais was barred. He assembled his army on ploughland made muddy by recent rain, with thick woods on either side which would make it difficult for the French cavalry to deploy. Some of the older and more experienced nobles in the French army, notably Marshal Boucicaut, advised against giving battle, but they were overruled by young nobles eager for glory and victory. On the next day, the English position held as the French front line advanced against it, and then, says the author of the *Gesta*, 'so great was the undisciplined violence and pressure' of the second line of Frenchmen, advancing on the first, 'that the living fell on top of the dead and others falling on top of the living were killed as well'.[7] The French suffered enormous casualties: the Constable, d'Albret, and the Dukes of Alençon, Bar and Brabant were killed, while the Dukes of Orléans and Bourbon together with the Counts of Eu, Richemont and Vendôme were captured. The Duke of Burgundy may have considered joining the battle, but in the event he never set out and he restrained his son Philip Count of Charolais from doing so. The Burgundians regarded the battle as a defeat primarily for the Armagnac faction, and many Armagnac nobles were killed or captured; but although the Duke of Burgundy probably hoped that the defeat would bring about a reaction in his favour in Paris, the Armagnacs maintained their hold on power.

On the English side the losses were light. The Duke of York and the Earl of Suffolk, who had inherited his title only a month earlier, were killed, together with perhaps three or four hundred men. News of the victory reached England a few days before the opening of parliament, and Bishop Beaufort was able to deliver a sermon on the trinity of divine judgements that had favoured the English cause in France: Sluys, Poitiers, and Agincourt. When parliament turned to more practical matters the commons voted Henry a new tax and agreed to grant him the customs revenue for life. Such a grant had been made only once before, when Richard II blackmailed the commons into agreeing to it in 1398, and their willingness to depart from the previously cherished principle of granting the customs for only a year or two at a time is a measure of their euphoria at victory and their enthusiasm for continuing the war. The euphoria induced by Agincourt reached its climax at the end of November 1415 when the City of London welcomed Henry to celebrate his triumph in deco-rated streets with choirs dressed as martyrs, prophets and virgins. Henry attracted praise for his modest bearing, and the celebrations culminated in the king making offerings at St Paul's and at the shrine of Edward the Confessor in Westminster Abbey.[8]

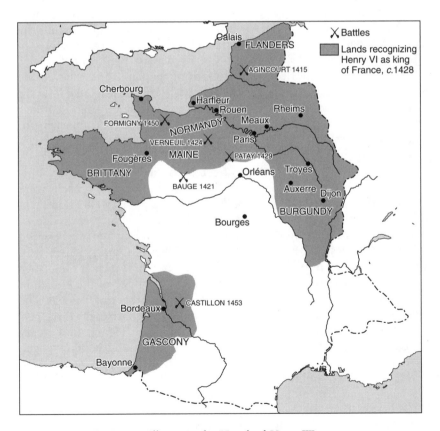

Map 3   France: to illustrate the Hundred Years War, 1415–1453

The Conquest of Normandy and the Treaty of Troyes

In France, the defeat not only destroyed many of the Armagnac leaders and demoralized the country, but it also created a belief in English invincibility in battle which was to influence military planning even in 1450 when they were poised to expel the English from Normandy. Henry hoped that the defeat might induce the French to reopen negotiations and offer substantial concessions, but his diplomacy was complicated by divisions amongst the Armagnac lords and by attempts at mediation on the part of the Emperor Sigismund. The Emperor believed that the work of the Council of Constance in seeking an end to the schism in the Church could be hastened by a settlement between England and France. Some of the Armagnac lords favoured a truce, but others, led by Bernard Count of Armagnac, wanted war to recover Harfleur. In the spring of 1416 the Armagnac forces established a blockade of Harfleur by land and sea, and the Earl of Dorset, the captain of the garrison, sent urgent messages to England for supplies and a relieving force. If the town were to remain in English hands the blockade had to be broken, and a naval force was therefore mustered in June, under Bedford's command. On 15 August Bedford defeated a French and Genoese fleet in the mouth of the Seine and relieved the town. The Armagnac policy perhaps made some sense from a military point of view, but their failure to regain the town simply exposed their duplicity in taking military action while at the same time appearing to negotiate with the English. While the Armagnacs were engaged in Normandy the Emperor Sigismund went to Paris and then to England, where he was received with great ceremony in May 1416. But Sigismund soon found that neither the English nor the French were prepared to be flexible, and that he had no hope of persuading them to reach a final agreement. The most he could induce each side to consider was a truce for three years accompanied by a meeting between Henry, Charles and himself. The *Gesta Henrici Quinti*, which may have been written to convince the Council of Constance of the justice of Henry's position, dwells at length on the duplicity of the French in keeping Henry engaged in talk while guilefully preparing for war. The point was not lost on Sigismund, and the Armagnacs' behaviour persuaded the emperor to align himself firmly with Henry. In a treaty concluded at Canterbury in August 1416 Sigismund acknowledged Henry's right to France and made it clear that he would be prepared to help him with military support.

Henry and Sigismund now planned to attract the Duke of Burgundy into their alliance, in the hope that together they could overthrow the Valois monarchy, and with England and France united under Lancastrian rule proceed to heal the schism in the Church.

John the Fearless responded to these overtures and agreed to meet Henry and Sigismund at Calais in October 1416. The negotiations took place in secret, and even contemporaries had little idea what happened. The author of the *Gesta* said that:

> what kind of conclusion ... these enigmatic talks and exchanges had produced went no further than the king's breast or the reticence with which he kept his counsel. I who am now writing know that the general view was that Burgundy had all this time detained our king with ambiguities and prevarications, and had so left him, and that in the end like all Frenchmen he would be found a double dealer, one person in public and another in private.[9]

There survives a draft treaty drawn up by the English Chancery which suggests that Henry hoped Duke John would recognize his right to the French throne, agree to give him military support, and 'do him liege homage and swear an oath of fealty to him as every subject of the King of France ought to do to his sovereign lord the King of France'.[10] Henry and Sigismund had much to gain from including Burgundy in their alliance: Henry would receive Burgundian military support in France, while Sigismund would benefit from a diversion of Burgundian interests away from expansion in imperial territory. It is much less clear, however, what Burgundy might expect to gain, for despite French statements to the contrary there is no evidence that Henry even offered Burgundy a share in his French conquests. Burgundy's interests were best served by avoiding any formal commitment to the alliance, though Duke John may have given Henry assurances that he would not oppose an English invasion of France. The negotiations at Calais ended without Burgundy's inclusion in the alliance, the draft treaty drawn up by the English was never agreed, and Henry now began to prepare another invasion of France.

Parliament met in October 1416 and heard a sermon from Bishop Beaufort on the theme, 'Let us make war so that we may have peace, for peace is the purpose of war'.[11] The commons voted two tenths and fifteenths, and the king conferred the dukedom of Exeter on the captain of the Harfleur garrison Thomas Beaufort Earl of Dorset. The peers not only approved the grant, but according to Walsingham suggested that the endowment of £1,000 a year which accompanied it was not sufficient 'for the worth of such a man'.[12] Earlier in the year Henry had reached agreement with the Scots over the ransom of Murdoch the Duke of Albany's son who had been captured at Homildon Hill in 1402. Murdoch was to be returned to Scotland for a ransom of £10,000 and Hotspur's son was to be allowed to return to England. Henry hoped by this move to secure his northern border against invasion by the Scots, and to eliminate the threat of further rebellions by disaffected supporters of the Percies. Hotspur's son was then granted the earldom of Northumberland, the wardenship of the East March, and the greater part of his grandfather's inheritance.

The campaign which Henry now planned was to be quite different from the plundering raids carried out under Edward III. His intention was to conquer and hold Normandy, and his experience of the Count of Armagnac's efforts to recover Harfleur the previous year led him to expect a long campaign encountering considerable resistance. Henry landed at Touques on the southern side of the Seine opposite Harfleur on 1 August 1417. The obvious strategy might have been to use his control of the Seine to move straight up to Rouen and seize the capital of Normandy, but instead he aimed first at Lower Normandy. He laid siege to Caen, which fell on 4 September and was subjected to looting by the English forces. By Christmas, Falaise, Argentan, Alençon and Verneuil had fallen. Cherbourg and Domfront were the only fortresses in Lower Normandy to hold out against him, and both gave him a hard time. Domfront did not surrender until July 1418, and Cherbourg resisted until September. The English faced some local counter-attacks, notably when Lord Talbot was routed at the mouth of the Vire after leading a raid into the Cotentin, and according to Adam of Usk he lost more than 500 men.[13] But the Duke of Burgundy took his forces to the Oise valley, whence they could threaten Paris, and where they provided a barrier behind which the English could continue their conquest of Normandy without fear of attack from the Armagnac princes. In early 1418 Henry moved towards the Seine, and on 29 June began the siege of Rouen. The Burgundians made no move to relieve the town, despite their presence no more than fifty miles away; it surrendered on 19 January 1419, and the rest of the duchy soon submitted. By the spring of 1419 virtually the whole of Normandy was in Henry's hands.

The conquest of Normandy was followed by the establishment of an English administration in the duchy and the settlement of Englishmen both in the captured towns and in the countryside. Some land was retained in the king's hands, to provide revenue and a reservoir of future patronage, but substantial grants were made to members of the titled nobility and prominent captains: in 1418–19, Henry granted the counties of Harcourt to Exeter, Aumale to Warwick, Perche to Salisbury, Tancarville to Sir John Grey, brother of the Southampton conspirator, Eu to Sir William Bourchier, and Longueville to Gaston de Foix, Captal de Buch. The Duke of Clarence received the viscounties of Auge, Orbec and Pont Audemer, and William de la Pole Earl of Suffolk, brother and heir of the earl who fell at Agincourt, was granted the lordships of Hambye and Briquebec. These were not perquisites to be enjoyed and exploited by absentee landowners:

Henry expected these nobles to undertake the defence and administration of the lands they received and to take responsibility for the
maintenance of the English conquest of Normandy. Most of those
who were granted estates in Normandy, however, were lesser men,
whom the king expected to live there and contribute to the defence of
the duchy. Many of these grants were made in tail male, an indication
that Henry expected his settlement to endure for several generations;
they carried with them an obligation to defend the property, and to
contribute a stated body of troops to serve the military needs of the
crown. It was Henry's eventual intention, it seems, to maintain only a
small number of paid troops in the garrisons of the principal towns in
Normandy, and to avoid the need to establish a permanent, professional army of occupation which would both drain the crown's financial resources and give the impression that English rule in Normandy
rested on force rather than acceptance of a just title.[14]

Although the settlement of Normandy provided the opportunity for
some men to enrich themselves, it is possible to exaggerate the extent
to which the duchy was exploited for the benefit of absentee English
lords. Sir John Fastolf, who had extensive estates in the Pays de Caux
and on the borders of Normandy and Maine, is probably an exception
upon whose career too many generalizations have been hung. For
most of those who settled in Normandy, their lands provided, in the
contemporary term, a 'lyvelode', a living, rather than the opportunity
to make substantial profits. For some, particularly perhaps those who
settled on the rich lands of the Pays d'Auge, the living would be good,
but it would be misleading to compare the creation of livelihoods for
English settlers in Normandy with the pillaging of the country under
Edward III. There was plenty of loot to be had during the campaign of
conquest: Adam of Usk reported that 'The booty taken in Normandy
was auctioned throughout England',[15] but once the initial conquest
was complete it is possible that the English derived less profit from
Normandy than they had done under Edward III. Even the titled
nobility did not necessarily profit greatly from their French possessions: for example, both Sir Henry Bourchier, who inherited Eu in
1420, and Humphrey Earl of Stafford, who was granted Perche
in 1431 after Salisbury's death, probably received less than the nominal value of their lands in Normandy, and as the fortunes of war
swung in favour of the French, their defence might even become a
liability.[16] For Henry, of course, the Normans were his subjects,
whether they were English settlers or Frenchmen who were willing
to swear allegiance to him, and they had to be protected as far as
possible from exploitation by the soldiery. Henry maintained strict
discipline in his armies, and sought to impose an administrative order
in Normandy which would contrast with the oppression of the Valois
monarchy and revive the duchy's pride in its ancient institutions.

Good government was to be a means of building up support in France for Lancastrian rule.

While Henry was engaged on the conquest of Normandy, John the Fearless embarked on a programme of sieges designed to win the principal towns around Paris. In the winter of 1417-18 Paris was surrounded by the Burgundians, and it fell on 28 May 1418, with the Dauphin escaping in his nightshirt. The Armagnac princes now began to consider an alliance with England, in the hope of recovering power from the Duke of Burgundy, and after Rouen fell both sides in the French civil war had an interest in seeking an agreement with Henry. In May 1419 John the Fearless and Queen Isabella met Henry at Meulan; Henry now offered to renounce the French crown in return for Normandy and a Greater Aquitaine, both in full sovereignty. These were the most moderate demands England had yet presented, but Burgundy and the queen felt unable to accept them. The negotiations were broken off, and a superficial rapprochement between the two French factions now took place. Burgundy and the Dauphin agreed to rule France jointly, and to make war on the English. Another meeting between the two was arranged for 10 September 1419 on the bridge at Montereau-sur-Yonne, but when the Duke of Burgundy arrived the Dauphin's retainers struck him down and killed him.

The murder at Montereau threw both sides in France into confusion, and placed Henry in a more commanding position than he could have hoped to achieve merely by force of arms. In the sixteenth century, the prior of the Charterhouse of Champmol, near Dijon, the burial place of the Dukes of Burgundy, said that the English entered France 'through the hole in the Duke of Burgundy's skull',[17] and Thomas Walsingham, writing only a few years after the event, believed that the murdered duke's heir, Philip the Good, became the king of England's liegeman out of a desire for revenge against his father's murderers.[18] Although the murder was greeted with revulsion in France, and although Philip was understandably grief stricken, the Burgundian decision to ally with England arose out of a clear calculation of interest as much as from a desire for revenge. Philip's councillors set out the arguments for and against an alliance with England with a degree of objectivity surprising in the circumstances, and the long-held view that Burgundy could not hope to gain much from a formal alliance with England clearly commanded some support. The clinching argument in favour of an alliance, however, was the strength of Henry's position and his determination to win the French crown: if Philip did not ally with him, then his enemies would certainly do so. Indeed, Henry made it clear to Philip that this would happen if Philip failed to meet Henry's terms. Philip agreed, and on Christmas Day 1419 the two sides concluded a formal alliance.

The upshot of this agreement was a treaty signed at Troyes on 21 May 1420 by Henry, Philip and Charles VI. This treaty settled the succession to the crown of France, and brought about 'a union of the crowns, but not the kingdoms, of England and France'.[19] Charles VI was to retain his throne for the rest of his life, but at his death it was to pass to Henry V, and he and his heirs were to rule both France and England. Henry was to become Regent of France immediately and the government of the country was to be handed over to him. Henry agreed to marry Catherine, Charles's daughter, who in effect became Charles's sole heir, for the Dauphin was disinherited. Henry and duke Philip undertook to conquer those parts of France which remained subject to the Dauphin. Normandy was to remain under English rule until Charles VI's death, when it was to be reunited with the crown of France, but Aquitaine was to remain separate from the French crown as the inheritance of the Lancastrians in their capacity as Kings of England. Although Henry and his heirs were to rule both kingdoms, each was to remain separate from the other. France was to retain its own institutions, it was to be ruled by Frenchmen, and those who gave their allegiance to the Lancastrian monarchy were to be permitted to retain their lands.

Contemporary English writers saw the Treaty of Troyes as a final peace, and it did of course mark the achievement of the ambitions of both Edward III and Henry V. Yet it cannot properly he presented as a treaty of peace: the Dauphin and his supporters were not parties to it, and indeed some of its terms were directed specifically against them. It committed Henry to continue the war against the Dauphinist forces, without the assurance of support from such powerful French nobles as the Duke of Brittany and the Count of Foix who were not included amongst those who swore to uphold the treaty. The treaty was really an Anglo-Burgundian agreement over the succession to the French crown. Although Henry and Philip persuaded the Estates-General and the *parlement* of Paris to ratify it, the Dauphin and his supporters could scarcely be expected to recognize its validity, and would seek both by diplomacy and by force to undo it.

In England, the treaty was placed before parliament in May 1421, and although the lords and commons approved it, doubts had already arisen about its implications. In December 1420 parliament expressed fear for the integrity of the English kingdom and concern lest the union of the crowns should lead to a union of the two realms in which France would inevitably appear the dominant partner.[20] The commons, too, were anxious about the financial consequences of a commitment to continue the war of conquest in France, and Henry's relations with parliament now seem to have become more difficult. As early as 1418 he had encountered some problems in raising money to continue the war, but the Treaty of Troyes ostensibly put an end to the war, and thus to the commons' commitment to finance it. When parliament met, in the presence of the king, in May 1421 it is possible that the commons refused to grant a subsidy, and Henry had to rely on loans raised from various towns and wealthy individuals, including bishop Beaufort, to finance the campaign of that year against the Dauphin on the borders of Maine.[21] The chronicles suggest that the loans were unpopular, and there is also evidence that Henry was finding it difficult to recruit troops for service in France: already there were signs of the strains which a long-drawn-out war would create. With characteristic hyperbole Adam of Usk wrote, 'No wonder... that the unbearable impositions being demanded from the people... are accompanied by dark – though private – mutterings and curses, and by hatred of such extortions', and in concluding his chronicle he prayed that 'my supreme lord may not, in the end, like Julius, and Ahasuerus, and Alexander, and Hector, and Cyrus, and Darius, and Macchabeus, incur the sword of the Lord's fury'.[22] Usk's prediction of discontent is revealing. The Treaty of Troyes did not produce the feeling of euphoria in England that had followed news of Agincourt, and Usk's fear that Henry might have overreached himself may have been widely felt.

It was unfortunate for Henry that news of the English defeat at Baugé in March 1421 reached England shortly before parliament was asked to ratify the Treaty of Troyes. The Duke of Clarence was killed in the battle, together with Lord Roos, Gilbert de Umfraville and John Grey, who had been granted the county of Tancarville in January 1419; the Earls of Somerset and Huntingdon and Lord FitzWalter were taken prisoner. The defeat had little immediate military importance, but it may have persuaded some French nobles who had hitherto been neutral that the English cause was not as invincible as it seemed. It is perhaps significant that shortly after the battle the Duke of Brittany concluded a truce with the Dauphin. Henry hastened back to France, where his personal presence did much to revive morale amongst the English, and the Dauphin's forces retreated to the Loire. Henry's immediate task was to mop up Dauphinist resistance around Paris, and in the winter of 1421 he laid siege to Meaux in the Marne valley. The town surrendered in May 1422, but during the siege Henry was struck down with dysentery. He died on 31 August 1422 without ever becoming King of France: his father-in-law Charles VI outlived him by seven weeks.

Henry's achievements were a triumph of will and determination. By the skilful exploitation of the division of his opponents, by the effective and ruthless exercise of military force and by persuading others that his ambitions were capable of realization he succeeded in establishing his grand design. He deliberately, and successfully, fostered harmony and unity amongst his people at home, and sought to eliminate the political tensions which derived from the events of 1399. Above all, perhaps, he was an outstanding soldier who inspired loyalty not just by his success but also by his self-confidence and by the moral authority which he established over his men. Yet the judgement of historians has not been unanimously favourable. The positive leadership he gave his people, and the enthusiasm with which they responded, stand greatly to his credit, and he attempted, with some temporary success, to restore order in the localities, not least by demonstrating a personal commitment to the enforcement of the law.[23] But the contrast between the euphoric aftermath of Agincourt and the more sober reception of the Treaty of Troyes is revealing. Already by 1421 the strains of war were showing: parliament had been generous in financing Henry's wars since 1415, but the reaction to the forced loans of 1421 showed that discontent was not far below the surface. It is possible, therefore, to argue that Henry underestimated the commitment he undertook by the Treaty of Troyes, and that it was a mistake for Henry to become heir to the crown of France rather than settling for territory within France. Perhaps the Treaty of Troyes represented an error of judgement, though it is of course impossible to know how Henry would have handled events had he lived.[24] By his early death he left the responsibility for the continuance of the war with his surviving brothers and the nobility. Over the next fifteen years, under Bedford as Regent in France, nobles such as Warwick, Salisbury, Suffolk, Talbot and Arundel were to devote most of their effort to the war in France. The nobility's commitment to continue the war had its roots not only in the need to protect the lands which many of them possessed in Normandy, but also in the sense of pride and cohesion which Henry's victories had given them, and a wish to complete the conquests on which he had embarked. Yet the commitment and the cohesion of the nobility serving in France was to be strained by the reluctance of Burgundy to commit money and manpower to the war, by disagreements over strategy, notably in 1429, and above all by financial and political difficulties at home during the long minority which now ensued.

The Minority of Henry VI

Nine months before Henry's death, Queen Catherine had given birth to a son, and this infant, Henry VI, became King of England in August 1422 and King of France in the following October. By a codicil which Henry added to his will on 26 August 1422, when he knew he was dying, he granted Gloucester the 'principal tutorship and defence' of his infant heir, and Exeter the responsibility for his upbringing and education. But Henry's will with its codicils was a personal document, and made no dispositions for the government of England and France after his death. The oral instructions which Henry gave on his deathbed survive only in the recollections of those immediately involved and in the accounts of some chroniclers, but it seems almost certain that Henry appointed Gloucester to have authority in England during his son's minority. The position in France was complicated by the fact that Charles VI was still alive and under the terms of the Treaty of Troyes would reign in France until his death. Henry appears to have asked Burgundy to act as Regent in France until Charles's death, while Bedford enjoyed authority as Lieutenant in Normandy. When Charles died on 21 October 1422, Burgundy relinquished the regency and Bedford assumed it, presiding at a meeting of the Paris *parlement* on 19 November. This too was probably in accordance with Henry's deathbed wishes, though as Professor Griffiths pointed out Bedford may well have wondered whether Burgundy would in the event surrender the regency to him.[25]

The transfer of power in France to Bedford thus proceeded smoothly enough; but Gloucester's position in England was challenged by the lords in November 1422. They rejected in principle the notion that the king could determine the governance of the realm by will, and declared that without the assent of parliament Henry had no power to 'commit or grant to any person the rule or governance of the land longer than he lived'.[26] Parliament eventually decided that Bedford should be Protector whenever he was in England, but that in his absence Gloucester was to act in his place, advised by a council named in parliament which was to be collectively responsible for exercising royal power until the king came of age. Most of the crown's powers of patronage, together with its power to appoint sheriffs, justices of the peace, escheators and customs officials were to be exercised by the council, and Gloucester was thus effectively deprived of the means of patronage which would have enabled him to build up a following and increase his own power. The council was to be broadly representative, and consisted of Gloucester and Exeter together with the three officers of state, the Archbishop of Canterbury, the Bishops of London, Winchester, Norwich and Worcester, the Earls of March, Warwick and Northumberland, the Earl Marshal, and five barons and knights.

It is unlikely that the council in parliament acted purely on principle in setting aside Henry V's arrangements for the government of England. Bedford had already made it clear that he would not tolerate Gloucester as Regent to the exclusion of his own claims, but Hardyng's Chronicle suggests that Henry Beaufort Bishop of Winchester took the lead in resisting Gloucester's pretensions,[27] and over the next fifteen years the rivalry between Gloucester and Beaufort was to be the dominant feature in English politics. Gloucester had had a distinguished military career, and had earned a reputation for good government when he had acted as Keeper of the Realm for Henry V between 1419 and 1421 and again in May and June 1422. But neither his father nor his brother had granted him substantial endowments and neither of his two marriages brought him any territorial gains in England. His lordship over men was neither as extensive nor as effectively exercised as that of his political rival. Beaufort had had much more experience of government than Gloucester. He had been a member of the council between 1409 and 1411, and had closely identified himself with the Prince of Wales's interests. He became Chancellor at Henry V's accession and played an important part in the affairs of the Council of Constance: indeed, he had the opportunity to make a career for himself in the international Church had he wished. In the duel between the two men, Beaufort was eventually to gain the upper hand, and he appears to have been the more wily and astute of the two. Gloucester enjoyed some genuine popularity with the commons and with the Londoners, but Beaufort was much the more effective as a political operator. Beaufort also had some influence in the royal household itself, through his brother Thomas Duke of Exeter who had responsibility for the person of the king, and the Beaufort family had extensive connections by marriage with the leading noble families.[28] The basis of Beaufort's position in English politics, however, was his wealth. His bishopric of Winchester was probably the richest see in England, bringing him an income of almost £4,000 a year. This was supplemented, to a limited extent, by profits from the export of wool, and no doubt by money received for personal favours during his long political career. He was thus as wealthy as some members of the titled nobility, with fewer calls on his income, and he used his wealth to sustain the Lancastrian regime over more than forty years.[29]

After the rebuff to his pretensions in 1422, Gloucester was for a time inclined to seek advancement elsewhere. Jacqueline, the daughter and heiress of the Count of Holland, Zeeland and Hainault, had taken refuge in England from an unsatisfactory marriage to the Duke of Brabant which the Duke of Burgundy had arranged in 1419. The marriage had considerable strategic advantages for Burgundy, since it served substantially to extend his influence in the Low Countries, but it lasted less than a year and in March 1420 Jacqueline fled to England, where she fell in love with the Duke of Gloucester. Gloucester saw an opportunity to make a future for himself in the Low Countries; Jacqueline obtained a dispensation annulling her first marriage, and the couple were married in 1423. Gloucester now styled himself Count of Holland, Zeeland and Hainault, and began to raise an army to invade the Low Countries and seize Hainault from Jacqueline's former husband the Duke of Brabant. Gloucester's ambition alarmed the Duke of Bedford, for it presented an obvious threat to the Anglo-Burgundian alliance. In April 1423 Bedford had concluded the Treaty of Amiens, which brought to a successful climax six months of negotiations with the Duke of Burgundy. Under the terms of this treaty Bedford agreed to marry Philip's sister Anne, and Philip agreed to give Bedford a wedding gift of 50,000 écus. This treaty breathed fresh life into an alliance which had shown signs of weakness. Philip already seemed to be standing back from wholehearted support for England, and was exploring the possibility of a settlement with the Dauphin. Through the mediation of the Count of Savoy, Philip had arranged truces with the Dauphin in the Mâconnais, on the border between ducal Burgundy and Dauphinist-held territory, and the Count of Savoy had even organized some negotiations between envoys of the duke and those of the Dauphin.

Gloucester's irruption into the politics of the Low Countries thus occurred at a moment of some sensitivity for the Anglo-Burgundian alliance, and his projected invasion of Hainault caused alarm in Burgundian circles, for his army would have to march across Burgundian territory to reach the country. But Gloucester managed to take his troops to Hainault without causing serious offence, and he and Jacqueline installed themselves in Mons in the autumn of 1424. Their triumph proved short-lived, however: a joint Burgundian and Brabançon army invaded Hainault in March 1425 and English resistance collapsed. Duke Philip brought the campaign to a halt by issuing a challenge to Gloucester to settle the issue by single combat. Gloucester accepted the challenge, but then withdrew to England, leaving Jacqueline behind in Mons but taking with him one of her ladies-in-waiting, Eleanor Cobham, who became his mistress. Bedford immediately began negotiations with Philip to ensure that the duel never took place, but Gloucester did not wholly abandon his ambitions in the Low Countries. He made two more attempts, in 1425 and 1427, to regain his wife's inheritance, but was finally thwarted in 1428 when Pope Martin V declared that Jacqueline's marriage to him was invalid. He promptly lost interest in the Low Countries, and consoled himself by marrying Eleanor Cobham.

The English occupation of Hainault had originally been popular in some circles, notably in London. But the eventual failure of Gloucester's ambition damaged his prestige, alarmed his brother and England's principal ally on the continent, and played into the hands of his domestic political rival, Bishop Beaufort. On Gloucester's return from Hainault in April 1425 the rivalry between the two erupted into violence. Beaufort tried to prevent Gloucester from lodging in the Tower, ostensibly because of the possibility of disturbances in London but in reality to keep him away from his supporters amongst the citizens of London. Beaufort raised an armed retinue, and according to Gloucester's subsequent allegation planned to seize the king at Eltham. Gloucester summoned the Lord Mayor of London and 300 armed men from the city to defend him, and after a skirmish on London Bridge on 30 October both sides agreed on a truce. Beaufort was surprised and, perhaps, alarmed by Gloucester's resistance: the following day he wrote to Bedford urging him to come home to prevent civil war breaking out and reminding him that 'the prosperity of France stands in the welfare of England'.[30]

In response to Beaufort's request Bedford returned to England in January 1426, but Gloucester proved reluctant to meet him and make peace. He declined to attend a council at St Albans and another at Northampton, and perhaps in the belief that he had support amongst the commons he refused to meet Bedford except in full parliament. Parliament was accordingly summoned to Leicester, well away from Gloucester's partisans in London, in February 1426, and Gloucester and Beaufort agreed to submit their dispute to a group of lords who would act as arbitrators. The lords' judgement required both parties to forgive one other and forget their accusations against each other, and Beaufort was formally declared a true and loyal subject of the king. But Beaufort had overreached himself by his actions in the previous year, and his public apology to Gloucester represented a personal humiliation. Shortly afterwards he resigned the chancellorship, and the Treasurer, the Bishop of Bath and Wells, was dismissed. Suspicion about the intentions of the two rivals still lingered, however, and in January 1427 the council asked both Bedford and Gloucester to confirm that they accepted the collective authority of the council during the king's minority. Both dukes acknowledged that they did, and Bedford returned to France in March 1427, accompanied by Bishop Beaufort who was on his way to Bohemia as Papal Legate.

Gloucester, however, was evidently dissatisfied by the outcome of Bedford's intervention and asked the parliament of October 1427 to define his powers more precisely. Parliament proved reluctant to do so, and only after Gloucester renewed his request in March 1428 did the lords reply, in a manner which cannot have pleased him, that he should be content with 'the affirmation that his powers were no greater than they would be when the king attained his majority'.[31] Although Gloucester enjoyed support amongst the Londoners, and probably had a following amongst the commons, the lords mistrusted him: they were determined to thwart his ambition for greater personal power, and to uphold the collective authority of the council. Few of the lords of the council wished to side openly with either protagonist: Humphrey Earl of Stafford (later Duke of Buckingham), for example, does not seem to have shown any marked preference for either side, while soldier-councillors such as Salisbury were concerned with the conduct of the war in France.[32] Stability and continuity with the previous reign were the principal objectives of most of the lay and clerical members of the council, and Gloucester's ambitions met with little sympathy.

The lords' declaration in March 1428 is especially significant for it was made in the absence of both Bedford and Beaufort. It suggests that it was not just Beaufort's ambition which prevented Gloucester from achieving a redefinition of his powers as Protector. Throughout the minority, the lords of the council remained committed to the principle of collective government by the council in the name of the young king. The antagonism between Gloucester and Beaufort was personal: the other lords of the council wished to prevent any magnate arrogating undue power to himself, and to ensure that power remained collectively in their own hands. For the most part they succeeded in both objects, and Gloucester's power was kept within bounds, however much he challenged the authority of the council.

In 1429, however, events in France compelled the feuding rivals to compose their differences for the moment. Although Gloucester's ambitions in Hainault had strained the Anglo-Burgundian alliance, English forces in France enjoyed considerable success in the early years of Bedford's regency. The Dauphin had established his government at Bourges, and all France south of the Loire, except Gascony, was under his control; but there were various pockets of Dauphinist resistance in northern France, and Bedford's first task was to eliminate them. In July 1423 a Dauphinist force moved north to try to reach Rheims and join others holding out in Champagne. The force did considerable damage to the countryside south of Rheims, but on 31 July the Earl of Salisbury defeated them at Cravant and forced them back to the Loire. There were bonfires and dancing in the streets of Paris when news of the victory arrived. The city was still loyal to the Anglo-Burgundian cause, but the Bourgeois of Paris commented soberly, 'How sad it was to think why the fires were lit! tears would have been better. It was said that three thousand or more Armagnacs had died in the battle and about two thousand taken and some fifteen hundred had drowned in trying to escape the cruel death their pursuers promised them.'[33] On the borders of Normandy the English took the war into Dauphinist territory with a march into Anjou in September 1423, but the march ended in disaster when the leader of the expedition, Sir John de la Pole, the brother of the Earl of Suffolk, was defeated and captured along with other English captains at Brossinière on the borders of Anjou and Maine.

In the following year the Dauphinists embarked on a counterattack, thrusting far into English-held territory on the borders of Normandy. However, on 17 August 1424 the Dauphinists, who had a substantial Scottish contingent in their army, were decisively defeated by the

Duke of Bedford and the Earl of Salisbury at Verneuil. Verneuil has sometimes been described as a second Agincourt, and although the losses on the English side were probably higher the immediate political effects were more substantial. The Dauphinist forces were destroyed, and they no longer presented a serious threat to Normandy. Verneuil made Normandy safe for the English, and shortly after their victory they pressed southwards into Maine. Salisbury entered Le Mans on 2 August 1425, and all Maine was soon in English hands. With the frontier now many miles to the south, the English settlers in Normandy enjoyed several years of peace, and English settlers began to establish themselves in Maine.

The Dauphin's ability to resist was at its lowest between 1424 and 1428. His army had been almost wiped out at Verneuil, and the atmosphere of intrigue and factionalism at his court weakened his authority. He made a truce with the Duke of Burgundy in 1424, but he lacked the military and political strength to exploit either the truce or the strains that developed in the Anglo-Burgundian alliance. By contrast, the English commanders in these years enjoyed great prestige through their successes at Cravant and Verneuil. Salisbury and Bedford in particular, but also Warwick, Sir John Talbot and Sir John Fastolf played a leading part in the defence of Normandy, the protection of the frontiers against Brittany, and the quelling of a revolt in Maine in 1428.

In the summer of 1428 the English commanders met in Paris to plan a major offensive. Bedford's proposal was to press southwards from Maine, take Angers, and reduce the county of Anjou to obedience. This was a cautious strategy, but one dictated by the small size of Bedford's army. He had only 5,000 men of his own, and the Burgundian contingent in the English army amounted to no more than 1,500 men: the strains in the Anglo-Burgundian alliance made the duke unwilling to commit a more sizeable force. But Salisbury, who had recently arrived from England with reinforcements, suggested attacking Orléans as a preliminary to a strike into the heart of Dauphinist territory. This bolder strategy carried the day, and Salisbury took up his position before Orléans on 7 October 1428. Less than a month after the siege began, Salisbury was killed by a stray cannon ball while on a reconnaissance expedition outside the city. His death was a major setback for the English: he was one of the most successful of the English commanders, and he had come to Orléans determined to capture it. Suffolk, his successor as commander at Orléans, was a man of much weaker will: he moved the English forces to winter quarters and thus gave some relief to the garrison at a time when continued pressure might have induced them to surrender. During that winter Joan of Arc persuaded the Dauphin, who was at Chinon, to march to the relief of Orléans. She restored the morale and cohesion of the

Dauphin's army, and entered Orléans at the head of a revitalized force on 3 May 1429.

Bedford had no doubt about the significance of the relief of Orléans. Writing to the king in 1434, he described the earlier English conquests in Brie, Champagne, Anjou, Maine and other territories, and said that 'al thyng there prospered for you tyl the tyme of the seige of Orleance takyn in hand God knoweth by what avys', and he attributed the relief of the city to 'a disciple and leme of the fende called the Pucelle that used fals enchantements and sorcerie'.[34] Bedford's bitter reflection on a change of policy that proved disastrous for the English cause in France suggests that hindsight made him more than ever convinced that his original strategy was right, and that the army which besieged Orléans should have been sent to subdue Anjou.

After the relief of Orléans the English suffered a series of setbacks. On 12 June 1429 Joan of Arc's army took the town of Jargeau, upstream from Orléans, and captured the Earl of Suffolk; six days later a small English force of 400 men under Sir John Fastolf was defeated at Patay and Sir John Talbot and Lord Scales were captured, though Fastolf himself escaped. The way now lay open for the French to strike either at Paris or Rouen; but Joan insisted that the Dauphin should move his army north-eastwards into Champagne. As he did so, the towns opened their gates to him and on 17 July 1429 he was crowned Charles VII in Rheims Cathedral. The coronation was a major psychological victory for Charles. The Treaty of Troyes had been recognized by both the Estates-General and the *parlement* of Paris, and there were many Frenchmen who had doubts about the legitimacy of Charles's claim to rule France. The coronation, in the traditional sacring place of French kings, resolved many of these doubts; and even the Duke of Burgundy thought it prudent to send representatives. After Charles's coronation his army remained active in northern France, and by the autumn of 1429 his forces had gained control of Laon, Soissons, Senlis, and Compiègne. But Joan of Arc had overstretched Charles's resources: he could not afford to keep his troops in northern France over the winter, and a faction at court led by La Tremoillé was determined to bring about Joan's downfall. The English persuaded the Duke of Burgundy to resume an active part in the war, and in February 1430 he agreed to serve against 'the Dauphin' in return for the county of Champagne, which was now in Charles VII's hands, and 50,000 gold saluts. The Burgundians laid siege to Compiègne; Joan of Arc marched to relieve the town, but was captured by a Burgundian force under John of Luxembourg, handed over to the English and executed in Rouen on 30 May 1431.

These setbacks can be explained partly in terms of the division of opinion amongst the English commanders about the wisdom of besieging Orléans, and partly by the misfortune of Salisbury's death and the misjudgement of Suffolk, his successor, in withdrawing his troops to winter quarters. But credit must be given to Joan of Arc for revitalizing Charles's army, and making Charles himself believe that he could win. How she did it remains beyond the power of historical analysis to determine, though it has produced a vast literature, and the influence she exercised over Charles was regarded at the time by some members of his own court with suspicion and hostility, despite her obvious success in reviving the French army as a coherent military force.

The reverses suffered by the English required them to make some response. In a letter discussed by the council on 15 April 1429, Bedford revealed the misgivings which he still had five years later, and he suggested that the young Henry should be crowned in France as soon as possible.[35] But a military effort was also necessary, and here the needs of the Regent of France were in competition with Beaufort's ambition to raise an army to go on crusade against the Hussites in Bohemia. At the same meeting the council in England considered a request from Bedford for reinforcements amounting to 200 lances and 12,000 archers; but the council agreed to send only 100 lances and 700 archers, whereas Beaufort was allowed to recruit 250 lances and 2,500 archers. Beaufort did not, however, choose to persist with a project which would almost certainly have gravely damaged his standing at home. On 1 July 1429 he agreed to place the forces he had recruited at the disposal of the Duke of Bedford, and his army was ordered to divert to defend Paris against the Dauphinists. The news of the relief of Orléans and the defeat at Patay had compelled the council to recognize the gravity of the English position in France, and Beaufort's crusading ambition had to be abandoned, though he was given permission to resume recruiting the following year.

In the autumn of 1430 the English began preparations for a major expedition to France which would culminate in Henry's coronation. The commons voted grants which were more substantial than any since 1418, and seven dukes and earls, together with thirty-three other captains, contracted to bring their retinues to the expedition. It was the greatest demonstration of support for the war by the nobility since the end of Henry V's reign, and the expedition numbered in all over 1,300 men-at-arms and 5,500 archers. Joan of Arc's victory had made the English more determined than at any time since the early 1420s to pursue the war with vigour. Despite the impressive force the English mustered, however, the coronation was perhaps an unwise move. The English had lost control of Champagne and thus the ceremony could not take place at Rheims Cathedral. It was held instead at Notre Dame Cathedral in Paris on 16 December 1431, and inevitably lacked, especially in French eyes, the special validity of a ceremony at Rheims. The coronation in Notre Dame could not undo the effects of Charles VII's coronation at Rheims, yet it served to reinforce the English commitment to the dual monarchy, and to make it even more unlikely that they would accept a negotiated settlement which involved surrendering the kingship now solemnly conferred on Henry. The Bourgeois of Paris, whose journal of the Anglo-Burgundian occupation of the city is a valuable eye-witness account, remarked on the 'Englishness' of the ceremony, as well he might when it turned out to be Cardinal Beaufort who placed the crown on Henry's head, much to the annoyance of the Bishop of Paris.[36]

The Duke of Gloucester, however, did not attend the Paris coronation. Although the protectorate had been wound up when Henry took the oath at his English coronation on 6 November 1429, Gloucester's powers were not fundamentally affected by this essentially formal change, and he remained in England as Regent during the king's absence. He took advantage of his position to resume his attack on Cardinal Beaufort. In November 1431 he arranged for a petition to be submitted to the council calling for Beaufort to be deprived of his see of Winchester because his tenure of it was incompatible with his position as a cardinal. The council allowed the petition and agreed to proceed against Beaufort under the Statute of Praemunire, but at the same time ordered that the proceedings should be stayed until Beaufort had had a chance to appear before the King in England, in view of his nearness to the King in blood and the many services he had rendered to the king.[37] Beaufort returned in February 1432, and Gloucester pressed home his attack. He had all the officials who supported Beaufort removed from office and replaced by those on whom he thought he could rely, and in a move which was even more obviously directed against Beaufort personally he had 6,000 marks' worth of the cardinal's plate and jewels seized.[38] When parliament met in May, however, Beaufort took the offensive. He offered to clear himself of the charges of treason which, he said, his enemies were bringing against him; but no one was prepared to maintain the charges, and the commons petitioned that in view of the many great and notable services he had done any charges against him under the Statute of Praemunire should be dropped. In return Beaufort agreed to lend the king £6,000, to postpone repayment of an earlier loan of 13,000 marks, and to pay £6,000 to recover his plate and jewels. Yet again he had used his wealth to buy himself out of an awkward political situation.

Beaufort's loans came at an opportune moment, for Bedford's government in France was urgently in need of money to stem the tide of French successes. In the spring of 1432 French forces under Richemont and Dunois were active in Maine and western Normandy; in April Chartres fell to the French and a French garrison at Lagny harassed English troops around Paris. Bedford's highest priority was to re-establish security in Normandy and Maine, but Gloucester was more concerned with the defence of Calais and the north-east. The two brothers met at Calais in April 1433 but failed to agree on the future conduct of the war. In June 1433 Bedford returned to England to put his plans for the war before the council and to raise money and men. On his return he automatically became 'chief of the King's Consail', and for a brief time he assumed a dominant position in England. He removed Gloucester's appointee as Treasurer, Henry Lord Scrope of Masham, replacing him by Ralph Lord Cromwell, and he sought to strengthen his authority in England by manipulating the appointments of sheriffs. Bedford had not expected to stay long in England, but in the November parliament of 1433 the commons sought to persuade him 'to abyde in this land'.[39] He agreed to do so, though only after some negotiations over the salary he was to be paid and on condition that he did not jeopardize the English position in France by remaining in England.

Bedford's powers were to be very extensive: he was to have the right to advise on appointments to the council and to the great offices of state, and to advise on when to summon parliament. His principal concern, however, was to raise money for the war in France. The Paris coronation and the military expedition which accompanied it had been very expensive, and there was an urgent need for money to re-establish the English position in France. The commons believed that once substantial parts of France had been conquered, their inhabitants should pay for the continuation of the war against the Dauphinsts. Throughout the 1420s and 1430s the Estates of Normandy regularly voted substantial sums for the war, though by 1433 the Norman Exchequer was in debt, and both the Estates of Normandy and local assemblies, which were by no means always compliant, began to voice objections to taxation. As far as England was concerned, the attempt to shift the cost of the war to Normandy was successful for some years: between 1422 and 1428 the English parliament had no need to make any grant of tax apart from the customs revenues, which were reduced for English exporters in 1422. The English Exchequer, however, was becoming steadily more burdened with debt, largely because of extravagance at home. Gloucester, for instance, drew the enormous salary of 8,000 marks a year as Protector, and other councillors used their position to procure favours for themselves, notably Lords Cromwell, Hungerford and Tiptoft. Beaufort's loans were an important source of income: between Henry VI's accession and 1435, he lent the Exchequer over £85,000, and until his death he used his wealth to underpin the Lancastrian regime. It is unlikely that Beaufort's loans were usurious: they were, perhaps, an expression of the obligation of a wealthy nobleman to assist the crown, but they also served to secure his political influence both during the minority of Henry VI and after the king assumed personal responsibility for government.[40]

When Lord Cromwell became Treasurer in 1433 he drew up a financial statement which revealed that although the gross annual revenue of the crown amounted to £54,000, accumulated debts were over three times the annual revenue and had reached £164,800. Cromwell concluded his statement by observing coolly that there was no money for the defence of the king's lands in France, and no money to maintain the king and his household. Cromwell complained particularly of the number of warrants for payments to lords and other persons, which amounted to much more than the annual revenue of the crown.[41] The exploitation of the financial resources of the crown for the personal advantage of the lords of the council was the underlying cause of the crisis, and no parliamentary grant of tax could solve the problem. In principle, the financial resources of the country were probably sufficient to sustain Bedford's needs, but the effective mobilization of these resources was impeded by the backlog of debt, which itself created a need for regular annual taxation. Yet the commons were disinclined to vote generous grants without some prospect of fundamental reform in the royal finances, and this perhaps required a firmer political will than the lords of the council were capable of exercising.

The attempt to reconstruct the royal finances was interrupted, however, by another dispute between Bedford and Gloucester. At a meeting of the council held at Westminster in April 1434, Gloucester argued that he could restore the position in France if he was granted £48,000 to finance an expedition there. Bedford interpreted this as an attack on his regency, and Gloucester took Bedford's reply as a slur on his own honour. The council required both of them to say no more about the matter, and Henry himself formally declared that no aspersion was intended on the honour of either duke. Gloucester's offer was refused, and by June 1434 Bedford had achieved some solution of the financial problem. The revenues of the Duchy of Lancaster had been paid since Henry V's death to a group of feoffees who held the estates in trust for Henry VI when he came of age. Excluding Queen Catherine's dower and other charges, the duchy revenues produced about £6,000 a year which Bedford proposed should be applied 'hooly to the defense of your royaume of France'.[42] Bedford also offered to use his own income from Normandy to pay for the war, and these proposals, if accepted, might have offered a long-term solution to the problem of maintaining an army in France. But the Duchy of Lancaster feoffees, who included Cardinal Beaufort, insisted on an alternative income, though they were prepared to hand over the surplus income of the duchy. In the event, Cardinal

Beaufort once again provided Bedford with the money he needed: he lent 10,000 marks for the defence of France and 3,000 marks to pay for Bedford's escort, the whole sum secured on the tax granted by parliament in 1433. Beaufort's conditions were severe: he required 7,000 marks' worth of crown jewels as security, the repayment of 5,000 marks lent in the previous year, and assurances about the repayment of other debts. The outcome of the financial crisis of 1433 was to strengthen still further Cardinal Beaufort's hold over the royal finances.

Bedford returned to France in July 1434, and England's military position momentarily improved. Lord Talbot, who had been released from captivity in 1433, led a successful campaign in the Oise valley, though the fact that he had to fight there at all showed how serious the French threat to Normandy had become. The Earl of Arundel recovered some ground in Maine, and a degree of security returned to Normandy. But the demand for an enormous grant of 334,000 livres from the Estates of Normandy in September 1434 precipitated open resistance in the form of a peasant rising in Lower Normandy, and in June 1435 Arundel was killed in a skirmish with the French only forty miles from Rouen.

At the same time, Charles VII, with Richemont rather than La Tremoille in the ascendant at his court, once again opened negotiations with the Duke of Burgundy. Early in 1435 Philip and the French ambassadors agreed to hold a meeting at Arras, to which representatives of Henry VI would be invited, in the hope that a general peace might be negotiated. The Duke of Burgundy told the French ambassadors that if the negotiations failed he would seek honourably to disengage himself from his English alliance. Burgundy's willingness to contemplate the abandonment of the English alliance represented no sudden change of stance: indeed, it is perhaps surprising that it had not happened earlier. From 1423 onwards Duke Philip had arranged a series of truces with Charles to protect the Mâconnais from attack, and in subsequent years truces were made which protected nearly all Philip's southern lands. Negotiations between the two sides never entirely ceased, even when the anti-Burgundian La Tremoillé was in the ascendant at Charles VII's court, and as early as 1424 Philip had accorded Charles the title 'King of France'. On the other hand, Philip had important reasons for remaining on good terms with the Duke of Bedford. His sister Anne was the duke's wife; the marriage was successful, and Anne may have used what influence she had to support the alliance. Philip also needed Bedford's good offices to restrain Gloucester from adventures in the Low Countries, and by 1431 Bedford was willing to pay Philip a pension of 3,000 francs per month to keep him on good terms. But the Duchess Anne died in 1432, and the English setbacks between 1429 and 1431 may well have led Philip to believe that Lancastrian France was a lost cause.

The peace conference which Philip and Charles had agreed upon opened at Arras in September 1435 under the presidency of Cardinal Albergati, the Papal Legate and Cardinal of Cyprus. Cardinal Beaufort led the Lancastrian delegation, and Richemont, the Duke of Bourbon and the Archbishop of Rheims represented the French. The English and French delegates never met one another, and the Cardinal President played a crucial role as intermediary between the two. He also had the power to absolve the Duke of Burgundy from the oath he had taken to Henry V in 1420 to uphold the Treaty of Troyes. The English took an uncompromising stand. They argued that no formal peace could be concluded while Henry was under age, but they were prepared to offer a lengthy truce accompanied by a marriage alliance between the Lancastrian and the Valois dynasties. They would not, however, recognize Charles as King of France, even though they were willing under the terms of the proposed truce to acknowledge his authority in much of his kingdom. The French were only a little less unyielding. They would not accept anything short of a conclusive peace: they insisted that Henry VI should renounce his right to the French throne, and although they were prepared to make generous territorial concessions to the English, any territory ceded was to be held of Charles VII by homage and fealty. The negotiations foundered, as had others before them, on the questions of English sovereignty over lands in France and the English king's title to the French crown. These obstacles were far from new, but they had become much more substantial by virtue of the conquest and settlement of Normandy and the coronation of Henry VI as King of France. The English accordingly left Arras empty handed on 6 September 1435.

After the departure of the English, the French and the Burgundians settled down to serious negotiations. Indeed for the French the detachment of Burgundy from the English alliance was perhaps the main purpose of the Congress of Arras, and they spared no effort to achieve their ends. Professor Vaughan published the text of a document[43] which reveals that Charles VII bribed the Chancellor of Burgundy, Nicholas Rolin, and other Burgundian officials. 'Bearing in mind', the document says, 'that this peace and reconciliation is more likely to be brought about by our cousin's leading confidential advisers, in whom he places his trust, than by others of his entourage', the king distributed 60,000 gold saluts to the Burgundians. Charles also offered to confirm Philip in his possession of a number of territories which he had annexed without the permission of the French king, and to mortgage the Somme towns to him. But the Burgundians were not easily persuaded. As Charles VII's letter had implied, some Burgundian councillors doubted whether an agreement with France was in

Burgundy's interests, fearing that the English might take retaliatory action by blockading Flanders and fomenting rebellion amongst the duke's Flemish subjects. The Governor of Holland in particular addressed an impassioned memorandum to Philip on the dangers of war with England. Nonetheless, Philip was persuaded by the Papal Legate that he could withdraw from his oath to uphold the Treaty of Troyes. He then agreed to a treaty with France which was promulgated on 21 September 1435 and which ensured Burgundian neutrality in the Anglo-French conflict. Six days earlier the Duke of Bedford had died at Rouen.

The Congress of Arras has often been seen as a turning point in the war, after which the dual monarchy ceased to be viable because Burgundian support was withdrawn. Yet Burgundy had contributed little to the English war effort for many years before 1435. Philip had made truces with Charles in the south and had had to be paid to fight him in the north, while the defence of Normandy, which was the primary English interest in France, was entirely in the hands of the English. Furthermore, Burgundy did not now begin to support Charles. Charles tried to escape from the undertakings he had given in the Treaty of Arras, and Burgundy opened negotiations with England to protect her trade with Flanders. Burgundian recognition of Charles VII as King of France weakened Henry VI's claim still further, but it is doubtful whether the treaty made any substantial difference to the ability or the willingness of the English to defend their remaining possessions in France, of which Normandy was now the most important.

The uncompromising stand of the English ambassadors at the Congress of Arras in 1435 disguised divisions within the English council and amongst the English commanders in France about the desirability of peace. In a memorandum which was probably addressed to the English envoys at Arras, Sir John Fastolf advised them not to consider making a treaty with the French, but rather to embark on a much more vigorous conduct of the war, with raids into Artois and Picardy and then through Vermandois, Champagne and Burgundy, 'brennyng and distruynge alle the lande'.[44] Fastolf asked for 500 lances to defend the borders of Normandy and to make war into Anjou, Maine and Chartraine. His belligerent stance may have represented the views of the English settlers and commanders in Normandy and perhaps public opinion in England too; but at the council in England more pacific views prevailed. Beaufort and Suffolk inclined to the view that a settlement with France was possible, and that the weakness of English resources made the pursuit of peace by diplomacy a more realistic policy than continued belligerence. Henry's title to the French throne and the English occupation of Normandy remained formidable stumbling blocks, however: for

Gloucester and his friends these were not negotiable, and Gloucester's uncompromising stand was favoured by many in England, including the Duke of York. Successful campaigns in the north in 1436 and 1437 suggested that a policy of belligerence still had some mileage left in it and a more flexible diplomatic approach was rebuffed at Oye in 1439 when the French refused to move from their two basic principles, that Henry should renounce his French title and that the English should hold their lands in France by liege homage. By 1445, however, the English negotiating position had changed substantially, and they were prepared to offer much more in return for peace. This change was the result of a new factor in English politics after 1437: the personal interests and the character of the king himself.

8
Lancaster and York, 1435–1461

The Surrender of Maine and the Loss of Normandy

Henry VI has suffered general condemnation both from his near contemporaries and from modern historians. Abbot Wheathampstead of St Albans described him, shortly after he had lost his throne, as 'his mother's stupid offspring, not his father's; a son greatly degenerated from his father, who did not cultivate the art of war...a mild spoken pious king but half-witted in affairs of state'. The theme of simple-mindedness has persisted through almost all judgements of the king: K. B. McFarlane said that he proceeded from first to second childhood without the usual interval, and that his inanity plunged the kingdom into war. More recent biographers, however, have taken a rather different view, emphasizing Henry's personal role in government. Dr Wolffe described him as a man 'of perverse wilfulness' whose chief characteristics were incompetence and untrustworthiness, while Dr Griffiths has taken a more charitable view, and has suggested that Henry was a well-intentioned man with laudable aspirations, but lacking in foresight, prudence, subtlety and political astuteness. More recently still, Dr Watts has once again questioned how far Henry himself was responsible for the policies of his reign, and has suggested that Henry's weakness of will allowed others to act in his name.[1] In political terms, however, these interpretations do not depart far from Mr McFarlane's notion of simple-mindedness: the king's lack of judgement, both of men and of political circumstances, seems to have been his most outstanding characteristic; and his compensating qualities of piety and generosity went some way towards ensuring his posthumous reputation. Yet the extent of Henry's personal responsibility for the disasters of his reign remains a matter for debate.

Once Henry came of age in 1437 his personality became the central feature of English politics. He could not be denied any of the traditional prerogatives of the monarchy: in principle, responsibility for the acts of government would ultimately rest with him, and he would enjoy the freedom to choose whom he wished as councillors. The lack of wisdom with which he exercised these freedoms was the underlying reason for the political instability which increasingly characterized his reign. Henry's personal involvement in government became significant in 1436, the year before he formally came of age. In Valois France it had become customary for a king to assume full power at fourteen years of age, and the constitutional changes which took place in 1436 and 1437 reflect this assumption. In May 1436 Henry's guardian, the Earl of Warwick, gave up his post and two months later Henry first exercised his own will in routine administration: significantly, it was a grant to Cardinal Beaufort. In November 1437 the king's formal assumption of power was marked by the appointment of a new council and the reservation to the king of powers such as appointments to offices and benefices, which had previously required ratification by the council. The council's authority was not greatly diminished by the king's coming of age, and there was little change in its composition. Both Gloucester and Beaufort remained members, together with the Earls of Huntingdon, Stafford, Northumberland and Suffolk, and there were no changes amongst the great officers of state. The new council, of course, now referred business to the king and acted on the king's advice, but it continued to govern, and lay magnates, including Gloucester, attended meetings assiduously between 1437 and 1443. The king's personal role in government gradually increased, however,[2] especially after 1439, and some signs of a new political alignment began to emerge in these years: the Duke of York, who stood next to Gloucester in precedence and who had been appointed Lieutenant in France in May 1436, was excluded from membership of the council, even though he returned to England in May 1437, while the Earl of Suffolk attended with increasing frequency, and thereby, perhaps, gradually increased his influence over the king.

After the failure of the Congress of Arras, the divisions in the council over the conduct of the war became more open and acute, with Gloucester taking the lead in opposing concessions to the French and advocating a more vigorous war policy. He enjoyed the support of the Duke of York and a number of veteran campaigners, and found himself drawn once again into conflict with Cardinal Beaufort, who favoured a more conciliatory approach to France. At the conference with the French held at Oye in 1439, the English negotiators offered to release the Duke of Orléans, who had been captured at Agincourt. Gloucester opposed this, and when it became clear that his opposition had not carried the day he issued a manifesto criticizing Beaufort and demanding his removal from the council. Gloucester gave his own account of the debate in the council and accused Beaufort of being willing to surrender the king's French title. He implied that only his opposition had prevented the council from adopting Beaufort's policy. But his attack on Beaufort went beyond the question of the concessions to he offered at Oye: he went back over old ground and revived his complaint about Beaufort's tenure of the see of Winchester; he accused Beaufort of financial dealings which defrauded the crown, and maintained that 'notwithstanding that the saide Cardinal hath noo maner of auctorite nor interesse into the coroune ... yeet he presumeth and taketh upon hym youre estate royal in cleping divers tymes youre counsaille to his owen hous, to grete abusion of al youre lande and derrogacion of youre high estate'. Gloucester dwelt extensively on Beaufort's misdeeds in taking advantage of the king's tender age to defraud the crown and provide advantage for himself. He argued that by estranging 'me youre seule oncle, my cousin of York, my cousin of Huntyngdon and many other lords of youre kyn' Beaufort was effectively preventing those who had a right by blood and birth to influence in his council from exercising it.[3]

The accusation of taking advantage of the king's tender age to usurp royal power was very similar to the argument used by the Appellants in 1388 against Richard II's courtiers, but Gloucester's grievances were essentially personal. Although couched in the language of baronial protests against misgovernment in earlier reigns, the essence of his complaint was his exclusion from power by the small circle around the king. He seems, however, to have commanded little support amongst the nobility, who were still unwilling to involve themselves in Gloucester's personal grievances, and his resources of money and manpower were insufficient to enable him to make an effective demonstration against the court group without the support of other nobles.

The court group, however, had entrenched its influence in the country: between 1437 and 1441 no less than eleven of Beaufort's associates became sheriffs. Such powerful men were not to be dislodged by a mere manifesto, however deeply felt and however much support Gloucester might have in London and amongst the commons. Gloucester lacked the 'good lordship', the ability to attract men to his following, which was essential to buttress his power. Nonetheless, Gloucester's enemies believed that his accusations merited a reply, if only to quell the 'noyse and grutching' among the people, and they issued a counter-manifesto which, while purporting to be a justification for their decision to release the Duke of Orléans, was in reality a defence of the policy of negotiation with France. It stressed that the king desired 'oon thing above alle othr erthly thinges, that is to saye, that the goode paix might be had, by the whiche the werre that longe hath contynued and endured, that is to saye, an hundreth yeeres and more... might cease and take ende', and it went on to set out the reasons why the king was so anxious for peace.[4] The content of the manifesto suggests that Beaufort and his friends were more afraid of popular anger about the release of Orléans and the proposed terms for a settlement with France than of Gloucester's general objections to Beaufort's rule, and the manifesto made no attempt to answer the charges of accroaching the royal power and taking advantage of the king's tender age.

The king's friends chose to deal with Gloucester not by counter-argument but by stirring up a scandal around him. At the end of June 1441 an astrologer named Roger Bolingbroke was arrested together with three accomplices and charged with predicting by sorcery the date of the king's death. Bolingbroke was a member of Gloucester's household whose dabblings in necromancy had allegedly aroused the interest of Gloucester's wife. Under examination Bolingbroke implicated the Duchess Eleanor, and she was accordingly arrested and brought before an ecclesiastical tribunal presided over by the Archbishop of Canterbury. Eleanor admitted her guilt, and was sentenced to perform public penance, followed by lifelong imprisonment. Bolingbroke himself was not so fortunate. He was hanged, while another of his accomplices, Margaret Jourdeman the Witch of Eye, was burnt, and a third, Thomas Southwell, died in prison. Eleanor may well have been guilty of the charges against her, but the purpose of the trial was political and its effect was to discredit Gloucester, who proved unable to protect his wife. The trial also raised doubts about his fitness to succeed to the throne in the event of Henry's death without a direct heir.

The dynastic motive may have played an important part in the decision to proceed against Eleanor: under the Act of 1406 which provided that the crown should pass to Henry IV's younger sons if the senior line failed, Gloucester was undoubtedly the heir to the throne; yet such a prospect may not have been acceptable to the king's intimates, and it is perhaps significant that discussions soon began about the king's marriage. Equally significant was Henry's patronage towards two members of the king's kindred, John Beaufort Earl of Somerset, and John Holand Earl of Huntingdon. Somerset was created a duke in 1443 with precedence over the Duke of Norfolk who had hitherto been senior to all dukes save Gloucester and York. Huntingdon became Duke of Exeter in 1444 with precedence over all except York. The first grant of precedence within the peerage had been made by Richard II in 1397, but the practice was not revived until these grants in 1443 and 1444. Grants of precedence should perhaps be seen as a means of patronage whereby the king could advance a particular duke or earl who enjoyed his favour. They were a highly visible form of patronage, since lords sat in parliament in order of precedence, and used unwisely such grants might give offence; but Henry's purpose was to emphasize the nearness to the royal line of those who received the grants.

Holand's claim to the throne was straightforward: he was the son of Henry IV's sister Elizabeth, and although the Act of 1406 did not define the succession beyond Henry IV's sons and their offspring, Holand was created duke specifically, according to his patent, because of his proximity in blood to the king. The Beauforts' position was more complicated. The family had been legitimized by Richard II in 1397, but in 1407, when Henry IV had renewed their patent of legitimization, he had added a clause debarring them from the succession to the throne. Henry VI was not prepared to propose anything so provocative as the repeal of the exclusion clause; but Somerset too was created duke because of his blood relationship with the king. It would have been foolish of the king to nominate either the Beaufort or the Holand line as his heirs if the Lancaster line failed and equally foolish formally to debar Gloucester from his right under the Act of 1406; but the nature of the king's preferences in the early 1440s is clear enough.

The Beauforts and the Holands, however, were not the only noble families with an interest in the succession. Edward Duke of York, who had turned his coat twice between 1399 and 1405, died at Agincourt, leaving no heirs. His brother Richard earl of Cambridge, who was executed for his part in the Southampton plot, had married Anne, sister and heiress of the Earl of March. Richard, the son of this marriage, became the representative of both the York and March lines when the Earl of March died childless in 1425, and he could trace his descent from Edward III's second son, Lionel Duke of Clarence. He became Duke of York in 1415 on his uncle's death, and had livery of his lands in 1432, when he was nineteen. He was knighted in 1426, and resided in the royal household from 1428 onwards. He succeeded Bedford as Lieutenant in France and Normandy in 1436, when he was twenty-five; in the following year he was replaced by the Earl of Warwick, but he served a second term of office from July 1440 until 1447. He appears to have enjoyed the confidence of the king and the council, and despite his claim to the throne the dynastic issue did not yet influence his relations with the court. Although it was now unlikely that Gloucester would have children, York, together with the rest of the nobility, no doubt assumed that Henry himself would marry and produce an heir. The dynastic issue seems to have been taken much more seriously at court than in York's circle, and it is ominous that a number of pedigrees drawn up in the late 1430s and early 1440s 'pointedly exclude all reference to the line of Lionel of Clarence'.[5] The Holands and the Beauforts may well have had designs on the throne and sought to bolster their positions by patronage and propaganda. At this stage York shared neither the pretensions of these two families nor their intimacy with the king, but the events of the late 1440s were to bring him much support outside the court circle.

The discrediting of the Duke of Gloucester enabled the king's friends to entrench themselves even more firmly in power, and the Earl of Suffolk now emerged as the chief beneficiary of the king's favour and patronage. Suffolk, the grandson of Michael de la Pole who had been ennobled by Richard II, had a modest inheritance of his own and added to it by grants of lands and offices in the 1440s, but his position as Steward of the Household, which he held until 1447, allowed him to influence appointments within the household and advance his dependants to positions of influence in the south and east of England especially.[6] Other magnates enjoyed the king's patronage, notably the Beauforts and the Staffords; but Suffolk established himself as the king's chief confidant. He had a strong base within the royal household, and he so manipulated his position that influence in the country rested very largely with him rather than with the king. Suffolk's ascendancy at court, and the disorder which went unpunished when it seemed to advance his interest, did much to undermine respect for the crown in the localities and to make men believe that the king could no longer uphold the law and maintain order.

Suffolk's influence over the king grew as that of Cardinal Beaufort, now an old man (he had been born c.1375), waned. Beaufort died in 1447, and well before then he appears to have moved into semi-retirement: he last attended the council in May 1444. Suffolk aspired to a more exclusive position in Henry's councils than Cardinal Beaufort had ever enjoyed, and he was to incur much greater unpopularity thereby than Beaufort ever had to endure. Yet Henry himself must bear the ultimate responsibility for the dominant position which Suffolk acquired. The king was free to choose what advisers he wished, and if he either failed to exercise that freedom at all, or exercised it unwisely, allowing one favourite to establish an ascendancy over him, then the fault lay with the king.

Suffolk's influence was felt in every aspect of royal policy, but it was over two matters, negotiations with France and the gradual breakdown of law and order, that he incurred most unpopularity. Gloucester's influence may have stopped the council agreeing to Cardinal Beaufort's suggestion that Henry's title to the French throne might be negotiable at the Oye conference; but after 1440 those who favoured saving Normandy and Gascony by a truce or a negotiated peace with France were in the ascendant and had the king's ear. York was reappointed as Lieutenant in Normandy in 1440, and his second term of office opened with some successes for the English: in 1441 he and Talbot drove the French out of the Oise valley and relieved the garrison at Pontoise. But York lacked the resources to follow up his success: he returned to Rouen, and in the autumn of 1441 Charles VII retook Pontoise by assault, while further south Evreux and Beaumont-le-Roger also fell. York's difficulties in Normandy were exacerbated by strained relations with the council in England. The defensive organization established by Henry V and Bedford had broken down in face of the unwillingness of many landowners to reside on their lands and contribute their due military service, and the lieutenants were forced increasingly to rely on professional soldiers paid by the council in England. York complained of shortage of money, and conciliar interference in military appointments in Normandy, but perhaps his real difficulty was that he lacked sufficient influence in the council both to ensure that Normandy remained England's chief military and financial priority in France, and to prevent those in the ascendant at court from manipulating military patronage in Normandy for their own advantage. The problem may, however, have gone deeper than that. The council in England, and indeed the political community more widely, perhaps lacked the will to defend Normandy. Although the English settlers there were dependent, by the 1440s, on money and troops from England to defend them, there were few in England who had any personal interest in the English settlement there. Most of the colonists in Normandy had only tenuous links with England, and for the council in England honour, and a continuing commitment to Henry V's achievement, rather than material benefit provided the main incentive to defend the duchy.[7]

Not just in Normandy but also in Gascony the French made substantial progress in the 1440s, and by the summer of 1442 Saintonge and the Landes had been lost, Bayonne was cut off, and the Médoc and Entre-Deux-Mers were threatened. The despatch of a relieving force was urgent, and as early as November 1442 the council had decided to send an army under Somerset. There were insufficient resources to send large armies to both Normandy and Gascony, and at a meeting of the council on 6 February 1443 the king sought to initiate a debate about whether Normandy or Gascony should be given priority, or whether it was possible 'to sende an armee for the secouring of both'. A month later, on 2 March, the Treasurer declared that 'it is unfaisible to make ii armees'.[8] Expeditions to both theatres at the same time were impossible on purely financial grounds, but the terms of Somerset's command reflect his influence over the king rather than good political or military judgement. For Somerset's commission was to wage a war of conquest in the lands between Normandy and Gascony. Henry granted him the governorship of Anjou and Maine for seven years, but this grant brought him into conflict with his younger brother Edmund Earl of Dorset who was already Governor of Maine. More seriously, it appeared to threaten York's position, for in 1440 he had been appointed Lieutenant-General and Governor of Normandy and the Kingdom of France. Somerset had in effect procured from Henry the right to take an army to carve out an appanage for himself in territory under French control, and to do so in a manner which would undermine York's confidence in the council and leave Gascony itself still exposed to French attacks, even though William Bonville took a small force to Bordeaux in March 1443. The council sought to persuade York that Somerset's command in Maine and Anjou would work to the advantage of Normandy and draw the French away from the duchy, in itself a not unreasonable supposition. But the council also told York that he would have to wait for the £20,000 due to him in 1442, since Somerset had used his influence with the council to ensure that his expedition had first call on the Exchequer's financial resources. Somerset's expedition proved a fiasco. He landed at Cherbourg in August 1443 with 8,000 men, led a raid into Brittany, and then meandered around Anjou without engaging in anything more demanding than local skirmishes. He appeared to have no plan of campaign; he was a sick man, and having spent seventeen years of his adult life in captivity in France after the English defeat at Baugé he had little experience to call upon in leading such a large and expensive expedition. He disbanded his army and returned to England, where he died in May 1444. It was rumoured that he had committed suicide.

The most substantial and expensive expedition to leave England since Henry VI had come of age, and one which the king should perhaps have led in person,[9] had come to nothing. Henry had shown poor judgement in his choice of Somerset to lead the expedition; and a lack of firm control in allowing Somerset in effect to embark on his own plan of conquest. He also showed a lack of political sensitivity in giving Somerset a position in France which made him appear a threat to York. Indeed, perhaps the only lasting result of Somerset's expedition was to increase the mistrust that York felt for those around the king who influenced his conduct of the war.

The failure of Somerset's campaign brought about a new approach to the war, in which, for the first time since the 1420s, the English sought seriously to negotiate a peace with France which would allow them to hold at least the lands that now seemed to be slipping away from them. But the initiative in reopening the negotiations came from the French, and this seems to have arisen partly at least from a deterioration in relations between France and Burgundy. In 1439 England and Burgundy had agreed to a commercial treaty which re-established normal trading links between England and Flanders, and this was reinforced in 1443 when the Duchess of Burgundy negotiated a perpetual truce with the Duke of York. Meanwhile the Duke of

Burgundy complained about the incursion of French troops into ducal lands and interference with ducal prerogatives by French officials. Charles VII vetoed a marriage between Margaret, daughter of René Duke of Anjou, and Duke Philip's nephew the Count of Nevers, fearing perhaps that an alliance between Burgundy and the House of Anjou, which had interests in Lorraine as well as in western France, would be contrary to French interests. Margaret was soon to become a candidate for Henry VI's hand.

In February 1444 Suffolk went to France with an English delegation which had power to negotiate an end to the war and the marriage of the king. Suffolk had originally been reluctant to go, fearing that any agreement he negotiated would increase his unpopularity in England; but the king insisted, and in the end Suffolk had to take responsibility for the terms which were agreed at Tours in May 1444. The two sides do not seem to have tried seriously to reach a final settlement. The questions of English sovereignty over Normandy and Aquitaine, and of Henry's title to the French crown, were rightly seen by both sides as intractable, and after little more than a fortnight a truce of two years' duration was agreed. The principal subject of discussion was Henry's betrothal to Margaret of Anjou, which was celebrated on 24 May. For Charles VII the marriage was a substantial achievement. It eliminated for the time being the prospect of another dynastic union between the houses of Lancaster and Valois. It ensured that there would be no alliance between Burgundy and Anjou; and above all it held out the prospect of the recovery of Maine, the patrimony of René of Anjou's younger brother Charles. It is less easy to see what the English gained from the marriage. A truce of only two years was insufficient to allow the English to regain their strength, and the marriage itself was unlikely to be popular in England. Margaret came with no dowry, and during the negotiations Suffolk gave the French envoys a hint that Henry might be prepared to give up his right to the French throne in return for Aquitaine and Normandy in full sovereignty.

The marriage of Henry and Margaret took place at Nancy in February 1445, with Suffolk acting as Henry's proxy. Rumours soon began to circulate in England that Suffolk had been persuaded while at Nancy to agree to abandon English claims to Anjou and Maine and surrender Maine to Duke René. On his return to England Suffolk made a declaration in parliament in which he denied that he had undertaken any secret negotiations; he may well have been telling the truth, but his denial was not widely believed. Suffolk's political survival now depended on his ability to negotiate a final and honourable settlement with France. In the summer of 1445 a French embassy arrived in England to resume negotiations in an atmosphere of some goodwill. The English offered the concession Suffolk had put forward at Tours, that they should hold Normandy and an enlarged Aquitaine in full sovereignty in return for abandoning Henry's claim to the French throne. The French were prepared to give way over Aquitaine, but negotiations foundered on the question of Normandy. The French argued that Henry III of England had renounced his rights to Normandy in the Treaty of Paris in 1259 'in exchange for which there was given [him] the duchy of ancient Guienne',[10] and they refused to contemplate the legalization of the English occupation of Normandy. The two sides agreed to extend the truce until 11 November 1446, and the English accepted a French proposal that the two kings should meet. Plans for the meeting went ahead, and it was agreed that it should take place near Le Mans in November 1446. These plans were viewed with some suspicion in England, for it was believed that Henry intended to make concessions to Charles VII which parliament would not accept. In the event the meeting never took place, but the suspicions about Henry's intentions were to be amply justified.

The French had, rightly, interpreted England's negotiating position in 1444 and 1445 as one of weakness, and in return for extending the truce for a longer period than they had hitherto accepted they hoped to obtain substantial concessions from the English. In November 1445 Charles VII sent envoys to Henry asking that the County of Maine should be granted to Duke René, in return for a truce lasting twenty years. He also thought that Queen Margaret might persuade Henry to agree to the cession. There is no evidence that Margaret possessed such influence over her husband at this stage, but she wrote to the French king in December 1445 saying that 'we will do for your pleasure the best that we can do, as we have always done'.[11] It is, however, probable that the decision to surrender Maine by 30 April 1446 was Henry's own. The letter agreeing to it went under the king's sign manual, and the queen had indicated in a letter to Charles VII that the decision would be Henry's own. It is, however, unlikely that Suffolk, the most intimate of the king's advisers, was kept in ignorance of the proposal. There is no evidence that the proposal originated with Suffolk but his supremacy on the council, and the exclusion from it of so many peers, inevitably meant that he received much of the blame for the surrender.

When news of Henry's intention to surrender Maine became public, it aroused anger not just in England, but also in Normandy and in Maine itself. Henry had simply given away territory which was of great strategic significance to the English, and which they had conquered only twenty years earlier, without receiving in return anything but a truce which was to last for twenty years. The agreement made no provision for English settlers and military commanders, who would presumably be required to leave, and lengthy negotiations took place in the autumn of 1447 about compensation for the departing English. There is little doubt that the English commissioners sent to implement the surrender tried to obstruct it, and gave way only when Charles VII, abandoning any hope that the English envoys would obey their king's instructions, massed an army and besieged Le Mans.

In Normandy itself the Duke of York's commission expired in September 1445 but his successor was not appointed until December 1446 and York thus remained in office for an extra fifteen months. There was no reason yet to doubt his support for the negotiations which had led to the truce of Tours, but during 1446 his relations with the king and the council rapidly deteriorated. He may well have had serious doubts about the wisdom of the surrender of Maine, which left the southern border of Normandy dangerously exposed. He also became involved in a financial scandal, of which he was eventually cleared, and in an altercation with Adam Moleyns, the secretary to the council, who accused him of maladministration and military incompetence. Moleyns was not the first English official to express doubts about York's ability as a commander, and there were some genuine grounds for criticizing his conduct as Lieutenant in Normandy; but York believed, no doubt with justification, that the charges against him were politically motivated, and he was politically damaged by them. At the end of 1446 Edmund Beaufort, the new Earl of Somerset, replaced him as Lieutenant in Normandy. Sir John Fastolf, who lost his barony of Cilly-Guillaume in the surrender of Maine, wrote a memorandum to Somerset in which he urged him to 'make you seure of your trew and stedfaste alliaunce of youre kynne and stedfast frendis in stedfast feithe and love to the kingis wele and the welfare of his royaume, that thei may, in youre absence, laboure and quyte hem truly unto you as nature, reason, and trouthe wolle in supportacion of the kingis righte and of your trouthe, yff any charge in tyme comyng myghte be ymaginede ayenst you'.[12] Fastolf knew only too well how important it was for the Lieutenant in Normandy to have the support of the council in England and to be able to exercise influence there. York's failures may have arisen in part from his own lack of ability, but, as Somerset's expedition of 1443 had shown only too clearly, York lacked the influence to ensure that the defence of Normandy was given priority in military expenditure.

After York returned to England in the winter of 1446 he was appointed Lieutenant in Ireland for ten years. Through his mother, York had inherited the Irish lands of the Mortimer family, and he might therefore be expected to play a leading part in the defence of the English lordship, as his Mortimer ancestors had done. He was granted almost palatine powers in Ireland, but York seems to have interpreted his appointment in political terms and evidently believed that it was an attempt to get him out of the way. He may, however, have been wrong about this. It is not clear that Henry and the court regarded York as an enemy at this time: indeed, they may have been trying to please him by giving him such extensive powers in Ireland. His absence might be convenient for the court, however. The king and Suffolk may well have feared that popular discontent over the cession of Maine would find a focus in either York or Gloucester, and while York was absent they intended to deal with Gloucester. The first parliament to be held since the agreement to surrender Maine became known was summoned to Bury St Edmunds in March 1447. The king mobilized substantial contingents of troops to counter any possibility of violence by his opponents, and when Gloucester arrived at Bury he was arrested and appealed of treason. In 1450 the commons accused Suffolk of instigating Gloucester's arrest, and although the evidence is slight, they were probably right. Suffolk, Lord Say and Bishop Ayscough apparently persuaded Henry that Gloucester was planning to raise a rebellion in Wales, and Henry may have intended that this should be the charge against him, false though it probably was. But Gloucester never came to trial: a week after his arrest he was found dead in his lodgings at Bury, and rumour soon spread that he had been poisoned on Suffolk's instructions.

Gloucester soon acquired a posthumous reputation as 'the good duke Humphrey', and a popular literature appeared extolling his virtues and suggesting that he had been put to death by the king's favourites. Such suggestions damaged Henry's government in the 1450s and played a part in bringing about the downfall of the Duke of Suffolk. However, although Gloucester may have been popular with the Londoners and with the commons, he was never able to use that popularity effectively to advance his own political position. He did not seem to understand the importance of building up a following through the exercise of good lordship, and the more he was excluded from the king's favour and patronage the more difficult it became for him to create and maintain a following. In his opposition to the court's policy of negotiation and concession in France he enjoyed genuine and widespread support, but he lacked both the means and the ability to translate that support into effective political power. Towards the end of his career he could not even protect his wife from politically motivated charges against her, and in his last years he appears an isolated figure, enjoying some prestige by virtue of his kinship with Henry V and his position as heir to the throne, but eventually easy prey for his opponents at court.

Gloucester's death was not, perhaps, so significant a turning point in English politics as has sometimes been supposed. He had been discredited since his wife's trial in 1441, and although opposed to the court's policy towards France it is doubtful whether he alone could have prevented the surrender of Maine. Nor did his death bring the dynastic issue more clearly to the fore: it must have been obvious for some years that he would have no legitimate heir, and there was no question of legitimizing his bastard daughter Antigone. Henry himself might reasonably expect an heir before long, and there is no reason to believe that York saw himself as either the dynastic or the political heir to Gloucester. Later events might make it expedient for York to claim to be both, but in 1447 there seemed no immediate prospect of the Lancastrian line dying out or being overthrown.

Gloucester's death served to entrench the power of the court still more deeply, though it was nonetheless becoming clear that the court was beginning to lose public support not merely because of its policy in France but also because of a growing sense that the administration of justice was partisan and influenced by faction. Lawlessness and the maladministration of justice were perennial problems in fourteenth- and fifteenth-century England. The ending of the unpopular but effective system of administering justice from the centre by sending out general eyres had left law enforcement in the hands of the justices of the peace, who were for the most part local gentry susceptible to local pressures and often under the influence of the great magnates of the shire. Complaints about the interference with the course of justice by the liveried retainers of great nobles went back at least to Edward III's reign, and Richard II had made an attempt to deal with the problem in 1388 and 1389 and by his ordinance on liveries in 1390. The nobility naturally resisted any attempt to bring their liveried retinues under statutory control: as John of Gaunt remarked in 1384, they believed they could maintain discipline in their retinues without legislation. Such statutes as were passed remained dead letters, and complaints from the commons about the evil of maintenance punctuate the parliamentary records of the first half of the fifteenth century. Henry V, however, had used his personal authority to enforce law and order more effectively than his predecessor, and during his absences from England after 1415 there were few outbreaks of serious disorder. Yet even Henry V's authority had its limits. Like all medieval kings, he depended on the co-operation of the local communities, particularly the gentry of the shires, for the maintenance of order, and not even Henry could remedy the defects of the legal machinery or eliminate the abuses perpetrated by the liveried retainers of the magnates.

Lawlessness was thus not a problem peculiar to the reign of Henry VI, though in the 1450s his father's reign was seen in retrospect as something of a golden age of good order and good governance. The revival of lawlessness perhaps seemed more acute in the light of the interlude of comparative tranquillity under Henry V. It may be, however, that the importance of disorder as a reason for the collapse of confidence in Henry VI's government has been exaggerated, while the importance of the collapse in France has been underestimated. Furthermore, as Dr Wolffe has pointed out, the medieval public 'was not naturally inclined to respect and obey the law',[13] and the fifteenth-century nobility and gentry regarded the law mainly as a means of advancing their private interests. The Paston Letters illuminate the problem of lawlessness in the 1440s and 1450s with an intensity unique in medieval England, and they suggest that the distinctive feature of these years was the manipulation of royal judicial power for their own ends by noblemen who enjoyed favour at court. In East Anglia, members of the king's household such as Sir Thomas Tuddenham and John Heydon enjoyed the protection of the Duke of Suffolk in committing acts of extortion: Margaret Paston wrote in April 1448 that 'no man ben so hardy to don nother seyn ayens my lord of Sowthfolk nere non that longyth to hym; and all that man don and seyd ayens hym, they xul sore repent them', and in the following year she observed that 'ye can never leven in pese wyth-owth ye have his (Suffolk's) godelordschep'.[14] Under Suffolk's protection corruption and extortion flourished, and although the king made several visits to East Anglia in these years, he never heard cases himself, and showed no interest in doing justice. His weakness of will was well illustrated by his neglect of his personal responsibility for justice, and the extent to which he allowed local judicial procedures to fall under the domination of Suffolk and the other great magnates. In this, as in so many other respects, Henry was the antithesis of his father.

The downfall of the Duke of Suffolk was brought about, however, not by discontent at the maladministration of justice but by the collapse of the English position in Normandy, and Suffolk must bear some of the responsibility for the events which precipitated that collapse. On 24 March 1449 François de Surienne, an Aragonese mercenary in the service of the English crown, took and sacked the town of Fougères in Brittany. Duke Francis of Brittany was in the French allegiance, and his reaction to the sack of Fougères was to demand compensation from the English, or to require the English to disown Surienne. The English government took no notice of his demands, and he therefore appealed to his suzerain, Charles VII. On 31 July, when negotiations over compensation had broken down, Charles assembled an army and invaded Normandy. There seems little doubt that both Suffolk and Somerset were implicated in the attack on Fougères: in Surienne's statement to the inquiry into the affair which was conducted at Rouen in the autumn of 1449 he recounted a conversation he had allegedly had with Suffolk at Monmouth in which Suffolk 'spoke to me of the enterprise of the said place of Fougères, and told me that if I could take it, this would be very well done'. He issued a challenge to anyone who wished to maintain that he had taken the fortress 'without the knowledge and consent of my said lord of Suffolk and my said lord of Somerset'.[15] The attack on Fougères was fundamentally ill-conceived, not least because it provided Charles VII with an excuse to denounce the truce with England and advance into Normandy.[16]

The English collapse in Normandy was remarkably swift. The 'list of towns, cities, castles and fortresses in France and Normandy taken from the English by the French during the administration of the Duke of Somerset' [17] is a catalogue of disaster. Some towns, such as Pont de l'Arche, fell to assault; at others, such as Pont l'Evêque, the English garrison fled, and between August and October 1449 more than twenty towns and fortresses surrendered by agreement. On 16 November Charles VII's army appeared before Rouen. After a fortnight of hard fighting the inhabitants of the city pressed Somerset to open negotiations and thus avoid the destruction and slaughter which would follow a French seizure of the city. Somerset agreed, and on 29 November he surrendered, having secured a safe passage out of the city for himself, his family and his retinue. He also agreed to surrender Arques, Caudebec, Tancarville, Lillebonne, Montevilliers and Harfleur, and to pay a ransom of 50,000 écus. As surety for the fulfilment of the surrender terms he agreed to leave eight nobles, including John Talbot Earl of Shrewsbury, as hostages. The terms of surrender were humiliating to the English and were recorded with bitterness by contemporary chroniclers. The English garrisons in Normandy had scarcely offered any resistance: the impressive array of siege artillery which accompanied Charles's army was sufficient to persuade many commanders to surrender before a shot was fired, and as the surrender gathered pace morale collapsed in those towns and fortresses that still held out. For the settlers in Normandy, the French reconquest was a catastrophe. Their livelihoods disappeared, and although some, who had married Frenchwomen, stayed on, most settlers, both military and civilian, had no alternative but to return to England. When John Lampet Esquire of the County of Suffolk surrendered Avranches 'he came into England and died of grief', and Oliver de Kathersby, Captain of Domfront, who was taken prisoner when the town fell to the French in August 1450, 'afterwards returned out of the enemy's prison into England, and for want of comfort and relief he died of grief of heart at Westminster near London, in very great poverty, in the year 1457'.[18] The fate of many others is unknown, though an investigation of what happened to the dispossessed settlers, both civilian and military, would prove very interesting. They expected the crown to help them out of its resources of patronage, as Fastolf had predicted in 1449, and Henry VI evidently felt some obligation towards them, but the over-committed resources of the crown were scarcely equal to the task of providing a livelihood in England for all the refugees from France.

The collapse in Normandy sealed Suffolk's fate. When parliament met in November 1449 there was much criticism of him for his supposed part in the loss of Normandy, though the commons voted a tax to finance a force led by Sir Thomas Kyriell which would attempt to hold on to what was left of English Normandy. The force was too small, and in any case its departure was delayed until March 1450. The common soldiers showed clearly enough where they believed responsibility for the collapse in Normandy lay when they murdered the Keeper of the Privy Seal, Adam Moleyns, at Portsmouth on 9 January 1450. Moleyns used his last moments to denounce Suffolk for the surrender of Maine, and when parliament resumed on 22 January Suffolk felt obliged to present a formal protest about the accusations that were being made against him. But the commons reacted by asking the king to commit him to custody, and on 7 February they began the process of impeaching him.[19] The first set of charges that the commons brought against him related to his conduct of foreign policy. He was charged with responsibility for the release of the Duke of Orléans and the surrender of Maine; giving military information and the secrets of the king's Council to the French; accepting bribes to hinder the despatch of troops to France, and causing the Duke of Brittany to enter the French allegiance. Just over a month later the commons brought in a second bill which contained eighteen further charges alleging that he had caused grants to be made that diminished the king's possessions, that he had allowed too many grants to be made in Gascony, that he had embezzled taxes, and, in a comprehensive attack on his influence in the localities, he was accused of manipulating the appointment of sheriffs 'to th'entent to enhaunce hymself and have over grete and unfittyng rule in this youre Reaume; whereof ensued, that they that wold not be of his affinite in their contreys were oversette, every mater true or fals that he favoured was furthered and spedde, and true maters of such persones as had not his favour were hyndred and put abakke'.

The commons made Suffolk the scapegoat for the failures in France and for misgovernment at home. But the surrender of Maine, and the foolish diplomacy which made concessions to the French without receiving anything substantial in return, were the king's policies, though Suffolk as the king's most intimate councillor had made no effort to persuade him to follow a different course. The charges of accroaching royal power and of using his influence to further his own interests had some substance, yet the responsibility for allowing Suffolk to behave in such a way rested with the king himself. Suffolk, of course, denied the charges, but before they could be heard Henry stepped in and ordered Suffolk into exile for five years, no doubt to save him from a worse fate. But the ship taking him to France was boarded by sailors from another English ship, the Nicholas of the Tower, and Suffolk was seized and beheaded. The sailors who murdered him did so in defiance of a safe-conduct granted by the king, and they declared that 'they did not know the said king, but they well knew the crown of England, the aforesaid crown was the community of the said realm, and that the community of the realm was the crown of the realm'.[20] They also asserted that they the sailors, and the community of the realm, would take and capture all traitors. The difficulty in believing that ordinary sailors could hold such an abstract view has led to suggestions that they were acting at the behest of discontented noblemen; but there is no good evidence for such a view, and their justification for murdering Suffolk should be seen in the context of the wider expressions of popular discontent that appeared in the summer of 1450.

While the commons were busy impeaching Suffolk, the final collapse took place in Normandy. Sir Thomas Kyriell's force landed at Cherbourg and marched south-eastwards to join Somerset, who had established his headquarters at Caen. But Kyriell's force was, as one chronicler remarked, too little and too late. It was intercepted at Formigny, west of Caen, on 15 April 1450 by Clermont and Richemont and defeated. Formigny marked the end of English rule in Normandy. In May, Bayeux and Vire surrendered; at the end of June, after a three-week bombardment, Somerset agreed to evacuate Caen; Falaise and Domfront followed, and on 12 August Cherbourg fell. In a letter to John Paston on 19 August James Gresham wrote, 'we have not now a foote of lond in Normandie'.[21]

The Rise of York

The spring and summer of 1450 were marked by outbreaks of popular disturbances in southern England, of which the most serious was Jack Cade's rebellion in Kent. Although this revolt has sometimes been likened to the Peasants' Revolt of 1381, it was essentially a political protest, and it was supported by many artisans and by minor landowners. Such people played a lesser part in local administration than the gentry, and were aggrieved by the corrupt behaviour of local officials who enjoyed the protection of the court and the Duke of Suffolk. Lying on the main route between London and the continent, Kent was perhaps the most politically aware of all English counties, but the rebellion extended through most of the counties of south-eastern and central southern England, and also into Suffolk. The rebels complained that 'the law serves for nought else in these days but to do wrong, for nothing is sped almost but false matters by colour of the law for bribery, dread, and favour, and so no remedy is obtainable in the court of conscience in any way', that France was lost, and that the king owed more 'than ever any King of England ought, for dauily his traitors about him, when any thing should come to him by his laws, at once ask it from him'. They demanded that the king should dismiss 'all the false progeny and affinity of the Duke of Suffolk', and that he should 'take about his noble person his true blood of his royal realm, that is to say, the high and mighty prince the Duke of York, exiled from our sovereign lord's person by the noising of the false traitor the Duke of Suffolk and his affinity'. They also asked that the king should include on his council the Dukes of Exeter, Buckingham and Norfolk, 'and his true earls and barons of this land'.[22]

The rebels' purpose was to obtain the punishment of those they believed responsible for misgovernment at home and collapse in France. They embodied their demands in a petition which they intended to present to parliament, but Henry prepared to use military force against them. His troops, however, refused to fight, insisting instead that the traitors round the king should be destroyed. At the end of June Henry gave way and retreated north. Lord Say, who had ruled Kent much as Suffolk had ruled East Anglia and who was especially unpopular with the rebels, was arrested along with William Crowmer the Sheriff of Kent and both were lodged in the Tower. By 4 July the rebels had gained control of London, and attracted sympathizers from Essex and from within the City itself. They managed to gain entry to the Tower and to seize Lord Say and William Crowmer, who were summarily executed. For forty-eight hours the rebels made free within the City, but on 6 July Lord Scales led the City militia in a counter-attack. He fought the rebels to a standstill, and then by the mediation of the two archbishops a truce was arranged and the rebels were offered a pardon which, unlike the pardon offered by Richard II in 1381, was honoured. Again in contrast with 1381, the government did not follow up the pardon with punitive judicial measures but instead sent a commission into Kent to investigate the rebels' grievances.

At the same time riots broke out in other parts of southern England. The Bishop of Salisbury, William Ayscough, who was the king's confessor and had been closely associated with Suffolk, was murdered by a mob while saying Mass at Edington in Wiltshire, while another mob ransacked his palace in Salisbury. In Hampshire, Gloucestershire and Suffolk adherents of the Duke of Suffolk were attacked. Although many of the gentry and some of the nobility sympathized with the grievances of the rebels, outside Kent most men took care not to associate themselves too publicly with mob violence against those who had close links with the detested court. Despite Cade's call to the king to heed the counsel of the Duke of York there is no reason to believe that York, who was in Ireland, was implicated in the revolt or that the rebels had tried to get in touch with him. However, the widespread animosity towards the court that the disturbances of June and July had revealed, together with the king's inept response, offered an obvious political opportunity to a magnate who was prepared to espouse the cause of reform, and the Duke of York was seen by many as the noble most fitted by blood and experience to deal with the traitors at court. He had not been tainted by association with the collapse in France and misgovernment at home, while his extensive territorial possessions and his kinship with the king gave him a strong position from which to attempt to exercise some influence over the king. Some even at this stage may have seen him as an alternative king, though the rebels' description of York as the 'true blood' of the realm should not be taken to mean anything more than that York had royal blood in his veins and was arguably the heir to the throne.

Towards the end of August 1450 York returned to England. His motive for doing so was not, in all probability, to take advantage of the political unrest in the country but rather to establish his own position at court now that the Duke of Somerset had replaced Suffolk as the king's chief confidant and councillor. Despite Somerset's involvement in the debacle in Normandy, he did not incur the hostility of the commons and soon rose high in favour at court. He had a powerful motive to retain his position at court, for most of the family estates had passed to his elder brother's daughter Margaret Beaufort, and he depended upon annuities from the Exchequer, where favour determined precedence amongst its creditors, for the greater part of his livelihood. John Wheathampstead, the Abbot of St Albans, believed that York was motivated in the years leading to the outbreak of civil war in 1455 by a desire for revenge against Somerset, whom he regarded as responsible for the collapse of English rule in Normandy. There is some validity in such an interpretation: York had had substantial personal interests in Normandy, which he retained after he ceased to hold office as lieutenant there in 1445, but which of course he had lost in the collapse of 1449–50. He also seems to have believed that Somerset had behaved dishonourably in face of the French invasion of the duchy, and now that both dukes were back in England politics over the next five years developed something of the character of a personal duel between the two dukes.[23] When York arrived in England he sought an interview with the king at which he urged Henry to deal with the remnants of the Suffolk faction and to heed the wishes of the commons in government. Henry returned a conciliatory answer. He agreed to establish a 'sad and substantial council', of which York should be a member, but only as the first among equals. York now turned his attention to the forthcoming parliament, which was due to meet on 6 November. He spent some time in East Anglia, working with his political ally the Duke of Norfolk to ensure the election of members favourable to his interests. At least five associates of York who had never sat in parliament before were elected for seats in the eastern counties, including his Chamberlain Sir William Old-hall who was elected for Hertfordshire and who was appointed Speaker when the commons met. York and Norfolk also gathered a substantial force of men of their affinity in East Anglia who would accompany them to parliament: a show of military strength was the indispensable accompaniment to the exercise of indirect political influence over parliament.

When parliament met, the commons, led by Speaker Oldhall, pre-sented a list of persons whom they wanted removed from court. Chief amongst them were the Duke of Somerset, the Duchess of Suffolk, and the queen's Chancellor, William Booth Bishop of Lichfield, but the list also included Lord Dudley, Sir Thomas Stanley, and twenty-five other members of the household. The commons demanded that these persons should also forfeit their lands, but the king ignored the demand for forfeiture; he agreed only that the ban should last for a year and insisted on so many exemptions that it was worthless. All lords, together with the king's personal servants, who 'shall be right fewe in nombre',[24] were to be exempted from the ban. The commons also petitioned that all grants made by the king since the beginning of his reign should be annulled. The king agreed to this, and the Act of Resumption which followed was, unlike its predecessors, made effect-ive by limiting severely the number of persons exempted from its scope. Several great lords, including York and Somerset, together with numerous members of the household, had to surrender their grants. The financial yield to the Exchequer from these resumptions was probably not sufficient to make any great difference to the royal revenue: the significance of the Act was its public demonstration that the flow of patronage emanating from the crown over the previous decade had been reversed.

By readily agreeing to the commons' request for an Act of Resump-tion and by ensuring that the Act was effective Henry recaptured the initiative from the Duke of York. Although York might have been popular with the commons, he enjoyed only lukewarm support amongst his peers, who had no wish to see York replace Suffolk and Somerset in domination over the king. The use made of his name by the Kentish rebels may have aroused suspicions about his loyalty in some minds, and his show of force in London during the first session of the November parliament lost him some moderate support. There was no sign yet amongst the lords of any substantial swing of loyalty away from King Henry.

The king's ineptitude was now to be demonstrated yet again, however, by his irresoluteness over the defence of Gascony. After driving the English out of Normandy, Charles VII turned his attention to Gascony and in the spring of 1451 rapidly reduced the principal English strongholds along the Dordogne and the Gironde estuary. The reconquest was completed when Bordeaux fell to the French on 30 June and Bayonne on 21 August. In the previous autumn Henry had appointed Lord Rivers Lieutenant in Gascony, and Rivers began to prepare a large expedition to defend what was left of English Gascony. But money to finance the expedition came in very slowly, and its departure was repeatedly postponed, allowing the French to proceed rapidly with the reconquest. By July 1451 Henry seems to have decided that Gascony was beyond hope and he switched the force to Calais, which he believed would be Charles VII's next target.

The loss of Gascony did not produce the same sense of shock and dismay in England as the loss of Normandy in the previous year. Few English knights and esquires had their livelihood there, and since 1420 it had generally taken second place to Normandy in English concerns. Nor could its fall readily be laid at the door of an unpopular courtier. William Worcester believed that the loss was due to the procrastinations of the council and the inability of the Exchequer to raise the necessary funds; the Duke of Suffolk's patronage of Jean de Foix, whom he persuaded the king to create Earl of Kendal, had weakened the loyalty to the English crown of a number of other Gascon lords, but it was difficult to implicate the king's new favourite the Duke of Somerset in the loss of the duchy.[25]

York did not make the same political capital out of the loss of Gascony as he had out of the collapse in Normandy, but he was still anxious to procure the removal of Somerset from the king's presence and ensure his own admission to the council. In the autumn of 1451 he made what amounted to a challenge to Henry's judicial authority by intervening with a force of 2,000 men in a dispute between the Earl of Devon and William Lord Bonville. Bonville had been a client of the Duke of Suffolk, and after Suffolk's fall he had established a link with another influential figure at court, James Butler, son of the Earl of Ormond, who was created Earl of Wiltshire in 1449. Devon had accordingly attached himself to York, who had become, as Professor Storey remarked, 'the natural focus for men with enemies in favour at the king's court'.[26] The origins of the dispute were obscure, and may have been personal; but by the autumn of 1451 it had escalated to the point where Devon was besieging Bonville in Taunton Castle. York persuaded Devon to abandon the siege of Taunton, and Bonville agreed to hand over the castle to York. The two lords were induced to settle their differences, and York gained a useful political ally. He had had no formal commission from the king to settle the dispute, though he could argue that as justice of peace for Somerset he had every right to intervene. But Henry made clear his displeasure at

York's action, and in January 1452 York issued a proclamation declaring his loyalty to the king.

In a sense, the siege of Taunton had been a diversion, however politically beneficial to York. York's main target was still Somerset, and in February 1452 he issued a manifesto appealing for support from the men of Shrewsbury. He accused Somerset of responsibility for the loss of Normandy, and he now tried to blame him for the loss of Gascony as well by arguing that the loss of Normandy 'has caused and encouraged the king's enemies to conquer... Gascony and Guienne'.[27] He went on to assert that Somerset was seeking his undoing, and the disinheritance of his heirs. Therefore he was 'fully determined to proceed in all haste against him', and sought aid from those to whom the manifesto was addressed. The implication of the manifesto was that York expected military support, yet so open an appeal was a misjudgement in that it enabled Henry to proclaim York a rebel and call on all loyal subjects to resist him. Henry raised an army that was probably three times as numerous as the forces York was able to muster, and the two sides confronted one another at Dartford on 1 March 1452. York was persuaded by a group of lords that he could not prevail against such a large royal army, and he agreed to submit to Henry on condition that Henry received a petition setting out a series of charges against Somerset, most of which related to his conduct as Lieutenant in Normandy. York evidently believed that the collapse of the dual monarchy was the most important count against Somerset, whose actions had resulted in 'losse of your lyvelode by yonde the see'.[28] Henry accepted the petition and undertook to place Somerset in the Tower until the charges against him were heard, but the king did not fulfil his side of the bargain. Far from being sent to the Tower, Somerset was a member of the armed group which now escorted York to London. York spent two weeks in custody during which he swore an oath of allegiance to the king and promised never to use armed force against the king or any of his subjects. York had been humiliated: his forces were outnumbered, and in the event he was not prepared to risk open conflict against the king in person.

Henry's defeat of York seemed to galvanize him into action. He began to make plans for an expedition to France, and he embarked on a lengthy judicial progress in the west of England to assert royal authority in person both in Somerset, the scene of York's recent efforts at mediation, and in Shropshire, the centre of York's influence. He also ennobled his Tudor half-brothers, conferring on Edmund the earldom of Richmond and on Jasper the earldom of Pembroke, giving them precedence over all other earls. Although neither of the Tudors had any claim to the throne, their advancement strengthened the influence of the king's kindred and provided the king with useful support in south Wales. For once, too, events in France played into

Henry's hands. Ever since the fall of Bordeaux in the previous summer an influential Gascon lobby had been at work in England seeking to persuade the king and the council to prepare an expedition to recover the city and the duchy. The king created a vested interest in a prospective reconquest by making twenty-two grants of lands and revenues in Gascony, and in September 1452 Talbot was appointed Lieutenant in the duchy with an army of 5,000 men. Supported by a group of Gascons who wanted to see the English connection reestablished, Talbot recaptured Bordeaux on 23 October 1452.

The parliament which assembled at Reading in March 1453 'turned out to be the most co-operative and generous one Henry ever met'.[29] His political reputation had risen to unprecedented heights after his resistance to the Duke of York's pretensions and Talbot's success in Gascony, which had removed (if only for a time) York's principal ground for criticizing the regime. The Speaker, Thomas Thorpe, who was an associate of Somerset, sought the attainder of Sir William Oldhall, the Speaker in the previous parliament and York's Chamberlain, and also the revocation of grants made to all persons 'who were assembled in the field at Dartford'. The commons then voted Henry the customs revenue for life, and made provision for the raising of a force of 20,000 archers 'for the defence of the realm'. The force was to remain in being for six months, and was to be mustered at four months' notice. It is not clear what the purpose of such a force was: four months' notice was too long to allow the force to be deployed against the Duke of York or rebels within the realm, and it may have been Henry's intention to deploy it in Gascony in support of Talbot's campaign of reconquest.

The commons perhaps hoped that Henry would take the field in person against the French; but the euphoric atmosphere of the Reading parliament was soon dissipated. The despatch of an expedition to Gascony to support Talbot was delayed because of the difficulty of raising money to finance it, and on 17 July 1453 Talbot was defeated and killed by the French at the battle of Castillon. Even then the rapid despatch of an expeditionary force might have saved Bordeaux, but Henry's attention was diverted first to the north by the outbreak of disturbances between Thomas Lord Egremont, a younger son of the Earl of Northumberland, and Sir John Neville, younger son of the Earl of Salisbury, and then to a much more serious quarrel between Somerset and Salisbury's son Richard Neville Earl of Warwick over the possession of lands in Glamorgan. The custody of these lands had been granted to Somerset in the spring of 1453 but Warwick was in possession and prepared to resist Somerset's attempt to remove him. At a meeting of the council on 21 July 1453 both sides were ordered to surrender the lands in dispute until the question of their custody could be settled, but Somerset was one of the councillors who made the order, and it is not surprising that Warwick refused to comply with it. Warwick now aligned himself with the Duke of York in the hope of ousting Somerset from his influence over the king, and the king's mishandling of this dispute marks the end of York's political isolation. Salisbury believed that Somerset might use his influence against him in the north, and thus both Neville earls had an interest in supporting the Duke of York.

Towards the end of July 1453, however, the whole political situation was transformed when Henry suffered the first attack of a mental illness which was to recur periodically for the rest of his life and render him incapable of action for long periods at a time. An accurate diagnosis of his affliction is impossible: it has certain similarities to the illness suffered by Henry's Valois grandfather Charles VI, and it may well have been an inherited condition. Modern opinion has held that catatonic schizophrenia or depressive stupor are the most likely diagnoses; to contemporaries the effect of the illness was only too apparent, and, as the author of Giles's Chronicle put it, neither doctor nor medicine could cure it.[30]

For several months the council tried to maintain the pretence that the king was still in control of government, but by October, when Bordeaux surrendered to the French for the second and final time, the need for effective direction of affairs was plain, and Somerset's position had been seriously weakened by the failure of the reconquest of Gascony. A great council was called for the end of October, to which York was not invited. He issued a strong protest and was eventually asked to attend, though he was warned to come with only a small entourage.

York's return to the council may have been facilitated by the news that the queen had given birth to a son on 13 October. The succession in the Lancastrian line was thus safeguarded, and York could no longer see himself, or be seen, as the heir to the throne. At the same time, the birth of an heir meant that Queen Margaret, who had never been popular in England, might seek to act as Regent for her infant son if Henry's incapacity proved permanent, and this possibility made some nobles draw closer to York as a more acceptable protector than the queen. Henry's illness and the birth of Prince Edward brought the queen to the forefront of politics, and henceforth her policy, in face of the increasing ineffectiveness of the king, was to seek to safeguard her son's right to the throne.[31] York's immediate purpose, however, was to strengthen his position on the council and settle accounts with Somerset. At a meeting of the council on 21 November the Duke of Norfolk, who had been York's ally since 1450, appealed Somerset of treason in a series of articles which related mainly to his conduct in France. The collapse in France was still the principal Yorkist count against Somerset. He was sent to the Tower, and at the same time the

Earl of Devon, another of York's allies, was released from Wallingford Castle where he had been confined since he had appeared in arms with York at Dartford in the previous year.

The council did not, however, resolve the question of who was to exercise royal authority during the king's illness. By January 1454 the queen had evidently begun to plan the transfer of power to herself by presenting to the council a bill of five articles 'whereof the first is that she desireth to have the hole reule of the land'; the next two proposed that she should have the authority to appoint the great officers of state, the sheriffs, and the bishops, while the fourth sought the provision of 'suffisant lyvelode' for her, the king, and the prince.[32] The author of the newsletter reporting the queen's proposals did not know what the fifth article was. Although such a transfer of power to the queen would have been without precedent in England, she had some influential supporters at court, who were prepared to fight to prevent York becoming protector. Somerset was said to be preparing to make himself 'as stronge as he kan', and the Earl of Wiltshire together with Lords Bonville, Egremont, Clifford and Poynings were arming their retinues. Both sides were preparing for war, and the opening of parliament, where the question of a protector would have to be settled, was postponed three times. In the event the issue was forced by the death of Cardinal Kemp, the Chancellor and Archbishop of Canterbury. It was essential, and urgent, to appoint a new Chancellor, and therefore to determine who had the authority to make such an appointment. York's political isolation became less marked when he joined twenty-one other lords in attesting the creation of Henry's son as Prince of Wales, thus recognizing the Lancastrian succession. His great territorial wealth and his kinship with the king gave him greater standing than the other lords, despite his political setbacks in the previous three years, and his claim to act as the representative of the enfeebled monarch could not easily he denied. On 27 March the lords created York Protector and Defender of the Realm, following the precedent of 1422 when the Duke of Gloucester had been given the same titles during the king's minority.

York's conduct of government during his period of office as Protector served to dispel some of the doubts about his political judgement which had arisen in 1450 and 1451. He avoided acting in too partisan a spirit, and did not even press for proceedings to be taken against Somerset, who was left to languish in the Tower. He appointed himself Captain of Calais in succession to the disgraced Somerset, but he obtained the consent of the council to his appointment and he also ensured that funds were earmarked for the defence of England's last remaining stronghold in France. The vacant office of Chancellor was filled by Richard Neville Earl of Salisbury, but otherwise York made few changes in the administration. The council was large and broadly representative, encompassing members of the household and friends of Somerset as well as allies of York. York was to be the first among equals rather than the leader of a narrow aristocratic clique, and on the precedent of 1422 the council collectively rather than York himself exercised the royal powers of patronage.

As Protector, York acquired the authority to settle disputes between magnates that in normal times belonged to the king, and in May 1454 he journeyed north to deal with the disorder in Yorkshire engendered by the quarrel between Egremont and Sir John Neville. Lord Egremont had received the support not only of his father the Earl of Northumberland but also of the Duke of Exeter, who perhaps believed that as the grandson of Henry IV's sister he had a greater right than York to be Protector of the Realm. Exeter led a rising with the object of seizing the Duke of York and murdering him, but on the approach of York's forces he fled to sanctuary in Westminster Abbey, whence he was later removed and imprisoned in Pontefract Castle. The rebels were treated leniently, and the most serious challenge to York's regime collapsed, but York did nothing to settle the quarrel between Egremont and Neville. This was resolved by force in a skirmish at Stamford Bridge on 31 October in which Egremont was captured and forced to pay Neville's father the Earl of Salisbury an enormous indemnity. He could not hope to find the sums required, and was imprisoned in Newgate.

York had no chance to make any significant impact on the troubled state of Yorkshire after putting down the Duke of Exeter's rising, for at Christmas 1454 the king recovered his wits and York resigned his protectorate. Henry's recovery of authority was followed by a series of partisan actions which made York and his supporters believe that they were being threatened. Somerset was released from the Tower and replaced York as Captain of Calais. The two lords agreed to submit their differences to a panel of arbitrators, but its composition was unlikely to make York believe that its judgement would be impartial, and in the event it never made an award. The Chancellor preferred to resign rather than agree to Somerset's release, and he was replaced by Thomas Bourchier Archbishop of Canterbury, while the Earl of Wiltshire became Treasurer. Both these officials were prominent courtiers. The Duke of Exeter was released from Pontefract Castle and welcomed back to court. Faced with the renewed ascendancy of Somerset and his friends, York and his Neville allies left court in April 1455, fearing that punitive action was being planned against them. Henry's partisanship had allowed the personal quarrel between York and Somerset to revive, and the animosity between them now led to civil war.

The court, however, had political rather than military action in mind in April and May 1455. A council was summoned to meet at

Leicester on 25 May 1455, and the king hoped to persuade the Yorkist lords to submit their grievances to the judgement of their peers. It was probably too late for arbitration, however, for York and the Neville earls were already massing an army. Their resort to arms took the court by surprise, and the king's friends hastily sought to summon military aid. On 19 May the king ordered York, Norfolk, Warwick and Salisbury to disband their army, but the Yorkist lords replied by drawing up a manifesto in the form of petitions to the king and the Chancellor in which they set out their grievances, declaring that their enemies, 'Such as abide and kepe theim self undre the wynge of your Mageste Roiall', had endeavoured to estrange them from the king, and they sought a meeting with the lords who were around the king to discuss the matter.[33] There was little hope, however, of a political settlement. Henry and the court now advanced in arms from Westminster towards Leicester, while the Yorkist earls moved south, perhaps hoping to reach London before the king left. The two armies met at St Albans on 22 May, and although the Duke of Buckingham, to whom Henry had entrusted command of his army, attempted to negotiate with York it was evident that York would accept nothing less than the sacrifice of Somerset, which the king refused to contemplate. According to the *Dijon Relation*,[34] probably a contemporary Burgundian account of the events which now ensued, York declared that he had come to punish the traitors around the king, and if he could not have them by agreement he would take them by force. The two sides joined battle in the streets of St Albans, and the Yorkists were victorious. Somerset was killed, probably deliberately, and the Earl of Northumberland and Lord Clifford also lost their lives. The king himself was captured, treated with every outward appearance of respect, and escorted to London by the Yorkist lords.

Somerset's death took much of the venom out of York's hostility to the court, and when parliament met on 9 July the Chancellor declared that its purpose was to heal the divisions amongst the lords. The king granted a pardon to all who had fought with York at St Albans, and allowed responsibility for what had occurred to be pinned on three people: Somerset himself, who was conveniently dead, and two minor figures, Thomas Thorpe and William Joseph. The Duke of Buckingham entered into substantial bonds for his good behaviour, and Exeter, whom York still saw as a serious threat, was placed in custody in Wallingford Castle. But York's aim was reconciliation, and on 24 July sixty lords spiritual and temporal took an oath of loyalty to the king and swore to protect him. Finally, on 31 July, the commons presented a petition asking the king to proclaim that Duke Humphrey of Gloucester had lived and died a true subject. Duke Humphrey was identified in the public mind with resistance to the French and opposition to the misrule of the court. By this proclamation York perhaps sought to make himself Duke Humphrey's political heir and identify himself with the cause of opposition to the court.

The studied moderation of the Yorkist settlement after St Albans was intended to ensure that York's regime was widely acceptable and that the king himself would acquiesce in what was done in his name. When parliament adjourned the king thanked the members in person, but by November, when it was due to reassemble, he had succumbed once again to his illness. The council came to the conclusion that he was too ill to preside at the reopening ceremony on 11 November, and after only five days' discussion between the council and a delegation from the commons it was agreed to appoint York Protector for the second time. The precedent of the previous year and the strength of his position after St Albans left little doubt that he would be asked to take up the office again. This time, however, he sought to consolidate his authority by insisting that he should hold office not during the king's pleasure, as on the previous occasion, but until relieved of it by the king in parliament with the advice of the lords. York formally took office as Protector on 19 November 1455, and three days later the council assumed responsibility for government during the king's illness.

In the event, however, York's second protectorate proved too brief for him to make any significant impact on government. He took steps to ensure that the Earl of Warwick was appointed Captain of Calais, which henceforward was to be a vitally important Yorkist base: but he was able to achieve little else before Henry had recovered sufficiently to appear in person before the third session of parliament on 25 February 1456 and relieve him of office. Henry did not immediately reverse the settlement of the previous summer. York remained as 'chief councillor and lieutenant', to the annoyance of the queen, who was widely believed to be intent on enhancing her own power. Warwick remained in office as Captain of Calais, and York was appointed to lead an army against James II of Scotland, who had broken the truce and had even offered to help make York king. Henry, with some generosity of spirit and an evident appreciation of his own weakness, was prepared to reign while York ruled as his principal councillor.

Such an arrangement, however, was unacceptable to the queen and to the heirs of the Lancastrian lords who had been killed at St Albans, and who now sought vengeance against the Yorkists. In the summer of 1456 the court moved to the midlands, and over the next three years the king made only occasional visits to Westminster. The queen's castles of Kenilworth and Leicester became the principal royal residences, and the queen seems to have been the driving force behind the changes in administrative personnel which took place in the autumn of 1456. Indeed, one chronicler remarked that 'the reame of Englonde was oute of alle good governaunce ... for the kyng was simple and lad by couvetous counseylle'. He went on to comment that 'The quene with such as were of her affynyte rewled the reame as her lyked, gaderyng ryches innumerable.'[35] The queen showed her hand when the Keeper of the Privy Seal resigned in September because of ill health. She appointed as his successor Lawrence Booth, who had been her Chancellor since 1451. In the summer of the following year Booth was appointed Bishop of Durham, in succession to Robert Neville, brother of the Earl of Salisbury, who died in 1457. A month after Booth became Keeper of the Privy Seal further ministerial changes were made at a great council held at Coventry. Viscount Bourchier was replaced as Treasurer by John Talbot Earl of Shrewsbury, a reliable if not fervent supporter of the court, and the king's confessor the Bishop of Winchester succeeded Archbishop Bourchier as Chancellor. The queen seemed intent on creating a narrow, partisan faction excluding York and his political allies. The harmony which had briefly prevailed after the battle of St Albans collapsed in face of a feeble king who now seemed incapable of taking up the reins of government, leaving them instead in the hands of the vengeful and ambitious queen who saw York as a threat not only to those around her at court but also to the rights of her infant son.

The governmental changes of September and October 1456 increased York's sense of insecurity, and indeed may have been designed to do just that. He left the council at Coventry incensed with the queen. Over the next three years the country was in effect governed from Coventry and Kenilworth, and the queen set about establishing a power base in Wales, the west midlands and the northwest. Sir Thomas Stanley, who was Chamberlain of the King's Household and had received numerous grants from the king in the 1440s and early 1450s, controlled the administration in Cheshire and north Wales and could call upon the loyalty of the lesser landowners of Lancashire and Cheshire. Jasper Tudor Earl of Pembroke controlled south Wales on behalf of the court, while in the west midlands several important courtiers had estates, and Warwick's influence in the county from which he took his title was substantially reduced.

The queen was not yet, however, prepared to take the field against her Yorkist enemies, and she lacked sufficient support to mount an effective political attack upon them. Indeed, no parliament was summoned between March 1456, when the long parliament which had been assembled in July 1455 was finally dissolved, and November 1459. This presented some financial problems for the government: no grant of tax had been made since 1453, and although the king had the customs revenue for life the government had to resort to such measures as distraint of knighthood, purveyance, and the exploitation of the crown's hereditary revenue to maintain the household. These expedients aroused resentment, for, as the author of Davies's

Chronicle remarked, all that came from such impositions 'was spended on vayne' since the king 'helde no households and meyntened no warres'.[36]

In October 1457 the king and the court returned to London, a move which may have coincided with some degree of recovery in the king's health. The king now used the authority granted him by parliament in 1453 to raise 13,000 archers from various counties in England. They were deployed round London, perhaps to overawe the Londoners, or possibly to protect the court against the disturbances which had been endemic in the city since the previous Easter. Henry's purpose in returning to London was to convene a great council which would try to reconcile the lords, and York, Salisbury and Warwick were summoned, together with the heirs of Somerset, Northumberland and Clifford. The council almost amounted to an armed confrontation between the two factions, and although Henry read the meeting a homily[37] on the evils of dissension amongst the lords it achieved nothing except an agreement on compensation for the heirs of those who had been killed at St Albans, and the establishment of a chantry at St Albans to pray for the souls of all those who fell there. Such reconciliation was hollow, and had no more than symbolic importance. Many of the nobility came to the council accompanied by substantial armed retinues, and despite the superficial reconciliation the country was moving towards civil war.

Over the winter of 1458–9 the court continued its military preparations. The household's store of weapons was reinforced, and three great serpentines were ordered which, Henry was assured, would be sufficient to complete the surrender of any castle held against him. The queen recruited a force of knights in Cheshire, to whom she gave her son's livery of the white swan, and on 10 May 1459 the king ordered a selective array of men for two months' military service. The king summoned a great council to meet at Coventry on 24 June; but York, Warwick, Salisbury, Arundel and the Bourchier brothers failed to appear. The queen thereupon insisted that they should be arrested, and both sides now gathered their forces. Salisbury moved south with a retinue of over 5,000 men to join York at Ludlow, but was halted at Blore Heath in Staffordshire on 23 September by a Lancastrian army under James Lord Audley which had been sent to arrest him. Audley's army may have been twice the size of Salisbury's, but in the bloody encounter which followed Salisbury was victorious, though he sustained heavy losses.

The king himself now moved with a sizeable force to Worcester and set off in pursuit of the Yorkist earls, who had advanced to Tewkesbury from their strongholds in the Welsh Marches. The Yorkists hesitated to confront so large a force, especially when it was led by the king himself. The two sides faced each other at Ludford Bridge on

12 October, but battle was never joined. York and the Nevilles retreated into Wales under cover of darkness, and the remnants of the Yorkist forces had no alternative but to submit and sue for pardon. From Wales York escaped to Ireland, while his son Edward, together with Warwick and Salisbury, sought refuge in Calais. The Calais garrison remained loyal to Warwick and refused admission to the new Duke of Somerset, who was appointed Captain of Calais in succession to Warwick on 9 October. In Ireland, where York was nominally by far the most important English landowner, the parliament refused to accept the court's dismissal of York from the lieutenancy and his replacement by the Earl of Wiltshire. York was able to recruit troops in Ireland, and he could communicate freely by sea with his supporters in Calais. Ireland and Calais were secure bases where the Yorkist forces could regroup out of reach of the queen and her party.

The rout at Ludford Bridge gave the queen and her supporters the opportunity they had been looking for to take political measures to crush the Yorkists. A parliament had already been summoned to meet at Coventry on 20 November 1459, and the newly appointed sheriffs, many of whom were clients of the court, did their best to ensure the return of a compliant commons. The main business of the parliament was the passing of an Act of Attainder against York and his supporters. York, his sons the Earls of Rutland and March, the Earls of Warwick and Salisbury, and many of their chief supporters were declared guilty of treason and sentenced to loss of all their lands and offices. The uncompromising mood of the queen and her supporters was well expressed in a propaganda tract published to justify the attainders, the *Somnium Vigilantis*.[38] The author of this tract declared that 'amonge many thinges by the whiche the commone welthe of a royaume stondyth, the most principall is this, a due subjeccion...to be yolden to the soverain in the sayd royame and that none incompatible astat be usurped by ony personne'. He went on to argue that the Yorkist lords had exalted themselves against the will of the sovereign, who alone had the power to introduce reforms if 'the good publique of this royaume hath ben vacillant in ony wyse and in perill of decay'. He wrote sarcastically of the Yorkist claim to be acting to maintain the well-being of the realm, and repudiated the idea that the magnates had any right or duty to intervene in government for the public good. The author's stress on the subject's duty of obedience to his sovereign was no novelty. Michael de la Pole had made the same point in his sermon at the opening on parliament in October 1383, and towards the end of his reign Richard II came to regard disobedience as amounting to rebellion. Such authoritarian ideas were a counter to the fourteenth-century argument that the nobility had a duty to act to restrain a king and to intervene in the government of the realm for the public good, yet whereas Henry V had been able to command obedience by virtue of his personality, theoretical arguments for obedience were unlikely to command much support in face of Henry VI's feeble government.

The Lancastrian triumph at Coventry proved short-lived. The most prominent victims of the 'parliament of devils' were all alive, and now had nothing to lose and much to gain by renewing the civil war. On 26 June 1460 the Earls of Warwick and Salisbury, together with York's son Edward, landed at Sandwich. They were joined by many men from Kent as they advanced towards London, which went over to them on 2 July. From London they issued a manifesto asserting their loyalty to the king and calling for an end to misrule. Once sure of London, they moved north to find the king. The two armies encountered each other at Northampton on 10 July 1460, and in a battle lasting little more than an hour the king was captured and several of his chief supporters, including the Duke of Buckingham and the Earl of Shrewsbury, were killed.

The victorious Yorkists now proceeded to establish their authority over the government. The household was purged of Lancastrian supporters, and Yorkist officers were installed in their places. Warwick's younger brother the Bishop of Exeter became Chancellor, and Viscount Bourchier Treasurer. Parliament met on 7 October, and repealed the attainders of the Coventry parliament. The consolidation of Yorkist authority after the battle of Northampton was essentially the work of Warwick and Salisbury. York himself did not leave Ireland until early September, but on his progress from Chester to London he assumed the trappings of royalty. All his outward display suggested that he had come to make himself king. He bore the arms of Lionel Duke of Clarence, and as he neared London he had the banner of England unfurled and a naked sword carried before him; on 16 October he formally laid claim to the crown.[39]

York evidently believed that after the attainders of the Coventry parliament neither he nor his supporters were safe as long as Henry reigned under the queen's domination. The queen could not be swept aside as an all-powerful favourite such as Suffolk or Somerset might have been, and even if the king himself were removed the infant Prince of Wales would inherit the throne and would remain under the domination of his mother until he reached adulthood. York's security therefore necessitated supplanting not merely the king but the dynasty, and he based his claim on his superior right of descent as heir general of Edward III. The lords, however, were most reluctant to accept York's claim. Many of them found the idea of repudiating the oath of allegiance they had taken to King Henry and setting aside a crowned and anointed sovereign unacceptable, and they balked at overturning the parliamentary entail of the crown on the heirs of

Henry IV. Some too, no doubt, could not swallow the implication of York's claim, which was that not just Henry VI but also his father and his grandfather had had no valid title to the throne. In the end the lords proposed a compromise which perhaps owed something to the Treaty of Troyes in 1420. Henry was to retain the throne for his lifetime, but his son was to be disinherited in favour of the Duke of York and his heirs. York was to receive all the endowments of the heir to the throne, and the lords took an oath to accept him as 'true heir of the kingdom'. Such a compromise was probably the only feasible solution to the problem. The lords would not agree to the deposition of a king to whom they had all sworn allegiance, yet they had little enthusiasm for the succession of his son, dominated by the unpopular queen. But although Henry accepted the arrangement with the same passivity as his Valois grandfather in 1420, the queen was determined to fight for her son's rights, and as long as she could count on the support of a substantial and powerful group amongst the nobility York could not consider himself secure.

Like the Dauphin in 1420, the queen had not been party to the agreement over the succession, and she fled to Scotland, where she bought the support of James III by agreeing to surrender Berwick. Her supporters meanwhile, chief amongst whom were the Dukes of Somerset and Exeter and the Earl of Northumberland, assembled an army at York which defeated York's forces at Wakefield on 30 December 1460. York and his second son Edmund Earl of Rutland were both killed in the battle, and Salisbury was captured and imprisoned in Pontefract Castle, only to be seized by the mob and executed. York's head was displayed over one of the city gates in York with a paper crown upon it. The defeat at Wakefield, however, proved only a temporary setback for the Yorkist lords. The king was still under Warwick's control in London, and under the agreement over the succession York's claim passed to his son Edward Earl of March. March, who was already in Shropshire safeguarding his family's interests there, gathered an army and at Mortimer's Cross, near the Mortimer stronghold of Wigmore in Herefordshire, he defeated a Lancastrian force led by the Earl of Wiltshire early in February 1461.

The Duke of York's death gave the queen the signal to return south to England. She placed herself at the head of the Lancastrian army and marched towards London to rescue the king from Warwick's clutches. On 17 February the Lancastrians defeated Warwick at the second battle of St Albans, and freed the king. Despite March's victory over Wiltshire the Yorkist cause seemed on the point of final collapse. But London refused entry to the queen, perhaps knowing already that March was advancing from Wales. He arrived in London on 27 February to a rapturous welcome, and over the next few days, in a series of carefully stage-managed ceremonies, he was proclaimed king. On 4 March at Westminster Abbey Edward IV ceremonially took possession of his crown and kingdom.

Edward had little alternative but to make himself king. Those who had doubts about such a move could salve their consciences with the thought that Henry had broken his oath over the succession by allowing his supporters to campaign against the Yorkist lords at Wakefield and St Albans, but Edward himself could not contemplate accepting Henry as king while he remained under the domination of the queen and her supporters. As long as the Yorkists had possession of the king they could rule through him and govern in his name; but after the second battle of St Albans, when they lost possession of him, they had no option but to establish their own king.

Once Edward had gained control of London, the queen's forces retreated northwards, but Edward needed a military victory over them to vindicate his title to the throne and establish it on a more secure basis than the support of London and his immediate political allies. A week after the ceremony in Westminster Abbey he set off in pursuit of the queen, and caught up with her at Towton in Yorkshire on 29 March 1461. The outcome was a decisive victory for the Yorkists. Henry, the queen and the Prince of Wales had remained at York, but when they heard of the Lancastrian defeat they fled to Scotland.

Edward's triumph did not rest solely on victory in the field. Indeed, a study[40] of the military aspects of the Wars of the Roses has suggested that the armies of both protagonists were neither large nor especially well trained, despite the experience that many of the captains had gained during the wars in France. Nor is there any reason to suppose that the Yorkist forces outnumbered their opponents: it is probable that the crown's military resources were the more substantial. The Yorkists suffered severe military reverses in 1460, and at Towton in March 1461 a majority of the lords fought for Henry.[41] But Edward himself was perhaps a better military leader than his father, and a good match for the young Duke of Somerset, the ablest commander on the Lancastrian side and a man with a high contemporary reputation for leadership in war. Over the previous four years, however, the Lancastrians had allowed their power base in the south, and especially in London, to weaken. Government from the midlands, supported by powerful nobles in Cheshire and Wales, had the grave disadvantage that it left the south-east exposed to Yorkist invasion both from Calais and from the Yorkist lands in the west, and the invasion of the south by the queen's forces in the winter of 1460–1 alienated still further a public opinion which had never warmed to the queen's cause.

On the other hand, Richard of York had never enjoyed widespread support amongst the nobility, as their reaction to his claim to the throne in 1460 clearly showed. The driving force behind his political ambition between 1450 and 1455 was a determination to remove Somerset from the royal presence and call him to account for the collapse of the dual monarchy. York's hostility to the court was formed by his experiences in France, and the loss of Normandy was the essence of his criticism of the king and his advisers. In holding the court responsible for failure in France, York struck a chord in public opinion, yet he failed, at least until the mid-1450s, to gather round him a substantial group of nobles who shared his opinion of the court. Unlike their predecessors in the reigns of Edward II and Richard II, the nobles showed little inclination to combine to force the king to dismiss and punish evil counsellors. Neither Gloucester nor York had much success in persuading their fellow nobles that their concern to free the king from evil counsellors was more important than their personal ambitions.

The catastrophic nature of the defeat in France should not be underestimated, and it is doubtful whether any government, let alone one as weak as that of Henry VI, could have survived such comprehensive defeat unscathed. Henry's loss of all that his father had won, as a contemporary chronicle put it, gave rise to a sense of humiliation and a feeling of disgust and contempt for the court which ensured much public support for York's attack on Somerset. Yet the nobles would not readily agree to Henry's replacement by York, and those nobles who had entrenched themselves at court in the 1450s would not give way easily. Their ascendancy, and their manipulation of the judicial powers of the crown to advance their own interests and protect their own followers, made their enemies look to York for protection, and in this way the alignments in the civil war, if not its origin, were determined by local feuds and rivalries. But as at other times in late medieval England when a group of nobles opposed the crown, the central issue was control of the king. As long as York and his allies had the king within their power they felt secure; but when he fell under the domination of the queen and her supporters, bent on vengeance, York concluded that only by making himself king could he prevent the ruin of his family and his allies. Despite Henry VI's manifest personal inadequacy the powers inherent in the office of monarch were so substantial, and so little susceptible to long-term control by a group of nobles, that York could survive only by seeking to assume those powers for himself.

Conclusion: The Yorkist Monarchy

The Yorkist victory at Towton and the coronation of Edward IV did not, however, lead immediately to a revitalization of the monarchy.

Although Edward was in many ways a contrast to Henry VI in personality, being young, vigorous and affable, with the prestige of success in battle behind him, the Yorkist monarchy was to prove dangerously dependent upon those families who had helped it to power and who now expected the due reward for their loyalty. The most important of these families, of course, was the Nevilles, and Richard Earl of Warwick was rewarded on such a scale that one contemporary chronicler remarked that he appeared to be insatiably greedy.[42] Warwick himself became the dominant territorial power in northern England, and his ambitions in south Wales were checked only by Edward's grant of authority there to Lord Herbert. His uncle was created Earl of Kent, and in 1464, after the suppression of Lancastrian resistance in Northumberland, his youngest brother was given most of the Percy lands in that county together with the title of Earl of Northumberland. The Neville family's capacity to raise troops made it essential for Edward to retain their loyalty, though in Warwick himself he had an ally who placed his own ambition and greed above his commitment to Edward. Edward also tried, not always successfully, to win the support of former Lancastrian sympathizers, and he also relied on a group of close personal friends and Yorkist retainers, notably Sir William Hastings who as Chamberlain of the Household was able to control access to the king's presence.[43] Edward's purpose may have been to base his rule on broader aristocratic support than Henry had ever managed to achieve, and to reconcile all but the hard core of Lancastrians to the Yorkist monarchy: yet within eight years he had been driven from his throne, and between 1469 and 1471 there ensued what Charles Ross called 'a period of political instability without parallel in English history since 1066'.[44]

Although Edward showed friendship and favour to Warwick from the very start of his reign, Warwick seemed unable to accept anything less than a dominant position in government and a preponderant influence even in foreign affairs. By 1469, relations between the king and Warwick had come under serious strain. The king's marriage in 1464 to Elizabeth Woodville, and the consequent influence at court of the queen's kin, aroused Warwick's jealousy, though Edward was careful to ensure that the Nevilles continued to enjoy royal favour and patronage. The breach between the two seems to have been provoked by disagreement over foreign policy. After 1464 the dominant theme in Edward's foreign policy was the re-establishment of the traditional friendship between England and Burgundy, perhaps as a preliminary to the renewal of the Anglo-French conflict. For despite the expulsion of the English from Normandy and the French reconquest of Gascony, there is no reason to believe that the Yorkists accepted the defeats of 1450 and 1453 as final. The Yorkist critique of Lancastrian misrule had made much of the incompetence and misjudgements which had led to the collapse in France, and it was expected both in England and in France that Edward would at some time seek to renew the war. Louis XI saw Edward's negotiations with Burgundy, which culminated in the marriage of Edward's sister Margaret to Charles, Duke Philip's successor, in 1468 as a step towards the renewal of war, and sought to undermine the Anglo-Burgundian friendship. Warwick, however, allowed himself to be persuaded by Louis XI that he might gain from an Anglo-French alliance against Burgundy: Louis's envoy in England dropped hints that his master might create a French appanage for the earl. Warwick swallowed the bait, and from 1464 onwards his understanding with Louis placed him at variance with the king over foreign policy.

In 1469 Warwick moved towards open rebellion; at the same time he won over the king's younger brother George Duke of Clarence, who married Warwick's daughter in the summer of that year. Warwick's revolt was initially successful, and for four months between July and October 1469 he ruled in Edward's name with Edward virtually a prisoner at Middleham Castle. The divisions within the Yorkist ranks, however, encouraged the remaining Lancastrians to instigate a rising in the north on behalf of Henry VI, and only the apparent closing of Yorkist ranks with the release and return to power of Edward himself enabled the rising to be suppressed. Warwick's policy had something in common with that of Richard of York in 1460: he first of all sought to establish his authority by ruling through a king who was under his control, but Edward's resumption of power in the autumn of 1469 put an end to this ambition, even though Edward treated Warwick with considerable leniency.

Warwick now sought to remove Edward and replace him with an alternative king who would be amenable to his wishes. In March 1470 he rose again, this time, evidently, with the intention of placing the Duke of Clarence on the throne; but Edward, with substantial support from the nobility, who had no wish to see Warwick in a position of supremacy ruling through a puppet king, put Warwick and Clarence to flight. They sought refuge in France, where Louis XI hoped to use them as instruments for the restoration of Henry VI and Margaret of Anjou. The bizarre spectacle of Warwick in alliance with Margaret and Henry VI suited Louis's diplomatic schemes, but it was unlikely to command conviction in England. The transient success of the invasion of England which Warwick launched in September 1470 owed much more to Edward's unpreparedness than to any genuine support for a Lancastrian restoration. Warwick landed at Dartmouth, and Edward, who had perhaps expected an invasion of northern England, was taken by surprise and fled to Burgundy rather than confront his enemies in battle. Political events in England were now to be determined essentially by the rival interests of Louis XI and Charles Duke of Burgundy. Henry VI was restored to the throne, but neither he nor Warwick enjoyed any widespread support; Warwick's position depended essentially on the military force that he and his family could deploy. Parliament refused to grant a subsidy for the war against Burgundy to which Warwick was committed, and Clarence moved towards a reconciliation with his brother now Henry occupied the throne which Warwick had intended for him the previous year. The remaining Lancastrian supporters could hardly be expected to place any real trust in Warwick, who had done so much to bring about their downfall ten years earlier, and the Duke of Burgundy's attitude to the restored Lancastrian regime became openly hostile when Louis XI declared war on Burgundy in December 1470. Charles allowed Edward to prepare an expedition to recover his kingdom, and furnished him with money and ships.

Edward's return to England in March 1471 shows some striking similarities to Bolingbroke's expedition in 1399: both landed at Ravenspur on the Humber, both faced a well-guarded and well-prepared kingdom, and neither could be sure of the attitude of the great nobles. Edward did not receive the same military support that the northern nobility had offered his predecessor in 1399, but they made no move against him. Warwick and his allies, however, were not prepared simply to accommodate themselves to the *fait accompli* of invasion, as the Duke of York, Edward's great-grandfather, had done in 1399. They gathered their forces, but Edward reached London and seized Henry VI without meeting a serious challenge. Warwick's army moved towards London, and on Easter Saturday, 13 April, Edward and the Yorkist lords who had rallied to him marched north to Barnet, where on the following day he won a decisive victory, in which Warwick and his brother John Marquis Montagu were killed. But Queen Margaret and her son Prince Edward had remained in France, and only landed at Weymouth on the day of Edward's victory at Barnet. They were joined by the Duke of Somerset, and moved towards the Severn. Edward was determined to prevent them raising support in the south-east, and took his army westwards, where he encountered the queen and her supporters at Tewkesbury on 4 May. This was the final battle: just as he had destroyed the Nevilles at Barnet, so now he decisively overcame the Lancastrians. Prince Edward and the Duke of Somerset's younger brother were killed in the battle, while Somerset himself was executed two days afterwards. On the day that Edward returned in triumph to London Henry VI was murdered in the Tower, and by his death and the death of his son the direct line of the House of Lancaster became extinct: 'no one now remained in the land of the living who could now claim the throne from that family'.[45] The Beauforts were also extinguished in the direct male line, leaving Henry Tudor as the senior representative of that family by his mother, the Duke of Somerset's cousin.

In his second reign, with his principal enemies eliminated and the prestige of these decisive victories behind him, Edward felt much more secure, and it is in these years, and particularly after 1475, that he made the greatest progress in the restoration of the authority and the financial stability of the crown. He also embarked in 1475 on the most substantial military expedition to the continent that an English king had mounted since the reign of Henry V. Public opinion in England was reminded not just of the king's claim to his French inheritance and the success which had attended those kings who had engaged in war, but also of the reputation of Edward III for victory abroad and good governance at home.[46] In spite of this careful preparation of domestic opinion, however, it remains doubtful whether, despite the scale of the mobilization for war, Edward intended to initiate a war of conquest.[47] With support from Burgundy he might nonetheless hope to exact territorial concessions from Louis, and the alliance with Burgundy was thus the cornerstone of his strategy. In the event, however, Charles of Burgundy let Edward down, by failing to bring the military support which he had promised, and in August 1475 by the Treaty of Picquigny Edward reached an agreement with Louis XI under which he agreed to leave France in return for an immediate payment of 75,000 crowns and an annual payment of 50,000 crowns. In addition, a number of the leading nobles who had accompanied Edward on the expedition received pensions and gifts from the French king. For Edward and his noble companions the expedition had been profitable, if not glorious, but its outcome was greeted with some dismay in England, and Edward lost face by his agreement with Louis. The contemporary French writer Philippe de Commynes believed that Edward had never been serious about the war, and that his lethargic disposition made him an unlikely leader of an English military revival.

Without Burgundian help it is hard to believe that Edward could have achieved much in France by force of arms. Despite the internal difficulties which Louis faced, notably the aristocratic combination against him in the League of the Public Weal, France was very different from the weak and divided realm which Henry V had invaded. Louis's resources of money and manpower were much more substantial than those of Edward IV, and apart from Calais Edward had nowhere in France which he could use as a port of entry. Burgundian assistance was crucial, and when it was not forthcoming Edward was probably wise to extricate himself as best he could. Two years later the death of Charles the Bold and the subsequent dismemberment of Burgundy inaugurated an era in which the western seaboard of Europe was to be dominated by two continental powers, Valois France and Habsburg Spain, whose resources far exceeded those which the Kings of England could deploy. By comparison England became a minor military power, and despite the exhortations of William Worcester[48] England could scarcely hope to revive the glories of Henry V's reign. Worcester was probably wrong to attribute this to the lack of bellicosity in the English nobility: the enthusiasm which greeted Edward's preparations for war in 1475 suggests that their bellicosity was not markedly diminished, and the real explanation for the abandonment of large-scale military ambitions on the continent after 1475 is to be found in the continuing domestic problems of the English monarchy and the rapid transformation of the political structure of the western European seaboard.

At home in his second reign, Edward's dependence on powerful noble families was substantially diminished. His recovery of his realm had been his own achievement, and no single family assumed so dominating a position as the Nevilles in Edward's first reign. But serious rifts began to develop amongst those nobles who were bound to the king by ties of blood or marriage, and the tension between the queen's kin, the Woodville family, and the king's youngest brother, Richard Duke of Gloucester, is the underlying reason for Edward's failure to ensure the undisputed succession of his son in 1483. Gloucester's position in the north was strong enough to enable him to gain control of the government by force if he chose to do so, yet his usurpation further exposed the strains within the network of Yorkist supporters, to the ultimate benefit of Henry Tudor.

The relationship between the crown and the nobility underwent more substantial change after 1485 than during the reigns of the Yorkist kings. Comradeship in arms, which had seemed for a moment as though it might become as important an element in the relationship between Edward IV and his nobility as it had been in the reigns of Edward III and Henry V, played an unimportant part in Henry VII's relationship with the nobility. The attainders and forfeitures of the previous twenty-five years brought into the hands of the crown very substantial resources of landed property, and Henry VII was under less pressure than Edward IV to use these resources as a reservoir of patronage to reward those who had helped him to the throne and to endow his kin. The restoration of royal finances, which had begun under Edward IV, made greater progress in Henry VII's reign, and although the resources available to Henry were small compared with those of his continental counterparts, there were no great subjects within the realm who could enjoy an income as large as the income the king derived, independent of parliamentary grant, from the crown lands. The restoration of royal finances was accompanied by the use of financial pressure against leading noblemen, in the form of bonds and recognizances, giving the king an instrument of political control by financial means which in a very general sense was not unlike the use made of financial pressure by Edward I.

The degree of authority which Henry established over the nobility should not, however, be exaggerated: he had to face several challenges to his title, though it is perhaps significant that two of these challenges were from fraudulent pretenders rather than from genuine scions of the House of York. Although the lack of an extensive royal family was an advantage in that no challenge to his rule could come from within it, and he had no brothers and only one younger son to endow, the risk that the dynasty might be extinguished, especially after Arthur Prince of Wales's death in 1502, did nothing to increase the king's sense of security: indeed, the question of the succession was to be a recurrent problem for the Tudor dynasty. Yet in the event Henry VII succeeded, where Henry VI, Edward IV and Richard III had failed, in holding on to the throne and ruling without undue dependence upon a small group of powerful subjects to whom the crown owed political debts. In this respect, at least, the advent of the Tudors marks a new phase in the history of the English monarchy.

Epilogue: New Perspectives, 1985–1999

The first edition of this book was written in the early 1980s and published in 1985. Since then, the approach to late medieval politics which it embodies, and which it shares with a number of other works on medieval English history which were written in the 1970s and early 1980s, has come under critical scrutiny from a variety of viewpoints. The argument of much of this book is that politics was in large part a matter of personal relationships between the king and his great nobles, and that these relationships were expressed in terms of leadership in war, patronage, choice of counsellors, and the maintenance of a court whose *mores* were acceptable to the nobility.[1] This perspective on the politics of late medieval England owes much to the work of the late K. B. McFarlane, whose standpoint is perhaps best encapsulated in a few well-known sentences from his 1953 Ford Lectures. Writing of Edward III, he argued that 'the real politics of the reign...were inherent...in Edward's daily personal relations with his magnates. The king's service was profitable; his favour the only sure road to honour and success; men went to court and to the royal camp, not to express unacceptable views, but for what they could get'. McFarlane went on to suggest that conflict between crown and nobility was not inherent in the structure of late medieval politics, but was most often the result of the unwise actions of a weak or foolish ruler. He reserved his harshest criticism for Henry VI, though he also regarded Edward II and Richard II as unable to 'get on with their magnates',[2] and were thus arguably unfit to rule.

Work on the political history of late medieval England in the 1970s and early 1980s showed many signs of McFarlane's influence, as Colin Richmond demonstrated in an important review article in 1983.[3] J. R. Maddicott argued in *Thomas of Lancaster* that conflict over patronage lay behind the magnates' grievances against Gaveston, while control of patronage was an important source of strength to the king himself, particularly in the middle years of the reign, and Natalie Fryde's study of the last years of Edward II's reign also stressed the importance of royal favour and patronage in determining the relations between the crown and the nobility. The present author argued that aristocratic resentment at the control and direction of patronage, especially between 1381 and 1386, was an important reason for the growth of hostility to Richard II. Henry VI, too, was seen as over-generous in his patronage towards his favourites and members of his household, and this served to alienate many of the nobility from his regime. By contrast, those kings such as Edward III and Henry V who exercised some caution in the distribution of patronage, and were not seen to reward favourites in too lavish a manner, enjoyed thereby a better relationship with the nobility.[4]

McFarlane, however, was not the only influence on historical writing in the 1970s. Some of the work on late medieval English political history might well be characterized as 'magnate history', for it assumed not only that the titled nobility were the dominant political group, but also that the gentry, bound to the great nobility by ties of affinity, had little political independence. Thus in 1957 G. A. Holmes wrote that 'The great magnates occupy a central position in the political and social history of England in the fourteenth century. The crises of politics were mainly in the relations of crown and magnates and in the relations within the magnate class itself'. In an important essay in 1972 T.B. Pugh discussed the emergence in the fourteenth century of a socially and politically powerful peerage numbering perhaps no more than sixty families, to whom the gentry looked for fees, annuities, and patronage in the form of grants of land and office. This approach underlay the argument of a number of works on late medieval history published in the 1970s, yet it is not a point of view with which McFarlane would have entirely sympathized. McFarlane argued that political influence was 'bound up with territorial influence', and that the worlds of the magnates and the gentry were interdependent. The main outlines of both local and central politics would thus emerge from a study of the country gentry and the network of their personal relationships with each other and with the nobility.[5] In recent years both local political societies and the affinities of some of the great magnates have been examined in detail in a number of major studies,[6] and although there is still debate about the significance of the county community as the political and social framework within which the gentry played out their careers, it is difficult now to accept the argument that the politics of late medieval England can be interpreted simply in terms of the relationship between the king and his most powerful nobles.[7]

The relationship between the crown and the titled nobility, however, remains of great importance in understanding political conflict in late medieval England, and it was always one of McFarlane's concerns, with patronage a key issue. In 1981, in the Introduction to his edition of McFarlane's collected papers, G. L. Harriss warned against the crude assumption (which McFarlane never believed) that the nobility were 'continually engaged in a struggle for royal patronage', though he went on to argue that baronial rebellion was generally grounded in fear that the crown might use its power in a way which was damaging to the interests and standing of the noblemen who rebelled.[8] However, in a paper given in 1989 but not published until 1994 E. Powell took issue with that element in the McFarlane interpretation which stressed the importance of patronage.[9] The title of his paper suggests that he regarded it as an inadequate explanation for political conflict, and in examining what he called the 'Poverty of Patronage' he observed in particular that it entailed the neglect of the study of constitutional history. He remarked that A. L. Brown's study of late medieval government stood almost alone in giving proper emphasis to the institutions of government, and he warned against too easily assuming that constitutional and institutional issues were peripheral to the main concern of the medieval nobility, the pursuit of self-interest. Christine Carpenter also argued the case for a renewed concern with constitutional history in her paper in the collection appropriately entitled 'The McFarlane Legacy'.[10] Both Powell and Carpenter suggested that an emphasis on patronage and on individual aristocratic interests provided but a partial understanding of late medieval England, and that it was necessary to return not to the rather artificial constitutional history of the Whig historians, but, instead, to examine the way in which contemporaries thought and wrote about government. In particular, they argued, the study of legal history might provide much valuable insight into contemporary views of government. In a notable work, John Watts has examined contemporary ideas about government and politics, and has constructed an ideological framework for a reinterpretation of the reign of Henry VI in which the determining issue is not simply the ineptitude of the king, but rather a constitutional problem, the inability of the monarchy 'to adjust to one of the possible extremes of human frailty'.[11]

Although too much emphasis has sometimes been laid on patronage as the essence of the relationship between the crown and the nobility, it would perhaps be equally mistaken to minimize it or to reject it entirely. There is plenty of contemporary evidence that access to royal favour and patronage on the part of the nobility, and access to magnate patronage by members of their affinities, were regarded as important by the political class. The Ordainers in 1311 attempted to control Edward II's patronage; so too did Richard II's opponents in 1386, and under Henry IV in particular the attempts by the commons in parliament to control the granting of annuities suggests that the financial implications of royal patronage were all too clear, even to those who individually might benefit from it. Equally, not only Henry IV but also other kings in adversity, such as Edward II after 1311, Edward III in 1376 and 1377, and Richard II after 1397 sought to gain and retain support by the exercise of patronage.

Nonetheless, the propensity of kings such as Edward II, Richard II and Henry VI to reward their unpopular favourites in too lavish a manner was criticized by the nobility not just out of self-interest but also on the grounds that the king's conduct was damaging to the interests of the kingdom and the well-being of the community. The development in Edward II's reign of the idea that the king and the crown were separate entities, and that the nobility's duty to the crown might entail placing restraints upon the king shows perhaps the growth of some concept of public duty which went beyond the personal relationships between king and nobles.[12] In the same way, in 1386 the Duke of Gloucester and Bishop Arundel reminded Richard II that they might apply an 'aid and remedy' if he did not remove his evil counsellors, and that if the king alienated himself from his people and refused to be governed by the laws and with the advice of the magnates of the realm, then the people might remove him from his throne. Such a theory of resistance was not new: the Ordainers used it to justify their imposition of measures of restraint upon Edward II in 1311, and in the final crisis of the reign the will of the people was held to justify the deposition of the king. In the reigns of both Edward II and Richard II the nobility showed themselves able to reflect upon their duty to the people when faced with kings who, as Gloucester and Arundel put it in 1386, chose to be guided by their own will or by malignant counsel.[13]

If the nobility saw the king as ruling within a framework of law and being subject to 'guidance' from the magnates of the realm were he to allow his own will too free a rein or set his will above the laws and customs of the kingdom, the response of the crown in the reigns of Edward II, Richard II and Henry VI was to stress the duty of obedience to royal authority and to develop the concept of treason to deal with subjects who accroached the royal power. Richard II went further than his predecessors in making such arguments explicit when he consulted his judges about his power in the summer of 1387, and they told him in effect that those who sought to constrain the royal prerogative should be punished as traitors. In the 1390s Richard dwelt increasingly on the duty of obedience and the wrongfulness of rebellion. For him, rebellion amounted to treason; his subjects, in deposing him after Bolingbroke's successful rebellion in 1399, drew a contrast between the king's view of his relationship to the law and that of the community. Henry VI also emphasized the duty of obedience (perhaps since there was no other obvious reason why subjects should obey so inept a king) and thus there runs through late medieval political conflict not just a rich vein of self-interest on the part of the nobility but also some sense of their public obligation to defend the interests of the community, and by contrast an authoritarian view of kingship. In the reigns of those kings whose relations with the nobility were for other reasons uneasy these two opposed views of kingship, law and the duties of the king's great subjects came into collision.[14]

Recent work on medieval kingship has, however, focused mainly on royal majesty and power rather than the political ideas of the nobility. In his analysis of the authoritarian nature of Richard II's kingship, Nigel Saul has discussed the language and imagery that Richard employed to emphasize his majesty, and Paul Strohm has examined the way in which Henry IV used language and symbols to sustain the legitimacy of his regime. Both Saul and Strohm have pressed into service a wider range of sources than those which the political historian has traditionally relied upon, and both have shown how much an analysis of art, literature and language can contribute to an understanding of the nature of late medieval kingship.[15]

While the nature of kingship has been a particular concern of those who have written on Richard II and Henry IV, the question of the impact of war on government and on the powers of the monarchy has underlain recent work on Edward III. The argument in the Introduction to the original edition of this book was that the experience of war in the fourteenth and fifteenth centuries served to weaken the English monarchy in some important respects, notably in giving parliament control of most of the financial resources of the crown, and in generating political conflict at home when the war went badly abroad. This was perhaps the conventional view in the 1970s, and it was reinforced in 1988 by R. W. Kaeuper's book *War, Justice, and Public Order: England and France in the Later Middle Ages*. This was essentially a comparative study of the impact of war on the two countries, with the emphasis mainly on the fourteenth century. Kaeuper argued that from the 1290s onwards both England and France were transformed into what he called 'war states'. In England, the great growth in royal power under the Angevins gave the king powerful financial and judicial institutions, yet the mobilization of the country's resources for war after c.1290 made the crown increasingly dependent on the wealth and goodwill of its subjects. War had the effect of seriously over-extending the English state, leading to a neglect of justice at home, and to the domination by the magnates of the local administration of justice. The king in effect became a warrior rather than a judge.[16]

The dependence of the king on the wealth and goodwill of his subjects for the prosecution of war was equally apparent in the fifteenth century. Looking at the war under Henry VI, J. R. Lander argued that the crown found it increasingly difficult to mobilize the resources it needed to sustain the English position in France, and that by then 'the idea of a military career was distinctly *passé*'. Lander placed his discussion of war finance in the context of a general 'retreat from taxation' and a growing demand for the king to live off his income from land and the customs duties. Under Henry VI the commons in parliament twice sought and obtained a reduction in the total assessment for the lay subsidy, and from early in the fifteenth century they made regular demands for the resumption by the king of lands that had been granted out. Fifteenth-century kings, not excepting Henry V, seem to have found it more difficult than Edward III to mobilize their subjects' resources for war.[17]

Such arguments about the impact of war on the English monarchy have, however, come under criticism, at least as far as the reign of Edward III is concerned. W. M. Ormrod argued in an article published in 1987 and in his book on the reign of Edward III[18] that the conventional view should be reconsidered. Although it is, of course, true that Edward III required the consent of the commons in parliament for taxation, Ormrod argued that Edward proved a skilful manager of parliament, and that until 1376 resistance to royal demands for revenue was virtually non-existent. Indeed, parliament's co-operation over taxation 'made the king an extremely wealthy man',[19] and his concessions to parliament and the magnates did not amount to a major diminution in the authority of the crown. Ormrod also argued that the demands of war did not, to any great extent, allow local government to slip into the hands of the magnates. Edward took an active part in the administration of justice in the 1350s and 1360s, and in the middle years of the reign the commons made few complaints about the abuse of power in the localities by the magnates.[20] The revival of such complaints in the 1370s, and again after Henry V's attempts to restore order in the localities, suggests that the problem of law and order was more a result of the personal inadequacies of Edward III in his last years, and of Richard II and Henry VI, than of a fundamental change in the nature of the English state under the impact of war.

Thus Edward III emerges from Ormrod's analysis as a king who maintained and even enhanced the authority of the monarchy, and the generalization that the demands of war in the later middle ages diminished the power of the crown therefore needs to be reconsidered. On the other hand, Richard II evidently believed that the financial needs of the crown for war damaged his relationship with his subjects,[21] and even though peace with France may not have been a pre-requisite for the development of Richard's ideas on kingship in the 1390s, the development certainly took place in the context of a cessation of hostilities which Richard had shown himself particularly anxious to achieve. The problem of the impact of war on English kingship and government may not be as straightforward as the Introduction to this book supposed,[22] at least as far as the fourteenth-century is concerned, but recent work on the fifteenth-century phase of the war sees little sign that the war after 1420 did anything but add to the difficulties of the English kings. In his biography of Henry V, Christopher Allmand argued that the Treaty of Troyes represented an error of judgement which burdened England with a commitment in France that proved increasingly difficult to sustain and which, as others have pointed out, the English nobility and gentry became increasingly reluctant to support, while the final collapse in Normandy in 1450 generated hostility between York and Somerset and contributed substantially to the political instability of the 1450s.[23]

There is nonetheless still a consensus that successful prosecution of the war in France required the support and active participation of the nobility and gentry. Here too recent work has questioned some earlier assumptions, including those of McFarlane, and has offered new perspectives on the motives that induced men to take part in the war. In two important papers,[24] McFarlane presented war as a business, with profit providing an important motive for service. He demonstrated how Sir John Fastolf invested the wealth he won in Normandy in the 1420s and 1430s in land and building projects in England, and in his analysis of an agreement between two English esquires in 1421 he showed how they agreed to share the winnings of war between them, and provide mutual support and aid if one of them should be captured by the enemy. McFarlane's examples came from the fifteenth century; but contemporary chroniclers provide numerous instances of the rich pickings that came from the successful English campaigns in France in the 1340s and 1350s, notably the campaigns in Aquitaine and the campaigns that culminated in the victories at Crécy and Poitiers. In an influential article Denys Hay examined the development of the rules for sharing the winnings of war between the ordinary soldier, his captain, and the crown, though his conclusions have recently been modified by Andrew Ayton.[25]

Thanks in large part to the work of Andrew Ayton and Anne Curry, we now know much more about the structure of the English armies in the fourteenth and fifteenth centuries, and recent studies of aristocratic affinities have extended our understanding of the aristocratic retinue in war as well as in peace.[26] In the light of this work, some of the broader generalizations about profit as a motive for participation in war should be modified. In his study of the Lancastrian affinity, Simon Walker accepts that in the fourteenth century war might still have been profitable, particularly when it was going well for the English, but both he and others have made the point that nobles such as John of Gaunt or Thomas of Woodstock, who engaged to serve with substantial retinues, might have to wait many years to receive payment in full from the Exchequer, and that these debts were sometimes passed on by delaying payment to those who served under them. Furthermore, although many men who served with Gaunt did so in the expectation of profit, 'it was an expectation frequently disappointed'. Therefore motives other than profit induced men to serve. For the great nobles, service was an obligation of their status and expressed their sense of themselves as the king's companions in arms. Lesser men, however, used service overseas as a means whereby they might come to the notice of their lord and gain his protection and patronage at home.[27] In this way, service abroad might have beneficial consequences for a man's standing at home as well bringing him some material rewards if he was lucky.

In the fifteenth century, however, as both Anne Curry and Maurice Keen have pointed out, the commitment which the English crown required from many of those who served in France was rather different. The conquest, settlement and garrisoning of Normandy and the other territories in France which came under English control after 1420 required the continuous presence in France of men who were expected to diminish, if not entirely sever, their ties with land and lordship in England. Although expeditionary forces still went out from England, they were different from the *chevauchées* which set off to campaign in France in the fourteenth century and, with luck, returned home with prisoners and plunder. Many of those who served in France after 1420 were resident there for lengthy periods and had expenses there which they had to fund out of their wages and whatever profits they could make out of the war. In a sense, by 1430, as Anne Curry has observed, the English came close to establishing 'a professional standing army' in Normandy. From this viewpoint, Fastolf and McFarlane's two esquires were perhaps, as Maurice Keen observed, the exception rather than the rule.[28]

Nonetheless, the memory of military success and chivalric honour under Edward III influenced men's attitudes towards war under Henry VI and the Yorkists. As Michael Jones demonstrated, chivalric considerations played a part in the conflict between York and Somerset, for York believed that Somerset had behaved dishonourably during the French invasion of Normandy in 1449–50. In face of the collapse of Lancastrian France, and the feebleness of Henry VI, Edward III's posthumous reputation became an element in political and military debate. As David Morgan has pointed out, Edward was seen as embodying the ideal of kingship, offering victory abroad and good order at home, and Edward IV's propaganda when he went to war in 1475 laid stress on the virtues and successes of his predecessor. The fifteenth-century view of Edward III, expressed in the language of chivalry, was perhaps over-idealized, but served to perpetuate the memory of English victories at a time when the whole venture in France had collapsed. In this way too, war was a formative influence on the outlook of late medieval Englishmen.[29]

Thus since 1985, much attention has been given to issues such as the nature of late medieval kingship, the importance or otherwise of patronage as a factor in conflict between crown and nobility, and the impact of war both on the English state and upon individuals. Yet although these broader issues have played an important part in recent debates, there is still a general acceptance that the medieval English monarchy was essentially personal in character, and that the personalities of individual monarchs are important in understanding the political history of their reigns. Here too work since the mid-1980s has proved illuminating, not least in a series of substantial scholarly biographies. In 1985 only Henry VI of the kings whose reigns cover the period dealt with in this book had received a modern, full-length scholarly biography, but since then Edward I, Richard II and Henry V have also been the subjects of major biographies.

Wolffe's biography of Henry VI confirmed the general consensus that Henry was a foolish and misguided king, though one whose own capacity for political action, even if disastrous, was rather greater than other historians had allowed. The issue of the extent to which Henry was merely manipulated by others is still a matter of debate, as Dr Watts's work on the king demonstrates, and both Watts and Richmond have commented on the difficulty of penetrating to the heart of Henry's personality.[30] Other kings are perhaps more readily comprehensible. Edward I emerges from Michael Prestwich's biography as a man who 'met most of the contemporary requirements for a king',[31] though his preference for confrontation rather than persuasion did not make for easy relations with his magnates, even if, in the last years of his reign, he eventually succeeded in getting his own way. A group of sermons on the death of Edward, possibly preached before pope Clement V at Poitiers, and analysed by D. R. d'Avray bears out Prestwich's judgement. Edward was described as a king who did justice to all his subjects, ruled with energy and wisdom of mind, and 'warred down his enemies', while one sermon brings out his restlessness as well as his energy as he sought to enlarge his kingdom.[32] Henry V, too, is now better known than he was in 1985. His reputation as an outstanding soldier is still intact, but recent work has served to emphasize how successful a king he was at home as well. Many aspects of his domestic policy came under review in the collection of essays edited in 1985 by G. L. Harriss, and Edward Powell has shown how Henry strove with some success, at least in the short term, to restore law and order within his kingdom.[33] Christopher Allmand's biography of Henry, published in 1992, gives due weight to his outstanding military career, though with the reservations discussed earlier, but also examines in detail his handling of his magnates, his relations with parliament, his financial policy and his concern for law and order. He also considers the language and symbolism of Henry's kingship, and argues that Henry encouraged his people to have pride in their achievements and a sense of their Englishness. In this, Allmand argues, Henry's encouragement of the use of the English language was vitally important as an expression of nationhood.[34]

If the language and symbolism of kingship and nationhood was important to Henry V, it was perhaps even more important to Richard II, though his emphasis was much more upon kingship and majesty than the idea of the nation. Nigel Saul's biography of Richard II offers an analysis of Richard's reign and personality which emphasizes his wish to find a new focus for unity and loyalty in place of the war which he sought to bring to an end. Unfortunately, his attempt to focus this new loyalty on his own prerogative and his own high and authoritarian view of kingship proved unacceptable to his subjects. He was perhaps too preoccupied with his own self-image as a king, to the extent that Professor Saul sees him as an 'essentially narcissistic' personality.[35] Saul's Richard is a complex, even contradictory, personality, but a man who was much more than merely a foolish king who could not get on with his magnates. His personality contained within it the seeds of his own destruction: his downfall was not merely the result of bad judgement and adverse circumstances, but was inherent in the nature of his approach to kingship.

In discussing the involvement of kings, nobles and gentry in war, the main focus has tended to be on France, though of course the English were involved during the period covered by this book in warfare in Ireland, Scotland and Wales and, for a shorter time, in the Iberian peninsula as well. In focusing on France, modern historians have perhaps reflected the preoccupations of contemporaries. After 1337 the English war effort was concentrated mainly on France, and the nobility of the fourteenth century believed that honour, fame and profit were pre-eminently to be found in France, though both Froissart and Sir Thomas Gray of Heton chronicled deeds of valour performed by English and Scottish knights in the northern theatre of war. Warfare in Wales and Ireland attracted less attention from chivalric chroniclers, and this probably corresponded to contemporary perceptions, notably perhaps that of the Duke of Gloucester in 1394.[36] Nonetheless, one of the more important historiographical developments since the late 1970s has been the establishment of a British rather than an English perspective on the history of these islands, and an appreciation of the totality of relationships between

England, Ireland, Scotland and Wales rather than looking at the latter three countries from a purely English standpoint. The concept of colonization has proved a useful tool for analysis of the English involvement with both Wales and Ireland. For Wales, the resulting tensions have been examined in some detail by R. R. Davies, both in general terms and, in particular, in his study of the revolt of Owain Glyn Dŵr, while in Ireland, where the English never achieved the degree of domination they established in Wales, the relationship between the English colony and Gaelic Irish society has been illuminated in several important studies.[37]

The position of Scotland was, of course, different from that of Wales and Ireland. The failure of Edward I and his successors to impose their will on Scotland meant that for most of the fourteenth century, and throughout the fifteenth, England was faced on her northern border by a coherent state whose kings possessed, though to a lesser extent than the English kings, the ability to organize for war and command the resources and manpower to make war. Recent work on the special characteristics of medieval frontiers and frontier societies has made comparisons between the Anglo-Scottish border and the frontier between the English and the Gaelic Irish in Ireland. Steven Ellis, for instance, has argued that both on the northern border and in the Pale the need to organize an effective system of defence had a significant impact on the economy and social structure of both regions. Yet, as Ellis acknowledged, important differences remained. On the Anglo-Scottish border two states confronted one another, and as Alexander Grant pointed out, even the Otterburn war of 1388, which Froissart chronicled in much detail, was not a private border raid but a campaign conducted with the knowledge and approval of Robert II, and which from the Scottish point of view marks the 'final, triumphant conclusion of Scotland's Wars of Independence'.[38]

Nonetheless, the northern frontier region of England had of necessity to respond to war in a manner that was different from the rest of the country. The north was the only part of England which actually became a theatre of war, and Colm McNamee has examined in much detail the effect that Robert I's raids into northern England had on the economy of the region in the early fourteenth century. McNamee's analysis, however, extends beyond northern England: he is concerned with the impact of Robert I's wars on the rest of the British Isles, particularly Ireland, and he adopts a trans-national approach: his perspective is British rather than merely English or Scottish. In this he is in the company of Robin Frame, whose account of political development in the British Isles seeks to relate events in all four countries to one another and to compare the frontiers of English lordship in the various parts of these islands.[39]

The ascendancy of England within the British Isles perhaps reached its zenith under Edward I, and its nadir in the early fifteenth century when Scottish independence was secure and English authority was challenged in Wales by rebellion and in Ireland by the expansion in the power of the Gaelic Irish rulers. R. R. Davies has argued that by the end of the thirteenth century England had developed an ideology of unity and domination within the British Isles. Edward I expressed this imperial ideology in his building work at Caernarvon and in his attempt to suppress the identity and destroy the symbols of the Scottish kingdom.[40] Yet the tide of English imperialism ebbed rapidly in the fourteenth century. By the end of the century, two organized monarchies were established in this island, and although they increasingly made use of two variants of the same language, they each stressed their own historical myths and developed their own symbols of kingship. Richard II's experience in Ireland in 1394–5 may, as Nigel Saul has suggested, have sharpened his thinking about rebellion and about the obligations of subjects to their king, but though clothed in the language of majesty his kingship seemed little concerned with ideas of domination over the other countries of the British Isles, even those which acknowledged his lordship, let alone Scotland. Nor was the dual monarchy of the Treaty of Troyes an expression of English imperialism. The symbolism of the Lancastrian monarchy in France stressed Henry VI's position as Charles VI's heir under the Treaty of Troyes, and perhaps one of the underlying weaknesses of the Troyes settlement was that while the French were unlikely ever wholeheartedly to accept the Lancastrian succession, the English too were lukewarm about it, and appear to have viewed their king's obligations in virtue of his French title with a degree of detachment, if not hostility. Henry V's kingship, as Christopher Allmand showed, emphasized the Englishness of his English realm: the imperial ambitions of Edward I had been transmuted, under the pressure of events, into a more specific sense of English nationhood.[41]

In these various ways, therefore, the approach to late medieval English political history which was adopted in the first edition of this book needs modification. Yet the relationship between crown and nobility, and the part played by war in shaping English government and politics and the English sense of themselves, remain at the heart of any interpretation of late medieval English politics. The issue is not whether the nobility were important, but rather what considerations determined their relations with the king and with the gentry, and how they reacted to inadequate or foolish kings. Furthermore, debates on war and the English state have focused on the questions of whether the influence of war was malign, whether it tended to strengthen or weaken the monarchy, and why men went to war in the service of the king and the great magnates. The importance of war itself is difficult to deny. The experience and the consequences of war for the crown, the nobility and the gentry remains a unifying theme for the history of late medieval England.

Notes

1 The Reign of Edward I, 1272–1307

1 *The Chronicle of Walter of Guisborough*, ed. H. Rothwell, London (Camden 3rd Series, vol. lxxxix) 1957, p. 213; T. Wright, *The Political Songs of England*, new edn with Introduction by Peter Coss, Cambridge, 1996, p. 128; *The Song of Lewes*, ed. C. L. Kingsford, Oxford, reprinted 1963, lines 440–5.
2 D. W. Sutherland, *Quo Warranto Proceedings in the Reign of Edward I 1278–94*, Oxford, 1963, pp. 6–7.
3 *Guisborough*, p. 216.
4 M. T. Clanchy, *From Memory to Written Record*, London, 1979, p. 22.
5 M. C. Prestwich, *The Three Edwards*, London, 1980, p. 20.
6 *Guisborough*, p. 218.
7 Ibid., p. 227.
8 J. G. Edwards, 'Justice in Early English Parliaments', *Bulletin of the Institute of Historical Research*, vol. xxvii, 1954, p. 40.
9 The most accessible English version of the Statute is in *English Historical Documents*, vol. III, ed. H. Rothwell, London, 1975, pp. 397–410.
10 *Calendar of Ancient Correspondence concerning Wales*, ed. J. G. Edwards, Cardiff, 1935, p. 84.
11 J. G. Bellamy, *The Law of Treason in England in the Later Middle Ages*, Cambridge, 1970, pp. 24–46.
12 Rothwell, *Documents*, p. 422.
13 *The History of the King's Works*, vol. I, ed. R. A. Brown, H. M. Colvin and A. J. Taylor, London, 1963, pp. 369–71; R. R. Davies, *Domination and Conquest: The Experience of Ireland, Scotland and Wales 1100–1300*, Cambridge, 1990, p. 127.
14 See J. E. Morris, *The Welsh Wars of Edward I*, Oxford, 1901, pp. 220–39 and R. R. Davies, *Lordship and Society in the March of Wales 1282–1400*, Oxford, 1978, pp. 259–60.
15 Davies, *Lordship and Society*, p. 264; Davies, *Domination and Conquest*, pp. 124–7.

16   Robin Frame, 'Aristocracies and the Political Configuration of the British Isles', in *The British Isles 1100–1500: Comparisons, Contrasts and Connections*, ed. R. R. Davies, Edinburgh, 1988, pp. 151–3; Alexander Grant, *Independence and Nationhood: Scotland 1306–1469*, London, 1984, pp. 120–43; A. Tuck, 'The Emergence of a Northern Nobility', *Northern History*, vol. 22, 1986, pp. 1–17.

17   Rothwell, *Documents*, pp. 467–8.

18   *Anglo-Scottish Relations 1174–1328: Some Selected Documents*, ed. E. L. G. Stones, Edinburgh, 1965, p. 54. For what follows, see *Edward I and the Throne of Scotland: An Edition of the Record Sources of the Great Cause*, ed. E. L. G. Stones and G. G. Simpson, 2 vols, Oxford, 1978.

19   Stones and Simpson, *Great Cause*, vol. II, pp. 248–9.

20   See below, p. 17.

21   Stones, *Anglo-Scottish Relations*, p. 65.

22   *Willelmi Rishanger Chronica et Annales 1259–1307*, ed. H. T. Riley, London (Rolls Series) 1865, p. 371; G. W. S. Barrow, *Robert Bruce*, London, 1965, pp. 74–96.

23   *Rishanger*, p. 373.

24   Quoted in E. M. Barron, *The Scottish War of Independence*, 2nd edn, Inverness, 1934, p. 117.

25   Michael Prestwich, *Edward I*, London, 1988, pp. 401–06; *Flores Historiarum*, ed. H. R. Ward, London (Rolls Series) vol. III, 1890, pp. 90, 275–6, but see Prestwich, *Edward I*, p. 405 note 12.

26   Prestwich, *Edward I*, p. 405.

27   *Bartholomaei de Cotton Historia Anglicana*, ed. H. R. Luard, London (Rolls Series) 1859, p. 322.

28   *Guisborough*, p. 290.

29   *Flores*, III, p. 101.

30   Prestwich, *Three Edwards*, p. 29.

31   *Flores*, III, pp. 295–6.

32   *Documents Illustrating the Crisis of 1297–98 in England*, ed. M. C. Prestwich, London (Camden 4th Series) 1980, p. 121.

33   Prestwich, *Documents*, pp. 115–17; Prestwich, *Edward I*, p. 421.

34   Prestwich, *Documents*, pp. 125–9.

35   Ibid., p. 138.

36   *Chronicon de Lanercost*, ed. J. Stevenson, Edinburgh, 1839, p. 190; *Guisborough*, p. 299; R. Nicholson, *Scotland: The Later Middle Ages*, Edinburgh, 1974, pp. 52–8.

37   Barrow, *Bruce*, p. 128.

38   Prestwich, *Documents*, pp. 154–5, 158–60.

39   F. M. Powicke, *The Thirteenth Century*, Oxford, 1953, p. 650; see also M. C. Prestwich, *War, Politics and Finance under Edward I*, London 1972, pp. 171–2.

40   *Guisborough*, p. 305.

41   Ibid., p. 325.

42   Ibid., p. 329.

43   Ibid.

44   Ibid., p. 330; Prestwich, *Edward I*, p. 520.

45 *The Chronicle of Bury St Edmunds*, ed. Antonia Gransden, London, 1964, p. 152; see also H. Rothwell, 'Edward I and the Struggle for the Charters, 1297–1305', in *Studies in Medieval History Presented to F. M. Powicke*, ed. R. W. Hunt, W. A. Pantin and R. W. Southern, Oxford, 1948, pp. 319–32.

46 *Guisborough*, p. 332.

47 Rothwell, *Documents*, pp. 496–501.

48 Prestwich, *Three Edwards*, p. 32.

49 Barrow, *Bruce*, p. 191; Davies, *Domination and Conquest*, chapter 6; *The Chronicle of Pierre de Langtoft*, ed. T. Wright, London (Rolls Series) 1868, vol. II, p. 264.

50 *Langtoft*, vol. II, p. 328.

51 M. C. Prestwich, 'Royal Patronage under Edward I', in *Thirteenth Century England*, vol. I, ed. P. R. Coss and S. D. Lloyd, Woodbridge, 1986, pp. 41–52.

52 *Guisborough*, p. 352.

53 *Rishanger*, p. 227.

2 Edward II and Thomas of Lancaster, 1307–1322

1   *Vita Edwardi Secundi*, ed. N. Denholm-Young, Edinburgh, 1957, p. ix.

2   Prestwich, *Three Edwards*, p. 80; *Guisborough* p. 382.

3   J. R. Maddicott, *Thomas of Lancaster*, Oxford, 1970, p. 6.

4   Pierre Chaplais, *Piers Gaveston: Edward II's Adoptive Brother*, Oxford, 1994; *Vita*, p. 15; *Annales Paulini*, in *Chronicles of the Reigns of Edward I and Edward II*, vol. I, ed. W. Stubbs, London (Rolls Series) 1882, p. 259. For the reliability of this source, see H. G. Richardson, 'The Annales Paulini', *Speculum*, vol. 23, 1948, pp. 630–40. J. S. Hamilton has no doubt about the homosexual nature of the king's relationship with Gaveston: *Piers Gaveston: Earl of Cornwall 1307–1312*, London, 1988, pp. 16–17.

5   *Vita*, p. 40.

6   Ibid., p. 1.

7   Ibid., p. 2.

8   Maddicott, *Thomas of Lancaster*, p. 73

9   *Ann. Paul.*, p. 260

10 Ibid., pp. 258–62; E. A. R. Brown, 'The Political Repercussions of Family Ties in the Early Fourteenth Century: The Marriage of Edward II of England and Isabelle of France', *Speculum*, vol. 63, 1988, pp. 582–3.

11 The text of the coronation oath is given in S. B. Chrimes and A. L. Brown, eds, *Select Documents of English Constitutional History 1307–1485*, London, 1961, pp. 4–5. For some discussion, see R. S. Hoyt, 'The Coronation Oath of 1308', *English Historical Review*, vol. lxxi, 1956, pp. 353–83.

12 *Ann. Paul.*, p. 262; *Vita*, p. 4.

13 *Vita.* p. 4.

14 Maddicott, *Thomas of Lancaster*, p. 79.

15 Ann. Paul., p. 260; Maddicott, Thomas of Lancaster, p. 86; Brown, 'Political Repercussions', p. 587.

16 Lanercost Chron., p. 212; Vita, p. 6.

17 Vita, pp. 7, 8; J. H. Denton, Robert Winchelsey and the Crown 1294–1313, Cambridge, 1980, pp. 258–9.

18 Vita, p. 8; Annales Londonienses, in Chronicles of Edward I and II, vol. I, p. 157.

19 Vita, p. 8; Maddicott, Thomas of Lancaster, pp. 95–102, 104.

20 Guisborough, p. 384.

21 Vita, p. 9.

22 Guisborough, p. 385.

23 Ann. Lond., pp. 168–9; Maddicott, Thomas of Lancaster, pp. 111–12.

24 Gesta Edwardi de Carnarvan Auctore Canonico Bridlingtoniensi (hereafter referred to as Ann. Bridl.), in Chronicles of Edward I and II, vol. II, p. 36.

25 Vita, p. 7.

26 Ibid., p. 10.

27 Lanercost Chron., p. 214.

28 Maddicott, Thomas of Lancaster, p. 115.

29 Ibid., pp. 114–15; T. Walsingham, Historia Anglicana, ed. H. T. Riley, London (Rolls Series) vol. I, 1863, p. 13.

30 Vita, p. 18.

31 Ann. Paul., p. 270; Vita, p. 19.

32 Rothwell, Documents, pp. 527–39; Hamilton, Gaveston, pp. 87–9.

33 See below, pp. 65–6.

34 Vita, pp. 11, 62–3; Maddicott, Thomas of Lancaster, pp. 119–20. For a discussion of Winchelsey's role, see Denton, Winchelsey, pp. 262–5.

35 For a discussion of the authorship of the Ordinances, see M. Prestwich, 'The Ordinances of 1311 and the Politics of the Early Fourteenth Century', in Politics and Crisis in Fourteenth Century England, ed. John Taylor and Wendy Childs, Gloucester, 1990, pp. 1–18, esp. pp. 13–15.

36 Vita, p. 23.

37 Ibid., p. 22.

38 Ann. Bridl., pp. 43–4.

39 Chronicon Henrici Knighton, ed. J. R. Lumby, London (Rolls Series) vol. I, 1889, p. 409.

40 Vita, p. 32.

41 Ibid., p. 37.

42 Ibid., p. 39.

43 The Brus, writ be Master Johne Barbour, Aberdeen, Spalding Club Edition, 1856, p. 253; Barrow, Bruce, pp. 291–6; C. McNamee, The Wars of the Bruces: Scotland, England and Ireland, 1306–1328, East Linton, 1997, pp. 60–7.

44 Flores, III, p. 338.

45 The campaign is discussed at length in Barrow, Bruce, pp. 301–32.

46 Chronicon Galfridi le Baker, ed. E. M. Thompson, London 1889, p. 7.

47 Vita, p. 53.

48 See below, p. 59.

49 *Vita*, p. 57; Maddicott, *Thomas of Lancaster*, pp. 160–5.

50 *Rotuli Parliamentorum*, i, London, 1783, p. 351.

51 *Vita*, p. 63.

52 J. R. S. Phillips, *Aymer de Valence: Earl of Pembroke 1307–1324*, Oxford, 1972, pp. 131–2.

53 *Vita*, p. 75; Phillips, *Aymer de Valence*, pp. 142–50.

54 McNamee, *Wars of the Bruces*, pp. 72–122; A. Tuck, 'War and Society in the Medieval North', *Northern History*, vol. 21, 1985, pp. 33–52.

55 McNamee, *Wars of the Bruces*, pp. 166–86; James Lydon, 'The Impact of the Bruce Invasion, 1315–27', in *A New History of Ireland vol. II: Medieval Ireland 1169–1534*, ed. Art Cosgrove, Oxford, 1993, pp. 275–94.

56 Ian Kershaw, 'The Great Famine and Agrarian Crisis in England 1315–1322', *Past and Present*, no. 59, 1973, pp. 3–50; Richard M. Smith, 'Demographic Developments in Rural England, 1300–48: a Survey', in *Before the Black Death: Studies in the 'Crisis' of the Early Fourteenth Century*, ed. B. M. S. Campbell, Manchester, 1991, pp. 25–77; W. M. Ormrod, 'The Crown and the English Economy, 1290–1348', in Campbell, *Before the Black Death*. pp. 149–83.

57 Phillips, *Aymer de Valence*, pp. 136–48; Prestwich, *Three Edwards*, p. 88.

58 *Vita*, pp. 97–9.

59 Walsingham, *Historia Anglicana*, I, p. 155; *Vita*, p. 104.

60 *Flores*, III, pp. 192–3.

61 *Vita*, p. 104.

62 *Cal. Anc. Corr. Wales*, pp. 219–20.

63 *Le Baker*, p. 11.

64 *Vita*, p. 112.

65 Walsingham, *Historia Anglicana*, I, p. 162.

66 G. L. Haskins, 'The Doncaster Petition, 1321', *English Historical Review*, vol. liii, 1938, pp. 478–85; B. Wilkinson, 'The Sherburn Indenture and the Attack on the Despensers, 1321', *English Historical Review*, vol. lxiii, 1948, pp. 1–28.

67 *Ann. Paul.*, p. 302; Maddicott, *Thomas of Lancaster*, pp. 302–3; Barrow, *Bruce*, p. 343.

68 *Cal. Anc. Corr. Wales*, pp. 219–20.

69 J. C. Russell, 'The Canonization of Opposition to the King in Angevin England', in *Haskins Anniversary Essays*, ed. C. H. Taylor, Boston 1929, p. 284.

70 *Vita*, p. 126; *Flores*, III, p. 206.

71 Nicholas Pronay and John Taylor, *Parliamentary Texts of the Later Middle Ages*, Oxford, 1980, pp. 133–91.

72 W. M. Ormrod, 'Agenda for Legislation, 1322–c.1340', *English Historical Review*, vol. cv, 1990, pp. 1–33.

73 K. B. McFarlane, *The Nobility of Later Medieval England*, Oxford, 1973, p. 274.

74 For some discussion of this subject, see C. Given-Wilson, *The English Nobility in the Late Middle Ages*, London, 1987, pp. 56–8.

3 The Abasement and Revival of the Monarchy, 1322–1337

1 *Lanercost Chron.*, p. 244; Bellamy, *Law of Treason*, pp. 49–52.
2 *Vita*, pp. 4, 17, 126; *Lanercost Chron.*, p. 244; Wendy Childs, 'Resistance and Treason in the *Vita Edwardi Secundi*', in *Thirteenth Century England* VI, ed. Michael Prestwich, R. H. Britnell and Robin Frame, Woodbridge, 1997, pp. 177–91; Jean Dunbabin, 'Government' in *The Cambridge History of Medieval Political Thought c.350–c.1450*, ed. J. H. Burns, Cambridge, 1988, pp. 492–501.
3 Rothwell, *Documents*, pp. 543–4.
4 *Vita*, p. 136; C. Given-Wilson, '*Vita Edwardi Secundi:* Memoir or Journal', in *Thirteenth Century England* VI, pp. 171–4; M. C. Buck, 'The Reform of the Exchequer, 1316–1326', *English Historical Review*, vol. xcviii, 1983, pp. 252–6.
5 Natalie Fryde, *The Tyranny and Fall of Edward II*, Cambridge, 1979, pp. 106–18, 163–4.
6 *Lanercost Chron.*, p. 249.
7 Fryde, *Tyranny*, pp. 134–48, 162, 180–5.
8 *A French Chronicle of London*, ed. G. J. Aungier, London (Camden 1st Series, vol. xxviii) 1844, p. 51; Fryde, *Tyranny*, pp. 185–6.
9 M. McKisack, 'London and the Succession to the Crown in the Middle Ages', in *Studies presented to Powicke*, p. 81.
10 R. R. Davies, *Conquest, Coexistence and Change: Wales 1063–1415*, Oxford, 1987, pp. 386–7, 397.
11 *Ann. Bridl.*, p. 87; *Knighton*, I, pp. 437–40; *Ann. Paul.*, p. 321.
12 *Lanercost Chron.*, p. 257.
13 Chrimes and Brown, *Documents*, pp. 33–8; for a discussion of the deposition proceedings, see R. M. Haines, *The Church and Politics in Fourteenth Century England*, Cambridge, 1978, pp. 168–76.
14 *Le Baker*, pp. 27–8.
15 Haines, *Church and Politics*, pp. 168–77; Haines, *Archbishop John Stratford*, Toronto, 1986, pp. 179–87; Edward Peters, *The Shadow King*, New Haven, 1970, esp. pp. 236–42; G. E. Caspary, 'The Deposition of Richard II and the Canon Law', Proceedings of the Second International Congress of Medieval Canon Law, Boston, 1965, pp. 189–201 (the term demagogic is Haines's: *Stratford*, p. 181).
16 *Le Baker*, pp. 30–4; G. P. Cuttino and T. W. Lyman, 'Where is Edward II?', *Speculum* vol. 53, 1978, pp. 522–43.
17 Nigel Saul, 'The Despensers and the Downfall of Edward II', *English Historical Review*, vol. xcix, 1984, pp. 1–33.
18 G. A. Holmes, *The Estates of the Higher Nobility in Fourteenth Century England*, Cambridge, 1957, pp. 13–14; Fryde, *Tyranny*, p. 206.
19 Fryde, *Tyranny*, pp. 209–11.
20 R. Frame, *English Lordship in Ireland 1318–1361*, Oxford, 1982, pp. 138–41; Lydon, 'Bruce Invasion', pp. 292–300; *Adae Murimuth Continuatio Chronicarum*, ed. E. M. Thompson, London (Rolls Series) 1889, p. 53; Sir Thomas Gray of Heton, *Scalacronica, a Chronicle of*

England and Scotland from 1066 to 1362, ed. J. Stevenson, Edinburgh, 1836, pp. 153–4.

21   *Murimuth*, p. 53; R. Nicholson, *Edward III and the Scots*, Oxford 1965, pp. 26–36.

22   Stones, *Anglo-Scottish Relations*, pp. 161–70.

23   J. Scammell, 'Robert I and the North of England', *English Historical Review*, vol. lxxiii, 1958, p. 402; McNamee, *Wars of the Bruces*, pp. 105–15, 240–6; Frame, *English Lordship*, p. 141.

24   *Murimuth*, p. 56, *Scalacronica*, p. 156; G. A. Holmes, 'The Rebellion of the Earl of Lancaster, 1328–29', *Bulletin of the Institute of Historical Research*, vol. xxviii, 1955, pp. 84–9; Fryde, *Tyranny*, pp. 217–22.

25   Fryde, *Tyranny*, pp. 219–21; *Calendar of Plea and Memoranda Rolls of the City of London*, ed. A. H. Thomas, Cambridge, 1926, pp. 79–83.

26   Holmes, 'Rebellion', pp. 84–9; *Plea and Memoranda Rolls*, pp. 79–83.

27   *The Brut, or The Chronicles of England*, ed. F. W. D. Brie, London (Early English Text Society) Part I, 1906, pp. 258–9.

28   C. G. Crump, 'The Arrest of Roger Mortimer and Queen Isabel', *English Historical Review*, vol. xxvi, 1911, pp. 331–2.

29   *Flores*, III, p. 178.

30   *Brut*, Part I, p. 271; *Le Baker*, p. 46.

31   *Rot. Parl*, ii, pp. 52–3.

32   *Knighton*, I, p. 454.

33   Holmes, *Estates of the Higher Nobility*, p. 17.

34   *Rot. Parl.*, ii, pp. 56–7.

35   Ibid.

36   *Brut*, Part I, p. 269.

37   *Scalacronica*, p. 158; Walsingham, *Historia Anglicana*, I, p. 193; *Murimuth*, p. 63.

38   *Scalacronica*, pp. 158–9.

39   Ibid., p. 159.

40   Ibid., p. 161; *Rot. Parl.*, ii, pp. 66–7.

41   For much of what follows, see Nicholson, *Edward III*, pp. 119–38.

42   Ibid., pp. 230–6.

43   Bruce Webster, 'Scotland without a King, 1329–1341', in *Medieval Scotland: Crown, Lordship and Community*, ed. Alexander Grant and Keith J. Stringer, Edinburgh, 1993, pp. 223–38; M. H. Dodds, *A History of Northumberland*, vol. xii, Newcastle upon Tyne, 1926, pp. 100–2.

44   *Rotuli Parliamentorum Anglie Hactenus Inediti*, ed. G. O. Sayles, London (Camden 3rd Series) 1935, pp. 224, 228.

45   *Chronica Monasterii de Melsa*, ed. E. A. Bond, London (Rolls Series), vol. II, 1867, p. 373.

4   The War with France, 1337–1364

1   This is, of course, a subject of much controversy. I have taken these estimates from B. H. Slicher van Bath, *The Agrarian History of Western Europe*, London, 1963, p. 80.

2   *English Historical Documents*, vol. IV, ed. A. R. Myers, London, 1969, pp. 62–3.
3   For a discussion of the succession problem, see R. Cazelles, *La Société Politique et la Crise de la Royauté sous Philippe de Valois*, Paris, 1958, pp. 48–57.
4   See above, p. 72.
5   Cazelles, *La Société Politique*, p. 51.
6   M. G. A. Vale, *The Angevin Legacy and the Hundred Years War 1250–1340*, Oxford, 1990, pp. 244–53.
7   Vale, *Angevin Legacy*, pp. 255–60.
8   Quoted in Prestwich, *Three Edwards*, p. 200.
9   G. L. Harriss, *King, Parliament and Public Finance in Medieval England to 1369*, Oxford, 1975, pp. 233–4. Dr Harriss regards it as certain that the king obtained 'specific assent to the war from prelates, magnates, and Commons'.
10 *Reports from the Lords Commissioners touching the Dignity of a Peer of the Realm*, vol. V, London, 1829, pp. 29–31.
11 T. F. Tout, *Chapters in the Administrative History of Medieval England*, vol. III, Manchester, 1928, p. 39.
12 *Murimuth*, p. 79.
13 *Scalacronica*, p. 168.
14 Robert of Avesbury, *De Gestis Mirabilibus Regis Edwardi Tertii*, ed. E. M. Thompson, London (Rolls Series) 1889, p. 309. Translated in Myers, *Documents*, London, 1969, pp. 66–7.
15 *Rot. Parl. Hactenus Inediti*, pp. 267–72; *Rot. Parl.*, ii, pp. 102–6, 114; Harriss, *Public Finance*, pp. 247–8, 253–65.
16 J. R. Maddicott, *The English Peasantry and the Demands of the Crown 1294–1341*, in *Past and Present*, supplement no. 1, 1975, pp. 64–5.
17 *Le Baker*, pp. 73–4; *Murimuth*, pp. 119–20.
18 W. M. Ormrod, *The Reign of Edward III*, New Haven and London, 1990, p. 101; Harriss, *Public Finance*, pp. 270–302.
19 *Murimuth*, p. 122; Harriss, *Public Finance*, p. 521.
20 *Brut*, Part II, 1908, p. 296; *Murimuth*, p. 123.
21 Froissart, *Chronicles,* selected and translated by Geoffrey Brereton, London (Penguin Edition) 1968, p. 76.
22 Froissart, *Chronicles.*, p. 92.
23 *Rot. Parl.*, ii, p. 159.
24 *Knighton's Chronicle 1337–1396,* ed. and trans. G. H. Martin, Oxford, 1995, pp. 52–3.
25 Froissart, *Chronicles* p. 77.
26 *Chronicon Angliae 1328–88,* ed. E. M. Thompson, London (Rolls Series) 1874, p. 26.
27 K. Fowler, *The King's Lieutenant*, London 1969, p. 72; R. Somerville, *Duchy of Lancaster*, vol. I, London, 1953, p. 35.
28 *Murimuth*, pp. 155–6.
29 Juliet Vale, *Edward III and Chivalry*, Woodbridge, 1982, pp. 76–91.
30 *Knighton*, ed. Martin, pp. 100–2; see also *The Black Death*, ed. and trans. Rosemary Horrox, Manchester, 1994.
31 *Le Baker*, p. 99.

32 W. M. Ormrod, 'The English Government and the Black Death of 1348–49', in *England in the Fourteenth Century*, ed. W. M. Ormrod, Woodbridge, 1986, pp. 175–88.

33 H. J. Hewitt, *The Black Prince's Expeditions of 1355–57*, Manchester, 1958, p. 101.

34 *Le Baker*, pp. 154–5; Froissart, *Chronicles* p. 143.

35 K. Fowler, *The Age of Plantagenet and Valois*, London, 1967, p. 61.

36 *Brut*, Part I, p. 225; M. R. Powicke, *Military Obligation in Medieval England*, Oxford, 1962, pp. 134–65, 182–212.

37 Andrew Ayton, 'English Armies in the Fourteenth Century' in *Arms, Armies and Fortifications in the Hundred Years War*, ed. Anne Curry and Michael Hughes, Woodbridge, 1994, pp. 21–38.

38 Andrew Ayton, *Knights and Warhorses: Military Service and the Aristocracy under Edward III*, Woodbridge, 1994, pp. 110–27.

39 PRO, Exchequer Accounts Various, E. 101/40/30.

40 Ayton, *Knights and Warhorses*, pp. 127–37.

41 BL Harleian Ms. 4840, fo. 303; C. Given-Wilson, 'Wealth and Credit, Public and Private: The Earls of Arundel 1306–1397', *English Historical Review*, vol. cvi, 1991, pp. 1–26.

42 *Ancient Petitions Relating to Northumberland*, ed. C. M. Fraser, Surtees Society vol. clxxvi, 1961, p. 160; Northumberland Record Office, *Swinburne Papers*, vol. 4, no. 60.

43 N. Saul, *Knights and Esquires: The Gloucestershire Gentry in the Fourteenth Century*, Oxford, 1981, pp. 52–9.

44 *Rot. Parl.*, ii, passim; Ormrod, *Edward III*, p. 165.

45 For this see Harriss, *Public Finance*, pp. 420–49.

46 *Rot. Parl*, ii, p. 229; Harriss, *Public Finance*, pp. 432–40.

47 J. S. Roskell, 'The Problem of the Attendance of the Lords in Medieval Parliaments', *Bulletin of the Institute of Historical Research*, vol. xxix, 1956, pp. 153–204; Harriss, *Public Finance*, pp. 255–6.

48 *Rot. Parl*, ii, pp. 158–9, 165.

49 J. Barnie, *War in Medieval Society*, London, 1974, p. 48.

50 *Chronicle of John of Reading*, ed. J. Tait, Manchester, 1914, p. 155.

51 Richard Bury, *Philobiblion*, ed. and trans. E. C. Thomas, London, 1888, pp. 55–64; but see also Scott L. Waugh, *England in the Reign of Edward III*, Cambridge, 1991, p. 235.

52 *Selections from English Wycliffite Writings*, ed. Anne Hudson, Cambridge, 1978, p. 28; Anne Hudson, *The Premature Reformation*, Oxford, 1988, pp. 367–70.

53 *Textes et Documents d'histoire du Moyen Age*, ed. J. Glenisson and J. Day, Paris, 1970, pp. 211–12.

54 Holmes, *Estates of the Higher Nobility*, p. 7.

55 J. M. W. Bean, *The Decline of English Feudalism*, Manchester, 1968, p. 212; Ormrod, *Edward III*, pp. 113–15.

56 F. R. Fairbank, 'The Last Earl of Warenne and Surrey', *Yorkshire Archaeological Journal*, vol. xix, 1907, pp. 193–264.

57 *Statutes of the Realm*, vol. I, London 1810, p. 310; Anthony Goodman, *John of Gaunt*, London, 1992, p. 33; *Knighton*, (ed. Martin), p. 185.

58 Myers, *Documents*, p. 403.

5 Military Stalemate and Political Conflict, 1364–1389

1 R. Delachenal, *Histoire de Charles V*, vol. III, Paris, 1931, pp. 551–3.
2 *Life of the Black Prince by the Herald of Sir John Chandos*, ed. M. K. Pope and E. C. Lodge, Oxford, 1910, lines 3877–96.
3 Froissart, *Chronicles*, p. 176.
4 Walsingham, *Historia Anglicana*, I, p. 322.
5 *The Sermons of Thomas Brinton*, ed. M. A. Devlin, London (Camden 3rd Series, vol. lxxxvi) 1954, p. 321.
6 C. Given-Wilson, *The Royal Household and the King's Affinity*, New Haven and London, 1986, pp. 146–60; Ormrod, *Edward III*, pp. 34–5.
7 Quoted in J. J. N. Palmer, *England, France and Christendom*, London, 1972, p. 6.
8 Anthony Goodman, *John of Gaunt*, London, 1992, p. 51; Ormrod, *Edward III*, pp. 116–17.
9 Walsingham, *Historia Anglicana*, I, p. 315; Froissart, *Chronicles*, p. 191; *The Anonimalle Chronicle 1333 to 1381*, ed. V. H. Galbraith, Manchester, 1927, p. 74.
10 G. A. Holmes, *The Good Parliament*, Oxford, 1975, pp. 56–62; Goodman, *John of Gaunt*, pp. 54–5.
11 Walsingham, *Historia Anglicana*, I, p. 319.
12 By Holmes, *Good Parliament*, pp. 100–58, and by C. Given-Wilson, *The Royal Household*, pp. 146–54.
13 *Anon. Chron.*, pp. 79–92.
14 T. F. T. Plucknett, 'The Impeachments of 1376', *Transactions of the Royal Historical Society*, 5th Series, vol. i, 1951, p. 53.
15 *Chronicon Angliae*, p. 74.
16 Goodman, *John of Gaunt*, pp. 57–62; Michael Bennett, 'Edward III's Entail and the Succession to the Crown, 1376–1461', *English Historical Review*, vol. cxiii, 1998, pp. 580–609.
17 *Chronicon Angliae*, esp. pp. 92–136.
18 Ibid., pp. 143–4.
19 Ibid., p. 164; N. Saul, *Richard II*, New Haven and London, 1997, pp. 27–30.
20 *Rot. Parl.*, iii, p. 34.
21 James Sherborne, 'The Cost of English Warfare with France in the Later Fourteenth Century', in his *War, Politics and Culture in Fourteenth-Century England*, ed. A. Tuck, London, 1994, pp. 66–70.
22 *Anon. Chron.*, p. 134; C. Oman, *The Great Revolt of 1381*, new edn with introduction by E. B. Fryde, Oxford, 1969, p. xvii.
23 *Rot. Parl.*, iii, p. 73.
24 There is a substantial literature on the Peasants' Revolt. The best recent general account is in Saul, *Richard II*, chapter 4. R. B. Dobson has edited and translated a selection of documents in *The Peasants' Revolt of 1381*, 2nd edn, London, 1981.

25 Palmer, *England, France and Christendom*, p. 10.
26 *Rot. Parl*, iii, pp. 99–101.
27 T. F. Tout, 'The Earldoms under Edward I', *Transactions of the Royal Historical Society*, vol. viii, 1894, p. 154; Walsingham, *Historia Anglicana*, II, p. 140.
28 *Annales Ricardi Secundi*, in *J. de Trokelowe et Anon. Chronica et Annales*, ed. H. T. Riley, London (Rolls Series) 1865, pp. 184–5.
29 *Rot. Parl.*, iii, pp. 216–17.
30 Walsingham, *Historia Anglicana*, II, p. 141.
31 A. Tuck, *Richard II and the English Nobility*, London, 1973, p. 76; C. Given-Wilson, 'Richard II and his Grandfather's Will', *English Historical Review*, vol. xciii, 1978, pp. 320–37.
32 *Knighton* (ed. Martin), p. 501; *The Kirkstall Chronicle 1355–1400*, ed. M. V. Clarke and N. Denholm-Young, *Bulletin of the John Rylands Library*, vol. 15, 1931, p. 128.
33 Walsingham, *Historia Anglicana*, II, p. 68.
34 *The Westminster Chronicle 1381–1394*, ed. and trans. L. C. Hector and Barbara F. Harvey, Oxford, 1982, p. 49.
35 *Westminster*, p. 53.
36 Ibid., p. 55.
37 Ibid., pp. 67–9.
38 Ibid., p. 69; Walsingham, *Historia Anglicana*, II, pp. 112–13.
39 *Westminster*, pp. 111–13.
40 Ibid., p. 115.
41 Ibid., p. 117.
42 J. J. N. Palmer, 'The Parliament of 1385 and the Constitutional Crisis of 1386', *Speculum*, vol. 46, 1971, pp. 477–90.
43 *Westminster*, p. 131.
44 J. J. N. Palmer, 'The Impeachment of Michael de la Pole in 1386', *Bulletin of the Institute of Historical Research*, vol. xlii, 1969, pp. 100–1.
45 The fullest source for this episode is *Knighton* (ed. Martin), pp. 352–62. For the possibility that Gloucester was Knighton's source, see ibid., pp. lxviii–lxix.
46 See for this J. S. Roskell, *The Impeachment of Michael de la Pole, Earl of Suffolk, in 1386*, Manchester, 1984.
47 R. G. Davies, 'The Episcopate and the Political Crisis in England of 1386–1388', *Speculum*, vol. 51, 1976, pp. 659–93.
48 The most accessible text and translation of the Questions to the Judges is *Westminster*, pp. 197–203.
49 Walsingham, *Historia Anglicana*, II, p. 161.
50 *Westminster*, p. 205.
51 Ibid., p. 211.
52 *Knighton* (ed. Martin), pp. 406–8.
53 *Westminster*, p. 229.
54 M. V. Clarke, *Fourteenth Century Studies*, ed. L. S. Sutherland and M. McKisack, Oxford 1937, pp. 91–5; Saul, *Richard II*, pp. 190, 385–7.
55 T. Favent, *Historia Mirabilis Parliamenti*, ed. M. McKisack (Camden Miscellany, vol. xiv, 1926), p. 14.

56   *Rot. Parl.*, iii, p. 236.
57   *Westminster*, p. 283.
58   Ibid., p. 285.
59   Ibid., p. 329.
60   Ibid., p. 333.
61   Palmer, *England, France and Christendom*, pp. 122–41.
62   Alexander Grant, 'The Otterburn War from the Scottish Point of View', in *War and Border Societies in the Middle Ages*, ed. Anthony Tuck and Anthony Goodman, London 1992, pp. 46–54.
63   Saul, *Richard II*, pp. 200–2.
64   *Westminster*, p. 393.

6   Richard II and Henry of Lancaster, 1389–1413

1   *Westminster*, p. 205.
2   Saul, *Richard II*, pp. 207–8.
3   *Oeuvres de Froissart*, ed. K. de Lettenhove, 25 vols, Brussels, 1867–77, vol. 14, p. 314.
4   *Westminster*, p. 519 Froissart, *Oeuvres*, vol. 14, p. 314; *Rot. Parl.* iii, pp. 313–14.
5   *Scalacronica*, pp. 197–8.
6   *Westminster*, pp. 491, 517–19; *Rot. Parl.*, iii, pp. 315–16; Saul, *Richard II*, pp. 221–24; A. Tuck, 'Richard II and the Hundred Years War' in *Politics and Crisis in Fourteenth Century England*, ed. John Taylor and Wendy Childs, Gloucester, 1990, pp. 117–31.
7   Tuck, *Richard II*, p. 161; Froissart, *Oeuvres*, vol. 16, p. 5.
8   *Annales*, p. 173.
9   Michael Wilks, 'Royal Priesthood: the Origins of Lollardy', in *The Church in a Changing Society*, CIHEC Conference, Uppsala, 1977.
10   Saul, *Richard II*, pp. 297–303.
11   A. K. McHardy, 'Haxey's Case, 1397: The Petition and its Presenter Reconsidered' in *The Age of Richard II*, ed. J. L. Gillespie, Stroud, 1997, pp. 93–114.
12   *Annales*, p. 199; *Chronique de la Traison et Mort de Richart II*, ed. B. Williams, London, 1846, pp. 3–6.
13   *Calendar of Close Rolls 1396–99*, p. 208.
14   *Traison*, pp. 1–2.
15   Froissart, *Oeuvres*, vol. 16, p. 6.
16   Saul, *Richard II*, pp. 375–6; *The History of Parliament: The House of Commons 1386–1421*, ed. J. S. Roskell, L. Clark and C. Rawcliffe, Stroud, 1992, vol. I, appendix C3.
17   *The Chronicle of Adam Usk 1377–1412*, ed. and trans. C. Given-Wilson, Oxford, 1997, pp. 22–4; *Historia Vitae et Regni Ricardi Secundi*, ed. G. B. Stow, Philadelphia, 1977, p. 140.
18   *Usk*, p. 34.
19   *Annales*, p. 223.

20 Ibid., pp. 218–19, 221.

21 *Usk*, p. 31.

22 *Rot. Parl.*, iii, p. 369.

23 Caroline Barron, 'The Tyranny of Richard II', *Bulletin of the Institute of Historical Research*, vol. xli, 1968, pp. 1–18, esp. pp. 13–14.

24 *Usk*, p. 52.

25 Ibid., pp. 38–40.

26 A. Tuck, 'Richard II and the Border Magnates',' *Northern History*, vol. 3, 1968, pp. 27–52.

27 C. Given-Wilson, 'Richard II, Edward II, and the Lancastrian Inheritance', *English Historical Review*, vol. cix, 1994, pp. 553–71.

28 Palmer, *England, France and Christendom*, pp. 222–6.

29 *Kirkstall Chronicle*, p. 132.

30 James Sherborne, 'Perjury and the Lancastrian Revolution of 1399', in his *War, Politics and Culture*, ed. Tuck, pp. 131–53.

31 Pole was the son of the impeached and exiled Chancellor. He was restored to his father's earldom in January 1398. For Henry's progress from Bristol to Chester, see *Usk*, pp. 53–8.

32 *Traison*, pp. 55–60.

33 *Usk*, pp. 62, 64.

34 Saul, *Richard II*, pp. 418–19; G. E. Caspary, 'The Deposition of Richard II and the Canon Law', Proceedings of the Second International Congress of Medieval Canon Law, Boston, 1965, pp. 189–201.

35 *Rot. Parl.*, iii, pp. 417–22.

36 Ibid., p. 424.

37 *The Dieulacres Chronicle*, ed. M. V. Clarke and V. H. Galbraith, *Bulletin of the John Rylands Library*, vol. xiv, 1930, p. 173.

38 *Traison*, pp. 70–1; J. J. N. Palmer, 'The Authorship, Date and Historical Value of the French Chronicles of the Lancastrian Revolution', *Bulletin of the John Rylands Library*, vol. lxi, 1978, pp. 49–53.

39 Bennett, 'Edward III's Entail', *English Historical Review*, vol. cxiii, 1998, pp. 580–609.

40 *Rot. Parl.*, iii, p. 423; G. O. Sayles, 'The Deposition of Richard II: Three Lancastrian Narratives', *Bulletin of the Institute of Historical Research*, vol. liv, 1981, p. 269.

41 Saul, *Richard II*, pp. 339–55, 384–90.

42 *Rot. Parl*, iii, p. 423.

43 J. L. Kirby, *Henry IV of England*, London, 1970, pp. 87–90.

44 R. R. Davies, *The Revolt of Owain Glyn Dŵr*, Oxford, 1995, pp. 65–93.

45 *Chronicle of John Hardyng*, ed. H. F. Ellis, London, 1812, p. 351ff.

46 *Calendar of Patent Rolls 1399–1401*, p. 458; A. Rogers, 'The Political Crisis of 1401,' *Nottingham Medieval Studies*, vol. 12, 1968, pp. 85–96.

47 *Eulogium Historiarum sive Temporis Chronicon*, ed. F. S. Haydon, London (Rolls Series) vol. III, 1863, p. 396.

48 *Incerti Scriptoris Chronicon Angliae*, ed. J. A. Giles, London, 1848, p. 33.

49 *Usk*, p. 174; see for this J. M. W. Bean, 'Henry IV and the Percies', *History*, Vol. 44, 1959, pp. 212–27.

50 *Historians of the Church of York*, ed. J. Raine, London (Rolls Series) vol. II, 1886, pp. 292–304; P. McNiven, 'The Betrayal of Archbishop Scrope', *Bulletin of the John Rylands Library*, vol. liv, 1971–2, pp. 173–213.

51 Quoted in F. Lehoux, *Jean de France Duc de Berry*, vol. II, Paris 1966, p. 420.

52 Kirby, *Henry IV*, p. 211.

53 *Annales Henrici Quarti, in J. de Trokelowe et Anon. Chronica et Annales*, ed. H. T. Riley, London (Rolls Series) 1865, p. 379.

54 Given-Wilson, *Royal Household*, pp. 231–3, 263–6.

55 T. Gascoigne, *Loci e Libro Veritatum*, ed. J. H. Thorold Rogers, Oxford, 1881, p. 228.

56 *Usk*, p. 242; *St Albans Chronicle 1406–1420*, ed. V. H. Galbraith, Oxford, 1937, p.29.

57 P. J. McNiven, 'The Problem of Henry IV's Health, 1405–1413', *English Historical Review*, vol. c, 1985, pp. 761–72, and the authorities cited there.

58 G. L. Harriss, *Cardinal Beaufort*, Oxford, 1988, p. 40.

59 R. Vaughan, *John the Fearless*, London, 1966, p. 92.

60 Giles's *Chronicle*, pp. 62–3.

61 T. Rymer, *Foedera, Conventiones et Litterae etc.*, 3rd edn, The Hague, 1745, reprinted 1967, vol. IV, part II, pp. 12–14; translation in Vaughan, *John the Fearless*, pp. 94–5.

62 B. A. Pocquet du Haut-Jussé, 'La Renaissance Littéraire autour de Henri V roi d'Angleterre', *Revue Historique*, vol. ccxxiv, 1960, pp. 329–38.

63 *St Albans Chronicle*, p. 65; P. McNiven, 'Prince Henry and the English Political Crisis of 1412', *History*, vol. 65, 1980, pp. 1–16.

64 J. D. Milner, 'The English Enterprise in France, 1412–13', in *Trade, Devotion and Governance. Papers in Later Medieval History*, ed. Dorothy J. Clayton, Richard G. Davies and Peter McNiven, Stroud, 1994, pp. 80–101.

65 McNiven, 'Political Crisis', pp. 13–16.

7   Henry V and the Dual Monarchy, 1413–1435

1 C. T. Allmand, *Henry V*, London (Historical Association) 1968, p. 18.

2 *Rot. Parl*, iv, p. 34.

3 Quoted in Vaughan, *John the Fearless*, p. 205.

4 P. McNiven, *Heresy and Politics in the Reign of Henry IV*, Woodbridge 1987, pp. 223–5; Allmand, *Henry V*, pp. 287–305.

5 T. B. Pugh, *Henry V and the Southampton Plot*, Gloucester, 1988, esp. pp. 109–17.

6 K. B. McFarlane, *Lancastrian Kings and Lollard Knights*, Oxford, 1972, pp. 126–7; C. T. Allmand, *Henry V*, London, 1992, pp. 83–5; *Gesta Henrici Quinti*, ed. F. Taylor and J. S. Roskell, Oxford, 1975, pp. 76–9.

7 *Gesta*, p. 91.

8 Ibid., pp. 101–13.

9   Ibid., pp. 173–5.
10 Quoted in Vaughan, *John the Fearless*, pp. 214–15.
11 *Rot. Parl.*, iv, p. 94.
12 *St Albans Chronicle*, p. 103.
13 *Usk*, p. 266 and note 2.
14 C. T. Allmand, *Lancastrian Normandy, 1415–1450*, pp. 50–80; R. Massey, 'The Lancastrian Land Settlement in Normandy', in *Property and Politics: Essays in Later Medieval History*, ed. A. J. Pollard, Gloucester, 1984, pp. 76–96.
15 *Usk*, p. 266.
16 Allmand, *Lancastrian Normandy*, pp. 70–1; C. Rawcliffe, *The Staffords, Earls of Stafford and Dukes of Buckingham 1394–1521*, Cambridge, 1978, pp. 109, 114–15; Linda Woodger, 'Henry Bourgchier Earl of Essex and his Family (1408–1483)', Oxford D.Phil. thesis, 1974, pp. 8, 13, 35–6.
17 Quoted in Otto Cartellieri, *The Court of Burgundy*, London, 1929, p. 9.
18 *St Albans Chronicle*, p. 124.
19 Allmand, *Henry V*, p. 146.
20 *Rot. Parl.*, iv, p. 127.
21 G. L. Harriss, 'The Management of Parliament', in Harriss, ed., *Henry V: The Practice of Kingship*, Oxford, 1985, pp. 148–51; Allmand, *Henry V*, pp. 375–7.
22 *Usk*, p. 270; A. Goodman, 'Responses to Requests in Yorkshire for Military Service under Henry V', *Northern History*, vol. 17, 1981, pp. 240–52.
23 E. Powell, *Kingship, Law and Society: Criminal Justice in the Reign of Henry V*, Oxford 1989, pp. 195–229; See also Allmand, *Henry V*, pp. 306–32.
24 Allmand, *Henry V*, pp. 438–43.
25 Patrick and Felicity Strong, 'The Last Will and Codicils of Henry V', *English Historical Review*, vol. xcvi, 1981, pp. 79–102; R. A. Griffiths, *The Reign of King Henry VI*, London, 1981, pp. 11–24.
26 *Rot. Parl.*, iv, pp. 326–7.
27 *Hardyng*, p. 391.
28 Harriss, *Cardinal Beaufort*, pp. 115–33.
29 Ibid., pp. 109–11, 411–13. See also K. B. McFarlane, 'At the Deathbed of Cardinal Beaufort', in his *England in the Fifteenth Century: Collected Essays*, with an Introduction by G. L. Harriss, London, 1981, p. 124.
30 Quoted in Griffiths, *Henry VI*, p. 77
31 *Rot. Parl.*, iv, pp. 326–7.
32 Rawcliffe, *Staffords*, p. 20.
33 *A Parisian Journal 1405–1449*, ed. Janet Shirley, Oxford, 1968, p. 189.
34 *Proceedings and Ordinances of the Privy Council (POPC)*, vol. IV, ed. N. H. Nicolas, London 1835, p. 223.
35 *POPC*, III, p. 322.
36 *Parisian Journal*, pp. 268–73; Harriss, *Beaufort*, pp. 212–3.
37 *POPC*, IV, pp. 104–5.
38 Harriss, *Beaufort*, pp. 216–22.

39 *POPC*, IV, p. 219.
40 Harriss, *Beaufort*, pp. 109–11, 392–4, 401–6.
41 B. P. Wolffe, *Henry VI*, London, 1981, pp. 73–4; *Rot. Parl*, iv, pp. 432–9.
42 *POPC*, IV, p. 227.
43 R. Vaughan, *Philip the Good*, London, 1970, p. 100.
44 *Letters and Papers Illustrative of the Wars of the English in France (L&P)*, ed. J. Stevenson, London (Rolls Series) vol. II, part ii, 1864, pp. 575–85.

8   Lancaster and York, 1435–1461

1 *Registrum Abbatiae Johannis Whethamstede*, ed. H. T. Riley, London (Rolls Series) vol. I, 1873, p. 415; B. P. Wolffe, 'The Personal Rule of Henry VI', in *Fifteenth Century England 1399–1509*, ed. S. B. Chrimes, C. D. Ross and R. A. Griffiths, Manchester, 1972, p. 44; Griffiths, *Henry VI*, pp. 253–84; John Watts, *Henry VI and the Politics of Kingship*, Cambridge, 1996, pp. 103–11. See also Christine Carpenter, *The Wars of the Roses*, Cambridge, 1997, pp. 87–90.
2 J. L. Watts, 'When Did Henry VI's Minority End?', in *Trade, Devotion and Governance: Papers in Later Medieval History*, ed. Dorothy J. Clayton, Richard G. Davies and Peter McNiven, Stroud, 1994, pp. 116–39.
3 *L & P*, II, ii, pp. 440–51.
4 Ibid., pp. 452–3.
5 R. A. Griffiths, 'The Sense of Dynasty in the Reign of Henry VI', in *Patronage, Pedigree and Power in Later Medieval England*, ed. C. D. Ross, Gloucester, 1979, p. 25.
6 Griffiths, *Henry VI*, pp. 336–7.
7 Anne Curry, 'The First English Standing Army? Military Organization in Lancastrian Normandy', in *Patronage, Pedigree and Power*, ed. Ross, pp. 193–208; Maurice Keen, 'The End of the Hundred Years War: Lancastrian France and Lancastrian England', in *England and Her Neighbours, 1066–1453*, ed. Michael Jones and Malcolm Vale, London, 1989, pp. 297–311; P. Johnson, *Duke Richard of York 1411–1460*, Oxford 1988, pp. 38–50.
8 *POPC*, V, pp. 223, 229.
9 See Wolffe's comment, *Henry VI*, p. 168.
10 *L & P*, I, p. 135.
11 Ibid., p. 166; Diana Dunn, 'Margaret of Anjou, Queen Consort of Henry VI: A Reassessment of Her Role, 1445–53', in *Crown, Government and People in the Fifteenth Century*, ed. Rowena E. Archer, Stroud, 1995, pp. 141–2.
12 *L & P*, II, ii, p. 592; Johnson, *Richard of York*, pp. 52–4.
13 Wolffe, *Henry VI*, p. 118; for law and order under Henry V, see Edward Powell, *Kingship, Law and Society*, Oxford, 1989, esp. pp. 265–75.
14 *Paston Letters and Papers (PL)*, ed. N. Davis, part I, Oxford, 1971, pp. 222, 236; Philippa C. Maddern, *Violence and Social Order: East Anglia 1422–1442*, Oxford, 1992.

15 *L & P*, I, pp. 283–4, 297.
16 See for this M. H. Keen and M. J. Daniel, 'English Diplomacy and the Sack of Fougères in 1449', in *History*, vol. lix, 1974, pp. 375–91.
17 *L & P*, II, ii, pp. 619–34.
18 Ibid., pp. 629, 633, 726. There is some discussion of this topic in Anne Marshall, 'The Role of English War Captains in England and Normandy 1436–1461', Wales MA thesis, 1974, pp. 153–8.
19 *Rot. Parl.*, v, pp. 177–82.
20 R. L. Virgoe, 'The Death of William de la Pole Duke of Suffolk', *Bulletin of the John Rylands Library*, vol. xlvii, 1964–5, pp. 486–502.
21 *PL*, part II, p. 42; Wolffe, *Henry VI*, p. 221
22 Myers, *Documents*, pp. 266–7; I. M. W. Harvey, *Jack Cade's Rebellion of 1450*, Oxford, 1991.
23 *Reg. Whethamstede*, p. 160; J. R. Lander, *Government and Community*, London, 1978, p. 190; M. K. Jones, 'Somerset, York and the Wars of the Roses', *English Historical Review*, vol. civ, 1989, pp. 285–307; Johnson, *Richard of York*, pp. 89–90.
24 *Rot. Parl.*, v, p. 216.
25 William Worcester, in *The Boke of Noblesse*, ed. J. G. Nichols, Edinburgh, 1860, pp. 38, 42; M. G. A. Vale, *English Gascony 1399–1453*, Oxford, 1970, p. 132.
26 R. L. Storey, *The End of the House of Lancaster*, London, 1966, p. 89.
27 Myers, *Documents*, p. 269.
28 Griffiths, *Henry VI*, p. 696.
29 Wolffe, *Henry VI*, p. 263.
30 Giles's *Chronicle*, p. 44.
31 Dunn, 'Margaret of Anjou', pp. 108–10, 143.
32 *The Paston Letters*, ed. J. Gairdner, vol. I, London, 1872, pp. 265–6.
33 *Rot. Parl.*, v, p. 281.
34 C. A. J. Armstrong, 'Politics and the Battle of St Albans, 1455', *Bulletin of the Institute of Historical Research* vol. xxxiii, 1960, pp. 1–72; Johnson, *Richard of York*, pp. 156–8.
35 *An English Chronicle of the Reigns of Richard II, Henry V and Henry VI*, ed. J. S. Davies, London (Camden 1st Series) 1856, p. 79.
36 Ibid.
37 *Reg. Whethamstede*, pp. 296–7.
38 J. P. Gilson, 'A Defence of the Proscription of the Yorkists in 1459', *English Historical Review*, vol. xxvi, 1911, pp. 512–25.
39 Johnson, *Richard of York*, pp. 211–18.
40 Anthony Goodman, *The Wars of the Roses*, London 1981, especially chapter 8.
41 Ibid., p. 52.
42 Charles Ross, *Edward IV*, London, 1974, p. 71.
43 Carpenter, *Wars of the Roses*, pp. 158–61.
44 Ross, *Edward IV*, p. 126.
45 Quoted in Ross, *Edward IV*, p. 175.
46 D. A. L. Morgan, 'The Political After-Life of Edward III: The Apotheosis of a Warmonger', *English Historical Review*, vol. cxii, 1997, pp. 856–81.

47 See Ross, *Edward IV*, pp. 223-4; J. R. Lander, 'The Hundred Years War and Edward IV's Campaign in France', in his *Crown and Nobility 1450-1509*, London, 1976, pp. 220-41.
48 *The Boke of Noblesse*, pp. 15-17, 25-6.

Epilogue: New Perspectives, 1985-1999

1 See above, Introduction, p. xv.
2 K. B. McFarlane, *The Nobility of Later Medieval England*, Oxford, 1973, pp. 120-1.
3 Colin Richmond, 'After McFarlane', *History*, vol. 68, 1983, pp. 46-60.
4 Maddicott, *Thomas of Lancaster*, pp. 79, 326, 330; Fryde, *Tyranny and Fall*, pp. 13-14; Tuck, *Richard II*, pp. 71-86; Griffiths, *Henry VI*, passim.
5 G. A. Holmes, *The Estates of the Higher Nobility in Fourteenth Century England*, Cambridge, 1957, p. 1; T. B. Pugh, 'The Magnates, Knights and Gentry', in *Fifteenth-Century England*, ed. S. D. Chrimes, C. D. Ross, and R. A. Griffiths, Manchester, 1972, pp. 86-128. McFarlane, *Nobility*, pp. 287-97. For an example of the influence of this approach, see Tuck, *Richard II*, pp. 1-2. For some differences of emphasis on the role of the Commons in the Good Parliament of 1376, see G. A. Holmes, *The Good Parliament*, Oxford, 1975, and C. Given-Wilson, *The Royal Household*, esp. p. 147.
6 See, for example, M. J. Bennett, *Community, Class and Careerism: Cheshire and Lancashire Society in the Age of Sir Gawain and the Green Knight*, Cambridge, 1983; Christine Carpenter, *Locality and Polity. A Study of Warwickshire Landed Society, 1401-1499*, Cambridge, 1992; S. J. Payling, *Political Society in Lancastrian England: The Greater Gentry of Nottinghamshire*, Oxford, 1991; Simon Walker, *The Lancastrian Affinity 1361-1399*, Oxford, 1990.
7 See, for example, the discussion in Carpenter, *Locality and Polity*, pp. 1-10.
8 K. B. McFarlane, *England in the Fifteenth Century: Collected Essays*, Introduction by G. L. Harriss, London, 1981, p. xxiv.
9 Edward Powell, 'After "After McFarlane": The Poverty of Patronage and the Case for Constitutional History', in *Trade, Devotion and Governance: Papers in Later Medieval History*, ed. Dorothy J. Clayton, Richard G. Davies and Peter McNiven, Stroud, 1994, pp. vii, 1-16.
10 A. L. Brown, *The Governance of Late Medieval England, 1272-1461*, London, 1989. Powell, 'After "After McFarlane"', p. 2; Christine Carpenter, 'Political and Constitutional History: Before and After McFarlane', in *The McFarlane Legacy: Studies in Late Medieval Politics and Society*, ed. R. H. Britnell and A. J. Pollard, Stroud, 1995, pp. 175-206. See also Christine Carpenter, *The Wars of the Roses*, Cambridge, 1997, pp. 16-26.
11 Watts, *Henry VI*, p. 366.
12 See above, p. 40.

13   *Knighton* (ed. Martin), pp. 355–61.

14   See above, pp. 164, 193–4, 196. On resistance and treason, see
     J. G. Bellamy, *The Law of Treason in England in the Later Middle
     Ages*, Cambridge, 1970, and Jean Dunbabin, 'Government', in *The
     Cambridge History of Medieval Political Thought c.350–c.1450*, ed.
     J. H. Burns, Cambridge, 1988, esp. pp. 493–8.

15   Nigel Saul, 'Richard II and the Vocabulary of Kingship', *English Histor-
     ical Review*, vol. cx, 1995, pp. 854–77; Saul, 'Richard II's Ideas of
     Kingship', in *The Regal Image of Richard II and the Wilton Diptych*,
     ed. Dillian Gordon, Lisa Monnas and Caroline Elam, London, 1998,
     pp. 27–32, and the other essays in that volume; Paul Strohm, *England's
     Empty Throne: Usurpation and the Language of Legitimation 1399–
     1422*, New Haven and London, 1998.

16   R. W. Kaeuper, *War, Justice and Public Order: England and France in
     the Later Middle Ages*, Oxford, 1988, esp. pp. 1–9; see also G. L.
     Harriss, 'Political Society and the Growth of Government in Late Medi-
     eval England', *Past and Present*, no. 138, 1993, pp. 28–57.

17   J. R. Lander, *The Limitations of English Monarchy in the Later Middle
     Ages*, Toronto, 1989, pp. 8–17, 60.

18   W. M. Ormrod, 'Edward III and the Recovery of Royal Authority in
     England, 1340–1360', *History*, vol. 72, 1987, pp. 4–19; Ormrod, *The
     Reign of Edward III*, New Haven and London, 1990.

19   Ormrod, *Reign of Edward III*, p. 201.

20   Ibid., pp. 110–13.

21   See above, p. 175

22   See above, Introduction, pp. xv–xvi.

23   Allmand, *Henry V*, pp. 438–43; Jones, 'Somerset, York and the Wars of
     the Roses', esp. pp. 303–7.

24   K. B. McFarlane, 'A Business Partnership in War and Administration
     1421–1445' (1963) and 'The Investment of Sir John Fastolf's Profits of
     War' (1957): both reprinted in *England in the Fifteenth Century*,
     pp. 151–97.

25   D. Hay, 'The division of the spoils of war in fourteenth-century
     England', *Transactions of the Royal Historical Society* (5th Series,
     vol. 4) 1954, pp. 91–109; Ayton, *Knights and Warhorses*, pp. 127–37.

26   Ayton, *Knights and Warhorses* and 'English Armies in the Fourteenth
     Century'; Curry, 'English Armies in the Fifteenth Century'; Anne Curry,
     'The First English Standing Army? Military Organization in Lancastrian
     Normandy, 1420–1450', in *Patronage Pedigree and Power in Later
     Medieval England*, ed. C. Ross, Gloucester, 1979, pp. 193–214; Walker,
     Lancastrian Affinity.

27   Walker, *Lancastrian Affinity*, pp. 58–80. (The quotation is from p. 75.)

28   Curry, 'The First English Standing Army?', pp. 205–8; Keen, 'The End
     of the Hundred Years War', pp. 304–5.

29   Jones, 'Somerset, York and the Wars of the Roses', pp. 285–307;
     D. A. L. Morgan, 'The Political After-Life of Edward III: The Apo-
     theosis of a Warmonger', *English Historical Review*, vol. cxii, 1997,
     pp. 856–81.

30   Watts, *Henry VI*, pp. 103–11; Richmond, 'After McFarlane', pp. 47–8.

31 Prestwich, *Edward I*, p. 559.

32 D. L. d'Avray, *Death and the Prince: Memorial Preaching Before 1350*, Oxford, 1994, p. 76.

33 G. L. Harriss, ed., *Henry V: The Practice of Kingship*, Oxford, 1985; Edward Powell, *Kingship, Law and Society: Criminal Justice in the Reign of Henry V*, Oxford, 1989.

34 Allmand, *Henry V*, esp. pp. 419–25.

35 Saul, *Richard II*, pp. 459–61.

36 See above, p. 178.

37 R. R. Davies, *The Revolt of Owain Glyn Dŵr*, Oxford, 1995; R. R. Davies, ed., *The British Isles 1100–1500: Comparisons, Contrasts and Connections*, Edinburgh, 1988; Terry Barry, Robin Frame and Katharine Simms, eds, *Colony and Frontier in Medieval Ireland: Essays Presented to J. F. Lydon*, London, 1995; see also Sean Duffy, *Ireland in the Middle Ages*, Dublin, 1997, esp. chapters 5 and 6.

38 S. G. Ellis, *The Pale and the Far North: Government and Society in two early Tudor Borderlands*, The O'Donnell Lecture, Galway, 1986. Grant, 'The Otterburn War', p. 54.

39 C. McNamee, *The Wars of the Bruces*, East Linton, 1997; R. Frame, *The Political Development of the British Isles, 1100–1400*, Oxford, 1990.

40 R. R. Davies, *Domination and Conquest: The Experience of Ireland, Scotland and Wales 1100–1300*, Cambridge, 1990, esp. pp. 120–28; see above, p. 10.

41 Allmand, *Henry V*, p. 425.

Bibliography

Primary Sources

Adae Murimuth Continuatio Chronicarum, ed. E. M. Thompson, London (Rolls Series) 1889.
Ancient Petitions Relating to Northumberland, ed. C. M. Fraser, Surtees Society, vol. clxxvi, 1961.
Anglo-Scottish Relations 1174–1328. Some Selected Documents, ed. E. L. G. Stones, Edinburgh, 1965.
Annales Ricardi Secundi et Henrici Quarti, in J. de Trokelowe et Anon. Chronica et Annales, ed. H. T. Riley, London (Rolls Series) 1866.
The Anonimalle Chronicle 1333 to 1381, ed. V. H. Galbraith, Manchester, 1927.
Avesbury, Robert of, *De Gestis Mirabilibus Regis Edwardi Tertii*, ed. E. M. Thompson, London (Rolls Series) 1889.
Bartholomaei de Cotton Historia Anglicana, ed. H. R. Luard, London (Rolls Series) 1859.
The Boke of Noblesse, ed. J. G. Nichols, Edinburgh (for the Roxburghe Club) 1860.
The Brus, Writ be Master Johne Barbour, Aberdeen, Spalding Club Edition, 1856.
The Brut, or The Chronicles of England, ed. F. W. D. Brie, London, Early English Text Society, Part I, 1906, Part II, 1908.
Bury, Richard, *Philobiblion*, ed. and trans. E. C. Thomas, London, 1888.
Calendar of Ancient Correspondence concerning Wales, ed. J. G. Edwards, Cardiff, 1935.
Calendar of Close Rolls 1396–99, London, 1927.
Calendar of Patent Rolls 1399–1401, London, 1903.
Calendar of Plea and Memoranda Rolls of the City of London, ed. A. H. Thomas, Cambridge, 1926.
Chrimes, S. B. and Brown, A. L. (eds), *Select Documents of English Constitutional History 1307–1485*, London, 1961.
Chronica Monasterii de Melsa, ed. E. A. Bond, London (Rolls Series) 1867.

The Chronicle of Adam Usk 1377–1421, ed. and trans. C. Given-Wilson, Oxford, 1997.

The Chronicle of Bury St Edmunds, ed. Antonia Gransden, London, 1964.

The Chronicle of John Hardyng, ed. H. F. Ellis, London, 1812.

The Chronicle of John of Reading, ed. J. Tait, Manchester, 1914.

The Chronicle of Pierre de Langtoft, ed. T. Wright, London (Rolls Series) vol. II, 1868.

Chronicle of Walter of Guisborough, ed. H. Rothwell, London (Camden 3rd Series) 1957.

Chronicles of the Reigns of Edward I and Edward II, vols I and II, ed. W. Stubbs, London (Rolls Series) 1882–3.

Chronicles of the Revolution 1397–1400, ed. and trans. C. Given-Wilson, Manchester, 1993.

Chronicon Angliae 1328–88, ed. E. M. Thompson, London (Rolls Series) 1874.

Chronicon de Lanercost, ed. J. Stevenson, Edinburgh, 1839.

Chronicon Galfridi le Baker, ed. E. M. Thompson, London, 1889.

Chronicon Henrici Knighton, ed. J. R. Lumby, vols I and II, London (Rolls Series) 1889–95, (see also below under *Knighton's Chronicle*).

Chronique de la Traison et Mort de Richart II, ed. B. Williams, London, 1846.

The Dieulacres Chronicle, ed. M. V. Clarke and V. H. Galbraith, *Bulletin of the John Rylands Library*, vol. xiv, 1930.

Documents Illustrating the Crisis of 1297–98 in England, ed. M. C. Prestwich, London (Camden 4th Series) 1980.

Edward I and the Throne of Scotland: An Edition of the Record Sources of the Great Cause, ed. E. L. G. Stones and G. G. Simpson, 2 vols, Oxford, 1978.

English Chronicle of the Reigns of Richard II, Henry IV, Henry V and Henry VI, ed. J. S. Davies, London (Camden 1st Series) 1856.

English Historical Documents, vol. III, ed. H. Rothwell, London, 1975.

English Historical Documents, vol. IV, ed. A. R. Myers, London, 1969.

Eulogium Historiarum sive Temporis, ed. F. S. Haydon, vol. III, London (Rolls Series) 1863.

Favent, T., *Historia Mirabilis Parliamenti*, ed. M. McKisack, Camden Miscellany vol. xiv, 1926.

Flores Historiarum, ed. H. R. Ward, vol. III, London (Rolls Series) 1890.

A French Chronicle of London, ed. G. J. Aungier, London (Camden 1st Series, vol. xxviii) 1844.

Froissart, *Chronicles*, selected and translated by Geoffrey Brereton, London (Penguin Edition) 1968.

Froissart, *Oeuvres*, ed. K. de Lettenhove, 25 vols, Brussels 1867–77.

Gascoigne, T., *Loci e Libro Veritatum*, ed. J. H. Thorold Rogers, Oxford, 1981.

Gesta Henrici Quinti, ed. F. Taylor and J. S. Roskell, Oxford, 1975.

Gray of Heton, Sir Thomas, *Scalacronica, a Chronicle of England and Scotland from 1066 to 1362*, ed. J. Stevenson, Edinburgh, 1836.

Historia Vitae et Regni Ricardi Secundi, ed. G. B. Stow, Philadelphia, 1977.

Historians of the Church of York, ed. J. Raine, vol. II, London (Rolls Series) 1886.

Incerti Scriptoris Chronicon Angliae, ed. J. A. Giles, London, 1848.

The Kirkstall Chronicle 1355–1400, ed. M. V. Clarke and N. Denholm-Young, *Bulletin of the John Rylands Library*, vol. xv, 1931.

Knighton's Chronicle 1337–1396, ed. G. H. Martin, Oxford, 1995. (See also *Chronicon Henrici Knighton* above.)

Letters and Papers Illustrative of the Wars of the English in France, ed. J. Stevenson, vol. II, part ii, London (Rolls Series) 1864.

Life of the Black Prince by the Herald of Sir John Chandos, ed. M. K. Pope and E. C. Lodge, Oxford, 1910.

A Parisian Journal 1405–1449, ed. Janet Shirley, Oxford, 1968.

The Paston Letters, ed. J. Gairdner, vol. I, London, 1872.

The Paston Letters and Papers, ed. N. Davis, part I, Oxford, 1971.

The Political Songs of England, ed. T. Wright, London, 1839, new edition, with Introduction by Peter Coss, Cambridge, 1966.

Proceedings and Ordinances of the Privy Council, ed. N. H. Nicolas, London, vol, 1834–7.

Registrum Abbatiae Johannis Whethamstede, ed. H. T. Riley, vol. I, London (Rolls Series) 1872.

Rymer, T., *Foedera, Conventiones, Litterae etc.* 3rd edn, 10 vols, The Hague, 1745, reprinted 1967.

Rotuli Parliamentorum, 6 vols, London, 1783.

Rotuli Parliamentorum Anglie Hactenus Inediti, ed. G. O. Sayles, London (Camden 3rd Series) 1935.

Reports from the Lords Commissioners Touching the Dignity of a Peer of the Realm, vol. V, London, 1829.

Selections from English Wycliffite Writings, ed. Anne Hudson, Cambridge, 1978.

Sermons of Thomas Brinton, ed. M. A. Devlin, London (Camden 3rd Series), 1954.

The Song of Lewes, ed. C. L. Kingsford, Oxford, reprinted 1963.

St Albans Chronicle 1406–1420, ed. V. H. Galbraith, Oxford, 1937.

Statutes of the Realm, vol. I, London, 1810.

Textes et Documents d'Histoire du Moyen Age, ed. J. Glenisson and J. Day, Paris, 1970.

Vita Edwardi Secundi, ed. N. Denholm-Young, Edinburgh, 1957.

Westminster Chronicle 1381–1394, ed. and trans. by L. C. Hector and Barbara F. Harvey, Oxford, 1982.

Willelmi Rishanger Chronica et Annales 1259–1307, ed. H. T. Riley, London (Rolls Series) 1865.

Secondary Sources

Allmand, C. T., *Henry V*, London (Historical Association) 1968.

Allmand, C. T., *Lancastrian Normandy 1415–1450*, Oxford, 1983.

Allmand, C. T., *Henry V*, London, 1992.

Armstrong, C. A. J., 'Politics and the Battle of St Albans, 1455', *Bulletin of the Institute of Historical Research*, vol. xxxiii, 1960, pp. 1–72.

Ayton, Andrew, 'English Armies in the Fourteenth Century', in *Arms, Armies and Fortifications in the Hundred Years War*, ed. Anne Curry and Michael Hughes, Woodbridge, 1994, pp. 21–38.

Ayton, Andrew, *Knights and Warhorses: Military Service and the English Aristocracy under Edward III*, Woodbridge, 1994.

Barnie, J., *War in Medieval Society*, London, 1974.

Barron, Caroline, 'The Tyranny of Richard II', *Bulletin of the Institute of Historical Research*, vol. xli, 1968, pp. 1–18.

Barron, Caroline, 'The Deposition of Richard II', in *Politics and Crisis in Fourteenth-Century England*, ed. John Taylor and Wendy Childs, Gloucester, 1990, pp. 132–49.

Barron, E. M. *The Scottish War of Independence*, 2nd edn, Inverness, 1934.

Barrow, G. W. S., *Robert Bruce and the Community of the Realm of Scotland*, London, 1965.

Barry, Terry, Frame, Robin, and Simms, Katharine, eds, *Colony and Frontier in Medieval Ireland: Essays Presented to J. F. Lydon*, London, 1995.

Bean, J. M. W., 'Henry IV and the Percies', *History*, vol. 44, 1959, pp. 212–27.

Bean, J. M. W., *The Decline of English Feudalism*, Manchester, 1968.

Bellamy, J. G., *The Law of Treason in England in the Later Middle Ages*, Cambridge, 1970.

Bennett, Michael, *Community, Class and Careerism: Cheshire and Lancashire Society in the Age of Sir Gawain and the Green Knight*, Cambridge, 1983.

Bennett, Michael, 'Edward III's Entail and the Succession to the Crown, 1376–1461', *English Historical Review*, vol. cxiii, 1998, pp. 580–609.

Brown, A. L., The *Governance of Late Medieval England 1272–1461*, London, 1989.

Brown, E. A. R., 'The Political Repercussions of Family Ties in the Early Fourteenth Century: The Marriage of Edward II of England and Isabelle of France', *Speculum*, vol. 63, 1988, pp. 573–95.

Brown, R. A., Colvin, H. M., and Taylor, A. J., *The History of the King's Works*, vol. I, London, 1963.

Buck, M. C., 'The Reform of the Exchequer, 1316–1326', *English Historical Review*, vol. xcviii, 1983, pp. 241–60.

Campbell, B. M. S. (ed.), *Before the Black Death: Studies in the 'Crisis' of the Early Fourteenth Century*, Manchester, 1991.

Carpenter, Christine, *Locality and Polity. A Study of Warwickshire Landed Society, 1401–1499*, Cambridge, 1992.

Carpenter, Christine, 'Political and Constitutional History: Before and After McFarlane', in *The McFarlane Legacy: Studies in Late Medieval Politics and Society*, ed. R. H. Britnell and A. J. Pollard, Stroud, 1995, pp. 175–206.

Carpenter, Christine, *The Wars of the Roses*, Cambridge, 1997.

Cartellieri, Otto, *The Court of Burgundy*, London, 1929.

Caspary, G. E., 'The Deposition of Richard II and the Canon Law', Proceedings of the Second International Congress of Medieval Canon Law, Boston, 1965, pp. 189–201.

Cazelles, R., *La Société Politique et la Crise de la Royauté sous Philippe de Valois*, Paris, 1958.

Chaplais, Pierre, *Piers Gaveston: Edward II's Adoptive Brother*, Oxford, 1994.

Childs, Wendy, 'Resistance and Treason in the *Vita Edwardi Secundi*', in *Thirteenth Century England* VI, ed. Michael Prestwich, R. H. Britnell and Robin Frame, Woodbridge, 1997, pp. 177–91.

Clanchy, M. T., *From Memory to Written Record*, London, 1979.

Clarke, M. V., *Fourteenth Century Studies*, ed. L. S. Sutherland and M. McKisack, Oxford, 1937.

Crump, C. G., 'The Arrest of Roger Mortimer and Queen Isabel', *English Historical Review*, vol. xxvi, 1911, pp. 331–2.

Curry, Anne, 'The First English Standing Army? Military Organization in Lancastrian Normandy', in *Patronage, Pedigree and Power in Later Medieval England*, ed. C. D. Ross, Gloucester, 1979, pp. 193–214.

Curry, Anne, 'English Armies in the Fifteenth Century', in *Arms, Armies and Fortifications in the Hundred Years War*, ed. Anne Curry and Michael Hughes, Woodbridge, 1994, pp. 39–68.

Cuttino, G. P., and Lyman, T. W., 'Where is Edward II?', *Speculum*, vol. 53, 1978, pp. 522–44

Davies, R. G., 'The Episcopate and the Political Crisis in England of 1386–1388', *Speculum*, vol. 51, 1976, pp. 659–93.

Davies, R. R., *Lordship and Society in the March of Wales 1282–1400*, Oxford, 1978.

Davies, R. R., *Conquest, Coexistence and Change: Wales 1063–1415*, Oxford, 1987.

Davies, R. R., ed., *The British Isles 1100–1500: Comparisons, Contrasts and Connections*, Edinburgh, 1988.

Davies, R. R., *Domination and Conquest: The Experience of Ireland, Scotland and Wales 1100–1300*, Cambridge, 1990.

Davies, R. R., *The Revolt of Owain Glyn Dŵr*, Oxford, 1995.

D'Avray, D. L., *Death and the Prince. Memorial Preaching before 1350*, Oxford, 1994.

Delachenal, R., *Histoire de Charles V*, vol. III, Paris, 1931.

Denton, J. H., *Robert Winchelsey and the Crown 1294–1313*, Cambridge, 1980.

Dobson, R. B., ed. and trans., *The Peasants' Revolt of 1381*, 2nd edn, London, 1981.

Dodds, M. H., *A History of Northumberland*, vol. xii, Newcastle upon Tyne, 1926.

Duffy, Sean, *Ireland in the Middle Ages*, Dublin, 1997.

Dunbabin, Jean, 'Government', in *The Cambridge History of Medieval Political Thought c.350–c.1450*, ed. J. H. Burns, Cambridge, 1988, pp. 477–519.

Dunn, Diana, 'Margaret of Anjou, Queen Consort of Henry VI: A Reassessment of her Role, 1445–53', in *Crown, Government and People in the Fifteenth Century*, ed. Rowena E. Archer, Stroud, 1995, pp. 107–43.

Edwards, J. G., 'Justice in Early English Parliaments', *Bulletin of the Institute of Historical Research*, vol. xxvii, 1954, pp. 35–53.

Ellis, S. G., *The Pale and the Far North: Government and Society in Two Early Tudor Borderlands*, The O'Donnell Lecture, Galway, 1986.

Fairbank, F. R., 'The Last Earl of Warenne and Surrey', *Yorkshire Aarchaeological Journal*, vol. xix, 1907, pp. 193–264.

Fowler, K., *The Age of Plantagenet and Valois*, London, 1967.

Fowler, K., *The King's Lieutenant. Henry of Grosmont, First Duke of Lancaster, 1310–1361*, London, 1969.

Frame, Robin, *English Lordship in Ireland 1318–1361*, Oxford, 1982.

Frame, Robin, 'Aristocracies and the Political Configuration of the British Isles' in *The British Isles 1100–1500: Comparisons, Contrasts and Connections*, ed. R. R. Davies, Edinburgh, 1988, pp. 142–59.

Frame, Robin, *The Political Development of the British Isles, 1100–1400*, Oxford, 1990.

Fryde, Natalie, *The Tyranny and Fall of Edward II*, Cambridge, 1979.

Gilson, J. P., 'A Defence of the Proscription of the Yorkists in 1459', *English Historical Review*, vol. xxvi, 1911, pp. 512–25.

Given-Wilson, C., 'Richard II and his Grandfather's Will', *English Historical Review*, vol. xciii, 1978, pp. 320–37.

Given-Wilson, C., *The Royal Household and the King's Affinity*, New Haven and London, 1986.

Given-Wilson, C., *The English Nobility in the Late Middle Ages*, London, 1987.

Given-Wilson, C., 'Wealth and Credit, Public and Private: The Earls of Arundel 1306–1397', *English Historical Review*, vol. cvi, 1991, pp. 1–26.

Given-Wilson, C., 'Richard II, Edward II, and the Lancastrian Inheritance', *English Historical Review*, vol. cix, 1994, pp. 553–71.

Given-Wilson, C., '*Vita Edwardi Secundi*: Memoir or Journal', in *Thirteenth Century England* VI, ed. Michael Prestwich, R. H. Britnell and Robin Frame, Woodbridge, 1997, pp. 165–76.

Goodman, A., *The Loyal Conspiracy*, London, 1971.

Goodman, A., 'Responses to Requests for Military Service under Henry V', *Northern History*, vol. 17, 1981, pp. 240–52.

Goodman, A., *The Wars of the Roses*, London, 1981.

Goodman, A., *John of Gaunt*, London, 1992.

Grant, Alexander, *Independence and Nationhood: Scotland 1306–1469*, London, 1984.

Grant, Alexander, 'The Otterburn War from the Scottish Point of View', in *War and Border Societies in the Middle Ages*, ed. Anthony Tuck and Anthony Goodman, London, 1992, pp. 30–64.

Griffiths, R. A., 'The Sense of Dynasty in the Reign of Henry VI', in *Patronage, Pedigree and Power in Later Medieval England*, ed. C. D. Ross, Gloucester, 1979.

Griffiths, R. A., *The Reign of King Henry VI*, London, 1981.

Haines, R. M., *The Church and Politics in Fourteenth Century England*, Cambridge, 1978.

Haines, R. M., *Archbishop John Stratford*, Toronto, 1986.

Hamilton, J. S., *Piers Gaveston: Earl of Cornwall 1307–1312*, London, 1988.

Harriss, G. L. *King, Parliament and Public Finance in Medieval England to 1369*, Oxford, 1975.

Harriss, G. L. (ed.), *Henry V: The Practice of Kingship*, Oxford, 1985.

Harriss, G. L. *Cardinal Beaufort*, Oxford, 1988.

Harriss, G. L., 'Political Society and the Growth of Government in Later Medieval England', *Past and Present* no. 138, 1993, pp. 28–57.

Harvey, I. M. W., *Jack Cade's Rebellion of 1450*, Oxford, 1991.

Haskins, G. L., 'The Doncaster Petition, 1321', *English Historical Review*, vol. liii, 1938, pp. 478–45.

Hay, D., 'The Divisions of the Spoils of War in Fourteenth- Century England', *Transactions of the Royal Historical Society*, 5th Series, vol. 4, 1954, pp. 91–109.

Hewitt, H. J., *The Black Prince's Expeditions of 1355–57*, Manchester, 1958.

Holmes, G. A., 'The Rebellion of the Earl of Lancaster, 1328–29', *Bulletin of the Institute of Historical Research*, vol. xxviii, 1955, pp. 84–9.

Holmes, G. A., *The Estates of the Higher Nobility in Fourteenth Century England*, Cambridge, 1957.

Holmes, G. A., *The Good Parliament*, Oxford, 1975.

Horrox, Rosemary, ed. and trans., *The Black Death*, Manchester, 1994.

Hoyt, R. S., 'The Coronation Oath of 1308', *English Historical Review*, vol. lxxi, 1956, pp. 353–83.

Hudson, Anne, *The Premature Reformation*, Oxford, 1988.

Johnson, P., *Duke Richard of York 1411–1460*, Oxford, 1988.

Jones, M., *Ducal Brittany 1364–1399*, Oxford, 1970.

Jones, M. K., 'Somerset, York and the Wars of the Roses', *English Historical Review*, vol. civ, 1989, pp. 285–307.

Kaeuper, R. W., *War, Justice and Public Order: England and France in the Later Middle Ages*, Oxford, 1988.

Keen, M. H., *England in the Later Middle Ages*, London, 1973.

Keen, M. H., and Daniel, M. J., 'English Diplomacy and the Sack of Fougères in 1449', *History*, vol. lix, 1974, pp. 375–91.

Keen, M. H., 'The End of the Hundred Years War: Lancastrian France and Lancastrian England', in *England and Her Neighbours, 1066–1453*, ed. Michael Jones and Malcolm Vale, London, 1989, pp. 297–311.

Kershaw, Ian, 'The Great Famine and Agrarian Crisis in England 1315–1322', *Past and Present* no. 59, 1973, pp. 3–50.

Kirby, J. L., *Henry IV of England*, London, 1970.

Lander, J. R., 'The Hundred Years War and Edward IV's Campaign in France', in his *Crown and Nobility 1450–1509*, London, 1976.

Lander, J. R., *Government and Community*, London, 1978.

Lander, J. R., *The Limitations of English Monarchy in the Later Middle Ages*, Toronto, 1989.

Lehoux, F., *Jean de France Duc de Berry*, vol. II, Paris, 1966.

Lydon, James, 'The Impact of the Bruce Invasion', in *A New History of Ireland vol. II: Medieval Ireland 1169–1534*, ed. Art Cosgrove, Oxford, 1993, pp. 275–302.

Lyman, T. W., 'Where is Edward II?', *Speculum*, vol. 53, 1978, pp. 522–43

Maddern, Philippa, *Violence and Social Order: East Anglia 1422–1442*, Oxford, 1992.

Maddicott, J. R., *Thomas of Lancaster*, Oxford, 1970.

Maddicott, J. R., 'The English Peasantry and the Demands of the Crown 1294–1341', in *Past and Present*, Supplement, no. 1, 1975.

Marshall, Anne, The Role of English War Captains in England and Normandy 1436–1461, University of Wales MA thesis, 1974.

Massey, R., 'The Lancastrian Land Settlement in Normandy', in *Property and Politics: Essays in Later Medieval History*, ed. A. J. Pollard, Gloucester, 1984, pp. 76–96.

McFarlane, K. B., *Lancastrian Kings and Lollard Knights*, Oxford, 1972.

McFarlane, K. B., *The Nobility of Later Medieval England*, Oxford, 1973.

McFarlane, K. B., *England in the Fifteenth Century: Collected Essays*, with an Introduction by G. L. Harriss, London, 1981.

McHardy, A. K., 'Haxey's Case, 1397: The Petition and its Presenter Reconsidered', in *The Age of Richard II*, ed. J. L. Gillespie, Stroud, 1997, pp. 93–114.

McKisack, M., 'London and the Succession to the Crown in the Middle Ages', in *Studies in Medieval History presented to F. M. Powicke*, ed. R. W. Hunt, W. A. Pautin and R. W. Southern, Oxford, 1948, pp. 76–89.

McKisack, M., *The Fourteenth Century*, Oxford, 1959.

McNamee, C. *The Wars of the Bruces. Scotland, England and Ireland, 1306–1328*, East Linton, 1997.

McNiven, P. 'The Betrayal of Archbishop Scrope', *Bulletin of the John Rylands Library*, vol. liv, 1971–2, pp. 173–213.

McNiven, P., 'Prince Henry and the English Political Crisis of 1412', *History*, vol. 65, 1980, pp. 1–16.

McNiven, P., 'The Problem of Henry IV's Health, 1405–1413', *English Historical Review*, vol. c, 1985, pp. 761–72.

McNiven, P., *Heresy and Politics in the Reign of Henry IV*, Woodbridge, 1987.

Milner, J. D., 'The English Enterprise in France, 1412–13', in *Trade, Devotion and Governance. Papers in Later Medieval History*, ed. Dorothy J. Clayton, Richard G. Davies and Peter McNiven, Stroud, 1994, pp. 80–101.

Morgan, D. A. L., 'The Political After-Life of Edward III: The Apotheosis of a Warmonger', *English Historical Review*, vol. cxii, 1997, pp. 856–81.

Morris, J. E., *The Welsh Wars of Edward I*, Oxford, 1901.

Nicholson, Ranald, *Edward III and the Scots*, Oxford, 1965.

Nicholson, Ranald, *Scotland: The Later Middle Ages*, Edinburgh, 1974.

Oman, C., *The Great Revolt of 1381*, new edn with an Introduction by E. B. Fryde, Oxford, 1969.

Ormrod, W. M., 'The English Government and the Black Death of 1348–49', in *England in the Fourteenth Century*, ed. W. M. Ormrod, Woodbridge, 1986, pp. 175–88

Ormrod, W. M., 'Edward III and the Recovery of Royal Authority in England, 1340–1360', *History*, vol. 72, 1987, pp. 4–19.

Ormrod, W. M., 'Agenda for Legislation, 1322–c.1340', *English Historical Review*, vol. cv, 1990, pp. 1–33.

Ormrod, W. M., *The Reign of Edward III*, New Haven and London, 1990.

Ormrod, W. M., 'The Crown and the English Economy, 1290–1348', in *Before the Black Death: Studies in the 'Crisis' of the Early Fourteenth Century*, ed. B. M. S. Campbell, Manchester, 1991, pp. 149–83.

Palmer, J. J. N., 'The Impeachment of Michael de la Pole in 1386', *Bulletin of the Institute of Historical Research*, vol. xlii, 1969, pp. 96–101.

Palmer, J. J. N., 'The Parliament of 1385 and the Constitutional Crisis of 1386', *Speculum*, vol. 46, 1971, pp. 477–90.

Palmer, J. J. N., *England, France and Christendom*, London, 1972.

Palmer, J. J. N., 'The Authorship, Date and Historical Value of the French Chronicles of the Lancastrian Revolution', *Bulletin of the John Rylands Library*, vol. lxi, 1978–9, pp. 145–81.

Payling, S. J., *Political Society in Lancastrian England: The Greater Gentry of Nottinghamshire*, Oxford, 1991.

Peters, Edward, *The Shadow King*, New Haven, 1970.

Phillips, J. R. S., *Aymer de Valence Earl of Pembroke 1307–24*, Oxford, 1972.

Plucknett, T. F. T. 'The Impeachments of 1376', *Transactions of the Royal Historical Society*, 5th Series, vol. I, 1951, pp. 153–64.

Pocquet du Haut-Jussé, B. A., 'La Renaissance Littéraire autour de Henri V roi d'Angleterre', *Revue Historique*, vol. ccxxiv, 1960, pp. 329–38.

Powell, Edward, *Kingship, Law and Society: Criminal Justice in the Reign of Henry V*, Oxford, 1989.

Powell, Edward, 'After "After McFarlane"': The Poverty of Patronage and the Case for Constitutional History', in *Trade, Devotion and Governance. Papers in Later Medieval History*, ed. Dorothy J. Clayton, Richard G. Davies and Peter McNiven, Stroud, 1994, pp. 1–16.

Powicke, F. M., *The Thirteenth Century*, Oxford, 1953.

Powicke, M. R., *Military Obligation in Medieval England*, Oxford, 1962.

Prestwich, M. C., *War, Politics and Finance under Edward I*, London, 1972.

Prestwich, M. C., *The Three Edwards: War and State in England 1272–1377*, London, 1980.

Prestwich, M. C., 'Royal Patronage under Edward I', in *Thirteenth Century England*, I, ed. P. R. Coss and S. D. Lloyd, Woodbridge, 1986, pp. 41–52.

Prestwich, M. C., *Edward I*, London, 1988.

Prestwich, M. C., 'The Ordinances of 1311 and the Politics of the Early Fourteenth Century', in *Politics and Crisis in Fourteenth Century England*, ed. John Taylor and Wendy Childs, Gloucester, 1990, pp. 1–18.

Pronay, Nicholas, and Taylor, John, *Parliamentary Texts of the Later Middle Ages*, Oxford, 1980.

Pugh, T. B., 'The Magnates, Knights and Gentry' in *Fifteenth-Century England*, ed. S. D. Chrimes, C. D. Ross, and R. A. Griffiths, Manchester, 1972, pp. 86–128.

Pugh, T. B., *Henry V and the Southampton Plot*, Gloucester, 1988.

Rawcliffe, Carol, *The Staffords, Earls of Stafford and Dukes of Buckingham 1394–1521*, Cambridge, 1978.

Richardson, H. G., 'The Annales Paulini', *Speculum*, vol. 23, 1948, pp. 630–40.

Richmond, Colin, 'After McFarlane', *History*, vol. 68, 1983, pp. 46–60.

Rogers, A., 'The Political Crisis of 1401', *Nottingham Medieval Studies*, vol. 12, 1968, pp. 85–96.

Roskell, J. S., 'The Problem of the Attendance of the Lords in Medieval Parliaments', *Bulletin of the Institute of Historical Research*, vol. xxix, 1956, pp. 153–204.

Roskell, J. S., *The Impeachment of Michael de la Pole, Earl of Suffolk, in 1386*, Manchester, 1984.

Roskell, J. S., Clark, L., and Rawcliffe, C., *The History of Parliament. The House of Commons 1386–1421*, vol. I, Stroud, 1992.

Ross, Charles, *Edward IV*, London, 1974.

Rothwell, 'Edward I and the Struggle for the Charters, 1297–1305', in *Studies in Medieval History presented to F. M. Powicke*, ed. R. W. Hunt, W. A. Pautin and R. W. Southern, Oxford, 1948, pp. 319–32.

Russell, J. C., 'The Canonization of Opposition to the King in Angevin England', in *Haskins Anniversary Essays*, ed. C. H. Taylor, Boston, 1929, pp. 279–90.

Saul, Nigel, *Knights and Esquires: The Gloucestershire Gentry in the Fourteenth Century*, Oxford, 1981.

Saul, Nigel, 'The Despensers and the Downfall of Edward II', *English Historical Review*, vol. xcix, 1984, pp. 1–33.

Saul, Nigel, 'Richard II and the Vocabulary of Kingship', *English Historical Review*, vol. cx, 1995, pp. 854–77.

Saul, Nigel, *Richard II*, New Haven and London, 1997.

Saul, Nigel, 'Richard II's Idea of Kingship', in *The Regal Image of Richard II and the Wilton Diptych*, ed. Dillian Gordon, Lisa Monnas and Caroline Elam, London, 1998, pp. 27–32.

Sayles, G. O., 'The Deposition of Richard II: Three Lancastrian Narratives', *Bulletin of the Institute of Historical Research*, vol. liv, 1981, pp. 257–70.

Scammell, Jean, 'Robert I and the North of England', *English Historical Review*, vol. lxxiii, 1958, pp. 385–403.

Sherborne, James, 'The Cost of English Warfare with France in the Later Fourteenth Century' in his *War, Politics and Culture in Fourteenth-Century England*, ed. A. Tuck, London, 1994, pp. 55–70.

Sherborne, James, 'Perjury and the Lancastrian Revolution of 1399', in his *War, Politics and Culture in Fourteenth-Century England*, ed. A. Tuck, London, 1994, pp. 131–53.

Slicher van Bath, B. H., *The Agrarian History of Western Europe*, London, 1963.

Smith, Richard M. 'Demographic Developments in Rural England, 1300–48: a Survey', in *Before the Black Death: Studies in the 'Crisis' of the Early Fourteenth Century*, ed. B. M. S. Campbell, Manchester, 1991, pp. 25–77.

Somerville, R., *The Duchy of Lancaster vol. I: 1265–1603*, London, 1953.

Storey, R. L., *The End of the House of Lancaster*, London, 1966.

Strohm, Paul, *England's Empty Throne: Usurpation and the Language of Legitimation 1399–1422*, New Haven and London, 1998.

Strong, Patrick and Felicity, 'The Last Will and Codicils of Henry V', *English Historical Review*, vol. xcvi, 1981, pp. 79–102.

Sutherland, D. W., *Quo Warranto Proceedings in the Reign of Edward I 1278–94*, Oxford, 1963.

Tout, T. F., 'The Earldoms under Edward I', *Transactions of the Royal Historical Society*, new series, vol. viii, 1894, pp. 129–55.

Tout, T. F., *The Place of the Reign of Edward II in English History*, Manchester, 1914.

Tout, T. F., *Chapters in the Administrative History of Medieval England*, vol. III, Manchester, 1928.

Tuck, A., 'Richard II and the Border Magnates', *Northern History*, vol. 3, 1968, pp. 27–52.

Tuck, A., *Richard II and the English Nobility*, London, 1973.

Tuck, A., 'War and Society in the Medieval North', *Northern History*, vol. 21, 1985, pp. 33–52.

Tuck, A., 'The Emergence of a Northern Nobility', *Northern History*, vol. 22, 1986, pp. 1–17.

Tuck, A., 'Richard II and the Hundred Years War', in *Politics and Crisis in Fourteenth Century England*, ed. John Taylor and Wendy Childs, Gloucester, 1990, pp. 117–31.

Vale, Juliet, *Edward III and Chivalry*, Woodbridge, 1982.

Vale, M. G. A., *English Gascony 1399–1453*, Oxford, 1970.

Vale, M. G. A., *The Angevin Legacy and the Hundred Years War*, Oxford, 1990.

Vaughan, R., *John the Fearless*, London, 1966.

Vaughan, R., *Philip the Good*, London, 1970.

Virgoe, R. L., 'The Death of William de la Pole Duke of Suffolk', *Bulletin of the John Rylands Library*, vol. xlvii, 1964–5, pp. 489–502.

Walker, Simon, *The Lancastrian Affinity 1361–1399*, Oxford, 1990.

Watts, J. L., 'When Did Henry VI's Minority End ?', in *Trade, Devotion and Governance. Papers in Later Medieval History*, ed. Dorothy J. Clayton, Richard G. Davies and Peter McNiven, Stroud, 1994, pp. 116–39.

Watts, J. L., *Henry VI and the Politics of Kingship*, Cambridge, 1996.

Waugh, Scott L., *England in the Reign of Edward III*, Cambridge, 1991.

Webster, Bruce, 'Scotland without a King, 1329–1341', in *Medieval Scotland. Crown Lordship and Community*, ed. Alexander Grant and Keith J. Stringer, Edinburgh, 1993, pp. 223–38.

Wilkinson, B., 'The Sherburn Indenture and the Attack on the Despensers, 1321', *English Historical Review*, vol. lxiii, 1948, pp. 1–28.

Wilks, Michael, 'Royal Priesthood: the Origins of Lollardy', in *The Church in a Changing Society*, CIHEC Conference, Uppsala, 1977.

Wolffe, B. P., The Personal Rule of Henry VI, in *Fifteenth Century England 1399–1509*, ed. S. B. Chrimes, C. D. Ross and R. A. Griffiths, Manchester, 1972.

Wolffe, B. P., *Henry VI*, London, 1981.

Woodger, Linda, 'Henry Bourchier Earl of Essex and His Family (1408–1483, Oxford D.Phil. thesis, 1974.

DAVID I
1124–53

Henry, Earl of Huntingdon

WILLIAM I
'The Lion'
1165–1214

ALEXANDER II
1214–49

ALEXANDER III
1249–86

Margaret = ERIC II of Norway
d.1283

MARGARET
'The Maid of Norway'
1286–90
(no issue)

David, Earl of Huntingdon

Margaret

Dervorguilla = John Balliol

JOHN BALLIOL
1291–6
d.1313

EDWARD BALLIOL
pretender to the
Scottish throne
1332–56

Isabel

Robert Bruce
'The Competitor'
d.1295

Robert Bruce
Earl of Carrick
d.1304

Elizabeth = (2) ROBERT I = (1) Isabella of Mar
de Burgh   1306–29   d.1316

DAVID II
1329–71
(no issue)

Marjory = Walter the Steward

ROBERT II
1371–90

ROBERT III
1390–1406

JAMES I
1406–37

Ada

Henry Hastings

John Hastings

Ada = Florent III
Count of
Holland

William I
Florent IV

William II
Florent V

Table 1   The Scottish Succession, 1286–1332
Names of those who claimed the kingdom 1291–2 are underlined.

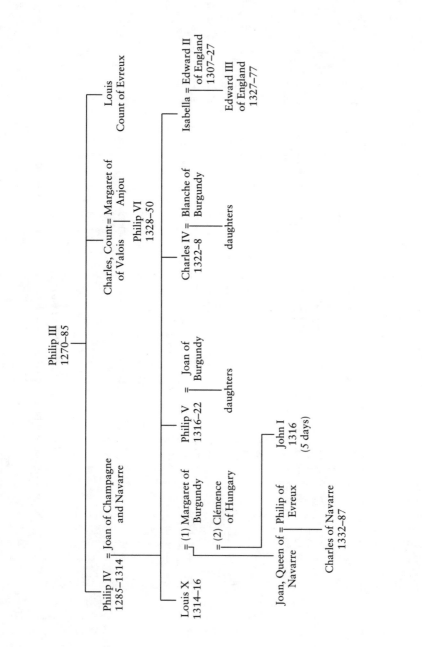

Table 2   The French Succession, 1328

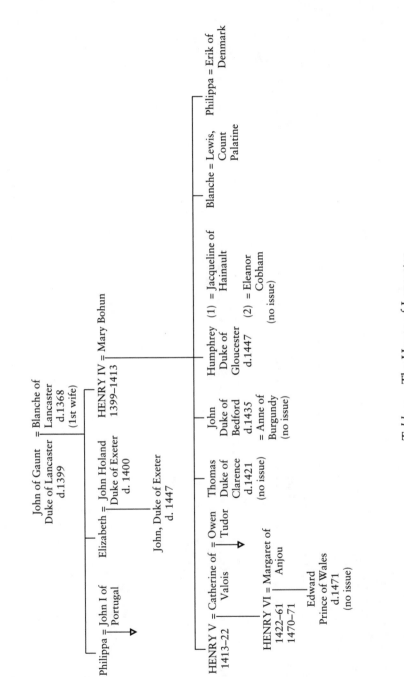

Table 3   The House of Lancaster

John of Gaunt = Katherine Swynford
Duke of Lancaster (3rd wife)
d.1399

John, Earl of = Margaret Holand
Somerset
d.1410

Henry, Earl of
Somerset
d.1418
(no issue)

John, Earl = Margaret
and Duke of   Beauchamp
Somerset   (daughter of
d.1444   Sir John
              Beauchamp)

Edmund Tudor, Earl of = Margaret
Richmond

HENRY VII
1485–1509

Henry, Bishop of
Winchester
d.1447

Thomas, Duke of
Exeter
d.1426
(no issue)

Joan = James I of
Scotland

Edmund, Duke = Margaret
of Somerset   Beauchamp
d.1455   (daughter of
               Earl of
               Warwick)

Henry, Duke of   Edmund, Duke
Somerset   of Somerset
d.1464   d.1471

Ralph Neville = Joan
Earl of Westmorland   d.1440
d.1425

Alice = Richard, Earl
Montague   of Salisbury
            d.1460

Richard, Earl
of Warwick
d.1471

Table 4 The Beaufort Family and their Neville Connections

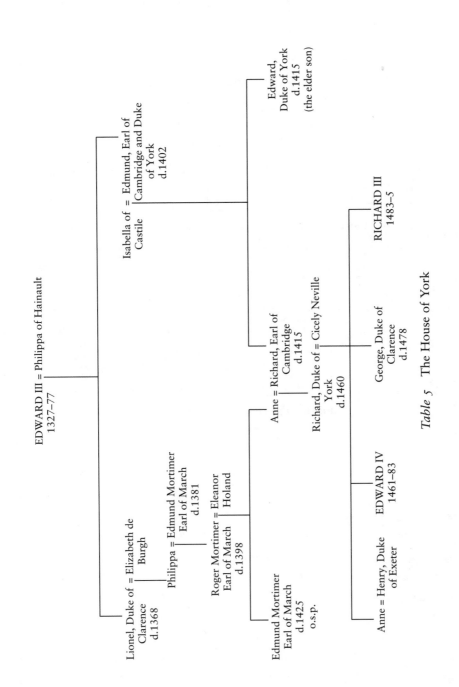

EDWARD III = Philippa of Hainault
1327–77

Lionel, Duke of = Elizabeth de
Clarence   Burgh
d.1368

Philippa = Edmund Mortimer
           Earl of March
           d.1381

Roger Mortimer = Eleanor
Earl of March   Holand
d.1398

Edmund Mortimer
Earl of March
d.1425
o.s.p.

Isabella of = Edmund, Earl of
Castile   Cambridge and Duke
             of York
             d.1402

Anne = Richard, Earl of
       Cambridge
       d.1415

Richard, Duke of = Cicely Neville
York
d.1460

Edward,
Duke of York
d.1415
(the elder son)

George, Duke of
Clarence
d.1478

RICHARD III
1483–5

Anne = Henry, Duke
       of Exeter

EDWARD IV
1461–83

Table 5   The House of York

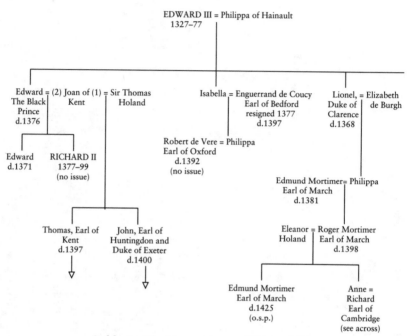

Table 6 The Descendants of Edward III

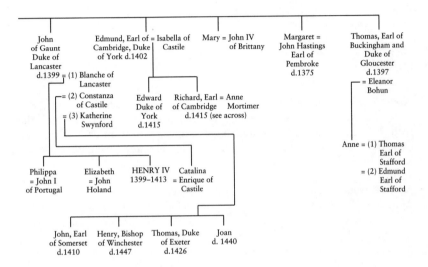

John
of Gaunt
Duke of
Lancaster
d.1399 = (1) Blanche of
Lancaster

= (2) Constanza
of Castile

= (3) Katherine
Swynford

Edmund, Earl of = Isabella of
Cambridge, Duke | Castile
of York d.1402

Mary = John IV
of Brittany

Margaret =
John Hastings
Earl of
Pembroke
d.1375

Thomas, Earl of
Buckingham and
Duke of
Gloucester
d.1397
= Eleanor
Bohun

Edward
Duke of
York
d.1415

Richard, Earl = Anne
of Cambridge Mortimer
d.1415 (see across)

Anne = (1) Thomas
Earl of
Stafford
= (2) Edmund
Earl of
Stafford

Philippa
= John I
of Portugal

Elizabeth
= John
Holand

HENRY IV
1399–1413

Catalina
= Enrique of
Castile

John, Earl
of Somerset
d.1410

Henry, Bishop
of Winchester
d.1447

Thomas, Duke
of Exeter
d.1426

Joan
d. 1440

Index

Note: Archbishops' and bishops' dates are those during which they held their sees. The dates for earls, marquises and dukes are those during which they held their earldoms, marquisates or dukedoms. Where an earl, marquis or duke held more than one title during his life, the dates during which he was known by each title are given.